Sowers and Reapers

For Alice, Anna and Tom

SOWERS AND REAPERS

A COMPANION TO THE
FOUR GOSPELS AND ACTS

EDITED BY

JOHN PARR

The Bible Reading Fellowship

Copyright © The Bible Reading Fellowship 1994

Published by
The Bible Reading Fellowship
Peter's Way, Sandy Lane West
Oxford OX4 5HG
ISBN 0 7459 2531 6
The Society for Promoting Christian Knowledge
Holy Trinity Church
Marylebone Road, London
ISBN 0 281 04821 5
First edition 1994

Acknowledgments

Revised Standard Version of the Bible copyright © 1946, 1952, 1971 by the Division of Christian Education of the National Council of the Churches of Christ in the USA.

New Revised Standard Version of the Bible, copyright © 1989 by the Division of Christian Education of the National Council of the Churches of Christ in the USA.

A catalogue record for this book is available from the British Library

Printed and bound in Great Britain by J.W. Arrowsmith Ltd, Bristol

CONTENTS

Preface	*John Parr*	**7**
The Gospels and Jesus	*John Parr*	**9**
Matthew	*Ivor Jones*	**37**
Mark	*Christopher Rowland and David Sanders*	**129**
Luke	*John Parr*	**187**
John	*Gordon Wakefield*	**282**
Acts	*Clare Amos*	**377**

PREFACE

Sowers and Reapers brings together material published over the last five years in the Bible Reading Fellowship's *Guidelines* Bible reading notes. As a companion rather than a verse-by-verse commentary, it is intended to be read alongside the four Gospels and the Acts of the Apostles. The contributors are all experienced biblical teachers who draw on current New Testament scholarship in order to highlight the main themes and emphases of theses foundational Christian writings.

Sowers and Reapers shares the overall aim of the *Guidelines* notes: to stimulate thought, prayer and action. Reading the Bible inevitably raises matters for further consideration, in both texts and readers. A feature of this volume is the regular invitation to think about some of the issues raised in the course of reading. This can only enrich our dialogue with the New Testament, and lead us into a deeper conversation with the living God. By allowing this to develop, we may hope to translate the impulses of the gospel into fresh and meaningful speech and action in today's world. And so the word of God produces yet another harvest.

John Parr
September 1994

NOTE: There is a companion volume to *Sowers and Reapers*. Entitled *Prophets and Poets*, it covers the prophetic books of the Old Testament, and is edited by Grace Emmerson, joint-editor of *Guidelines*.

CONTRIBUTORS

Clare Amos has lived and taught biblical studies in Jerusalem, Beirut and Cambridge, to both clergy and laity. Currently she is Editor of Partners in Learning, an ecumenical journal which provides resources for All-Age Worship. She also lectures in Old and New Testament at the Roehampton Institute in south London, and to ordinands in Kent.

Ivor Jones is Principal of Wesley House, Cambridge. He has written widely on biblical and musical subjects.

John Parr is Director of Studies at Ridley Hall, Cambridge. He teaches New Testament and liberation theology in the Cambridge Federation of Theological Colleges and Cambridge University.

Christopher Rowland is Dean Ireland's Professor of the Exegesis of Holy Scripture at Oxford University. He is an Anglican priest who has a long-standing interest in the Church's response to the poor and the contribution of liberation theology to biblical interpretation and Christian discipleship.

David Sanders is a Dominican who has taught theology in Jamaica. He now teaches in Cambridge and takes part in theological education further afield.

Gordon Wakefield is a Methodist minister. He is a former Principal of Queen's College, Birmingham, an ecumenical college. He has written widely, mostly on spirituality.

THE GOSPELS AND JESUS

— FROM JESUS TO THE GOSPELS —

The fulfilment of promise

Jesus of Nazareth began his ministry around AD30 in the northern regions of a small but strategically significant province of the Roman Empire at the eastern end of the Mediterranean. As a Jew, he belonged to a nation that was deeply conscious of its heritage as the chosen people of the one true God. Their God had bound himself to them in a sacred covenant, and they lived out their obligation to him by obeying the Law he revealed to Moses. They believed their God had given them the sole right to occupy the land he promised to the patriarch Abraham, a land their ancestors laid claim to after their God had released them from slavery in Egypt. Israel's history had reached its zenith a thousand years before Jesus, when the borders of her territory achieved their greatest reach under king David, and his son Solomon built a temple in Jerusalem to symbolize God's dwelling among his people. But within 400 years David's kingdom had long been divided, and the Promised Land was all but lost when much of its population was deported to Babylon (modern day Iraq). The Jews had struggled to re-establish their nation and identity following their release from exile. By the time of Jesus, they had been exposed to Greek culture for the best part of 350 years, as it spread around the Mediterranean into their ancestral land. During that period the land of the Jews had been the object of successive imperialist interests, though a successful rebellion against foreign rule around 160BC under Judas Maccabeus eventually led to eighty years of relative freedom prior to Pompey's capture of Jerusalem in 63BC. As Jesus was beginning his ministry, the memory of the Maccabean revolt still fired Jewish hopes that, despite appearances to the contrary, God's ancient

9

promises might yet be fulfilled in her liberation from the powers that occupied her land.

Jesus' brief ministry was largely confined to rural Galilee, though he visited Jerusalem as a pilgrim. He was not a politician or a supporter of violent revolution, but he managed to disturb the delicate balance of power in Jewish Palestine to the extent that the leaders of his own people in Jerusalem—the guardians of the temple, who under their Roman overlords had a political as well as a religious role in Jewish life—saw fit to have him executed. Yet within a generation small communities owing their allegiance to him had been established around the Mediterranean. Their roots were in the Jewish synagogues, and they also traced their ancestry back to Abraham. But their membership was increasingly drawn from a cross-section of urban Gentile society. These 'Christians' believed that God's ancient promises to Israel had at last begun to be fulfilled—though in a surprising and hardly obvious way—and the whole world, not just the Jewish people, stood to benefit.

Impressions of Jesus

Around the middle of the Jewish war against Rome (AD66–74), the first surviving written account of Jesus' ministry appeared in the Gospel of Mark. This anonymously issued collection of stories and sayings traced the course of Jesus' career from Galilee to Jerusalem, and concluded with the promise that the risen Jesus would meet up with his scattered followers once more in Galilee. Mark produced a literary novelty. In calling his account a 'Gospel', he was borrowing a military term for the announcement of a king's victory. The Jewish historian Josephus (c. AD37–100) saw the beginning of the emperor Vespasian's reign in AD69 as 'gospel' because he managed to restore peace to an empire beset by civil war. Mark may have been countering the extravagant claims currently being made for Vespasian by insisting that the story of Jesus, not Vespasian, was a genuine 'gospel' for the empire. In this he was no doubt influenced by earlier Christian usage—in Romans 1:16 Paul used 'gospel' as shorthand for the Christian message of all that God had achieved in the death and resurrection of Jesus. Mark, though, used it for the first time as the title of a *written account* of the words and deeds of Jesus—'the gospel of Jesus Christ, the Son of God'.

Within a generation, the other three New Testament Gospels were written. Like Mark, they are all anonymous—later Christian tradition is

10

responsible for seeing 'Mark' as the interpreter of Peter, 'Matthew' as the tax-collector who became a disciple, 'Luke' as one of Paul's travelling companions, and 'John' as the beloved disciple. Two of these Gospels owe something to Mark's seminal work, the other is less directly related. Matthew's Gospel, with its strongly Jewish flavour, is an expansion of Mark. Luke's account is less dependent on Mark (though he probably used it at some stage in the process of writing his Gospel), and his second volume—the Acts of the Apostles—extends the story of Jesus into that of the movement he founded. The Gospel of John is very different from the other three (the so-called 'synoptic' Gospels, because they follow a common synopsis of Jesus' ministry). It omits some of their characteristic features, and introduces many of its own. Yet it can be seen as a development of the traditions that lie behind the synoptics, and there are times when John brings us closest to the historical Jesus.

Though the four Gospels share the same main character, they are hardly biographies in the modern sense. They are far too brief for that, and leave out much of the kind of material that fascinates biographers. Only Matthew and Luke reveal anything about Jesus' birth and early life, and even then the details are scant. All the evangelists leave us guessing about Jesus' moral, spiritual and psychological development, and none of them discusses the people and events who had a great influence on him. Even their information about the course of Jesus' ministry is sparse—we could well imagine the events they describe occupying a matter of weeks rather than years. They include typical examples of actions and teachings rather than full accounts. Like Monet's series of grainstacks painted at various times of the day and year, and his images of the façade of Rouen Cathedral in different lighting conditions, the Gospels offer impressionistic pictures of Jesus, rather than literary portraits. Their subject is the same historical figure, but the evangelists have viewed him in a variety of local conditions.

Sowers and reapers

Unlike Monet, the evangelists reveal little of how they produced their impressions of Jesus. John acknowledges that he has selected from the available material about Jesus, and claims that his account is rooted in the testimony of the mysterious 'disciple whom Jesus loved' (20:30–31; 21:24–25). In his prologue, Luke refers to oral and written traditions about Jesus, with their source in the memories of those who witnessed the events of his ministry (Luke 1:1–4). If we draw on the imagery of one of the best-known parables of Jesus, we might say that the Gospels are the result of the processes of sowing and reaping that go back to Jesus himself. The seeds planted by the sower bore fruit in the lives of those who met and followed him throughout Galilee and Judea. The characteristic sayings and themes of his ministry were remembered and repeated. In their turn apostles, evangelists and teachers also became sowers and reapers. They established the earliest churches by planting what had been remembered of Jesus' words and deeds in new soil, and nurturing what sprang up as a result. But this sowing and reaping—like the work of an artist—was highly creative. It involved a dynamic relationship between the 'Jesus tradition' and the new settings of Christian mission. As they were told and re-told in the spread of the gospel and the consolidation of Christian faith, the stories about Jesus were honed into shape like stones made smooth by the sea. With the distancing of the memory of Jesus' words and deeds from his ministry in Galilee and Judea, the original contexts of many incidents were forgotten. New situations shed fresh light on inherited material, and even modified its meaning. For example, Matthew 10:26 and Luke 12:2 record a saying of Jesus: 'Nothing is covered up that will not be uncovered, and nothing secret that will not become known.' The wording is identical, but in Matthew it refers to the contrast between Jesus' private instruction of his disciples and their later public ministry, whereas in Luke it refers to the Pharisees' hypocrisy that will one day be brought out into the open. Even where the original context was remembered—as in the case of the words over the bread and wine at the Last Supper—there was clearly a degree of freedom in reproducing what Jesus said. The eucharistic traditions in the synoptics and Paul (1 Corinthians 11:23–26; the Fourth Gospel omits the institution of the Lord's Supper altogether) are characterized both by substantial overlap and significant differences, which may well reflect the liturgical practices of the churches which preserved this material. Liturgical practice may also account for the different versions of the Lord's Prayer in Matthew 6 and Luke 11. The prayer Jesus taught his disciples was not only *remembered*, it was also *used*, and used differently, as we might expect from the variety of versions which abound in today's churches.

Longer collections of Jesus' teaching may have been made early in the life of the Church. Some scholars believe that the so-called 'Little Apocalypse' in Mark 13 (compare Matthew 24 and Luke 21) was put together as early as AD40, and that an early version of the passion narrative was written down around the same time. A more extended collection of Jesus' teachings—used by Matthew and Luke—was made in Palestine soon after. Sayings and incidents from the life of Jesus were linked by common themes or catchwords, such as the series of conflict stories in Mark 2:1—3:6. The fact that Luke reproduces this whereas Matthew breaks it up suggests that the evangelists made no attempt to provide information of the exact course of Jesus' ministry. What others had joined together, Matthew was free to separate. This warns us against taking some of the longer collections of Jesus' teaching at face value. The Sermon on the Mount in Matthew 5–7 includes most of the Sermon on the Plain from Luke 6:20–49; some of Matthew's Sermon is found elsewhere in Luke (and also in Mark), though parts of it are unique to Matthew's Gospel; and the two Sermons begin and end almost identically. It would be difficult to maintain that either Matthew or Luke recorded an actual sermon of Jesus. It is more likely that his sayings were collected, adapted and edited, and that the evangelists have played their part in shaping and modifying them so that they could speak afresh to new audiences.

Trustworthy impressions?

We can imagine, then, that the evangelists in their turn became sowers, as they scattered into new soil the seeds that had fallen from the harvest of the 'Jesus tradition' in the earliest Christian communities. They succeeded in developing new strains of gospel seed out of the dynamic interaction between what they inherited and the situations they served, and this accounts for some of the distinctive emphases of each of the Gospels. We may well wonder about the implications of this creativity for the reliability of the Gospels as historical sources for the ministry of Jesus. Some place so much stress on the power of ecclesiastical inventiveness that they are sceptical about the ability of the Gospels to tell us much about Jesus. They look to Paul as an ally: 'Even though we once knew Christ from a human point of view, we no longer know him that way' (2 Corinthians 5:16). If the apostle showed no interest in the historical Jesus, why then should we? But this is to misinterpret Paul, who was arguing against members of the Corinthian church who judged true apostolic ministry according to human standards of power and influence. Paul maintained that in the new creation brought about by the death and resurrection of Jesus, the human tendency to judge by outward appearances counted for nothing. He no longer judged Jesus by the ignominy and shame of his execution, but saw him as the revelation of God's reconciling love. It is not that Paul was not interested in the historical Jesus, but that he now saw him in a different light. Indeed, if Paul had known nothing about Jesus' ministry, we might wonder how he could ever have come to see the crucified Jesus—to the Jew a shameful image of God's rejection and curse—as the embodiment of God's reconciling love (Romans 5:6–11; 2 Corinthians 5:14–19).

There are several good reasons for believing that the early Church was interested in preserving the memory of the ministry of Jesus of Nazareth.

◇ Luke's reports of Peter's and Paul's preaching reveal a concern for the beginnings of the story of the Church on the part of the apostolic sowers of the word (Acts 2:22ff; 10:36ff; 13:23ff). The outline of Jesus' ministry here—baptism by John, anointing by the Holy Spirit, mighty works in Galilee, ministry in Judea and Jerusalem, rejection by the Jewish leaders, execution and resurrection—corresponds with the story told in the Gospels. The resurrection was clearly understood as God's vindication of the one who was rejected by the Jerusalem authorities, but it is significant that such vindication was not merely seen as a reversal of Jesus' death but extended to his whole career—hence the importance of remembering its details.

◇ The New Testament writers betray an interest in those who could well have been guardians of the 'Jesus tradition'. Matthias, Judas' replacement, was chosen from among those who had followed Jesus from the time of his baptism by John (Acts 1:21). We are told nothing further about Matthias—his sole significance lay in the fact that he accompanied Jesus throughout his ministry, and would therefore have had firsthand experience of his work. Likewise, when Paul reminded the Corinthians of the teaching he had received and handed on to them, he mentioned that the risen Jesus appeared to 'Cephas, then to the twelve' (1 Corinthians 15:5). They were not actually the first to see the risen Jesus (Mary Magdalene could claim that honour), but it is likely that they soon came to be regarded as the principal guardians of the 'Jesus tradition'. As those who had been privy to the whole of Jesus' ministry, they were the natural ones to safeguard Jesus' teaching, by remembering, interpreting and passing it on.

◇ Jesus taught in Aramaic, but the Gospels were written in Greek. When we compare the synoptic Gospels, we find that there is substantial verbal agreement between parallel passages. In some cases this is because one evangelist has used another's Gospel; in others the evangelists were drawing on common sources. The degree of verbal correspondence between the Greek of the Gospels suggests that the evangelists' common sources must have been written in Greek—no two translators from Aramaic into Greek would agree quite so closely. So the material about Jesus assumed an established form before the Gospels were written. This is an indication of continuity between the Gospels and the earlier stages of the 'Jesus tradition'. On the further assumption that in an oral culture people were more accustomed to remember what they heard, such continuity can be extended back to the very beginnings of the 'Jesus tradition', and the argument for a substantial historical basis to the Gospels is considerably strengthened. This is not to say that the evangelists only ever provide the 'hard facts' about Jesus. Parallel Gospel passages also have their differences—of length, detailed wording, emphasis or interpretation. But there is clearly a common core of historical material about Jesus which the evangelists and their predecessors regarded as being of great importance.

The willingness of the Gospels to preserve material about Jesus that might prove embarrassing to the early Church can be used as an argument for the overall historical trustworthiness of the 'Jesus tradition'. In Matthew 19:28 (also Luke 22:30) Jesus promised the Twelve that in the coming kingdom of God they would sit on thrones judging the twelve tribes of Israel. No one in the early Church could have imagined these words being fulfilled, in view of Judas' betrayal. Jesus' prediction of the destruction of the temple was right in general but wrong in detail: it was not pulled down but destroyed by fire in AD70 (Mark 13:2). Jesus' admitted ignorance about the future course of events sits uneasily alongside the Church's developing belief in his divinity (Mark 13:32, Matthew 24:36; Luke, together with some manuscripts of Matthew's Gospel, omits the reference). There are three larger blocks of material that bring this embarrassment factor into sharp focus.

◇ All four Gospels note Jesus' early associations with John the Baptist. Mark and Matthew tell us that Jesus approached John and asked to be baptized; Luke is more reticent; but if we only had the Fourth Gospel, we would not assume that Jesus was actually baptized by John. The potential for embarrassment in Jesus' baptism is obvious. By identifying with those who wanted to be baptized as a sign of repentance, was Jesus admitting his own sinfulness? By submitting to the baptism of John, was Jesus recognizing his authority over him? Matthew has John hesitate when Jesus stands before him; in the end Jesus' insistence that he perform the act 'in order to fulfil all righteousness' (a favourite Matthean term) wins the day. The Fourth Gospel includes only the Baptist's testimony to the Spirit descending on Jesus and remaining on him; John the Baptist is no more than a witness to Jesus. The evangelists' willingness to preserve material about the links between Jesus and John the Baptist demonstrates their ability to put us in touch with the historical core of Jesus' ministry, as well as revealing their own ways of dealing with the implications of Jesus' baptism. These stories are a good example of the way in which the Gospels tell us something about the concerns of the evangelists, but without losing sight of Jesus.

◇ All four Gospels tell the story of Jesus' crucifixion. Jews found the whole idea of crucifixion scandalous, more an indication of God's curse than his blessing; there is no evidence that they were expecting a crucified Messiah. For Gentiles it was ridiculous even to mention divinity in the same breath as crucifixion, which the Romans frequently used to suppress insurrection. It is inconceivable that anyone would dream of launching a new religious movement with the publicity provided by Jesus' execution, unless of course it was authentic. But like the stories of Jesus' baptism, the passion narratives contain variations in detail which reflect the concerns of the evangelists. The words of Jesus from the cross are a case in point. Though these are often strung together as the 'seven last words from the cross' and used profitably as the basis of Good Friday devotions, they reflect different understandings of Jesus' death on the part of the evangelists. Mark does not shrink from presenting the reality of Jesus' suffering. As he dies he feels God-forsaken, like all who suffer unjustly, and his final cry of desolation draws on Psalm 22: 'My God, my God, why have you forsaken me?' Only Matthew repeats this, though his passion narrative is keen to demonstrate the majesty and authority of Jesus even in the face of death. Throughout his passion story, Luke insists that even the prospect of death cannot diminish the stature of Jesus. He dies as he had lived, full of confidence and faith in his Father, again using words from the Psalms: 'Into your hands, O Lord, I commit my spirit.' John goes even further by having Jesus end his earthly life with a triumphant flourish: 'It is finished.' The accounts of Jesus' passion are therefore of a piece with those of his baptism. They undoubtedly preserve the historical core of the story of Jesus. But the evangelists weave into their narratives their own understandings of the meaning of Jesus' crucifixion.

◇ All four Gospels give women pride of place in the stories of Easter morning. In Jewish society, the testimony of women carried no legal weight, and it is significant that in 1 Corinthians 15 Paul does not mention the women in his list of those to whom the risen Christ appeared. But they play a key role in the Gospel traditions. The synoptics not only name them, but also identify them as those who witnessed Jesus' death and burial. John's Gospel takes great care to underline the importance of Mary Magdalene's testimony, which is confirmed by Jesus' subsequent appearances to the disciples; Mary is the first apostle of the resurrection. Like the crucifixion itself, the testimony of women would hardly have strengthened the early Christians' case for the resurrection of Jesus; its inclusion is a mark of authenticity. The differences between the resurrection narratives indicate that they too are shot through with each evangelist's interpretation of the significance of Easter. According to Mark's mysterious ending—so much in keeping with the rest of his Gospel—the risen Jesus is still ready to meet his followers in the way of discipleship. For Matthew the resurrection of Jesus confirms his authority as the one who inaugurates a new age for the people of God. Luke shows how the presence of the risen Jesus is mediated through the Scriptures and the common meals of the Christian community. John insists that faith in Jesus' resurrection is possible on the strength of the testimony of others, without the confirmation of sight or touch. If the resurrection narratives interpret Easter through the experiences of the early Christian communities, who knew that the risen Lord was with them, the prominence they give to the testimony of women is further evidence that the evangelists have not lost sight of the historical core of the story they tell.

The case for the general reliability of the Gospels is strengthened by archaeological and literary evidence suggesting that at the time Mark was written—nearly forty years on from the story it tells—Galilee was not the region it had been at the time of Jesus. Mark depicts Jesus moving freely through Galilee, and crossing the borders into Gentile territory with ease. This would have been possible during the reign of the client king Herod Antipas (4BC–AD39), who is mentioned in the Gospels, but not in the years leading up to the Jewish War, when there is evidence of hostility towards Jews in Galilee. Though Mark does not provide a detailed picture of Galilean life, the impression he gives is essentially consistent with what we know from historical sources. Of course, to maintain that the Gospels are generally trustworthy is not the same as saying that they conform to today's standards of historical accuracy at all points. But there are clearly good reasons for thinking that they put us in touch with the one on whom Christian faith is based, as well as revealing something of his continuing impact on the earliest generations of the Christianity. To return to the 'sowing and reaping' imagery of Jesus' parable, we might say that the continuity between the ministry of Jesus, the memories of his first followers, the oral and written collections of his words and deeds, and the narratives we now call 'Gospels'—a continuity that allows us to believe that the 'Jesus tradition' has a substantial historical core—lies in the nature of the seeds that were sown and harvested in different soils around the Mediterranean. They were all developed from the 'Jesus' variety, and they proved their vitality by the multitude of crops they produced whenever they were planted in good soils.

— FROM THE GOSPELS TO JESUS —

It is one thing to make a case for the general historical trustworthiness of the Gospels, but another to go on and use them to re-tell the story of Jesus. Those who do so must work within the constraints common to all historians. We have no direct access to the past, only what the past has delivered to us. This means that we can only ever offer a reconstruction of the past based on the evidence available. In this, imagination as well as critical judgment come into play, together with a range of perspectives, interests and values. There is no final, objective version of events; each reconstruction is placed in the public domain where it can be scrutinized. We do not escape the limitations of historical reconstruction when we use the Gospels as the basis of our understanding of Jesus. Indeed, we should not expect to, if we are drawing on genuinely historical sources whose main character is a flesh-and-blood figure of history.

Attempts to recover the Jesus of history over the past two hundred years have taught us that a degree of modesty is in order on the part of those who claim to have discovered the real Jesus. About him, as about any historical figure, there is a certain elusiveness, which in his case is heightened by the mystery of what Christians believe he of all people reveals most fully. So we must be content with a degree of provisionality in our picture of him. The results of the quest for the historical Jesus (as the scholarly enterprise of the past two hundred years has been called) are paralleled by the sheer range of contemporary images of him in the many cultures in which the seeds of the gospel have been sown. As fresh evidence from the past comes to light, and as new questions and issues are brought to the Gospels, the appearance of their main character alters—sometimes quite considerably. It would be irresponsible of anyone to claim that they have discovered him as he really was.

What follows is no more than an outline sketch of one way of reconstructing 'the historical Jesus'. It is based on the work of scholars who, over the past twenty or so years, have read the Gospels in the light of what we can know of the world of Palestinian Judaism during the lifetime of Jesus. Had I been writing as a member of a Third World church committed to the struggle for a more just society, my account would have been more heavily accented in favour of Jesus' relationship with the economically poor. Had I been a woman caught up in the struggles against patriarchal prejudice as well as poverty, I would

19

doubtless have been more sensitive to the place of women in the Gospel narratives. What I find fascinating and challenging is that these admittedly more political readings of the Gospels have considerable overlap with the emerging picture of Jesus as one who gave himself for the renewal of Israel at a time of acute crisis for his own people.

The one to redeem Israel

It has become commonplace in recent years for both Jewish and Christian scholars to stress the Jewishness of Jesus. This is not merely a statement of the obvious regarding his ethnic, cultural and religious background, but an indication of where we should locate him in relation to the particular struggles of human history. The Palestinian Jewish world in which he lived and died was marked by diversity, social fragmentation and separatism. When Josephus referred to the four Jewish philosophies of the Sadducees, the Pharisees, the Zealots and the Essenes, he was not referring to what we might understand as four schools of thought. These were alternative versions of what it meant to be God's covenant people, a series of responses to the extension of Greek culture and Roman imperial rule into the Promised Land itself. The presence of a bigger world on the Jews' own doorstep, denying as it did all that lay at the heart of Jewish belief, provoked the crisis to which the ministry of Jesus was but one response.

The Jews were united in their core beliefs—one God, Israel as his covenant people, the Law of Moses as the supreme revelation of his will, the land he promised to Abraham as their eternal possession, their temple in Jerusalem as God's dwelling place; but living under the double occupation of Athens and Rome raised the issue of their true identity. What did it mean to be the people of a holy God? Ever since the return from exile in Babylon, there had been a tendency to ward off the pressures of assimilation by paying particular attention to those parts of the Law that emphasized separation. By giving a high profile to the observance of circumcision, sabbath and dietary regulations, zealous Jews were able to keep a distance between themselves and Gentile culture; the Law's demand for holiness meant separation. But history saw to it that zeal for the Law could not guarantee unanimity in its interpretation. If the Jerusalem temple were to be the symbolic centre of Jewish life, what happened if the price of maintaining its worship and priesthood were some degree of compromise with one or other of the foreign powers who staked a claim on the Jews' land? Some were willing to pay that price, others were not. If God had given the land to the children of Abraham, and warned his covenant people against foreign defilement, how should the Jews respond when Gentile defilement reached into every part of their land? Jews with a common concern for holiness were divided in their attitudes to foreign rule and culture, and as a result developed different strategies to enable them to hold on to their identity as the people of God.

The Sadducees were the Jewish political leaders, aristocratic land-owners from whose ranks the high-priestly families came. They were prepared to pay price of compromise with Rome (who appointed the high priest) in order to maintain the temple and the authority of its priesthood. Their conservative religious beliefs served their political interests well. They did not hold with the idea of the resurrection of the dead, because it was a symbol of the new world order that would put an end to their political and religious power, dependent as it was on Rome. Their belief in free will meant that they were prepared to seize power with both hands, drawing on the help of God by helping themselves. Their stress on the sole authority of Moses allowed them to keep their distance from the Pharisees, whose teachings applied the Law to every last detail of life. The Pharisees were a renewal movement rather than an official body. Their programme involved extending the priestly laws of ritual purity beyond the temple into the whole of life, to create enclaves of holiness within the unclean Gentile-dominated world. Some Pharisees accepted Roman rule as long as it did not interfere with their separatist piety; others supported the more revolutionary Jews like Judas the Galilean, who led the revolt against the census in AD6. It would be a mistake to imagine an organized Jewish resistance movement at the time of Jesus. Josephus' 'Zealots' were one of a number of groups whose religiously-inspired zeal encouraged them to turn the frustrations of economic hardship into violence in order to rid their land of foreign defilement. Insurrection was always a possibility during the period of Roman rule, though outbreaks of violence coincided with the deaths of political leaders, or the provocation of the Jews by those in power over them. The Essenes were in some ways a more radical version of the Pharisees, with whom they may have had common roots in the third century BC. They too applied the Law to every detail of life in the pursuit of holiness, but this led them to a stricter form of separatism. Their monastery at Qumran, on the northern shores of the Dead Sea, was the mother-house of a broadly based movement whose writings suggest that they were unhappy with Roman occupation, Sadducean compromise and Pharisaic toleration. Inspired by Isaiah 40:3 ('In the wilderness prepare the way of the Lord, make straight in the desert a highway for our God'), the Essenes were preparing for the coming of the Messiah. They saw themselves as the true Israel, the faithful covenant community, the true temple now that the one in Jerusalem was defiled. Until it could be purified, and Israel's enemies defeated, God would accept their sacrifices of prayer, discipline, study and writing, rather than the burnt offerings of Mount Zion. The Qumran settlement was destroyed by the Romans during the Jewish War in AD68, and the Essenes disappeared from history.

It is not difficult to discern the inevitably political character of the pursuit of holiness as a response to Israel's double occupation. By the time Jesus began his ministry, prolonged exposure to foreign culture had stamped Palestinian Judaism with the hallmarks of separation and fragmentation. In addition, Roman taxation policies succeeded in creating a class of non-observant Jews, who could not afford to pay tithes to the temple in addition to the poll tax. These 'sinners' were despised by the zealous, because they allowed Jewish identity—defined by commitment to the Law's demand for separatist holiness—to be undermined. Zealous Jews regarded the worst of the 'sinners' as no better than Gentiles, either because they belonged to such notoriously wicked groups as prostitutes or because their occupations were deemed to be particularly defiling. Tax-collectors (who of necessity collaborated with Rome) and shepherds (whose work prevented scrupulous observation of the purity laws) were included in the latter group. Antipathy towards Rome was fuelled by the relatively recent memory of faithful Jews who had resisted foreign powers out of faithfulness to the Law. The Maccabean revolt gave the Jews a taste of comparative freedom for nearly a century, until the Romans captured Jerusalem in 63BC. The cleansing of the temple following its defilement by Antiochus Epiphanes in 167BC was celebrated at the annual festival of Dedication (Hanukkah), and of course the liberation from Egypt was celebrated at Passover. So the Jews were not without encouragement to hold on to their hopes for freedom from the oppression brought about by living in doubly occupied territory.

A text from Luke's Gospel provides a clue to the way Jesus was perceived by those closest to him. Two disciples were travelling home from Jerusalem to Emmaus after an unforgettable Passover. They told the stranger they met on the road about one whose violent death had given way to reports that his tomb had been found empty and that he was alive. Of this man the travellers confessed, 'We had hoped that he was the one to redeem Israel' (Luke 24:21). Jesus of Nazareth was seen as one who promised the freedom Jews were looking for. But how did he envisage this? Can we discover anything of his aims and intentions?

Your kingdom come, your will be done

The petition that lies at the heart of Matthew's version of the Lord's Prayer can help us to understand how Jesus envisaged his mission. According to Matthew and Mark, he began his Galilean ministry by announcing the nearness of 'the kingdom of God'. The term is not explained anywhere in the Gospels. In common with his contemporaries, Jesus saw the kingdom of God not as a territory, but as the rule or reign of God. 'The kingdom of God is at hand' means that God is drawing near in strength to redeem his people; Israel's hopes for redemption are beginning to be fulfilled. Jesus dared to believe that God's universal reign over the world was starting to take shape in the liberation that his own ministry was bringing to Israel.

Jesus was keen to distance himself from some of the alternative strategies currently on offer. Because he did not see military victory over Israel's foreign enemies as the vehicle of the coming of God's kingdom, he gave no support to people of violence. He did not make common cause with those who ran Jerusalem and its temple. Neither did he align himself with the Essenes in their protest against the temple's defilement. He did not endorse the Pharisees' desire to extend the purity laws beyond the temple, to create a sacred sphere free from Gentile contamination. What he did do was to identify early in his career with John the Baptist. The Gospels depict John as an Elijah-like figure, the forerunner of a new order in Israel. He announced the imminence of God's judgment, soon to be followed by a salvation mediated by 'one mightier than I'. It is significant that John was preparing for the coming salvation in the wilderness, a place of new beginnings for Israel according to Hosea 2:14. He was using water baptism as a sign of Israel's readiness to participate in the new order. The wilderness was not Jerusalem, and John's baptism was not the temple cult. According to John, the restored Israel would no longer be centred on Jerusalem and its temple, neither would it be constituted by descent, because God could turn stones into children of Abraham. Unlike the Pharisees and the Essenes, John offered no vision of a renewed Israel based on separatist holiness. Unlike the revolutionaries, he did not advocate violence. Jesus was drawn to the Baptist's vision of Israel's salvation, and received his call as John baptized him. According to the Fourth Gospel, he was one of John's disciples and collaborators, and first met some of his own disciples among the people drawn to John (John 1:35ff; 3:22ff). Jesus, then, began his public ministry in close association with a prophet who was preparing for the restoration of Israel. He identified with the Baptist because he recognized that John was laying foundations on which he himself could build. We have here, then, an early clue about Jesus' own aims and intentions.

Herod's arrest of John the Baptist marked the start of Jesus' Galilean ministry, and with it his demonstration of what it meant for the reign of God to begin to take shape in Israel. The diverse group of twelve men whom he called to identify totally with his mission symbolized his intention to restore the twelve tribes, that is, Israel as a whole. He gave them a share in his ministry (Matthew 10:6) and promised them a role in God kingdom (Matthew 19:28). We have some idea of what Israel's restoration looked like to Jesus from three aspects of his ministry—his table fellowship; his healing and exorcism; and his attitude to the temple. Jesus' habit of sharing meals with outcasts as well as respectable members of the Jewish community provoked both delight and shock. The meal table provided zealous Jews with the opportunity to rehearse their understanding of what it meant to be God's covenant people in the face of foreign defilement. They were careful to eat only kosher food; sharing meals with Gentiles, or Jews who were deemed unclean, was taboo. The Essenes refused to allow the maimed, the lame and the blind to share their community meals, which ran entirely contrary to Jesus' practice and advice (Luke 14:23). Anyone who subverted the distinctions between clean and unclean, as these were publicly demonstrated in table fellowship, was questioning a fundamental understanding of Israel's identity and challenging the politics of holiness. So it is not surprising that Jesus' social behaviour should have scandalized those Jewish groups who were particularly concerned with the strategies of separatism. This was one of his ways of demonstrating God's desire to embrace *all* Israel.

This same desire is also expressed in Jesus' ministry of healing and exorcism. The Jewish scholar Geza Vermes has compared Jesus with

contemporary Galilean 'holy men' mentioned in the rabbinic literature. These charismatic figures operated on the edges of mainstream
Judaism. They were men of prayer who sensed the immediacy of God,
owing their inspiration to God's Spirit rather than the Jewish scribal
schools. They were more concerned with the general principles of the
Law than its detailed application, and they were known for their
healing, exorcism and power over nature. Vermes has helped us to
understand Jesus' healing and exorcism as a type of activity we might
expect from such charismatic figures, though there are significant
differences between Jesus and them. Jesus' mighty works were an
integral part of his strategy for Israel's renewal, which cannot be said of
the Galilean charismatics. Their spectacular actions only enhanced their
religious authority, but Jesus consistently refused to heal or exorcise in
order to increase his public credibility. Instead he interpreted what he
was doing as signs of God's reign. They demonstrated that the hopes of
the prophets for a new order in Israel were at last beginning to take
shape (see Isaiah 35; 61). To those who saw his works as manifestations
of the power of evil, he issued the counter-claim that they revealed the
renewing power of the Spirit of God (Matthew 12:27ff; Luke 11:15ff).
It is important to recognize that all sections of Israel benefited from
Jesus' healing and exorcism—his ministry crossed social, religious and
economic divisions, and occasionally embraced Gentiles too. Like his
habit of sharing meals across the many divisions he encountered, his
healing and exorcism enabled him to signal God's intention to
overcome the disintegration which had resulted from Israel's double
occupation. And like his table fellowship, his mighty works provoked a
strongly negative response from those who were particularly concerned
to keep the boundaries between insiders and outsiders in place.

Jesus' attitude to the temple can also be seen as a sign of his intention
to redeem Israel. The Gospels reveal a degree of ambivalence towards
the temple on the part of Jesus. He assumed that his disciples would
offer sacrifice there (Matthew 5:23ff), but reminded his hearers of the
limitations of its cult (Matthew 12:6–7; Mark 12:33–34; John 4:20–
24). We should perhaps interpret Jesus' declaration of forgiveness in
Mark 2:5 in this light: he is deemed blasphemous because he denies the
necessity of the temple as the mediator of God's mercy. The evangelists
agree that Jesus announced the destruction and replacement of the
temple, though not by another building (Mark 13:2; Mark 14:58;
Matthew 26:61; John 2:19–22). It is possible that we should understand

Jesus' words to Peter in Matthew 16:18—'you are Peter, and on this rock I will build my church'—as meaning that faith in Jesus as Messiah is to replace the rock on which the Jerusalem temple was built as the foundation of the restored Israel. There is evidence that some Jewish groups, disenchanted with the current state of affairs in Jerusalem, were expecting a new temple in the age of salvation. Some Jewish texts see the new temple as a community rather than a building, and one of the Essene writings envisages the Messiah as its builder. So it is conceivable, though not certain, that Jesus intended to create a different kind of temple, one that fitted into his vision of Israel as a redeemed and restored community, in covenant with God.

According to Jesus, then, the appearance of God's kingdom would not precipitate the end of the world, nor would it come about by a glorious victory over Israel's enemies. Jesus believed that God was more interested in forgiveness and healing than winning military battles, and his kingdom would come through prayer rather than force of arms. God was not the guarantor of the politics of holiness, and his concerns could not be narrowed down to those who managed to avoid, or at least deal with, the contaminating power of what zealous Jews considered to be impure—like foreigners, or marginalized members of their own people. Jesus believed that in all that was taking place through him, Israel's God was beginning to write a new chapter in the story of his relationship with the world through his chosen people. In the face of a threat to the very existence of the Jews in the land they had always believed was God's gift to them, Jesus saw himself and his cause starting to fulfil the ancient hopes of his people for freedom, though not without some surprises. Israel's salvation would reverse the positions of first and last (Matthew 19:30); tax-collectors and prostitutes would enter the kingdom ahead of those whose ideology of holiness was essentially separatist (Matthew 21:31); the blessings of God's reign would embrace the poor rather than the rich (Luke 6:20; Mark 10:23; compare Luke 1:52ff). In the imagery of the parables in Luke 15, he interpreted his particular response to Israel's crisis in terms of searching for the lost so that the divided family of Israel could be made whole. This was the texture of the kingdom that he encouraged his disciples to pray for.

Marks tells us that Jesus began his ministry with a call for repentance. The first to heed this were fishermen, who 'immediately left their nets and followed him' (Mark 1:18). Because there is nothing inherently sinful about earning a living by fishing, Jesus must have envisaged something other than turning *aside* from sin. His call for repentance was a summons to a decisive turning *towards* the kingdom as it was taking shape through and around him. What exactly did he have in mind? Many of his parables are like pictures painted with broad brush strokes of the kind of response he was looking for: alertness, responsibility, persistent prayer, generosity, humility, faith, forgiveness and so on. But if we want a sharper image of his understanding of what God was expecting from Israel in her time of crisis, we need to pay heed to the way he used the Law to define the will of God.

Jesus does not appear to have sanctioned breaking the Law of Moses. According to Matthew 5:17, he had no wish to abolish the Law. On occasions, he commended the commandments to those who wanted to be sure of salvation (Mark 10:19; Luke 10:25ff). But he recognized that there was no universally recognized way of interpreting the Law in Israel—he asked the lawyer who enquired about eternal life in Luke 10:26, 'What is written in the law? *What do you read there?*' Jesus did not so much challenge the authority of the Law of Moses as take issue with some of the ways of *reading* it among his contemporaries. His legal disputes focused on those parts of the Torah that were used by the more zealous Jewish groups to define what it meant to be a true member of the covenant people. As we have seen, preoccupation with identity had proved to be divisive, and the differences between Jewish groups were not simply matters of after-dinner debate. This area of intra-Jewish tension, which sometimes spilled over into violence, provides the context within which we should understand Jesus' attitude to the Law of Moses.

Jesus differed from his opponents in Galilee (usually Pharisees and their legal experts) in his grasp of what was of central importance in the Law. He saw holiness not in terms of separatist purity but 'the weightier matters of the Law'—justice; mercy; love of God, neighbour and even enemies; faith (Matthew 9:11; 12:7; 23:23; Mark 12:28ff; Luke 6:27ff; 10:25ff; 11:42). He used these as keys to open up the heart of Israel's Law. Many Jews believed that when salvation came, the world would be returned to the pristine state of the original creation. Convinced that his ministry instituted the time when Israel's hopes for a new future were being fulfilled (Mark 1:15; Luke 4:21), Jesus advocated an interpretation of the Law that expressed God's original intention for creation. This comes across in his teaching about divorce in Mark 10:2ff. The questioner wanted to know where he stood in the debates between Jewish groups on the matter. Some maintained that Moses' permission for a husband to divorce his wife should be granted only if he discovered that she was not a virgin when he married her; others allowed him to divorce her if he were not satisfied with her cooking. Reading the whole Law through the 'weightier matters' of justice, mercy and love allowed Jesus to bring a critical eye to the divorce law. The Mosaic permission bred injustice in a society which treated the wife as the property of her husband. 'From the beginning' (v. 6) God did not intend a social order in which women were regarded as disposable commodities, but one in which male and female were treated alike as bearers of the divine image. On this understanding, marriage was originally intended to express the equality and complementarity that belong with being 'one flesh'. Jesus' reply suggests that the Torah-based practice of divorce in a society where women were mere chattels did not conform with God's intention 'from the beginning'. He offered an interpretation of the Law that matched his belief that the age of salvation was dawning; the renewal of Israel was nothing less than the restoration of the ideal order of creation.

We can see, then, how Jesus' strategy for the kingdom of God and his grasp of the will of God informed each other. He interpreted the Torah in such a way as to draw out the values that would establish his vision of God's reign in Israel, and thereby permit a more creative response to Israel's crisis, as she struggled to come to terms with the bigger world emanating from Greece and Rome. Rather than fastening onto those parts of the Law that promoted separatism and fragmentation, Jesus saw the will of God in terms of a new spirit to transform individuals and society, rooted in unlimited divine mercy (Matthew 5:38–48; Luke 6:27–36). The heart of Israel's God was full of longing to search for those who had strayed from the paths of justice, mercy and love, and to draw them into a renewed Israel which reflected his intentions for the whole of creation. Jesus' critique of separatist holiness was part of a wider challenge to what had become conventional wisdom in Israel—equating wealth with God's blessing; seeing the patriarchal family as sacrosanct; measuring honour by social recognition. Jesus saw these conventional values as a broad way leading to destruction (Matthew 7:13–14). He discerned that there was more violence in understanding holiness in terms of purity than Israel could bear if God's covenant people were to have a future: separatism, with its various strategies, would ultimately destroy itself. His alternative was the narrow way that led to life—an *inner* purity, a transformation of the heart that enabled people to live trustfully before God (Mark 7:14ff; Matthew 6:35ff). And he continued to press the claim that his vision of the will of God—rooted as it was in his own Spirit-filled experience of the intimacy of God as *Abba*—carried ultimate authority in Israel.

Who do people say that I am?

In setting out his vision of the reign and will of God, did Jesus see himself as the expected Jewish Messiah? This is not an easy question to answer, for a number of reasons. First, in contemporary Judaism there was no single concept of 'the Messiah' to which Jesus' ministry might be compared. Expectations abounded of a military leader, or a priestly figure, or a heavenly judge, or some combination of these; some Jewish texts even envisaged salvation coming to Israel without the help of a Messiah. Then, the Gospels indicate a degree of reserve on the part of Jesus towards any public acknowledgment that he might be the Messiah (see Mark 8:30). This should not be surprising, in view of his rejection of violence. He had a following in rural Galilee, where the outbreak of revolutionary violence was always possible. Publicity about any messianic aspirations that he might have for himself, or that others might wish to project onto him, could only hinder rather than help his cause. It is significant that he used the images of seed and yeast to picture the coming of God's kingdom in his own work (Matthew 13:24–33). These suggest that unlike the triumph of an army, God's reign can easily be overlooked; it can appear small and trifling, though its impact is undeniable. The uncertainty surrounding Jesus and messianic expectations is reflected in the enquiry of the imprisoned John the Baptist, whose disciples asked Jesus: 'Are you the one who is to come, or are we to wait for another?' (Matthew 11:2). In his reply, Jesus invited them to compare his teaching and actions with the prophetic pictures of the age of salvation (with Matthew 11:5 and Luke 7:22, compare Isaiah 29:18–19; 35:5–6; 61:1). This certainly suggests that he saw himself as the instrument of Israel's promised salvation. If he also believed that he had been anointed by the Spirit of God for this role (as is suggested in Mark 1:10, Matthew 12:28 and Luke 4:18), then he could conceivably have thought of himself as the messianic agent of salvation—the root meaning of 'Messiah' is 'one who is anointed by God'—without committing himself to any of the particular messianic strategies currently abroad in Israel. He appears to have been more concerned to persuade his contemporaries that his understanding of 'your kingdom come, your will be done' carried ultimate authority than to align himself with the hopes of one Jewish group or another for the redemption of Israel.

The messianic reserve in the synoptic Gospels is striking in view of the beliefs about Jesus that sprang up among his followers so soon after Easter. But it is not necessary to write off the early Church's faith in Jesus as 'the Messiah/Christ' as groundless. The Acts of the Apostles and the Epistles testify to the way in which the resurrection of Jesus provided the foundation for the belief that God had vindicated all that Jesus had lived and died for, despite his humiliating and shameful death. Such vindication included his sense of being the divinely authorized and anointed instrument of the messianic age. Jesus' ambivalent attitudes to messiahship can be interpreted as part of his desire to redefine the shape of salvation—the direction of the reign of God, the purpose of the Torah, the role of the agent of Israel's redemption. In the face of the various competing visions of a new future for the people of God, early Christianity continued the process of redefinition that began with Jesus. Its leading lights sought to persuade the sons and daughters of Abraham that the messianic age of Israel's promised redemption really had started to take shape in and through Jesus and his community, rather than any of the other options currently being pursued by Jewish groups. It is this continuity of redefinition—beginning with Jesus and taken up by his followers after Easter—that allows us to ground the earliest beliefs in the messiahship of Jesus in the faith of Jesus himself.

The kingdom of heaven has suffered violence

The prophets had warned that Israel's salvation would be preceded by upheaval (Micah 7:6f; Ezekiel 38:18ff; Zechariah 14:13ff). Because Jesus did not set out to paper over the cracks in Jewish society, his ministry of renewal by redefinition only exacerbated Israel's crisis (Matthew 10:34; Luke 12:51). Given the degree of fragmentation he encountered in Jewish Palestine, he could hardly have expected to gain a widespread endorsement for his vision of the rule and will of God. If the crowds who were attracted by his teaching and healing were capable of misunderstanding his intentions, with his closest followers occasionally outspoken in their stubborn resistance to his chosen path, then those who openly opposed him could not have remained content with a 'live and let live' attitude to his vision of Israel's salvation. The potential for intra-Jewish tensions to spill over into violence might shed light on an enigmatic saying preserved in Matthew 11:12: 'From the time of John the Baptist until now, the kingdom of heaven has suffered violence, and the violent take it by force.' Though the meaning of this saying is not clear, Jesus may have been suggesting that the messengers of God's reign, like John the Baptist and himself, could not expect an easy passage. John was of course arrested by Herod Antipas, client ruler of Galilee. According to Josephus, this was because the Baptist's ability to attract crowds made him a threat to public order. Mark tells us that Herod's supporters made common cause with some Pharisees in Galilee, against Jesus (Mark 3:6). These two groups shared an interest in keeping the peace in Galilee, thus preventing any need for Roman interference in Galilean affairs. Jesus' challenge to separatist ways of ordering the world, backed up by his popularity among the rural poor, threatened the delicate balance of political power. By drawing out the violence that was necessary to maintain the status quo, he put his own life at risk.

The Gospels give the impression that the intensity of the violence directed against Jesus increased the closer he was to Jerusalem. In the synoptics, his single visit to the holy city at Passover-tide constituted the climax of his challenge to Israel, and gave the guardians of the temple a golden opportunity to get rid of him. The Fourth Gospel shows how Jesus' teaching in the temple courts on his regular visits to Jerusalem for the pilgrim feasts provoked the hostility of 'the Jews' (that is, the Jewish leaders), not least because his claim to speak and act in the name of God challenged their right to exercise any authority in Israel (John 5:1–47; 7:14–36; 8:12–59). After several unsuccessful attempts to stone him, they finally decided on a course of action to prevent the inevitable Roman interference in Jewish affairs should Jesus' popularity with the crowds persist (John 11:47ff). Ironically, it was the raising of Lazarus which propelled Jesus' opponents along the road that brought about his execution. If we allow the synoptics and the Fourth Gospel to shed light on each other here, they allow us to see Jesus as a Galilean teacher who was well-known in Jerusalem before his fateful visit. His opponents were aware of what he stood for, and that he had a following in his native Galilee. He may well have seen what turned out to be his final visit to the holy city as a further chance to appeal to the leaders of his people to embrace his vision of the rule and will of God before it was too late. His

31

so-called cleansing of the temple was a symbolic action in the best prophetic tradition, directed against an institution whose very architecture represented the policies of separatist holiness. He attacked what he saw as the centre of Israel's defilement—did he see the temple as a 'den of robbers' because its authorities were creaming off the wealth of the Jewish regions and using it to support their place in the religious and political power structure? Whatever his reasons, his action left the Jewish leaders with no choice other than to enlist the support of the Roman governor to have him removed. The atmosphere in a city bulging with Passover pilgrims, celebrating God's liberation of their forebears from foreign oppression, was too volatile to risk allowing Galilean sparks to fly freely. Jesus' crucifixion would not only remove an irritant from the body politic, it would also deter his supporters against doing anything rash. The violence of the gibbet was a price worth paying to preserve the delicate politics and fragile peace of the holy city from the brutality of Rome.

The cup, the baptism and the Son of Man

According to the Gospels, Jesus predicted his death and interpreted it in relation to Israel's crisis and her hopes for salvation. It was a 'baptism' he had to endure and a 'cup' he must drink (Mark 10:38–39). He expected to meet his end in the calamitous flood that would engulf Israel should his way be rejected. If there were overtones of divine judgment in this imagery (as in the Genesis flood, and the cup of Psalm 75:8), then Jesus may have seen his own death, not that of Israel's enemies, as somehow cleansing the world in preparation for the coming salvation. Clearly he did not see his death as an isolated event—those who threw in their lot with him in the hope of participating in Israel's salvation would likewise drink his cup and share his baptism.

Jesus hardly needed supernatural insight to realize what would happen to him should he persist in his challenge to Jerusalem. He need only recall the history of the prophets, in whose line he saw himself (Luke 13:34ff). Material from one particular prophetic book— Daniel—has made a deep impression on the synoptic passion predictions (Mark 8:31; 9:31; 10:33–34). Even if their wording owes more to later reflection on the actual course of events, there are good reasons for believing that these sayings bring us close to the mind of Jesus as he anticipated his passion. Josephus tells us that first-century Jews held that

Daniel was a prophet for their own time. The book's stories and visions—originally compiled to encourage an earlier generation of Jews, in the aftermath of Antiochus Epiphanes' assaults on their land and temple some 200 years before the ministry of Jesus—summed up the bitter lesson of Israel's turbulent history. God would indeed vindicate the faithful remnant of his people, but they would not enter the promised new world of justice and freedom without first enduring the distress of foreign oppression. The vision in Daniel 7 provided the imagery and ideas that articulated the hopes of some Jewish groups in the first Christian century. Four menacing beasts, representing earthly rulers, appear before the judgment seat of 'the Ancient of Days'. The fourth is especially terrifying in its violence and arrogance. A human figure, 'one like a son of man', is presented before God's throne and promised everlasting universal dominion. By contrast, the beasts are stripped of their power and the fourth is utterly destroyed. In the interpretation of the vision, the 'one like a son of man' is said to represent 'the Holy Ones of the Most High', who have suffered greatly under the rule of the fourth beast (which presumably originally referred to Antiochus Epiphanes). They are vindicated, while their oppressors are consumed by God's judgment.

Jesus drew on these images to give voice to his own faith as he faced the prospect of suffering and death. However much violence he had to endure for the sake of God's reign and will, he believed that God would vindicate him and his cause. As in the book of Daniel and the stories of the Maccabean martyrs, he not surprisingly envisaged such vindication in terms of resurrection from the dead (Daniel 12:2–3; 2 Maccabees 7). But Jesus put his own slant on Daniel's vision, in four ways. First, his 'Son of Man' did not merely represent suffering Israel before God; he actually suffered as a faithful Israelite. He expected God to vindicate his willingness to give everything for the sake of the kingdom. Secondly, his reference to the suffering 'Son of Man' is followed by words about discipleship: his followers must take up their cross and risk their lives for his sake if they want to reap the benefits of God's reign (Mark 8:34–38). This suggests that Jesus did not see himself suffering in isolation from his followers. They too must expect their faith in God's kingdom to be severely tested; and like Jesus they can expect their own faithfulness to be vindicated (Mark 13:9–13). Thirdly, Jesus dared to identify Israel's enemies (the oppressors of the Son of Man) not with foreign rulers but the Jewish leaders in Jerusalem. He believed that *his* vision of God's reign and will, not theirs, would usher in the messianic age—a claim which he pressed before the high priest following his arrest, and one which not surprisingly met with hostile rejection (Mark 14:61–64). Fourthly, a further 'Son of Man' saying offers a critique of worldly power, in speaking of the beneficial impact of Jesus' Passion as the fruit of the Son of Man's self-giving. 'The Son of Man came not to be served but to serve, and to give his life as a ransom for many' (Mark 10:45). His whole life, culminating in his death, would be the means of overcoming the powers of the old, unredeemed order and restoring Israel for the day of salvation. In this way he would be the true Israelite, and stamp his pattern on the life of the redeemed community, for whom power was to be exercised in service rather than tyranny (Mark 10:42–44).

The fact that these 'Son of Man' sayings—like those of the baptism and the cup—link Jesus' Passion with the way of discipleship, and place these in the broader context of Israel's impending crisis in the face of the struggle for her salvation, suggests that Jesus saw his Passion as the leading edge of the promised new world. He was willing to face the consequences of his all-embracing call for repentance, come what may. He trusted that God would vindicate him and establish the cause for which he had lived and would die. He believed that God would bring him through his suffering and death, together with all who identified with him, into the new order of resurrection. His words over the bread and the cup at the Last Supper give further substance to the faith that Jesus articulated with the help of the prophet Daniel. 'This is my body . . . my blood of the covenant'—the sacrifice of his own life would seal God's commitment to establish the new covenant with his people, promised in Jeremiah 31:31–34. Eating and drinking enabled the disciples to identify with all that he had given himself for. His suffering would not be in vain, but would bear fruit 'for many' in the coming of God's kingdom, in which he and his followers would once again drink 'the fruit of the vine'.

Among Jesus' last recorded words are his prayer in the garden. 'Let this cup pass from me; nevertheless not my will but your will be done' expresses not only his devotion to the reign and will of God, but also his readiness to entrust to God all that he had lived for. He went to his death prepared to leave the outcome of his cause in God's hands. On the cross Jesus felt just as God-forsaken as anyone else who is forced to suffer unimaginable and unbearable pain. Whether the last words from the cross were a cry of desolation (Matthew and Mark), faith (Luke) or victory (John), the one who uttered them had not been overcome by the violence of those who sought to deflect him from his course. He had proved to be utterly faithful in his witness to the coming of God's kingdom and the revelation of God's will for the redemption of Israel from the consequences of her double occupation. In the event, Good Friday gave way to Easter and Pentecost. God did not abandon the one who had truly lived and died for Israel's salvation. The Spirit that had animated his life and ministry from the beginning was released into the wider world, and the seeds of his gospel were blown into new and distant soil around the empire. Communities sprang up owing their allegiance to Jesus as Messiah, and understanding themselves as a renewed Israel. Her new temple, built and held together by the Messiah, had no courts to separate the holy from the unclean. In the Messiah's body, conventional understandings of race, gender, social standing, power and wisdom counted for nothing. This covenant community did not identify itself by the markers of separatist holiness, but only by faith in the crucified and risen Jesus as Israel's long-expected Messiah. It measured the holiness to which it was called by God in terms of the fruit of the Spirit, who was transforming the covenant people from within by writing the Law of love in their hearts.

Early Christianity's redefinition of Israel can fairly claim to be a creative response to the crisis facing the covenant people of God. It opened up the possibility of using the Jewish Scriptures as the foundation for a world-embracing faith, but at a price—the loss of Jewish identity. The Christian movement grew further and further away from its Jewish roots, and history saw to it that the two ways eventually parted. In a world that has in some ways, though not in others, moved on from the first century, Jewish interest in Jesus and Christian interest in Judaism are signs of hope. The politics of holiness are still with us, in one form or another. The violence needed to keep separatism in place regularly spills over into conflict, but now the stakes are higher than they were 2,000 years ago. The world has shrunk as much as our capacity to destroy ourselves has expanded. Living as we do under the occupation of all manner of powers that fragment societies and divide nations, we are in no position to push to one side Jesus' vision of restoration and transformation. The substance of his prayer—'your kingdom come, your will be done'—still holds out the possibility of renewal.

For further reading

Marcus J. Borg, *Jesus: A New Vision. Spirit, Culture and the Life of Discipleship*, SPCK, 1993

John H. Charlesworth, *Jesus Within Judaism. New Light from Exciting Archaeological Discoveries*, SPCK, 1988

Elizabeth Schüssler Fiorenza, *In Memory of Her. A Feminist Theological Reconstruction of Christian Origins*, SCM Press, 1983

Anthony Harvey, *Jesus and the Constraints of History*, Duckworth, 1982

John Riches, *The World of Jesus. First Century Judaism in Crisis*, Cambridge, 1990

Ed Sanders and Margaret Davies, *Studying the Synoptic Gospels*, SCM Press/TPI, 1989

Ed Sanders, *The Historical Figure of Jesus*, Penguin, 1993

Jon Sobrino, *Jesus in Latin America*, Orbis Books, 1987

Graham Stanton, *The Gospels and Jesus*, OUP, 1989

Gerd Theissen, *The Shadow of the Galilean. The Quest of the Historical Jesus in Narrative Form*, SCM Press, 1987

Geza Vermes, *Jesus the Jew*, SCM Press, 1983

Geza Vermes, *The Religion of Jesus the Jew*, SCM Press, 1993

N.T. Wright, *The New Testament and the People of God*, SPCK, 1992

N.T. Wright, *Who Was Jesus?* SPCK 1993

MATTHEW

Matthew's Gospel was probably written in the last decade of the first century AD. All the surviving manuscripts of the Gospel are headed 'According to Matthew', and the name appears twice in the text. Mark's 'Levi son of Alphaeus', sitting at the tax booth (Mark 2:14), is named 'Matthew' in Matthew 9:9; the same man appears in Matthew's list of the twelve apostles in 10:3 (compare Mark 3:18 and Luke 6:15). While this does not prove authorship, it might lend some support to the second-century belief that the Gospel was written by Matthew the tax collector-turned-disciple. One of the most striking features of Matthew's Gospel is its Jewishness: its five great collections of Jesus' teaching may have been intended as counterparts of the five books of Moses, and its twelve fulfilment quotations root its narrative in the Jewish Scriptures. The Gospel's attitude to Judaism is both strongly positive and harshly critical, and it is at times open to the Gentiles. This suggests a good deal of complexity in the relationship between the Gospel and those for whom it was first intended, and in the way it came to be written.

Scholars have traditionally assumed that Matthew used Mark as his primary source. Matthew includes most of Mark's Gospel; Matthew's Greek is considerably better than Mark's, and much of the time Matthew follows Mark's order. As well as Mark, Matthew is supposed to have used a collection of the sayings of Jesus (also used by Luke) and material that was unique to his account. Careful attention to the actual text of Matthew's Gospel suggests an alternative account of its composition to one which sees the evangelist using written sources. Matthew apparently made little attempt to reconcile some of the divergent traditions he drew on. Jesus was sent only to the 'lost sheep of the house of Israel' (10:6; 15:24)—or was he (8:5–13)? He came to fulfil the Law, which should not be altered in the slightest (5:17ff)—or should it (9:13; 12:7)? He expected his disciples to fast (6:16–18)—or did he (9:14ff)? He sanctioned unlimited forgiveness for an erring member of the Church (18:21ff)—or did he (18:15ff)? He announced that the Son of Man would come to establish his kingdom within a generation (16:28)—or would he (24:48; 25:5, 19)?

One way of accounting for these divergencies is to understand Matthew's Gospel as a reflection of the emphases of different Christian groups living in a mixed background. The Church's mission was expanding in a region inhabited by Jews and Gentiles. Some Christian groups were more rooted in Judaism, while others were more open to Gentile cultures. The author of the Gospel collected the traditions about Jesus that were held by the various Christian groups in his area. His narrative—based on a developed form of the Marcan tradition—is a statement of the entire tradition held by the various communities, with all its rough edges. It attempts to enable each group to become conversant with a richer and more varied story of Jesus than their own. By building into its story opportunities for mutual understanding, the Gospel reconciles the tensions between these groups and serves their mission. Matthew stresses continuity with the past and openness to the future: the story of Jesus Christ fulfils God's work in the history of Israel, but in such a way as to enable Israel to embrace and welcome the Gentiles. Jesus is the way for Jew and Gentile alike to discover and fulfil the will of God. Many of Jesus' sayings and parables implied personal and corporate responsibility before God. Matthew presents these in such a way as to stimulate a thoughtful approach to discipleship, with a freedom to find and respond to the will of God as disclosed in Jesus Christ. That way the different Christian groups Matthew wrote for would find a common purpose.

As to the setting for which the Gospel was written, Matthew sees the events he narrates in Galilee and Judea taking place on the other side of the Jordan (4:15; 19:1). Antioch in Syria is a possible location; this was a metropolitan area with many different social and religious communities. We know from an earlier period (see Galatians 2:11—14) that there were Christian groups there who found it hard to reconcile their approaches to the Jewish Law and mission among Gentiles. After the Jewish War (AD66—74) and the fall of Jerusalem (AD70), both Jews and Christians had to come to terms with a radically new situation, in which both communities were wondering what it meant to be God's covenant people now that the temple was no more. Matthew's Gospel can usefully be read against the mixed background of an area surrounding Syrian Antioch towards the end of the first century AD. It can thereby help today's readers—whether individuals or communities—to discover new and unanticipated ways forward in Christian discipleship, in an ecumenical and multi-cultural setting.

The translation used is the Revised English Bible.

Further reading

Margaret Davies, *Matthew. Readings: A New Biblical Commentary*, JSOT Press, 1993

R.T. France, *Matthew—Evangelist and Teacher*, Paternoster Press, 1989

Ivor H. Jones, *The Gospel of Matthew*, Epworth Press, 1994

J.D. Kingsbury, *Matthew as Story*, Fortress Press, 1988

Outline of Matthew's Gospel

The fulfilment of Israel's hope	1:1—2:23
The Baptist and the Son of God: Israel's restoration begins	3:1—4:25
The first discourse: Living in God's way in God's world (The Sermon on the Mount)	5:1—7:29
The authority and power of the healing Messiah	8:1—9:38
The second discourse: Labourers in the harvest of God's mission	10:1—11:1
The words and works of God's wisdom	11:2—12:50
The third discourse: Revealing God's secrets in parables	13:1–52
Rejection and compassion	13:53—16:12
The Son of God is the Son of Man	16:13—17:27
The fourth discourse: Life in the kingdom	18:1–35
Jesus in Judea: questions and parables	19:1—20:34

The Messiah in Jerusalem   21:1—22:41

The fifth discourse: Final and abiding warnings   23:1—25:45

The Son of Man is delivered up to be crucified   26:1—27:66

The crucified Messiah is raised to
universal authority   28:1–20

— THE FULFILMENT OF — ISRAEL'S HOPE

Widening the horizons   *Matthew 1:1–17*

Matthew has a different kind of opening from the other Gospels. Mark's introduction mentions 'gospel'; Luke refers to his 'account'. Matthew calls his work a 'book of the genealogy of Jesus Christ' (some translations of verse 1 omit the word 'book'). From the beginning, in verse 2, he links this story with another very significant narrative: the book of Genesis. Like Genesis his book is full of surprises. As Genesis offers an expanding vision of God's creative work, so Matthew notes the expansion of the vision of the Messiah ('son of David') in the universal promises to Abraham ('son of Abraham'). He includes immediately four women within the genealogy, some of them of doubtful repute (Tamar, Rahab, Ruth and the wife of Uriah—vv. 3, 5, 6) and all considered at that time to be non-Jews. All these Matthew links with Jesus Christ, in whom God's new and surprising work has begun.

But that work is not without due preparation. This will be a theme of the whole Gospel and particularly of the opening two chapters. God's hand has been at work preparing the way for this new opportunity. Verse 17 sees God's hand in the numerical perfection of the generations which have led up to this time (fourteen from Abraham to David, fourteen from David to the exile, fourteen from the exile to the Messiah). What Israel has experienced over forty-two generations is an integral part of the book which Matthew is writing. But new this present opportunity certainly is. The Messiah will gather up the history of Israel, with its periods of greatness and of humiliation. He will show that the story includes the dispossessed, the outcasts, the aliens, the misjudged. It is a story of new

40

hope and encouragement, written so that Matthew's own generation might widen its own horizons. The story of the Messiah is for all. Salvation, hope, wisdom and responsibility are the key elements of his story. They are part of a universal heritage. So future generations too will read in this Gospel about the reliability of all God's ways and works and be amazed at the vistas of God's purposes as they continue to unfold.

Astonishment and obedience   *Matthew 1:18–25*

How does humanity discover this divine hope? Is not the distance between the human and the divine too great? Are we not limited to our own vision and understanding? This opening story provides an unexpected answer. Indeed this section is full of surprises. We are expecting the story of the birth of the Messiah (v. 18). But first comes the story of Joseph, a 'man of principle' (v. 19). There is no difficulty for Joseph in discovering the divine purpose. He has come to a clear judgment on the problem which confronts him: he must stand by his principles, but he must also save Mary from cruel tongues. Then comes the dream, which reveals the role of the Holy Spirit in the conception of Jesus. God's work of salvation has been planned and is linked with the naming of 'Jesus' (v. 21). There is the promise of the divine presence in Jesus, Emmanuel—'God with us' (v. 23). The situation has changed dramatically. Again the book of Genesis is recalled in the first of five references to dreams (see also 2:12, 13, 19, 22), such as those that guided Moses, Jacob, Joseph and others of the patriarchs. The directness of the communication is staggering. Joseph receives the divine assurance personally and without any external mediation. The message contains also some very significant elements. Joseph is addressed as 'Son of David' (v. 20); the messianic story already involves him. He is offered comfort and encouragement and the evidence of a prophecy that 'a virgin will conceive' (v. 23; compare Isaiah 7:14). The dream may have the authority of its own immediacy. But there is a good deal more to the dream than that. Its message is evidently consonant with the ways and purpose of God revealed in the Old Testament tradition.

It is difficult to know where the emphasis lies in this astonishing introductory story. There is much to be said for noting the content of the dream. The message of Emmanuel, God with us, appears here in the opening story and finally in the concluding verse of the Gospel. It is also confirmed in the promise made in 18:20, where Christ promises his presence among the ' two or three who meet in his name'. There is also much to be said for placing some emphasis on verse 24: 'When he woke, Joseph did as the angel of the Lord had directed him.' Matthew, like Paul, is concerned that vision and insight, revelation and privilege, should be perfected in actual obedience.

Fulfilment in homage and contrasts   *Matthew 2:1–12*

As the Joseph narrative provided insights into the coming of the Messiah, so the story of the astrologers does the same here. Like Joseph they too are already part of the messianic story. One of the Old Testament promises associated with the coming of the Messiah concerns an oracle 'from the mountains of the east' that 'a star will come forth out of Jacob; a comet will arise from Israel' (Numbers 24:17). The astrologers come because they have associated a star with a royal promise. As in the case of Joseph's dream there is no hint of criticism or caution about the astrologer's methods. Matthew simply narrates that they came, and that the scribes in Jerusalem confirmed the nature of the promise. 'A ruler' is to come, but he will be from Judah, from lowly Bethlehem. These Gentiles have been drawn to Jerusalem, as the book of Isaiah promised they would be (Isaiah 66:20). But the fulfilment is not there; it is in Bethlehem.

Part of the fascination of Matthew's Gospel is why the Gentile astrologers are given pride of place as the first to seek out the new-born king to pay him homage. Perhaps Matthew is writing to Jewish Christians and wants to warn them against excluding Gentiles from their company. Perhaps he is writing to both Jewish and Gentile Christians to encourage them to coexist. Of crucial importance is the role of the others in the story. Sometimes it is suggested that the scribes appear here as a warning that Gentiles can see the light where the Jews in Jerusalem do not (as the people of Nineveh are a warning in Matthew 12:41). The text does not actually say that. One of the great tragedies in the reading of Matthew's Gospel has been the damage which some interpretations have caused to Jewish-Christian relationships. There are problems to be faced in the reading of Matthew in the context of contemporary Jewish-Christian relationships, but that is no reason for reading them into the text here.

The giving of homage to Jesus Christ is another link between the beginning of Matthew's Gospel and its ending (compare v. 11 with

28:17). This is a characteristic theme of the Gospel. Sometimes it is insincere, as with Herod here. But one of the features of the story of the astrologers is that homage is brought 'with great joy' (v. 10). The gold, frankincense and myrrh can be treated symbolically. Gold points to a royal birth, frankincense to divinity, and myrrh to the coming cross and passion. Perhaps the gifts are prophetic in a different way. Rather than prophesying what is to happen to Christ, the gifts point to what many Gentiles will contribute to the Christian worship. Moreover they demonstrate that the moment Israel has been expecting has arrived. God's time of fulfilment is with us. Psalm 72 had looked forward to as much: 'All kings will do him homage . . . He will redeem their lives from exploitation and outrage . . . May gold of Sheba be given him!' (vv. 11, 13, 14). This Messiah is not a tyrant, like Herod: 'He will not snap off a broken reed, nor snuff out a smouldering wick . . . In him the nations shall put their hope' (Matthew 12:20–21, quoting Isaiah 42:3–4). Contrasts are part of Matthew's good news—between the prestige of Jerusalem and the lowly status of Bethlehem, between astrologers and infant, between vicious tyrant and merciful Messiah.

Superbly narrated, the story of the astrologers brings its own beauty to Matthew's presentation of Christ's birth. In its theme of homage, in its contrasts between joy and pain, humility and blessing, it is a preparation for the story ahead. It is also about the practical and down-to-earth, so much a feature of Matthew's Gospel. As we read further, we shall see that the kingdom of Heaven is about money, the cup of cold water, the help given to a prisoner.

Another contrast: providence and tyranny
Matthew 2:13–18

Joseph's obedience is now tested by a further dream. This time he is required to take Jesus and his mother to the safety of Egypt. They are to rehearse again what many before and many since have experienced in order to escape from tyranny or famine: the life of a refugee. God has been preparing us for his new moment, as Matthew has already noted in chapter 1. Providence had been at work during Israel's history. Now providence becomes a feature of the life of God's son, as Herod's plan is forestalled by means of a vision. The pattern for the refugees' escape was that of Jacob's flight from famine in Canaan into another Joseph's protection in Egypt (Genesis 45). The timing of their departure at night and the mention of Herod's death evoke a different feature of Israel's time in Egypt: the experience of Pharoah's tyranny. It was by night that the Israelites escaped from Pharoah—the Pharaoh who murdered the Israelites' children. Matthew tells the story as if the providential events of the exodus were being relived in the life of Jesus. What God promised then is being fulfilled now. However, the quotation from Hosea 11:1, 'Out of Egypt have I called my son', is being used to recall yet another feature of this story of Palestinian refugees. The messianic claim of Jesus was being extended and enlarged. Jesus' first visitors came from abroad. Here his first summons came while he was abroad. No refugee is outside divine concern and care. This particular refugee ensured that once and for all.

The slaughter of the innocents is surely one of the most poignant passages in Matthew's Gospel. The story of the birth of the Messiah has begun. Visions and dreams have provided providential care and guidance. The visiting astrologers have reacted with joy to finding the Christ-child. Into the story is inserted the human cost of ruthless tyranny, the apparently pointless venting of frustrated rage. Why does the story stand here? Some suggest that the solution is to be found in the Old Testament, in Jeremiah 31, the chapter that promises a new covenant written in the heart. It is a chapter of hope and promise. Even the reference to Rachel weeping for her children in Jeremiah 31:15 is immediately followed by the return of the lost children (see vv. 16, 17). But in Matthew there is no such happy ending. The massacre in all its horror remains unpublished and irreversible. Tyranny is part of the Matthean story. It is part of the disorder from which the Messiah promises deliverance. It is part of the human cost of living with those who know no mercy. It helps to explain why the Messiah must redeem us from exploitation and outrage. It shows why only the one who 'will not break the crushed reed' can be a hope for the Gentiles. This Messiah is the Son of Man, who will judge by standards of mercy (see 25:31f), but who was himself subjected to an unjust trial (27:1—2). The slaughter of the innocents is not just a background to the story of salvation. It is part of that story, to be faced in all its hideous folly and grief. There is a pattern of destruction within God's world. Those who are responsible for it must hear Matthew's words of judgment. And no Gospel sets out that judgment more clearly.

Fulfilment in the coming of God's servant *Matthew 2:19–23*

It has been said that the first two chapters of Matthew are concerned to establish who Jesus is and where he came from. That is a useful summary, although we have seen that there is rather more to the geographical references than such a simple summary might suggest. Certainly the story takes us via another dream back to the land of Israel. Because of Archelaus' ascension in place of his father Herod, and a further dream, Joseph settled the family into Galilee. The Galilee narratives begin from there. Does the name 'Galilee' suggest a quiet, peaceful country area? We shall soon read Matthew's description of Galilee, or at least a part of the region. It is the place where the Gentiles live, where people living in darkness have now seen a great light (4:13–16). Part of our picture of Galilee is of Jesus' home in Nazareth. We fill in the details with our imagination. We see Jesus in the carpenter's shop and reconstruct his life there. Matthew's interest in Nazareth was somewhat different, and at first slightly less helpful. He suggests that the move there was in fulfilment of another prophecy: 'He shall be called a Nazarene' (v. 23). But which prophecy does he have in mind here? Is this yet another illustration of how providentially God has prepared the way for Jesus?

The answer to these questions is by no means clear. No one particular Old Testament passage seems to fit Matthew's quotation exactly. It looks as if it is the result of a good deal of contemplation of the Old Testament in the light of Christ's coming, and meditation on the life of Jesus based on Scripture, providing illuminating insights into Christ's mission and work. The three key insights are:

◇ '(He) . . . shall be called holy' (Isaiah 4:3)—holiness and being 'a Nazarite'(Numbers 6:2ff) went together;

◇ 'I have called you a righteousness' (Isaiah 42:6), with a similar passage in Isaiah 49:6, which might be read as 'a Nazarene restoring Israel';

◇ the traditional meanness of Nazareth (compare John 1:46).

Putting these together we can see how Matthew understood Jesus, the Nazarene. The Messiah is none other than the servant of God, dedicated and led by the Holy Spirit, called to bring restoration to

Israel. Restoration for Israel and hope for the Gentiles were linked together, at least in Matthew's understanding. So verse 23 summarizes a great deal of the first two chapters of Matthew. This is the story of Jesus, the Christ, the son of David, son of Abraham, deliverer, redeemer, judge, on behalf of all humanity.

> We can see two striking features in the opening of Matthew's Gospel. In the coming of Jesus, God is widening the horizons of what it means to be his people Israel. At the same time he makes use of what may be to us surprising channels of communication.
>
> ● Do we maintain barriers comparable with the divide between Jew and Gentile? Are they insuperable?
>
> ● What are the ways in which God draws **us** into partnership? If it was by dreams and vision then, how does it happen now?

THE BAPTIST AND THE SON OF GOD: ── ISRAEL'S RESTORATION BEGINS ──

The gospel and the forerunner   *Matthew 3:1—6*

Jesus is very close to John the Baptist in Matthew's Gospel. Their message is identical: 'Repent, for the kingdom of Heaven is upon you!' (compare v. 2 and 4:17). The kingdom which they both serve is one and the same. They have the same word of judgment. They both present in their different ways the words of divine wisdom (see 11:19). They both draw large crowds. They each recognize that a similar fate awaits them. There is a partnership between them which each acknowledges and values. 'Among all who have ever been born,' says Jesus, 'no one has been greater than John the Baptist' (11:11).

There are, nevertheless, differences. Jesus speaks of them in this way: 'John came neither eating and drinking, and people said: "He is possessed"; the Son of Man came eating and drinking, and they say, "Look at him! A glutton and a drinker, a friend of tax-collectors and sinners!" ' (11:18—19). Despite their closeness, John is different in his

46

style of life and availability. He is moreover only a forerunner who prepares the way (v. 3). Crucially important events in which Jesus takes centre stage will take place without John, who will be in prison, or already beheaded. In those respects he misses out on so much. But to have been the herald of the Messiah, to have witnessed the messianic activity and recognized it, that is honour enough. To have prepared the crowds for the day of the Lord, and to have done so faithfully and effectively, is more than most of us could hope to achieve, or have the opportunity to achieve.

One could say that John has absolutely the right approach. He does not think of himself. He gives way. He speaks God's word whatever the cost, persevering to the bitter end. And this is rather more than a right approach. These are gospel attitudes. Maybe he is too early to share in the benefits of Christ's work. He is a witness to the way of Christ all the same. Not merely is he the forerunner, a voice crying aloud in the wilderness. He prepares the way of the Lord by the way he lives as well as by what he says. In Matthew's view his way of doing right and proclaiming right makes him the ideal witness. He shows that it is obedience to the divine call that matters. Doing the divine will is supremely important. Little wonder that Jesus spoke so highly of him.

Prophets of judgment   *Matthew 3:7–12*

According to Matthew, Jesus and John taught in the same way. John spoke of the winnowing-shovel being ready. The chaff has been cleared from the threshing-floor; it is ready for burning. This is not a message which John alone delivers. It is not a question of John proclaiming judgment and Jesus proclaiming mercy—Jesus too preaches judgment: 'Every tree that fails to produce fruit is cut down and thrown into the fire' (7:19). 'The men of Nineveh will appear in court when this generation is on trial, and ensure its condemnation, for they repented at the preaching of Jonah; and what is here is greater than Jonah' (12:41). And to the disciples Jesus says, 'You also will sit on twelve thrones, judging the twelve tribes of Israel' (19:28). The preaching of judgment, begun by John the Baptist, is to be continued by Jesus. In this respect John and Jesus both stand in the prophetic tradition. They sound like Old Testament prophets: God's day of judgment is near; God will exact punishment on those who practise injustice; there is no protection for Israel or Judah. John the Baptist's warning sounds very like that. Like

Ezekiel he warns that once a tree has ceased to produce fruit nothing can be done with the wood except to burn it (Ezekiel 19:14). His hearers may claim to be Abraham's children (v. 9). But the divine power can form descendants for Abraham from the desert stones.

In one particular respect John the Baptist recognizes that Jesus will continue his words of warning. He adds this about Jesus' work: 'He will baptize you with the Holy Spirit and with fire' (v. 11). This sentence is translated in many different ways according to how strongly the translators are prepared to emphasize the element of judgment. Some understand it to mean: 'He will baptize you with the fire of the Holy Spirit.' It probably means: 'He will baptize you with the Holy Spirit and with the fire of judgment.' In other words, when Jesus teaches, God's Holy Spirit will be at work confronting his hearers with the peril of their position and warning of judgment if they will not listen and respond. John does not expect Jesus to depart from the prophetic pattern. All the more so will this be true of Jesus because God's Holy Spirit will be in him. The fire of judgment will be proclaimed and known.

The gracious obedience of God's son   *Matthew 3:13–17*

Jesus persuades John to baptize him. There could be no better indication of Jesus' high regard for John than that. Despite John's disclaimer in verse 14, Jesus insists that John baptize him. The reason that Jesus gives for this is unique to Matthew's Gospel. In the Revised English Bible verse 15 is translated: 'Let it be so for the present; it is right for us to do all that God requires.' Literally, the answer of Jesus reads: 'Let it be for now; for thus it is fitting for us to fulfil all righteousness.' Righteousness is human conduct consonant with the divine will, a rightness of life before God which is pleasing to him. It is a way of life which is a natural response to divine grace. So, 'It is fitting for us to do all that God requires' is not just an acceptance by the Messiah of what God requires. It is a recognition of the divine work of grace. And within that gracious work the submission of the Messiah to John's baptism had its proper place. God's new work is beginning, and for this Jesus' association with John has an essential role.

The baptism of Jesus is marked by the open heaven, the descent of the Spirit and the voice from heaven. Matthew slips easily from the prophecy of John to what happens at the baptism. He has prophesied that Jesus will baptize with the Holy Spirit. What happens in fact is that the Spirit descends on Jesus. From now on he will confront humanity with divine authority. When he heals, or warns, or forgives, it is God at work. The voice from heaven—'This is my beloved Son'—is confirmation of the divine sonship, and a relationship which has one special feature among many others: Jesus is the obedient and loving Son. He has already shown this in his conversation with John. He has recognized the gracious nature of what God is doing and willingly submitted himself to whatever is necessary: 'It is right for us to do all that God requires.' He has recommended to John that they should fall in with the divine purpose. The cost will be great, but his obedience will illustrate and expound the nature of the divine will. Jesus will be its expositor, just as he is its fulfilment. Because of his obedience and his humility, those who listen to him will discover the true nature of the divine will. They will find God's way revealed in him.

The way of the servant Son   *Matthew 4:1–11*

The first of the temptations begins 'If you are the Son of God . . .' (v. 3). Jesus is hungry. Like the Israelites in the wilderness he is tempted to take matters into his own hands. What is at issue is the nature of his sonship. 'If you are the Son of God, tell these stones to become bread.' He has the power to make provision for himself. This he refuses to do. His answer is to refer to the divine will revealed in Scripture. Sonship consists in seeking and doing God's will. Scripture provides the way to seek that will. Any other kind of sonship than obedience would be a snare and a delusion. The second temptation also concerns sonship: 'If you are the Son of God . . .' But this time the temptation is more subtle. Scripture is the way to discern the divine will. But Scripture offers a way of testing God's faithfulness: 'If you are the Son of God, throw yourself down; for Scripture says, ''He will put his angels in charge of you . . .'' ' Jesus affirms Scripture, but rejects the devil's interpretation. Scripture offers a promise of God, not a way of testing God. To turn the promise into a test is to falsify the relationship. It is to turn filial trust into a kind of doubt. The third temptation gathers up the issues of power and authority. Herod has given evidence of what power can do. What the devil offers is unlimited control. The condition is that Jesus worships him. What Jesus rejects is power for himself. God alone is to be given homage (v. 10). That again is the direction which Scripture requires.

49

Guided by Scripture Jesus chooses the way of the Servant Son, claiming nothing for himself and giving all the honour to God.

So the temptations in Matthew clarify what happened at the baptism of Jesus. There Jesus committed himself to God's way. He would seek and do God's will. The temptations help to clarify what this means. At the baptism itself it meant fulfilling with John the purpose which they both recognized. The temptations show its deeper aspects. Seeking God's way is a relationship of trust in which there is no place for personal gratification and aggrandizement. Matthew recognizes that this has practical consequences for Christian living. He is also aware of what the temptation story says about the nature of the Son's revelation. The divine will is known in the obedience and trust of a filial relationship with God—in the way of the Servant Son.

The dawning of the Messiah's ministry   *Matthew 4:12–17*

John's imprisonment leads to Jesus' withdrawal to the Galilean town of Capernaum, which now becomes the centre of operations. It is where Andrew and Peter lived. It becomes Jesus' own city, where his public ministry is about to begin, and where many miracles are done. Matthew pauses to reflect at this moment in the story on where the ministry began. Capernaum is described as 'in the district of Zebulun and Naphtali'. These two names come from the tribes which were the first to go into exile (2 Kings 15:29). Ancient Christian tradition saw it as appropriate that the first proclamation by Jesus of the restoration of the kingdom should be where the exile first began. Freedom begins where slavery first started.

The quotation from Isaiah 9 in verse 15 picks up those two names. Isaiah 9 is a very significant passage for Matthew. First, it includes one of the great messianic prophecies: 'Wide will be the dominion and boundless the peace bestowed on David's throne and on his kingdom, to establish it and support it with justice and righteousness from now on for evermore' (Isaiah 9:7). Secondly, it contains the description of the dawn driving away the darkness, which Matthew quotes here in verse 16. Thirdly, it carries a reference to Zebulun and Naphtali. The Isaiah oracle offers the hope of a new leader to a broken people and specifies the different areas affected by the Assyrian deportation. Matthew is less interested in the different areas. For him what matters is the fulfilment of Isaiah's prophecy. As Isaiah said, 'Honour is bestowed on Galilee of the

Nations' (Isaiah 9:1). It is indeed where the Messiah has begun his work.

Fulfilment is a rich word in Matthew's vocabulary. It is not so much a matter of predictions made long ago and now at last coming true. It is rather that God's promises of hope and restoration given through the prophets have now at last been realized. God has been faithful to his promises. His providence has been continually at work. Faithful servants have assured God's people of this in time of disaster and in exile. Now, in the ministry about to begin, these promises have come to fruition. 'From that day,' writes Matthew in verse 17, 'Jesus began to proclaim the message.' It is a decisive moment. The story reaches a climax here; from this moment on the ministry of the Messiah begins to unfold.

The responsibility and cost of discipleship *Matthew 4:18–25*

Matthew describes the calling of Peter and Andrew, and James and John. Like the Gospel itself, the story of the calling of the disciples is one in which the end is known before the story begins. Matthew paused to reflect on the momentous arrival of Jesus in Capernaum and meditated on that moment in the light of the unfolding story of the Messiah. Now he tells of the disciples' call. Among Matthew's readers the names of these disciples were well known. Perhaps some, like Peter, had been their leaders. The consequences of their obedience in following Jesus were now evident. For Peter it had meant martyrdom. The stories about the disciples are to be rehearsed in the Gospel. They will give a curious impression of discipleship: failure, distress, insight, courage, betrayal, denial, repentance, forgiveness, misunderstanding, a little faith. The cost will have been evident to the first readers, as it is to us.

The responsibility carried by these few will also have been evident. The humble beginnings of these leaders is in no way disguised. They were fisherfolk. Their status is clearly that of disciples. They are classed with learners. They belong with prophets, martyrs, scribes and sages, not with rulers, officials and rabbis. And yet they have carried heavy responsibilities. They have had to understand, live by, interpret and apply the teaching of Jesus, and give guidance to Christian communities across the Palestinian, Syrian and Eastern Mediterranean regions. Their responsibilities have not been accompanied by official status. In this respect their work—which began with the act of obedience to Jesus Christ when he called them by the Sea of Galilee—has carried the seal of their servant Messiah.

The conclusion of chapter 4 is a summary. It can be read as a simple message. The story so far has been of promises, of prophets, of forerunners, of providence, of potential. Now all that John had proclaimed and sensed is happening. The Baptist had promised that one would come after him who would baptize with the Holy Spirit and with fire. He had baptized Jesus so that between them God's will might be performed. Now travel, the proclamation, the healing, the exorcisms, the crowds all witnessed to the coming of the Servant Messiah into Galilee, in the power of the Spirit, and with the message of repentance and faith. The restoration had begun.

> The relationship of John the Baptist and Jesus gives much food for thought; in particular the varieties of approach and attitude between the two central figures of Matthew's early chapters. The issues of status emerge strongly in these two chapters. We have seen them as the first readers might have faced them. Within the kind of society we know, how do these early stories relate to our questions of status, leadership, responsibility and government?

THE FIRST DISCOURSE: LIVING — IN GOD'S WAY IN GOD'S WORLD —

The divine endorsement   *Matthew 5:1–12*

The Sermon on the Mount (chapters 5–7) is the first of Matthew's five blocks of Jesus' teaching. It begins with two groups of listeners. There are the disciples gathered around Jesus, and the crowds, whose attention is not stated but only implied. Sometimes the Sermon on the Mount has been regarded as so demanding that only the most rigorous of disciples could begin to match up to its demands. Sometimes the demands have been regarded as too heavy for any but those who throw themselves on divine mercy for forgiveness. There is, however, a way of listening to the Sermon which recognizes both disciples and crowd as potential hearers, as we shall see.

The Beatitudes in Matthew have two distinctive features. First, several of the blessings are given in this form: 'Blessed are *the* sorrowful: *they* shall find consolation.' This contrasts with Luke's more direct: 'Blessed are *you* who now go hungry; *you* will be satisfied' (Luke 6:21). Where Luke uses the second person, Matthew has the third. Secondly, the blessings concern those with particular qualities of life: the gentle, the merciful, the pure, the peacemakers. Matthew hears the Beatitudes as confirmation of the qualities of life which Jesus himself showed. Consider for example, 'Blessed are the gentle' (v. 5, REB). The word translated as 'gentle' is used by Jesus of himself: 'Take my yoke upon you, and learn from me, for I am gentle and humble-hearted; and you will find rest for your souls' (11:29). It is also applied to Jesus on his entry into Jerusalem on a donkey: 'Here is your king, who comes to you in gentleness, riding on a donkey . . .' (21:5). Does this mean, then, that Matthew hears the Sermon on the Mount in terms of Jesus presenting a moral message, about qualities of behaviour and attitude?

The translation 'gentle' is in one sense misleading. For behind the word stands a fundamental approach to God, and to the world as belonging to God. 'Gentle' in verse 5 has more to do with 'peace and the integrity of creation' than softness and adaptability. It assumes that we are alive in God's world, and discovering that fact is an essential basis for living. Most of the terms used in the Sermon on the Mount are of that kind. Jesus is saying: those who learn to live in God's way in God's world (with the qualities of life, privileges and suffering which that implies) discover now or later a divine endorsement.

Bringing glory to God   *Matthew 5:13–20*

For Matthew these verses summarize the Beatitudes in three striking pictures which move and shift in the mind, helping us to see ourselves and the world in new ways. That is how Jesus used picture language. *Salt* is about the righteous preserving God's order. *Light* is what Christ brought to Zebulun and Naphtali (4:15); it connects with the picture of the hilltop *city*. For did not God promise that the Jerusalem set on a hill would be a light to the nations (Isaiah 60:1–3)? But that is not all. For salt and light are given a universal significance: 'You are salt to the world' (v. 13); 'You are light for all the world' (v. 14). The promise that Jerusalem would be a light to nations is fulfilled in the people who are salt and light. The city on the hill cannot be hidden. Living in God's way in God's world brings God's glory.

Salt is associated with costly discipleship. It is effective; it cleanses; it purifies. But salt can lose its qualities. It is then good for nothing; it is thrown away (v. 13). Here another theme is rehearsed, which occurs in Matthew frequently. Hearing is not enough; action, obedient action is required. Otherwise disciples are like tasteless salt. The Sermon on the Mount moves towards this same conclusion (7:24–27).

What Jesus says about the Jewish Law here is difficult. The right action, the true qualities depend on right teaching; and the foundation of right teaching according to this passage is 'the Law'. The emphasis on every dot and letter of the Law must surely be the kind of exaggeration by which Jesus regularly taught. The Law is important, Jesus is saying. But the Law must be heard alongside the Prophets. The Prophets remind us of justice and mercy, so that the Law is never to be used in ways which disqualify justice and mercy. Furthermore the Law is understood as being completed in Jesus Christ. The way in which he lived and taught becomes the new test for understanding, teaching and obedience, the new way of interpreting the Jewish Law. And living according to the way of the servant Son is what enables disciples to glorify God as salt and light, the people who are now the hilltop city of Jerusalem.

Living with each other in God's world   *Matthew 5:21–32*

The moral teaching of Jesus depends on two pillars. Human reflection is one. When Jesus talks about anger his hearers are well aware of what that means. They know its destructive power. He uses the language of everyday anger and compares it with murder. The exaggeration stimulates the mind. It is more effective than talking about 'destructive power'. Anger and murder are set side by side. This is not of course a full-scale treatment of anger. It has one focus only, anger as murder. Matthew is well aware of other aspects of the subject and in due course he will introduce other features of Jesus' teaching. They will indicate the positive aspects of some forms of anger, and how these other forms can be prevented from deteriorating into 'murder'. For the moment the single focus is enough.

Human reflection is one pillar for moral teaching; the divine world is the other. This is a perspective which Jesus himself presents in a fresh way. It can be illustrated first from the 'gift on the altar' (vv. 23–24). Property belonging to one party has been misappropriated by another. The Law recommends a remedy: the offer of a sacrifice. Jesus makes explicit the need for the property to be returned as well. But that is not the end of the matter. The reconciliation should take place first; then the sacrifice should be offered. We live and work at complex levels, with each other and in God's world. Both are given a fresh perspective in the teaching of Jesus.

The verses on settling legal matters out of court (vv. 25–26) illustrate another aspect of the same approach. These verses can be treated on the level of practical commonsense advice: 'you would be well advised to keep out of the courtroom if you possibly can'. Alternatively they can be treated as referring to the divine courtroom: 'you will be judged at the end, so you will be well advised to settle your affairs with God before it comes to that'. But Jesus does not seem to be making that kind of distinction. The commonsense level and the divine courtroom level are not so easily separable. The decisions made at the former level have much to do with the latter. We are to make the practical decisions as those who are living in God's world. Of course the world as we know it and God's world are not exactly identical. The distance between those is part of what Jesus Christ reveals.

Jesus goes on to set lust and adultery side by side in verses 27–30. Just as anger and murder were given an unwelcome association in the last reading, so are lust and adultery here. What follows is the most blatant piece of exaggeration in the New Testament, and all the more memorable for that: cut off what is causing offence! These are serious matters. Whether we are dealing with pornography or flirtations, the language of Jesus will not let us belittle the issue. He insists that these are life and death issues and he is willing to shock us out of our complacency.

We may wonder what is at issue in Jesus' words about divorce in verses 31–32. Jesus appears to be setting his own ruling alongside the Jewish regulations—something that was expected of teachers. The regulations on divorce in Deuteronomy 24 were so imprecise that, in the arguments over the rights and wrongs of a particular separation, authoritative clarifications were essential. Who could give the clarifications except the teacher or the rabbi? In Matthew the formulation is: 'If a man divorces his wife for any cause other than unchastity he involves her in adultery' (v. 32). Jesus appears to be restricting the right of divorce to cases involving a serious misdemeanour. There is to be no quick divorce on the grounds of passing preference or trivial excuse, as some of the more lax rabbis taught: 'My wife burned the cakes last week.'

But Jesus is doing more than simply adjusting an Old Testament ruling by means of a clarification of the wording. He appears to be introducing a much more fundamental adjustment, one of human relationships. We are to treat one another as responsible *persons*. It is not even a matter of whether or not a woman had the right to initiate divorce in court. There is evidence that she may have had that particular right in Jewish as well as in Roman legal systems. What Jesus introduces into the discussion is a mutuality of responsibility. Each is responsible to and for the other. This is part of what it means to live in God's world and to live with each other as if this is in every respect God's world.

Straightforward language   *Matthew 5:33–37*

The change of attitude which Jesus requires also influences our use of language. The straightforward 'Yes' or 'No' answer is what is required. The usefulness of this was evident in the early days of the Church. Plain 'Yes' or 'No' had much to commend it (James 5:12). Each generation has its own particular problems with language, and one of the most common of these concerns oaths. Oaths can of course be invaluable. They add to the element of responsibility in evidence given in litigations. They were required in ancient courts of law. But however much additions to oaths increase their impressiveness, in the end they are self-defeating. They reduce the reliability of language as a means of communication. They may also involve the blasphemous and the irreverent. Oaths sworn by God, or by Jerusalem or some other holy thing, are self-defeating in another sense as well. They rely on the holiness of that by which the oath is sworn to provide a sense of reliability for a statement or a piece of evidence. If the evidence is unreliable then an oath devalues what is holy.

But what does it mean to say that a plain 'Yes' or 'No' is *required*? Required by law? Required under pain of eternal punishment (v. 37)? Of course not. The exaggeration is obvious. No law could enforce straightforward language, unless perhaps to a limited extent in court-room proceedings. And oaths, unless they involve blasphemy, cannot be said to deserve eternal damnation. The motivation has to be different; it has to be personal. And the character of Jesus' language is disturbing because it is aimed at precisely that change of attitude. Unless we can see for ourselves what fools we are, we are unlikely to believe anyone else. Our habits are going to take some shaking, particularly when it comes to so personal a matter as how we speak and how we try to communicate.

A surprising way of living in God's world *Matthew 5:38–48*

The early Church did not succeed in fulfilling literally this part of the teaching of Jesus. Essentially Jesus is saying , 'Do without your rights!' He gives three examples in verses 39–41: Do without your right to hit back; do without your legal right to retain one piece of clothing to cover you; do without your right to limit the demands which authority places on you. In Corinth the issue arose of taking a Christian to court for a secular hearing (1 Corinthians 6). Paul advised against it, but introduced a reference to Jesus' teaching on rights. Paul tells them that they seem to have fallen short already by standing on their rights. Certainly in Corinth they did not succeed in fulfilling literally what Jesus taught. Verse 42 is an unwise piece of advice to give in many circumstances. Most of us would refuse to comply with it. So what kind of teaching do we have in these verses? It would be possible to understand all these examples in a general way: do not lend with the sole intention of gaining further profit or advantage for yourself; do not comply with regulations merely to the letter. At least that would be better than treating Jesus' teaching as frankly impossible.

However, behind these examples and the advice to love enemies there is something more radical. We are invited to a surprising style of life. It will be one capable of surprising the world. It will not fit in with normal expectations. People usually stand on their rights. There is a different way, and on occasion it might just be right. The invitation to discover this comes from one who himself showed the power of the unexpected response. Prayer for those with whom we are at war is never easy. But it might just be the way forward. A second pillar of Jesus' teaching is, as we have seen, discovering how to live in God's world. The surprising feature of that world is that it does not work as we might have expected it to. We anticipate that because God is just and right and good, that will be reflected in the nature of the cosmos. Instead we discover that there is no such distinction when it comes to rain and sun. The rain falls equally on the evil and on the good; similarly the sun shines for those who are wicked as well as for those who are virtuous. The moral is clear. If God is like that, does not this question the way we usually respond to each other? We discover that living in God's world is a surprising place to be!

Living and praying from the heart   *Matthew 6:1–15*

Inner motives are central to this section of the Sermon on the Mount. In
giving charitably or in prayer, what matters is that God sees. The private
character of religion in this part of the Sermon seems to conflict with the
emphasis on public recognition in the earlier part (see especially 5:13–
20). But it was public recognition for God's work and not for human
achievement. The temptation to show off will always be with us. It has to
be resisted. What matters is what comes from the heart.

  The Lord's Prayer provides a summary of so many of the concerns in
the Sermon on the Mount. It begins with the nature of God as Father. He
is Father of all, and that includes those who are evil as well as those who
are good. The hallowing of God's name belongs with the restriction of
oath-taking. The prayer for the coming of the kingdom is central to the
proclamation of Jesus. It is what is meant by living in this world as it if is
God's. The commitment to doing God's will is a silver thread
throughout the whole Sermon. 'On earth as in heaven' draws together
the need to change this world, truly to live in this world as if it were
God's.

  Two elements of the prayer will become of increasing importance in
the remainder of the Gospel: the practical needs of human existence
(our prayer for daily bread), and our vulnerability to evil ('Deliver us
from evil'). Our need to forgive and to be forgiven is again a matter of
heart. The parable of the unforgiving servant in chapter 18 expands in
story form our need to receive and show forgiveness. Forgiveness has to
become part of us. If it does not, in the end we become unable to respond
from the heart (18:35). Our capacity to limit forgiveness is real, but the
divine forgiveness holds the key. Only because of God's forgiveness is it
possible for us to see how we can ourselves be forgiven and how others
can be forgiven. Only there are the real limits to forgiveness overcome,
and the world opened up to the divine mercy.

Glad fasting *Matthew 6:16–18*

Matthew recognizes that there is a place for fasting. He returns to the subject on several occasions. In 9:15 he seems to accept that it will be a continuing feature of the Church's life. The recommendation here is for 'glad fasting', which is characterized by the inner attitude of repentance and humility before God, and the avoidance of morose impressions and ostentatious expressions. 'Glad fasting' will link together joy at the forgiveness which is offered and our inner homage to God.

An enslaving though transient power *Matthew 6:19–24*

These two sections warn against too great an attachment to money. The first stresses its transient character and its capacity to enslave. The second considers its exclusiveness. It is a master which allows no rival. This apparently negative approach to money has parallels in the other Gospels. In Matthew there are other ways of discussing property and finance. Earlier in this chapter we read that alms given with the right motive deserve a heavenly reward (v. 4). There are parables in Matthew which use finance as a means of understanding God's kingdom. One of them, the parable of the talents (25:14–30), seems to imply that money is among the gifts which we need to use well. We should not bury our talent in the earth. These two approaches, the one highly critical of money, and the other highly positive, are by no means inconsistent. They are part of a realistic estimate of Christian responsibility. Money can enslave and it is transient. It would be very easy for those who deal in financial matters to lose track of whose world this is. In order to correct that kind of fault the sacrifice indicated in the story of the rich enquirer might be required. In Matthew's version of the story (19:16–22) he is told to 'Sell your possessions and give to the poor.'

There is a long-standing tradition that Matthew's Gospel was used in monastic circles. There are hints that Matthew recognized two levels of Christian responsibility, one for the crowds and another for those who missionary work required poverty. The latter had to leave everything behind, and depend on the hospitality that was offered. They could take no gold, silver or copper with them, nor a pack for the road (10:5–10). For these the radical warning against money had a different significance. They had turned from the one master to serve the other wholeheartedly, with a single mind (v. 24).

Providence and the way of the kingdom   *Matthew 6:25–34*

This passage has been linked with the previous section on money. Those who have to leave everything behind and go on Christ's mission without food or money do not need to be anxious. The provision which God will make for them will be as ample as the provision he makes for all his creation. The argument from the natural world is used here. There is a natural providence which preserves the lives of the birds and allows the flowers to grow. Their beauty is given to them even though their lives are so short. Why then should human beings be anxious, supported by so gracious a providence?

This fits well with verse 33: 'Set your mind on God's kingdom and his justice, and all the rest will come to you as well.' Those who commit themselves to a life of poverty are able to seek justice for others, and in doing so will discover that they receive more than enough in return. The word 'justice' expresses the practical side of obedience to Christ. It is a concept which we met earlier in the story of Jesus' baptism, where it meant 'the doing of the divine will and purpose'. But surely Matthew could not have restricted the 'doing of the divine will' to those who commit themselves to a life of poverty? What he has to say is certainly relevant to those with a particular calling to poverty. But it also speaks to everyone called by Christ to follow him.

Contentment and determination to do the divine will are not the prerogative of the few. If Matthew recognized that there were missionaries living on the generosity of local people, he was also aware that his Gospel would be heard by many whose daily responsibilities were of a different kind. For them he advises: do not lose sight of the kingdom; the kingdom involves doing the will and purpose of God. The Gospel with its parables will help such people to see every part of their daily lives in terms of the kingdom. The decisions they make, the way they spend their money, their enjoyment of social relationships, their homes and their employment will be an arena for seeking justice. That is also the place where they can do God's will.

Judgment and generosity   *Matthew 7:1–12*

It is clear that living in God's world requires careful judgments. Living in the Christian community requires discrimination too. Later Matthew considers what should be done about those whose teaching is false or those who reject the common standards of Christian life together (7:15ff). Judgment is necessary, even sometimes to the extent of expelling a member who will not listen. Whatever verse 1 means—'Do not judge, and you will not be judged'—it does not imply avoiding judgment altogether. It must surely say, simply but firmly: we are all tempted to be judgmental; we are all tempted from time to time to judge hypocritically; we are all capable of banding together to criticize and exclude. These are temptations which we must be aware of. Again we find Jesus confronting us with a radical requirement. There is no way in which we can avoid the directness of what he says. He gives us the picture of the man with the plank in his eye criticizing his colleague for having a speck in his. The message could not be clearer.

Verse 6 is a puzzle. Perhaps it is about failing to make distinctions: what is holy and what is profane should not be mixed. But that would be the opposite of what Jesus seemed to be saying in the last chapter. Perhaps it is about restricting the time we spend with outsiders. But that again does not fit with the secularity of the Matthean parables. Perhaps it is about keeping one form of teaching for the disciples and another for the crowd. But that does not seem to be what Matthew is emphasizing here. Perhaps he felt that this was a useful warning about what happens to Christians who teach in the local market-place. It may be that one of the values of Matthew's work is that he included the whole tradition that came to him, even when small parts were not relevant or were even contradictory to his general approach.

The parallel between the Father of all and a human father in verses 9–11 leads to a positive version of the golden rule. Just as the natural world provides an insight into the generosity of God, so also human relationships suggest that the Father of all will not be less generous than we are at our best. To treat others as you would like them to treat you—the positive version of the golden rule—is by no means only a secular guideline; as Paul also recognized, it is a useful focus for the whole Jewish tradition (Galatians 5:14).

Teachers of faith and the narrow way   *Matthew 7:13–23*

We are to behave as if only a few could enter life. This registers the seriousness of the enterprise. It also registers its difficulty. The way to life is narrow; it is not easy to find. That is a hard saying, but it is not without its parallels. There is the famous saying that 'It is easier for a camel to pass through the eye of a needle than for a rich man to enter the kingdom of Heaven' (19:24). To live in this world as if in God's world is hard—the Sermon on the Mount has illustrated the problems. To find the narrow gate and enter life through it means finding a new basis for living and for action. We do not like change. We resist change in ourselves and there is much in our circumstances which might snare us or hold us back. But the teaching of Jesus encourages and challenges us, helping us to see in God's world new hope and new possibilities. The world of divine providence and generosity points us in this direction, as does our own experience of the world, if only we will reflect on it.

Among the difficulties we have to contend with are those people who appear to be speaking God's message but are in fact as misleading and dangerous as wolves. Verse 15 sounds as if Matthew has a specific group of teachers in mind. That impression is reinforced by the verses which follow. Such people can be judged by their actions and their words. They call repeatedly on their Lord, claiming all manner of achievements. Perhaps they are like the Christians found in Corinth who identified miraculous activities as infallible signs of faith (1 Corinthians 12:29). Such teachers would make the task of seeking and doing God's will all the harder. They would divert attention and energies from finding the narrow gate, and make the broad gate to destruction seem all the more attractive. The way through the narrow gate is demanding and difficult, and lacks the public acclamation which the miraculous attracts. Judgment is never far away in the Sermon on the Mount. At this point it becomes explicit. There is the fire that burns the fruitless trees (we met the imagery of verse 19 in the teaching of John the Baptist in 3:19). There is the Lord who says, 'I never knew you! Out of my sight; your deeds are evil!'

The foundations of wisdom and folly   *Matthew 7:24–29*

The final parable of the Sermon on the Mount is that of the two houses. In Matthew it is a contrast between the wise person and the fool. The wise person builds on rock; the fool builds on sand. Wisdom consists in hearing and doing; folly consists in hearing and not doing. The parable therefore links closely with the previous verses, as it also does with the opening of the Sermon. In a way, it summarizes the whole Sermon, which is about hearing and doing.

It is particularly important what the wise person hears—this is where the introduction to the parable places the emphasis. The wise person hears the words of Jesus, and it is these words which alone provide the solid foundation for those who hear and act. Those who only listen and whose understanding does not lead to action have only a foundation of sand. The two foundations hold until the time of testing, symbolized here by the storm. Rain, floods and a driving wind batter the houses, testing the quality of the foundations. The rock holds firm; the sand gives way, and disaster follows. Reflected in the narrative of the parable is the time of God's judgment. It is the time when the false teachers appeal to their Lord and receive the answer that he does not know them (v. 23).

Here then is a powerful picture of apparent safety suddenly and totally disrupted. For readers in Antioch (see page 38) the story would have awakened memories of thunderstorms in the mountains above, sending destructive torrents on to the streets below. The words of judgment in Matthew are powerfully expressed. The dangers are very great. The difficulties are many. Only those who hear and are obedient will find life. Little wonder the Sermon ends with a note of amazement from the hearers.

We have reached the end of the first of the five great discourses in Matthew, all of which are composed of words of Jesus. This suggests that it is not only the Sermon on the Mount that provides the firm foundation on which the wise can build their lives. Here and in the other four discourses, Matthew's task in passing on Jesus' teaching is to enable it to be heard. It is the hearers' responsibility to turn this into a new kind of living.

One of the great commentaries on the Sermon on the Mount is Dietrich Bonhoeffer's The Cost of Discipleship (SCM Press). It begins with the famous theme of 'costly grace' and ends with the vision of Christ the image of God.

It is only because he became like us that we can become like him. It is only because we are identified with him that we can become like him. By being transformed into his image, we are enabled to model our lives on his. Now at last deeds are performed and life is lived in single-minded discipleship in the image of Christ and his words find unquestioning obedience . . . The disciple looks solely at his Master. But when a man follows Jesus Christ and bears the image of the incarnate, crucified and risen Lord, when he has become the image of God, we may at last say that he has been called to be the 'imitator of God' (Ephesians 5:1).

THE AUTHORITY AND POWER
OF THE HEALING MESSIAH

The authority of Jesus' humanity *Matthew 8:1–13*

Matthew now moves from 'sayings' material to 'narrative' material: from the Sermon on the Mount to the healing of the diseased man and the centurion's servant. There are various ways in which this move from sayings to actions can be understood. It could be to provide a set of messianic actions to corroborate the messianic words which we have just heard. This could be a helpful approach to chapters 8 and 9, which together with the Sermon on the Mount substantiate the outline of Jesus' ministry given in 4:23–25. These next two chapters contain a great deal about the healing activity and authority of Jesus. But it is also possible that the traditions which Matthew assembles are to be explored in other directions. Matthew 8:1–4 raises the problem of impurity, and the crowds who follow Jesus are offered a complex testimony (v. 4: 'for a proof to the people', RSV) which seems by turns to infringe and then uphold the ceremonial law. The man is restored by an illegal touch but told only to reveal what has happened through the actions enjoined in Leviticus 14.

The healing of the centurion's servant emphasizes the authority of Jesus with great clarity. The centurion uses his own experience of giving orders to give expression to his profound faith in what Jesus can do. A word from Jesus is all that is necessary: 'Give the word and my servant will be healed' (v. 8; see also v. 16). And the centurion's confidence is fully justified. Jesus gives the word and the child is healed. But the end of the story (and in this Matthew differs from the Lucan and Johannine versions—Luke 7:1–10, John 4:46–53) exposes a different framework for it: a Gentile has demonstrated faith and many others will follow his lead. People will come from all over the world to share in God's victory feast (v. 11; see also Psalm 107:3). By contrast 'those who were born to the kingdom' (v. 12) will be excluded from it.

Matthew's Gospel is often regarded as a conservative document: Jesus is presented as strict and law-abiding, giving firm instructions and offering a clear example for his followers. These two stories confirm our earlier suspicions that this is only part of the truth. The examples are there to be followed: the humility of Jesus crosses the traditional boundaries of action and expectation. Jesus' authority is of a new and distinctive kind, one which is expressed in his style of life. This is important, as the following verses will illustrate.

The cost of Jesus' authority   *Matthew 8:1–22*

Verses 19–20 contrast the Son of Man with animals and birds, which despite their wandering or migrant existence are nevertheless able to make homes for themselves. The Son of Man has nowhere to lay his head. Sometimes the Son of Man is spoken of in terms of dignity and glory. Here it is in terms only of human loneliness and homelessness. In Luke's Gospel (Luke 9:57–62) the contrast between the Son of Man and the animal kingdom is made in the context of missionary journeys. These demand incessant movement, without any seasonal breaks. They do not even allow room for farewells to one's family; they may even result in rejection or persecution. Perhaps in Matthew the reason why the Son of Man has no home is that he is given no respite by friend or foe; he warns his disciples to expect the same. The lot of the Son of Man and the lot of the disciples is one and the same (10:25).

This does not mean that the disciples and the Son of Man are indistinguishable, far from it. The Son of Man has authority, especially over his followers. It is an authority which resides in the style of his ministry and the immediacy of his claims over those who hear and answer his call (10:24). Like Elijah the prophet, he may require an allegiance above that of family life and duties. This does not mean that family links are irrelevant. He heals Peter's mother-in-law (vv. 14–15). But it does mean that the claims of discipleship must take first place.

Central to this sequence of stories is another fulfilment quotation: verse 17 quotes Isaiah 53:4. The passage from Isaiah is translated in several different ways in modern versions, and the differences suggest the variety of ways in which the text can be understood. The quotation has two parts and the Revised English Bible translates both parts as having the same force: 'He took our illnesses from us and carried away our diseases.' Jesus healed the people; he got rid of their sickness. Both parts of the verse have the same emphasis. The Good News Bible translates the first part with an alternative nuance: 'He himself took our sickness and carried away our diseases.' 'Took our sickness' is ambiguous. Does it imply that there was a cost to himself in healing

65

others? Did the healing of the man with a skin disease imply a double risk: of infection and of impurity, of danger to health and reputation? There is sufficient about the sufferings of the Son of Man in the passage which we are studying to warrant a studied ambiguity in the translation of verse 17: he removed suffering—at personal cost. His style of life is integral to his healing ministry, as we shall see later in 12:17–21, another quotation from an Isaianic 'servant' passage.

Reactions to Jesus' messianic power *Matthew 8:23—9:1*

Matthew now records two stories which in Mark and Luke appear at a later stage of the narrative: the stilling of the storm and the healing of the Gadarene demoniacs. The stilling of the storm is about divine power. Immediately after the pictures of the suffering Son of Man comes an example of power, in this case a power over nature such as only God possesses. The response of the disciples in verse 27 is astonishment: 'What sort of man must this be?' It is partly amazement at the raw power displayed—'Even the wind and the sea obey him'— and partly amazement at the wider sequence of events of which that demonstration of power was a part. Jesus was responsible for their being on the lake (v. 18); he was the one they naturally appealed to (v. 25: 'Save us, Lord; we are about to go under!'); his reaction to their panic was a reprimand: 'You haven't much faith, have you?' Both his extraordinary power and the circumstances of their deliverance prompted the question, 'What sort of man must this be?' He seemed to take for granted so much which they did not.

If Jesus' attitude is central to the story of the stilling of the storm, the Gadarene narrative is concerned with the attitude of others to him. The fierce demoniacs bar his way but find themselves confronted by someone who threatens them with a premature fate. They identify who this Jesus is: the Son of God who spells doom for all that is evil. They recognize his authority and scatter at his peremptory 'Off with you!' (v. 32), carrying a distant herd of pigs over the precipice into the sea. The herdsmen and the compatriots are similarly and not unnaturally ill-disposed towards him. To judge by the name 'Gadarene' and the reference to pigs (see Leviticus 11:7) these are, according to Matthew's version, Gentiles. They too want nothing to do with this disturbing character. The herdsmen scatter as their herd drowns, giving an account of the events which causes the whole city to appeal for Jesus to go.

At the beginning of Matthew's Gospel we saw the messianic hopes of Israel being broadened and deepened. That is true here also as the healing aspect of messianic expectations appears. After all, was not Solomon, the great healer, David's son (1:6)? Messianic expectations included healing and wholeness, yet these are taken to a new level through a narrative of the powerful Son of God offering healing for all. But even at the beginning of the Gospel the premonitions were there of tyranny, inhumanity, rejection and misunderstanding. The cost for the obedient son will be great. A Gentile city will have nothing to do with this healer; and the disciples will be a people of 'little faith'.

The authority of mercy   *Matthew 9:2–13*

Matthew reverts to the sequence of healings which in Mark are found at the beginning of Jesus' ministry. Faith shown by the friends of a paralysed man finds a response in Jesus' words of forgiveness: 'Take heart, my son; your sins are forgiven.' In the subsequent debate the issue turns on how Jesus could make such a declaration. It is an authority accompanied by Jesus' power to heal. So his authority is unmistakable. But the end of the story is puzzling. Instead of the people praising God for the authority granted to Jesus, they praise God for the authority granted to 'men' (v. 8). Why the plural, and why the general word 'men' instead of the specific name 'Jesus'? One possible reason is that the Gospel writer was aware of an important question: given the authority of Jesus to declare sins forgiven, how available is that forgiveness now? The narrative as Matthew records it gives a clear answer to such a question: God has made forgiveness available now, and Jesus' authority is a sign of that gift.

The call of a tax-collector has provided a name for the Gospel as a whole. Why the tax-collector is given the name Matthew here in place of the Marcan name of Levi (Mark 2:14) is a mystery. Certainly we need to assume that Matthew (as well as Levi?) was known to be a tax-collector. The flavour of the word 'tax-collector' can be judged from traditional associations betrayed in 18:17: 'Treat him as you would a tax-collector or a pagan.' So whatever we conclude about Levi and Matthew, it is the traditional associations of his office which matter here, and Jesus' refusal to go along with them.

He refuses because central to his work (according to this Gospel) is the quotation from Hosea 6:6—'I require mercy, not sacrifice.' Three times this appears: here in verse 13, at 12:7 and again at 23:23. In each

67

case mercy is associated with a perspective on life and people. It is about not excluding others, not condemning those who are innocent, putting people above matters of legal principle. Mercy is a perspective on life and the attitudes that grow from it. Jesus expressed his acceptance of sinners by eating with them, and recommended this as a pattern of life. As in 5:7, showing mercy and the experience of mercy belong together.

The relationship between old and new   *Matthew 9:14–26*

As we saw earlier in 6:16–18, the Gospel of Matthew recognizes fasting as an appropriate activity. Naturally, for a disciple of Jesus Christ, it needs to express the joy of the gospel, as verse 15a makes clear, but providing that the heart is right, fasting can be an aid to discipleship. It can be a reminder of what it costs to follow the one who was taken by force and crucified: 'The time will come when the bridegroom will be taken away from them; then they will fast' (v. 15b). Fasting was, of course, a feature of the Jewish religion. The disciples of John fasted (v. 14) and Jesus seems in this passage to be approving their practice but seeking a different basis for it. The external practices of religion can be preserved, as long as there is a change to what is internal. Verses 14–15 can be read in that way. However, this solution seems to be in direct contradiction with verses 16–17, which say that it is no use hanging on to the old and external because what is new is bound to destroy it.

The relationship between the old and the new is a subject to which Matthew keeps returning (see, for example, 13:52). It includes the great theme of promise and fulfilment: the old prophecies seen in relationship to the new activity of God in Jesus. In that case there is no question of dispensing with the old as if it were a piece of thin fraying cloth. The old has its honoured place: 'this had to happen so that what was spoken by the prophet might be fulfilled' (8:17; 12:17). The subject of things old and new also covers the old Law and its new interpretation: 'You have heard that our predecessors were told . . . But I say to you . . .' (5:21–22, 27–28). Again, there is no question in Matthew or in Mark (2:18–22) of dispensing with the Law as if it were a stiff old wineskin. In both, the Law has its honoured place. Why then does Matthew retain these two pictures, the patch and the wineskins, both of which set the old over against the new? One of the more important problems with which the Gospel of Matthew wrestled was the relationship between the Church on the one hand and Judaism on the other. In that argument it was the new which for him displaced the old, partly because in the new the chief actors of verses 18–38 would have a new role.

A conclusion and a new beginning   *Matthew 9:18–38*

The four healings in these verses bring the major section in chapters 8 and 9 to a conclusion. The account of the first two—the healing of the official's daughter and of the woman with the haemorrhage—is a considerably longer in Mark 5:21–43 and Luke 8:40–56. It is not clear in Matthew whether the girl's father is a religious of civil official (elsewhere he is the ruler of the synagogue). Jesus' dismissive words to the professional mourners gathered at the house indicate the reversibility of death: for believers it is no more than 'sleep' (compare 1 Corinthians 15:20ff; 1 Thessalonians 4:13ff). Acting as Elijah did (1 Kings 17:19), Jesus restores the girl in private. This is another sign of his healing for the nation, promised in Isaiah 26:19–21 and performed publicly on other occasions (10:8, 11:5). By now the woman with the haemorrhage has also been cured (vv. 20–22). Matthew's brief account shows Jesus crossing the boundaries from normality into areas of mystery and holiness, as a ritually unclean woman who believes she only needs to touch the fringe of Jesus' cloak is recognized without a word being spoken, and declared whole.

Next to be healed are two blind men, who address Jesus the healer as Messiah: 'Have pity on us, Son of David!' Once again faith is operative, though in the healing of the dumb demoniac which follows there is no mention of it. We should not make the mistake of thinking that healing automatically follows on from faith, or that lack of healing is an indication of inadequate faith on the believer's part. Within Matthew's Gospel as a whole, the ultimate test of faith is not whether the miracle or act of healing occurs, but whether the Father's purpose is fulfilled (26:39). Though Jesus tried to limit the publicity generated by his healings in verse 30, the comment in verse 33—'Nothing like this has ever been seen in Israel'—suggests he had less success on other occasions. Verse 35 then summarizes the activity of Jesus exactly as 4:23 had done: it involved teaching in the synagogues, proclaiming the good news, curing every kind of illness.

But to that summary is attached a fresh comment, which is rather fuller than in Mark. Mark 6:34 simply uses the language of Micaiah's prophecy in 1 Kings 22:17, declaring what will happen when the people

69

have no true leader (Numbers 27:17): they will be 'like sheep without a shepherd'. In verse 36 Matthew amplifies the comment: they are 'like sheep without a shepherd, *confused and exhausted*'. To see the people in this state fills Jesus with pity and love. The words translated here as 'confused and exhausted' have a subtle link with the descriptions earlier of those 'struck down' by illness, 'prostrate' and 'paralysed' (4:24). He meets their needs with healing, but also with the encouragement of the good news of the kingdom. Perhaps there is an implied criticism in the comment. The leadership had failed the people, leaving them vulnerable and helpless. To that extent the stories of healing have a metaphorical aspect. Jesus is working for the healing of the nation as well as for the healing of the physically and mentally ill. And that will mean confrontation with a false and unconcerned leadership which has left the people to struggle with their own problems without lifting a finger to help.

So a new start has to be made. The task has been stated; acts of healing have been witnessed; their results have varied. Sometimes people were surprisingly antagonistic, although perhaps we ought not to be surprised. Physical healing, like the healing of a nation, can provoke opposition; it can infringe taboos and challenge deeply held convictions. In the terminology of verse 37, 'the harvest is large, but there are few workers to gather it in.' A new beginning is envisaged. The new start includes a fresh commissioning of labourers to work in this area of human need and opportunity. Verse 38 instructs disciples to pray for such a commissioning. What is prayed for here is fulfilled in chapter 10, the second of five great discourses in Matthew, often called the mission discourse.

Healing stirs many controversies today. The financing of medical care is one source of argument and disagreement. There is the very considerable expenditure of medical care in the Western world over against the crying needs of hospitals and medical services in economically poorer areas of the world. There is the debate over the character of health care in the Western world. How the healing of body and mind is related to the health of the nation is another massive question.

Fred Kaan's hymn 'For the healing of the nations' offers a thought-provoking prayer which is appropriate to several aspects of Matthew chapters 8 and 9.

For the healing of the nations,
Lord, we pray with one accord;
For a just and equal sharing
Of the things that earth affords.
To a life of love in action
Help us rise and pledge our word.

Lead us, Father, into freedom;
From despair your world release,
That, redeemed from war and hatred,
All may come and go in peace.
Show us how through care and goodness
Fear will die and hope increase.

All that kills abundant living,
Let it from the earth be banned;
Pride of status, race or schooling,
Dogmas that obscure your plan.
In our common quest for justice
May we hallow life's brief span.

You, Creator-God, have written
Your great name on humankind;
For our growing in your likeness
Bring the life of Christ to mind;
That by our response and service
Earth its destiny may find.

Hymns and Psalms, Methodist Publishing House, number 402

THE SECOND DISCOURSE: LABOURERS ── IN THE HARVEST OF GOD'S MISSION ──

The first commission   *Matthew 10:1—15*

The disciples are authorized and empowered, named and commissioned. The commission that they are given, however, provides one of the most difficult problems in Matthew's Gospel. It is geographically limited: 'Do not take the road to the Gentile lands, and do not enter any Samaritan town.' Moreover verse 23 adds a further limitation, one of time. It suggests that the disciples will be moving at high speed, so that there will not be time before the Parousia of the Son of Man for any wider mission than the geographically limited one in verse 5. It will remain strictly a mission within the Israelite area. There will be no time for anything more.

Other parts of Matthew tell a different story. There are two passages worth particular note. In Matthew, as in Mark, it is clearly stated that before the Parousia can happen the mission to all nations must have been completed (Mark 13:10; Matthew 24:14). Then again Matthew's Gospel ends with the great commission, which sets no limitations on missionary work except that of 'the end of time': 'Go therefore to all the nations and make them my disciples . . . I will be with you always, to the end of time' (28:19—20).

How then are the two commissions related? How can the first set limits of place and time on missionary work, while the latter revokes at the very least the geographical limits? The most obvious solution is that the first reflects strictly and exclusively the original commission which Jesus gave to his disciples. Jesus planned a swift movement through the towns of Israel; there was no need for loose change or extra clothing; it could all be completed barefoot and without a stick. The healing of the nation required nothing less. But for the future the commission would be different. Future disciples like ourselves would have a wider brief. They would be dispatched across the world to make disciples of all the nations.

Depending on the teacher and the Spirit   *Matthew 10:16—25*

In these notes on Matthew 4:18—25 we looked at discipleship. There we saw that the humble beginnings of the disciples are never disguised. Nor is their humble status. They are classed as learners, permanently. This is presented here in three different aspects.

First, they are learners in the sense that they never overtake their teacher. However much they may learn, they retain the status of a pupil. Later, in Matthew 23:10, Jesus says that they should avoid being called a teacher ('Nor must you be called a teacher; you have one Teacher, that is the Messiah'), for the very reason that they depend on the teacher as the source of their teaching and will continue to be dependent.

Secondly, they are learners in the sense that what happens to their teacher will happen to them: 'The pupil should be content to share the teacher's lot' (v. 25). They must learn a way of living which includes homelessness and danger. They must learn that these are unavoidable in the course of their mission. They are one with their master and their colleagues in this (23:8). So they need to be 'wary as serpents, innocent as doves' (v. 16). What is required is not primarily that they should know their place. Rather they should develop those qualities which their teacher's lot demands and their teacher's work and example inspire.

Thirdly, they can never be fully prepared for what they will have to face. The prospect is too daunting for self-confidence. Verses 17–18 outline what may be anticipated: legal prosecutions, public punishment, tyrannical intimidation. Verse 21 hints at what might not have been anticipated and could cut even more deeply into personal confidence: family feuds, the generation gap, the poignancy of family betrayal. In today's pluralistic culture we are agonizingly aware of the cost to individuals who depart from their family's tradition of piety. Verse 25b notes the religious dimensions to this horrifying prospect: since Jesus was called the prince of demons, can anything better be expected by his followers? They will literally be damned. The one comfort which the disciple has illustrates perfectly dependence on the master. Self-confidence wilts before the prospect and cost of mission. But just as Jesus could answer his accusers in the power of God's Spirit and presence, so the disciples will not merely be given what to say in a moment of helplessness and danger; they too will be the mouthpiece of the Father's Spirit (v. 20).

Mission: cost, encouragement & rewards *Matthew 10:26–42*

The prospects and dangers of mission are restated: there will be enemies under one's own roof. That illustrates one of the most disturbing of the sayings of Jesus. 'I have not come to bring peace, but a sword' (v. 34).

The divisiveness of religious commitments is one of the significant issues which the disciples of Jesus must face. Where such a commitment overrides personal, family and national expectations conflict may well result, and it will be of the most profound kind possible. How the disciple faces up to that issue in all its complexity is nothing less than a matter of life and death (vv. 37–39).

Encouraging aspects of mission are also restated in verses 26–31. Where such conflict arises, what matters above all is the truth, and the struggle to make known publicly the unveiling of human life which has taken place in Christ's life and work. The rest can be left to the Father's providential care. Alongside the disturbing saying about 'not peace but a sword' are the words that 'even the hairs on your head have all been counted' (v. 30)!

As well as restating powerfully what we have already heard, this passage takes us a significant stage further. It presents the disciple's learner status in a fresh light. There are enormous benefits to be gained from a disciple who in forgetfulness of self and commitment to the truth follows the way of the Lord. The conclusion of the mission discourse sets this out in verses 40–42. That there are benefits is clear. The word 'reward' is repeated three times. Precisely what the verses mean is less certain. Most likely it is this: whoever welcomes a prophet, recognizing that such a person can point to God's will and purpose in the world, will receive the blessing which belongs (by divine commission) to a prophet's work; similarly a good person, in the same way as a prophet, has distinctive benefits of guidance and wisdom to offer. Indeed any disciple, being nothing less than a representative of God, has great riches to confer, once even the meanest service has been provided. The challenge here to values commonly accepted in Matthew's world and our own is unmistakable.

THE WORDS AND WORKS
OF GOD'S WISDOM

John and Jesus—agents of God's wisdom   *Matthew 11:1–19*

The Gospels of Luke and Matthew both contain material on the relationship between Jesus and John the Baptist (see the notes on

Matthew 3). The corresponding passage to this one in Luke 7:18–34 follows on from Jesus' healing activity. Though in Matthew this sequence is interrupted by the Mission discourse, the parallels are sufficient to show that early Christians understood John the Baptist and Jesus to be in close relationship. John the Baptist sends disciples to ask if Jesus is the 'coming one' (vv. 2–6). The answer which they receive is unexpected, in two particular ways. First, Jesus points by way of a reply to acts of healing; these correspond in part to some of the narratives which we have met in chapters 8 and 9, and illustrate his messianic authority. Secondly, Jesus does not specify that these are his actions and his alone. Is this because the disciples have been authorized by Jesus to perform the same tasks of healing (10:8)? Is Jesus providing an answer based on all the messianic activity associated with his mission?

The problem is, as the following verses indicate, that messianic activity of every kind can be misinterpreted or misunderstood. That is true of the work of Jesus and of his disciples; it is also true of John as forerunner and herald. Here again the close relationship between John the Baptist and Jesus is stressed: what both of them do has been criticized. The works which God has been doing in both of them have met with misunderstanding. They have very different lifestyles and roles. But it makes no difference to the people around them who they are or what they do. The works of God are misinterpreted or dismissed, whatever kind they are. John the Baptist and Jesus are both greeted with petulance. People find an excuse to dismiss them both. Yet they are both expressions of divine wisdom. Different though they may be, both John and Jesus are forms of divine activity and vindications of how God works (v. 19). In what sense this is so will become apparent as we read further.

Fierce concern for the unrepentant   *Matthew 11:20–24*

The works of God witnessed by the cities of Galilee are a decisively new context for the common proclamation of John the Baptist and Jesus. Jesus has been teaching and healing in the towns and villages of Galilee (4:23); his mission has also been broadened to include the whole nation (9:35–36). Like John he has been proclaiming: 'Repent, for the kingdom of heaven is upon you!' (3:2; 4:17). Now his mission of preaching and healing has spread far and wide. Earlier the people have been spoken of as harassed and helpless. Now it is implied in verses 20–24 that they are unrepentant. Despite all the preaching and healing, repentance has not happened.

This new situation is expounded by means of two fierce contrasts. The first is between two Galilean villages and two Gentile cities. Words of judgment were spoken on Tyre and Sidon by the Old Testament prophets, yet the two Gentile cities are said to be more easily brought to repentance than the Galilean. They would have responded more vigorously to Jesus' mission than Galilee has. The second contrast is between Jesus' own home town (Capernaum—see 4:13) and Sodom, the most notorious place in the biblical tradition. Capernaum is characterized by another allusion to an Old Testament prophet, this time rather specific. Isaiah had prophesied that Babylon's pride would be its downfall (Isaiah 14:13–15). Jesus applies those very words to Capernaum. Its pride would also be its downfall. What is so fierce about these contrasts is the wholesale and unqualified character of condemnation. Jesus sounds like an Old Testament prophet, but his generation has far less excuse than that addressed by those prophets. This generation's responsibility is greater and the judgment on them will be correspondingly severe.

These contrasts do not make for easy reading. They are hard to reconcile with the picture of Jesus as the forgiving friend of sinners. But the problem which Jesus identifies in Capernaum's case is a serious matter and his language has to be sharp and direct for his concern to be heard. Repentance is required and repentance is possible. But when people assume for themselves a position of privilege, repentance becomes very difficult. Self-satisfaction blinds our eyes. Fierce and uncompromising criticism may then be a measure of true concern and care.

The teacher who embodies wisdom *Matthew 11:25–30*

Matthew presents John the Baptist and Jesus as sharing the same message and a similar fate. They are both expressions of the divine wisdom. Different though they are, they represent the one God and embody the one divine wisdom. Jesus does so particularly as a teacher of wisdom, declaring what God has revealed (vv. 25–27). The relationship of father and son explains his ability to reveal the Father's mind. He can expound God's will. He also calls with wisdom's voice. He encourages people to listen and respond (vv. 29–30). He understands their problems as a good teacher should and helps them to gain a new level of self-understanding. Every teacher knows that hearers can fail or refuse to listen, and so the teacher looks for ways to help the hearing and learning process. One of the chief reasons why we often fail to listen is the belief that we know it all. As the example of Capernaum reminded us, pride makes people blind to the truth; it makes them unreceptive and over-confident. The humility of a quiet mind makes for a good learner; pride destroys the capacity to learn. So the questions about pride and humility belong with the questions about folly and wisdom.

But Jesus is more than a teacher of wisdom. He embodies wisdom. He illustrates the obedience and humility in the way that he teaches and by the way he lives. He does not merely teach that the humble in heart will be blessed (5:5). He is himself humble of heart (v. 29). Responsive to the Father, he sets the pattern for all God's children. Those who claim to be God's children though social or religious privilege may close themselves to such influences. They will not feel at home and at peace. By contrast those who are willing to receive may find their burdens lightened. The way of Jesus, apparently demanding at first sight, becomes ultimately a way of healing and release. A clue therefore to God's way of working is the responsiveness that goes with humility. That is one reason why God's wisdom is vindicated by its results. We can see the sense of it. We may also experience the results of it.

The revelation of God's will and purpose in his Son, in this strangely humble Messiah, is the continuing interest of the following chapters.

> Our pretensions simply add to the burdens which others have to carry. Matthew's Gospel presents to a harassed and vulnerable people one who is without pretensions and who therefore can reduce the burdens of others. He expects the same of those who represent him. The late Gonville ffrench-Beytagh pictured the meaning of the cross and his own experience of helplessness using the image of a neutron star, burning itself out, becoming a total emptiness, a still centre, yet capable of drawing everything to it. Being empty of pretensions is a mark of Christ-like freedom, and so of the ability to liberate others.

Gentleness and justice in God's servant   *Matthew 12:1–21*

Matthew shares with Mark the two stories of the disciples in the cornfield and the healing on the sabbath (compare Mark 2:23–3:6). In Matthew they illustrate one particular way in which the yoke of Christ is lighter. With other teachers of his day he brought a humanitarian concern to the

77

interpretation of the Law, especially the sabbath laws. Human compassion directs how the law may be understood. Compassion for the hungry can override ritual regulations; compassion for an animal can override restrictions on sabbath movement or work. In both cases Scripture provides the warrant for the exceptions. Scripture itself authorizes compassion: 'I will have mercy and not sacrifice' (Hosea 6:6).

Matthew also shares with Mark a note about some healings by Jesus: 'He gave strict instructions that they were not to make him known' (v. 16). This is the theme of secrecy, which in Mark enfolds something of the mystery of God's work in Christ. The seed growing secretly, the message which is hidden from some and revealed to others, the silence of Christ before the high priest: all these show how distinctive gospel standards are. In Matthew the theme of secrecy is understood by means of a quotation from Isaiah 42:1–4 about God's servant. Part of that quotation reads: 'He will not strive, he will not shout, nor will his voice be heard in the streets' (v. 19). This is the servant's secret way, his humble demeanour, his avoidance of show. The quotation continues: 'He will not snap off a broken reed, nor snuff out a smouldering wick . . .' (v. 20). This too belongs to the servant's secret way: a gentleness with the weak and unpromising. The theme of secrecy in Matthew focuses on undervalued qualities of life and behaviour.

But alongside these gentle qualities is the complementary motif of justice—'He will proclaim justice among the nations' (v. 18), and 'until he leads justice on to victory. In him the nations shall put their hope' (vv. 20–21). There is a revolution of world proportions in this servant's vocation. Hidden within the humility of the servant is a massive potential which will uproot the tyrant and avenge innocent blood.

The eternal significance of thoughts and words
Matthew 12:22–37

Here the paradox of weakness and strength appears in another form. Jesus' critics ascribe his healings to demonic authority with their claim that he is operating on behalf of the prince of demons. By means of three parables Jesus denies the charge, facing his critics with the abyss which is opening up in front of them. The charge is nonsensical: Satan would not destroy his own powers. Such binding of evil powers is well enough known; if a house is to be plundered the owner must be roped down first. So the opposite way of looking at Jesus' healing has to be considered. On that view the charge is also blasphemous; those who make it will discover that they are slandering God to his face, and the penalty for that is unthinkable. The Son of Man may appear weak and vulnerable; not so the divine strength operating in him.

All this sounds unrelated to everyday life. But it is characteristic of Matthew's Gospel to bring together the massive issues of world significance and issues of day-to-day living. That is the case here. The critics of Jesus are risking the unthinkable; they are calling God evil to his face. But in fact this comes down to the practical matters of language and speech. Words betray the reality of what is in the heart. Foolish and blasphemous charges would not have been made if the whole person were not rotten to the core. 'Good people from their store of good produce good; and evil from their store of evil produce evil' (v. 35). So, concludes Jesus at this most practical of levels, 'Out of your own mouth you will be acquitted; out of your own mouth you will be condemned' (v. 37).

What makes possible this link between the everyday and world affairs is the reality of judgment. What is said has the ring of intentional exaggeration about it: 'Every thoughtless word you speak you will have to account for on the day of judgement' (v. 36). But the exaggeration makes a real point. In terms of human responsibility before God what we say and do matters, and matters eternally; what we say and do has wide implications which spread far beyond the immediate time and place.

Further warnings for those who seek God's will
Matthew 12:38–50

The final section of this chapter has three parts, each of which recalls an earlier part of the Gospel. It is as if Matthew had several particular interests and the narratives reflect now one, now the other. The first recalls the fierce contrasts of 11:20–24, where Jesus stated that Gentile towns would have reacted more favourably to his mission than Israelite towns. This time the point is made in a slightly different way. There are two contrasts again. The first is that the ancient pagan city of Ninevah repented when Jonah warned them of God's judgment; whereas this 'wicked generation' is in danger of judgment yet neglects the signs that have been given them. Jonah is a sign to them of resurrecting and prophetic power, with the Ninevites as a permanent rebuke; and there is the greater sign of resurrecting and prophetic power in the Son of

Man. The second contrast is gentler: see the trouble which the Queen of Sheba took; she too is a permanent rebuke to this generation.

The second part of this final section is a kind of parable or fable. It continues the earlier discussion about expecting bad fruit from bad trees (v. 33). It has the same general message as a fable like *The Fox and the Hedgehog*: 'Get rid of one, and the rest will arrive, all hungry!' Jesus is saying: 'Get rid of one evil spirit and the rest will soon arrive, all eager to take up residence.' The point here is simple: unless you build up the qualities of Christian living (watching your language, cultivating a receptive frame of mind, taking up the cross, and so on) you will be under continual threat from the powers of evil.

The third story is the disconcerting picture of Jesus making the Father's will the key test of close relationships. Earlier (10:34–37) Jesus had warned that he had not come to bring peace but a sword, and that a person's enemies would come from the family household. Now he uses family relationships to depict the new relationship which commitment to the Father's revelation will forge. As the mission of Jesus demands of the disciples that they should leave their homes and relatives, it also provides a new kind of family and a new set of personal loyalties (19:29).

THE THIRD DISCOURSE: REVEALING — GOD'S SECRETS IN PARABLES —

Hear and understand the
word of the kingdom
Matthew 13:1–23

Chapter 13, the chapter of parables—although it includes (or concludes?) the third great discourse—lacks a clear structure. Like Mark 4 it presents parables of proclamation and faith, which help us to reflect on how we respond to the good news of Jesus Christ. But perhaps even more than Mark, Matthew 13 gives added weight to the contrast between privilege and possible failure. The parable of the sower in verses 3–9 illustrates the point well. Whereas in Mark the parable ends with an ascending scale of success (Mark 4:8), Matthew's version ends with the law of diminishing returns (v. 8). It is as if the story is saying:

the possibility of a rich harvest is there, but take care that it does not turn into a failure. The responsibility is yours.

This fits with what is said about the purpose of parables. They provide a rich opportunity for grasping the revelation which the Son of God has brought (v. 11). This is a privilege which many people have wanted to share (vv. 16–17). Yet so many simply will not hear and understand. Some may perhaps hear but their understanding does not produce the practical results of commitment to Christ. Even then all is not lost. Thanks to the teaching of Jesus in the parable, verse 15 holds out the possibility that some may repent and change their ways.

The interpretation of the parable of the sower (vv. 18–23) adds some practical detail to the reading of the parable. As in Mark and Luke the concern is particularly that external pressures, such as persecution and threats, competing attractions and anxieties might cause a relapse. The question of money arises. Matthew, like Mark, warns against the 'false glamour of wealth' (v. 22 REB). This becomes a major concern of the Gospel, and we shall see later how this concern is worked out, particularly through the use of many parables. Luke's interpretation asks for perseverance through all the trials and tribulations (Luke 8:11–15). Matthew's emphasis, in line particularly with the previous chapter, is more on maintaining particular qualities of life and action (v. 23).

Weapons in the struggle against evil   *Matthew 13:24–43*

The problem of evil dominates the parable of the darnel and its interpretation. Why should there have been darnel among the wheat? Was it introduced by an evil power? What are we to do about the darnel? These are not just theoretical questions. They concern how life is to be lived, and by what standards. They relate to practical matters, and that is why the Gospel of Matthew introduces them. It is very difficult to know how the writer would have answered the questions from a theoretical point of view. We do not know enough of the writer to make a judgment on that issue. Some people think that Matthew saw God and Satan as competing powers. Others recognize that for Matthew the kingdom of heaven is about the sole and supreme responsibility and power of God.

Matthew's concern is severely practical. There are many forms of evil which endanger the disciples' faith and many safeguards which can be built into our lives to counter them. We have already seen that the disciple needs to develop qualities of Christ-like living for this very purpose. There are matters of personal discipline. One of the important safeguards against evil is that of a corporate discipline, for which chapter 18 expresses a concern. One way of understanding the parable of the darnel is to hear it in relation to the practical question of whether or not the corporate body of Christians should take action together for protection against evil. For example, should they expel someone who does evil? Or should they try to retain such a person within the Christian company, in the hope that repentance and forgiveness may provide a chance for rehabilitation? The parable of the darnel appears to support the latter: 'Let them both grow together until harvest' (v. 30).

The parables themselves are an important weapon in the struggle against evil. The Old Testament quotation in verse 35 treats the parables as revelation, as a disclosure of what has been 'kept secret since the world was made'. They are part of the Son of God's revelation, and as we listen to them and study them, new resources for the struggle emerge.

Effort and gift in the kingdom of heaven   *Matthew 13:44–52*

The Sermon on the Mount introduced us to an important feature of Matthew's Gospel: strenuous efforts are required, but always against a background of the opportunities being offered. That is true of this chapter, especially of the twin parables in verses 44–45. The language of the parable of the treasure hints at the strenuous efforts necessary to take advantage of the kingdom's privileges. There is a level on which the kingdom has to be won. Perhaps that level includes the commerce to which the parable alludes. One the other hand, the finding of a buried treasure usually has something of the fortuitous about it. It is by no means all a matter of effort and struggle. The same can be said of the parable of the pearl. There is something in this parable which is akin to the saying about 'the one who seeks will find' (7:7). A merchant searching for a pearl is eventually rewarded by the finest find of all.

The last of the parables resembles the parable of the darnel. It opens up the fearsome character of rejection, and pictures the separation of bad from good. Like the final parable in Matthew 25 it envisages this as taking place at the Last Judgment. What is meant by bad and good is not made clear. Earlier in the chapter hints were given about the criteria of judgment; what is particularly evil is to behave as if the Law did not matter. But these are only hints and for more detail we must wait for the fascinating disclosures of the parable of the sheep and goats (25:31–46).

Jesus asks the disciples if they have understood the parables, and they give an affirmative answer. They are not outright failures, whatever mistakes they may make. Jesus' reply is rather like a riddle, and half the fun of a riddle is making up your own mind how to understand it. It is a riddle about one of Matthew's favourite themes: the old and the new. Can you make sense of what God has done and is now doing? Can you make sense of what you have been taught and are not being taught, of the old law and Jesus' new interpretation? Well, if you can then you deserve the name of a 'discipled scribe'!

> Reflect on the kind of teacher Jesus was. He is like wisdom, teaching with real attention to the identity and needs of his disciples. He offers stories, fables, riddles—and therefore the responsibility to work out what is important. In all his teaching, Jesus summons us to what the Puritans called 'serious religion'.

— REJECTION AND COMPASSION —

A prophet without honour   *Matthew 13:53–58*

At this point in the narrative a note of opposition to Jesus appears, from a surprising quarter—his home town. Mark and Luke have similar stories (Mark 6:1–6; Luke 4:16–30). In Nazareth the extraordinary character of Jesus' words and deeds does not square with what is known to be the ordinariness of his family background. He is merely the son of a carpenter, and his mother, brothers and sisters are well known to the hearers. Though Jesus has a high reputation elsewhere, as the proverb in verse 57 suggests, he cannot count on that in his home town. Matthew sees this response to Jesus as an example of unbelief. His audience cannot connect his humble and ordinary background with the wisdom and power God has given him. The link between faith and healing has been made on many occasions (8:10; 9:22, 29). In Nazareth the lack of faith inhibits Jesus' healing work.

Villainy and compassion—
pointers to Jesus' Passion

The Baptist's death is a paradigm of the fate of the righteous, and evidence of the villainy of kings and princes. But there is more to it than that. The story begins and ends with Jesus: Herod identifies Jesus as a resurrected John, in order to explain Jesus' powerful acts; and John's martyrdom is reported to Jesus by the very disciples who had earlier acted as messengers between the imprisoned John and Jesus (11:2). In this way the narrative hints that the fate of John and the fate of Jesus are intertwined. The Gospel has presented them both as proclaimers of the kingdom of heaven; it has associated them both with divine wisdom. Now their common fate is recognized. The narrative of the beheading of John points forward to the trial and passion of Jesus.

Matthew ascribes to Herod a desire to kill the Baptist, but he is reluctant to do so because of his fear of the people. Perhaps in this respect Matthew's version of the story is nearer the truth than Mark's. Mark simply speaks of Herod's fear of John (Mark 6:16). The political realities favour Matthew's version. The people would certainly have been on John's side in this particular dispute. Herod had courted disaster by an action which caused intense hatred from both outside and inside the kingdom. Nevertheless, in both Matthew and Mark, Herod is the villain. Whatever the actual historical circumstances were, the Gospel record lays the blame firmly on the king. That is even clearer if verse 9 means that Herod Antipas was not simply sorry but appalled at the potentially calamitous consequences of his rash promise. Here was tyranny painted in its darkest colours.

The narrative of the feeding of the five thousand can be read in many different ways. One possibility is to contrast Jesus' care for the people with the villainy of Herod, and even with the unimaginativeness of the disciples. Matthew notes Jesus' concern for the sick here (compare verse 14 with Mark 6:34, which is echoed in Matthew 9:36, again in the context of Jesus' concern for the sick). One of the curious features of Matthew's version of the feeding as compared with Mark's is that mention is made only of the bread as the disciples distribute food to the men, women and children (v. 19; compare Mark 6:41). Some take this to mean that the feeding of the multitude, like the death of John, points forward to the passion of Jesus. It anticipates Jesus' final prophetic supper with his friends.

Resources

The modern reader finds it difficult to get past the initial impressions left by this story. It is about actions of Jesus, some of which have little parallel in our normal experience. Some of the features of the story are, however, entirely familiar. The movement of the narrative from verse 13 has been as follows: Jesus is searching for peace and quiet; this is interrupted by the arrival of a crowd; his concern for them leaves him no option but to provide for their needs. Having done this he makes a further attempt to secure some peace, and spends the night in prayer alone, as Matthew twice indicates in verse 23. So Jesus himself fulfils the pattern of prayer commended in 6:6. This requires a degree of firmness. First the disciples have to be dispatched to the other side of the lake; then the crowds have to be persuaded to break up and go home. But the firmness with which Jesus dispatches the disciples for an evening crossing of the lake enables him not merely to secure peace and quiet. It also creates the scenario for what is to happen next: 'he urged them strongly to embark . . . between three and six in the morning he came to them . . .' (vv. 22, 25).

This is where the story ceases to resemble our normal experience and we encounter problems in our interpretation of it. That would not have been true of the first readers. They would have sensed its significance immediately. In so far as they knew the Old Testament they would have recognized what Jesus did as a divine activity. It is God who walks on the face of the waters; he alone strides across the waves of the deep (see Job 9:8, Psalm 77:19, Isaiah 43:16). When the narrative reaches this point and Jesus approaches his disciples walking on the water, the first readers would have sensed the majestic claim implicit in the Gospel narrative. The one who sent the disciples on ahead and strode across the water to help his disciples moved with divine resourcefulness. It is not simply that the situation or circumstance is within his power to control and direct. All that is happening falls within his purpose and design.

Signposts

We have already noticed the role of the disciples in Matthew. Among them Peter has a distinctive place, often as one who poses key questions (14:14, 18:21) or as the one who, as here, takes the initiative. A special authority is given to him by Christ (16:19), although this appears to be shared with the other disciples in 18:18. Peter also shares with all the disciples a certain fallibility. This is represented in several Matthean narratives and dramatically in the story of Peter coming to Jesus on the water. He begins well, but then starts to sink and cries out in fear. The fallibility of the disciples, and especially of Peter, is both warning and comfort. The reader is warned against Peter's errors, but encouraged by Peter's periodic acts of faith.

Peter's fear is particularly important. He cries out in terror as he begins to sink. Fear is a recurrent theme of Matthew's Gospel. We have already seen that there is much which might inspire fear. In 13:23 the fear concerns failure to produce fruit; in 25:25 the fear immobilizes the servant and makes him unable to credit his master with kindly motives. Sometimes the fear is justified, as in 17:6 where the disciples are terrified by the awesome events of the transfiguration. The circumstances of Christian living can sometimes provoke a fear. If as here in verse 30 it is a paralysing fear, then the reader is made aware that deliverance is possible. Christ catches hold of Peter and brings him safely to the boat. Such a deliverance depends on divine resourcefulness.

The story is a parable of deliverance. It introduces a series of other stories in chapters 15–17 in which our attention is drawn to the participants. It is not only the parables which help us respond to the Gospel in fresh ways; these narratives also have a similar function. Like the participants in the parabolic stories who engage our interest, our sympathy or our disapproval, the participants in the following chapters do the same. Peter is not the only person whose reactions call us to a deeper faith and commitment. Nevertheless those narratives concerning Peter show how someone with little faith became, in dependence on Christ, a reliable testimony to Christ. They are signposts on the route of discipleship.

When religion becomes an excuse   *Matthew 15:1–14*

This is in some ways a distasteful area of Matthew. Jesus attacks the Pharisees with a disturbing degree of ferocity (vv. 1, 12–14). There can be no disguising the antipathy toward the Pharisees which is revealed here.They are described as hypocrites (v. 7; compare 23:13), as blind guides (v. 14; compare 23:16). They are not the heavenly Father's planting (v. 13). But this antipathy is not unique to the Gospel of Matthew. It is found elsewhere also. It is true that sometimes the author of this Gospel is held to be responsible for creating this distasteful impression. But a comparison with Mark and Luke suggests otherwise. The Pharisees are treated harshly here too (compare Matthew 12:24 and Mark 3:22; Matthew 23:25 and Luke 11:39). The condemnation of the Pharisees has a long history.

There is however another side to the picture. What Jesus has to say about the Pharisees in Matthew is not all bad. They are even commended on one occasion, and the commendation is genuine: 'The scribes and Pharisees occupy Moses' seat; so be careful to do whatever they tell you' (Matthew 23:3). Moreover our sense of distaste at the fierceness of the attack on the Pharisees in Matthew 15 is actually reflected in the Matthean text itself. The disciples express it in verse 12: 'Do you not know that the Pharisees have taken great offence at what you have been saying?'

What then could have caused so profound a disagreement—a disagreement which, even after the word of caution from the disciples, had to be repeated ever more forcefully? It is almost impossible to answer that question. We know too little and in insufficient detail about the arguments between Jewish groups at the time of Jesus and at the time of Matthew's writing. We can only guess at who these 'Pharisees' really were and at how representative or otherwise they might have been of the teachers of their day. All we can deduce from verses 4–9 is that for some people ritual dedication of family funds was sufficient excuse for evading family responsibilities, whereas for Jesus that was too superficial a response. It was lip-service, tantamount to finding a religious excuse to evade God's demand. It meant turning religion into something external, superficial and ungodly. The temptation for one single group to do that in one single instance was a fundamental challenge. Little wonder the disagreement was profound—it concerned the nature of true religion.

Common wisdom   *Matthew 15:15—28*

True religion in Matthew's Gospel is down-to-earth. It is a matter of the words we say and write, of seeing the everyday in a fresh light. Far from being irrelevant to that which is spiritual, this is of the very essence of religion. That is the interpretation given to the saying of Jesus in verse 11: 'No one is defiled by what goes into the mouth; only by what comes out of it'. The interpretation echoes and expands what we read in 12:36: 'Every thoughtless word you speak you will have to account for on the day of judgment.' Words are significant because they are a test of personal

87

honour; they reveal what we think and who we are. They are also a test of social honour; they betray the real state of our spoiled and disfigured relationships. These are the pointers to true religion, which cannot be defined merely in terms of ritual actions and prescribed activities. Once again we are back in the arena of the Sermon on the Mount, where we are required to act and speak responsibly in the world which belongs to God.

The narrative which follows is an astonishing commentary on speech, conversation and silence. It begins with an appeal from a non-Israelite on behalf of her daughter. She pleads for a messianic act of healing. Jesus does not even answer. To judge by the conversation that follows, the disciples want an act of healing too—to get rid of this plague of a woman! For Jesus reminds them that he is only sent to Israel (see the note on 10:5 on page 72). How can he help her? The exchange between Jesus and the woman cuts to the heart of what religion is about. Religious requirements appear to mean that Jesus cannot help. She is not a Jew. He is only sent to Jews: he must save the food for 'the children'. But, as the woman says, that does not mean that there will not be scraps for the animals. Common wisdom opens up religious requirements to a fresh critique. We are back to what real religion is about. Jesus challenged others to meet responsibilities laid upon them by God and to refuse any religious evasion of them. That is the way, at her prompting, he acted himself. The disciples had their wish—but not before the Canaanite woman had been commended for her faith. And her faith was expressed in a piece of common household wisdom.

Again and again   *Matthew 15:29–39*

You may feel as you read this passage that you have heard it all before. The healing of the lame, the blind, the dumb and the crippled, and the feeding of the large multitude are apparently a repetition of what we read in 4:24, 8:15, 9:35 and 14:21. That is our modern Western way of reading: we respond to the text by feeling that we have read it all before. The Gospel was written out of a context very different from our own. There repetition was not a weakness, a loss of interest, a failure. It had the value of a reminder, a reinforcement, a recapitulation. It prevented the mind from losing track of the essentials. It helped to give the Gospels a clear focus.

This does not mean that the repetition is without variation. On the contrary, the very fact of the repetition allows us to spot the differences and to savour them. Take for example the function of the disciples in this passage. In both 14:19 and 15:36 the disciples are given food by Jesus and told to serve it to the multitude. But in 14:14–15 it is the disciples who show the initiative by suggesting that it is time for the people to go, whereas in 15:32 it is Jesus who shows the initiative. His concern shows itself in sharing the problem with them. In 14:15 the disciples want to send the crowd off to buy food for themselves. In 15:33 they despair of finding enough to answer the problem which Jesus has posed. In these ways the apparent repetitions serve to highlight different relationships between Jesus and the disciples. They are always the ones who serve with and on behalf of Jesus. Perhaps they do so without being able to recollect what has happened before. Surely they could have remembered what Jesus did previously! Do they perhaps, like the readers, quickly forget what has happened, extraordinary and memorable though it was?

A review of chapter 15 can take this reflection a stage further. Around Jesus are different kinds of people responding to him in different ways. The participants in the stories are varied enough to draw us into the narrative and help us make the story our own. The variations further help to secure our involvement. Even the crossing of the lake once more is given a new touch—this time it is to Magdala (where Mary Magdalene came from), or as Matthew called it, using its more traditional name, Magadan.

Religion is a powerful system. It builds up over the centuries, growing richer in its resources of symbolism and insight. Over against this is the danger that it becomes lip-service, superficial, essentially ungodly, and needing to be opened up to criticism and reviewed by common sense.

A prayer

O God, who are your honoured guests in your tent? . . .
Those who do the thing that is right, who speak the truth
from their hearts . . . who recognize the outcast as the one
whom they need, who forgive seventy times seven. Those
who do these things shall never be overthrown . . . They are
faithful and blessed, God's sisters and brothers and friends.

Prayer in the Morning

Seeing and understanding *Matthew 16:1—12*

The story begins with the request for a sign from heaven. It is part of Jesus' controversy with the upholders of a false religion. The very act of requesting a sign illustrates the problem. They have not used their eyes to see what is happening around them. If they had they would have begun to repent. The illustration from weather conditions fits the controversy well. The Pharisees (and Sadducees also here) know how to use their eyes, as everyone else does, in forecasting weather conditions; but they have seen the multitudes fed and healed and still ask for a sign. In some modern translations verses 2—3 are placed in the footnotes, because early witnesses to the text of Matthew omit the passage. That could be because the original version of Matthew (which of course we do not possess) did not have it. Alternatively the original could have had the illustration and a scribe failed to transcribe it because in his part of the world red sky in the morning did not signify rain.

Leaven can signify either a good influence, as in bread-making, or something bad, as in examples of cultic impurity. Here it is the second, although there is a reference to the first. Jesus warns his disciples to beware of the influence of those who represent a false version of religion. The background is the sea crossing and the failure to take food with them. The disciples assume that Jesus' reference to leaven is occasioned by their failure to carry bread. A clue to the discussion lies in Jesus' directions about mission in 10:9—11. They have been told that there is no need to worry about food; it will be provided. But they misunderstand what Jesus says about the leaven of the Pharisees and so indicate that they have not taken on board the assurances which he gave earlier.

The difficulty is not simply that they have failed to take on board Jesus' assurances. In one way they are no better than the Pharisees and Sadducees, for like them they too have not used their eyes. At least they could have remembered the two feedings of the multitude. They would then have realized that they need not worry. The disciples needed to watch out for the destructive leaven in themselves.

THE SON OF GOD IS
THE SON OF MAN

Believing and deciding
Matthew 16:13–20

Peter makes the historic confession that Jesus is the Messiah, the Son of the living God; and Jesus responds by affirming Peter's place in the battle against lawlessness and evil. That battle is being waged victoriously by God and within it Peter is the rock, a defence against the powers of chaos and destruction. With him is linked the Church. They stand together in the final battle against evil and the final victory over it, as in the parable of the house on the rock (7:24–25). They are the foundation and building. The discussions as to whether or not the foundation is Peter or Peter's confession are largely irrelevant. These have of course figured largely in the debate between Protestant and Catholic scholars. Who succeeds Peter—Pope or believer? But such an argument overlooks the context, which stresses the unity of Peter and the Church, both in their struggle and in their victory.

The unity of Peter and the Church is explained in relation to heaven and earth. Heaven and earth in Matthew are not geographical areas. They are different but related ways of understanding existence. Revelation from heaven brings light into human existence. This is the way in which Matthew has presented the Son of God: the Son has revealed the wisdom of God and the way of God (11:25ff). Peter could make his confession only in so far as it was revealed to him from heaven (v. 17) . But there are other aspects to this relation of heaven and earth. Responsibility is a trust given from heaven to earth. We have already recognized this in the notes on Matthew 9:8 (see page 67). An authority has been given which extends from the work of Jesus and involves many others because of him. In verse 19 this responsibility includes the making of decisions. Decisions on earth have to be made which have validity in heaven. Precisely what kind of decisions these might be is not stated with any clarity. They may include decisions about the Christian way or about the life of the Church. But what is clear is that human responsibility is a gift from heaven and to be used accordingly. Little wonder that the responsibility is given to Peter here, and to the disciples in 18:18. It is a responsibility given from heaven and shared on earth.

Responsibilities

In Mark's version of the Caesarea Philippi episode (Mark 8:27—33), Jesus shifts the discussion from himself as Messiah to himself as suffering Son of Man. Peter has proclaimed him as Messiah and this must not be disclosed. Instead Jesus gives a threefold prophecy: the Son of Man will be rejected, executed and eventually vindicated (Mark 8:31). In Matthew, Peter proclaims Jesus as the Messiah, the Son of the living God, and as in Mark this must not be disclosed. Thus far Mark and Matthew are running parallel. But what follows in Matthew does not immediately mention the Son of Man (v. 21). Matthew uses the same three prophetic pillars of suffering, execution and vindication, but they are given a different setting. Perhaps Matthew has already said so much about the revelation of the Son of God that the contrast between Messiahship and the Son of Man is different in his Gospel from what it is in Mark.

The different setting in Matthew of the Caesarea Philippi confession includes two particular features. The first is that the argument with Peter is more intense. In Mark's Gospel Peter takes exception to what Jesus says about the Son of Man and is rebuked by Jesus with the words 'Out of my sight, Satan!' (Mark 8:33). In Matthew Peter says that what Jesus foretells cannot be, and the rebuke to Peter is 'Out of my sight, Satan; you are a stumbling block to me.' In Matthew the responsibility given to Peter is greater than in Mark; and this means that he is exposed to a greater danger. The second feature which distinguishes the Matthean context this: In Mark the warning to keep silent and the prophecy about the Son of Man lead into a description of discipleship: discipleship involves taking up one's cross; it means shame shared here but glory shared with the Son of Man at his (apparently) imminent coming. In Matthew, the sequence is similar, but there are differences. First, the reward will be 'to each according to what each does' (this is obscured in some modern translations of v. 27). This serves to underline the importance of Christian behaviour: the one who gives us responsibility to act for him is none other than the powerful heavenly Lord. Second the final phrase in verse 28 refers to the coming of the Son of Man in his kingdom (compare the parallels in Mark 9:1 and Luke 9:27). Perhaps Matthew suggests that Peter, James and John (three of those standing there) are to glimpse this kingdom momentarily in the next incident.

Vision and suffering

The powerful heavenly Lord is glimpsed by the disciples in the transfiguration. In a heavenly vision which fills them with fear they see the true nature of the one with whom they live and work. He is the one who will come as judge of all. God had affirmed Jesus as Son at his baptism; now he reaffirms that vocation in the transfiguration (v. 5). This is for the sake of the disciples in particular. They are to listen to him; his words carry divine authority. This applies both to what Jesus has taught them and to his words of comfort and encouragement: 'Stand up; do not be afraid' (v. 7).

The experience of the disciples is made more awesome still by the presence of Moses and Elijah. They are representative figures. Jesus fulfils the Law and the prophets, and their presence confirms that. But their presence is rather more than that of representative persons. This is also true of Mark's version of the transfiguration (Mark 9:2–13). But it is demonstrated much more clearly in Matthew. Their presence is symbolic. In both Mark and Matthew, Moses and Elijah point to suffering and vindication. They both suffered in obedience to God's purpose. They were both part of God's purpose for Israel; they suffered and were persecuted because of it. Although this is true in Mark's account, in Matthew the role of Elijah is specifically underlined.

The discussion about Elijah has a distinctive ending in Matthew. Verse 13 reads: 'Then the disciples understood that he meant John the Baptist.' Not only is Elijah the prophet present at the transfiguration as testimony to Jesus' fulfilment of the work of all the prophets, he is also there as the one who was expected to inaugurate the fulfilment: 'Elijah will come and set everything right.' What the disciples now came to realize was that in a sense Elijah had come; the fulfilment had been inaugurated. They had seen it for themselves. Their own eyes had witnessed it. It was John the Baptist, the one who had suffered and been persecuted for proclaiming repentance, who had said, 'The kingdom of heaven is upon you!' The perspective of John the Baptist—as preparing the way, as living out gospel values, as an expression of the divine wisdom—gives the transfiguration a historical thrust. The vision of the heavenly Lord of glory has its counterparts on earth: what happened to the forerunner is not far off for the Messiah (vv. 22-23, and compare 16:21).

Faith and the Messiah's presence

In comparison with the Marcan story of the epileptic boy (Mark 9:14–29), the Matthean account is brief. It is as if the contrast between the glory of the disciples' experience and the bathos of their inability to help (v. 16) needs no elaboration. The contrast is made simply, with a minimum of detail. It is the familiar picture of a descent from the mountain-top experience to the realities of the valley below. They have witnessed the power of their Lord; but they remain fallible and helpless.

But the brevity of the Matthean story gives it another dimension. It brings into close proximity the disciples' failure and Christ's authority: 'Then Jesus spoke sternly to him; the demon left the boy, and from that moment he was cured' (v. 18). Such a stark contrast might strike the reader as unhelpful if repeated again and again. We are left with the sense that there is nothing we can do. But in this story Matthew has something else in mind. His shorter narrative serves to highlight the tension between the disciples' inadequate faith ('What an unbelieving and perverse generation!'—v. 17) and the power of faith even when it is no bigger than a mustard seed (v. 20).

Mark is concerned in his story of the descent from the mountain to stress the importance of prayer (Mark 9.29), and there are many passages where the same can be said of Matthew. Prayer is the means by which the disciple receives strength; in order to match the demands of the disciples' vocation, time alone with God is essential. Both Mark and Matthew agree on that. But Matthew seems to provide the reader with a further key to the healing narratives. It is not so much that we are fallible and Jesus is the great healer; it is more that the great healer never departs from our company. He continues with us and amongst us. So even the beginnings of faith can see the enormous possibilities in Christ's presence with us (v. 20; compare 18:20, 28:20). Because of Christ's presence, faith 'laughs at impossibilities and cries, "It shall be done!"' (from a hymn by Charles Wesley).

Free choice

The story of the coin in the fish's mouth is another incident in which Peter figures conspicuously. He is questioned about Jesus' attitude to the temple tax. The half-shekel mentioned in this passage was a payment due from each Israelite according to Exodus 30:13–15. There was considerable debate as to whether or not the payment of this could be required by all Jews. The Pharisees believed it could, but others objected. We have evidence of this from the Dead Sea Scrolls. It would seem that Jesus here is siding with the objectors; he was willing to pay the half-shekel on a single occasion with out accepting liability for its regular payment.

According to the narrative, Jesus takes up the issue with Peter and appears to assert for himself and his followers the kind of freedom from external authorities claimed by all who are Jews: ' "Yes", said Jesus, "and their own people [i.e. the Jews] are exempt" ' (v. 26). This is the first time in the Gospel that the theme of freedom has been explicitly stated and it is interesting that it appears in the context of Jewish practice. Although it is explicitly stated only here, the concept of freedom stands behind much of what we have read so far in the Gospel. We have often used the notion of responsibility, and responsibility and freedom go together. The one makes little sense without the other. We are free to consider the possible patterns of Christian obedience and to act in accordance with the decisions we make. That was one of the findings of our work on the Sermon on the Mount.

Freedom includes the freedom to pay the half-shekel tax. That is how the narrative ends. Peter is told to go and catch the fish with the coin in its mouth. Providing that the payment is not imposed, and that a single payment is not understood as acceptance of the tax in principle, there is no reason why the miraculous coin should not be paid on behalf of both of them. Their freedom is not infringed thereby; it is enhanced by the free decision to pay on that one occasion. Freedom in the New Testament has these important elements: it belongs with responsibility; it includes the freedom to decide, and that may be exercised in obedience as well as in resistance. Like Jesus, we may choose not to cause offence.

> We have been considering several aspects of our responsibility before God. Let us pray with peoples emerging into political freedom that with them we may discover the true nature of freedom.
>
> We are aware that democratic freedom implies a great obligation. It is necessary for us to learn to live in freedom. The attainment of new structures does not yet resolve the spiritual struggle. The new orientation of life in our country needs the message of the Gospel.
>
> Christians in Czechoslovakia

THE FOURTH DISCOURSE:
— LIFE IN THE KINGDOM —

A child is the greatest   *Matthew 18:1–5*

The fourth of the five great discourses in Matthew begins with a question—'Who is the greatest in the kingdom of heaven?'—and much of the chapter provides various aspects of the answer. The first answer is given as an immediate response: 'Whoever humbles himself and becomes like this child will be the greatest in the kingdom of heaven, and whoever receives one such child in my name receives me.' The openness of a child to divine revelation was often recognized by Jewish divines. The biblical pattern is provided by Samuel in the temple (1 Samuel 3). His elders were able only to advise; he alone heard the call of God. Humility, then, means the willingness to live in the world as God's world and to be open to the divine revelation by whatever means it may come. That is where greatness lies, according to the values of the kingdom. It is not about status, power or authority, but about the aptitude and attitude of the learner.

The presentation of a child provides an acted parable of these values of the kingdom. Jesus sets a child in the middle of the disciples and says that only those who change and become like a child will enter the kingdom of heaven. Matthew is not alone in citing such an entry qualification. In John's Gospel, Nicodemus is told that he must be born 'again' or 'from above' if he is to enter the kingdom (John 3:3ff.) The helpless potential of a little child carries hope beyond our adult dreams. A child can also become Christ to the welcoming host (v. 5). What this means has been argued in many different ways. Perhaps the best way is to approach the passage through the many other contexts in which Christ is spoken of as present— he is present in his disciples (28:20), in his little ones (25:40), in his community (18:20). A child is special in being a symbol of all who need care, attention and protection, and who are vulnerable and defenceless. In Matthew's Gospel there is a one-to-one relationship between such a person and Christ himself. In serving such a one we serve Christ. Sometimes scholars have argued that a claim like this could only be made if the child represents a Christian missionary or a Christian church member. Verses 1–5 do not seem to know that kind of qualification.

Little ones

However a qualification does appear in verse 6: the little ones *who believe in me* can be given offence. A recurrent motif in this section of chapter 18 is that of 'offence'. Translators have difficulty here because the Greek term, from which our word 'scandal' derives, is capable of so many variant translations. We have already met it in Jesus' rejoinder to Peter: 'You are an offence (or a stumbling block) to me' (16:23). It can refer to anything which trips us up. In verses 6–9 some translators take it in a spiritual sense: 'cause to sin', or 'cause to lose faith in me'. This follows from the definition of the little ones as 'those who believe in me'. Other translators prefer a more general translation, such as 'be a hindrance to'. The passage can then have a wider sense: 'whoever prevents the development of, offers a bad example to, puts temptation in the way of these little ones who believe in me . . .' Those who cause such offence are given stern advice. We found it in the Sermon on the Mount, where right decisions are so important that the best way to grasp their importance is through overstatement. Verses 6b–9 should be compared with 'Go and amputate yourself!' in 5:29–30. This is the level of importance that the teacher must attach to work with the vulnerable.

Verse 10 adds a further reason for caring for the 'little ones'. No one is quite sure what is meant by the verse. It could mean that the 'real selves' of these little ones are close to God. Or the angels could be guardian angels, keeping personal watch over each individual from birth onwards. Or these are angels of the divine presence whose care for the 'little ones' ensures God's close acquaintance with their fate. Whichever of these is correct, the point is that offence caused to 'little ones' is all the more serious because of the value placed upon them in the heavenly realm. Once again the interaction of heaven and earth is an important factor in our daily lives. Perhaps the strongest argument for the last alternative, 'the angels of the presence', is that chapter 18 ends with a story where those who have 'the king's ear' relate to him the offence done to one of his servants. They perform on earth the task which the angels perform in heaven.

The return of the stray

The parable of the straying sheep ends in Matthew with a reference to the Father's will. It is not God's will that any of these little ones should perish (v. 14). This makes the parable a conclusion to the first half of the discourse, which is concerned with God's little ones—their place in the kingdom and the dangers facing those who might cause them harm. The parable confirms God's purpose in caring for them and protecting them. The identity of the 'little ones' is not defined at the beginning of the chapter, but it becomes clear from verse 6 onwards that these can be understood as Christian believers. Why are they called 'little ones' is not clear. It could be because they are young in years, or young in faith. They may be vulnerable in themselves, or live in a situation which makes them vulnerable, or perhaps they have strayed into places which make them vulnerable.

Three times Matthew's version of the parable uses the verb 'wander': 'if one of them should wander', 'look for the wanderer', 'rejoice over that one rather than over the ninety-nine which did not wander'. The Matthean parable is therefore more about a wandering sheep than a lost sheep. The sheep has gone astray. The concern is for little ones who are vulnerable because they have strayed into dangerous places or even been led astray into them. The dangers highlighted in 13:22, together with the 'scandal' language of the earlier part of the chapter, suggest the power of worldly cares, the glamour of wealth and the excesses of the flesh to lead the vulnerable astray.

There are two facets to the return of the straying sheep, both of them found in the version in Luke 15:3–7. The first is the joy over the discovery of the stray. We shall find that several of the parables later on in Matthew emphasize this theme. Matthew's parables are not just about judgment. They also have a lot to say about the joy of the kingdom. Faithful servants are told in 25:23, 'Enter into your Lord's joy'. The second facet is the contrast between the one and the ninety-nine, with the emphasis on the finding of the one. This coincides with the interest we discovered in Matthew 13:15—return is possible.

The sinner who goes astray   *Matthew 18:15–17*

The second half of the chapter begins with an example of someone going astray. It is the specific case of a sinful act. Jewish tradition about how to deal with such a situation has a long history, going back to Leviticus 19:17–18. Basically, Leviticus says four things: the sinner should be reproved; anger is dangerous; guilt is contagious; the motivation should be love. To follow all four suggestions is quite a feat. Few people can manage it. So in the course of Jewish history the tradition suggested various stages. For example, reprove the sinner person-to-person, but try to make it up before the sun goes down; if that proves unworkable or ineffective then try giving the matter an airing before a larger group. What is presented here in Matthew is a three-fold pattern: person-to-person, before two or three witnesses, before the Church as a whole.

But what happens if the sinner, after being reproved in all the three ways, still refuses to listen? There is a danger of contagion and a problem of intransigence. The sinner endangers the life of the Christian community, and fails to see the necessity of putting the matter right. An ultimate act of discipline is then essential. It is necessary to treat the sinner as you would 'a pagan' or a 'tax-collector' (v. 17). The language has the ring of Jewish discipline about it. It involves exclusion from the community.

But is the exclusion to be permanent? Perhaps in some communities it was. Paul did not think of it as an irrevocable act. For him the final level of discipline was exclusion from the community, but still it was aimed at eventual restoration. In 1 Corinthians 5:5 he writes of 'consigning someone to Satan', with the hope that salvation may ultimately result. In Matthew 18 the aim of exclusion is not made clear. Nor is it apparent whether this was a tradition of discipline which had been handed down and might need adjustment and modification. What is clear, though, is that the remainder of chapter 18 concerns forgiveness. According to this second half of the chapter, forgiveness has no limits, unless these are imposed by the sinner. In this case, forgiveness could be offered again and again, and the refusal to be forgiven could mean exclusion and ultimate disaster. There seems to be no way back from a self-imposed hell.

The power to forgive   *Matthew 18:19—20*

In 16:19 we saw how Peter was given the responsibility of 'binding' and 'loosing'. The nature of this cannot be defined with any certainty. It could refer to making decisions about the Christian way or the Christian community. Here the responsibility is explicitly a shared one. 'Whatever you bind' in verse 18 has a plural reference. It means that all the disciples share the binding and the loosing. The context in chapter 18 is rather more specific than in chapter 16—as we have seen, it concerns forgiveness. Peter asks Jesus how often he is to forgive his brother. There is a passage in John's Gospel which sounds very like

Matthew 18:18. In John 20:22–23 the Holy Spirit is breathed on the disciples and they are given new powers. These sound similar to those in Matthew 18:18, but instead of defining them by the verbs 'binding' and 'loosing', John uses the similar but more specific terms of 'forgiving' and 'retaining'. So the parallel in John 20:23, along with the context in Matthew 18, suggest that 'binding' and 'loosing' in verse 18 might mean 'declaring forgiven' and 'declaring unforgiven'.

We saw earlier in Matthew 16:19 that what is done in heaven and on earth affect each other: what is bound or loosed in heaven is bound or loosed on earth. Verse 19 makes the same point, although the relationship between earth and heaven is expressed differently. Here the promise is given that requests made on earth by the agreement of two will be honoured in heaven. Presumably this means that the request that God would forgive made by two in agreement with each other would be honoured by the heavenly Father. The grounds for the honouring of such a request on earth are stated in verse 20: Christ is present in the midst of even two or three who are gathered in his name. 'I am there' has a divine ring to it. It recalls the mention of God's presence in 1:23 and anticipates the promise in 28:20: 'I will be with you to the end of time'. Christ's presence, linking heaven and earth, means that the agreement on earth already has the divine sanction.

The depths of forgiveness   *Matthew 18:21–35*

Peter now asks about the limits to forgiveness. Jesus' response suggests that at least in personal relationships there is no limit. But the parable of the unmerciful servant adds a caveat. As the story begins it sounds as if the parable is about the unlimited nature of forgiveness. The lord hears his servant's plea and releases him from an enormous debt. The second part, however, depicts the servant well-nigh throttling a fellow servant, deaf to his entreaties, and demanding on pain of imprisonment that he should settle a paltry debt. The parable has become a story not about release from an enormous debt, but about a servant released from an enormous debt who refuses to show mercy to a colleague. There is a final twist to the tale and the last part of the parable abounds with Matthean cross-references. The unmerciful servant's colleagues report the matter to the lord, who revokes his act of mercy and requires the debt to be paid in full. The parable has become a story of judgment on an unmerciful servant who will find that no mercy will be shown to him.

The end of the chapter offers a comment on the parable. God will respond as the lord did if we do not show mercy to others. Those who are forgiven must discover the way to forgive. Verse 35 takes us still deeper. It is not only a matter of forgiving because we have been forgiven. We are told to forgive *from the heart*. That is a startlingly difficult requirement. Like the Israelite called on to reprove a sinner but told that he must reprove without anger and love his neighbour as himself (Leviticus 19:17–18), we are asked to consider our motives. Forgiveness has to come from the heart and this is impossible unless we discover how we may truly love our neighbour. The stories in Matthew often appear to be direct and simple. The more we read them, the more searching we find them. Like the Sermon on the Mount they require of us responsible decisions and fresh attitudes.

> *Chapter 18 as a whole raises an important question: Is the care of the young adequate in secular or church contexts without attention to the deep questions about why and how forgiveness is possible?*
>
> *Most merciful and holy God, may your mercy penetrate the depths of our being and make us again in your likeness.*

JESUS IN JUDEA: — QUESTIONS AND PARABLES —

There have been indications of Jesus' journey to Jerusalem since 16:21. This section has Jesus moving south from Galilee to Judea, moving ever nearer to the holy city.

Divine grace and human responsibility   *Matthew 19:1–30*

We have already seen some of the teaching about marriage and divorce in Matthew (see notes on 5:32, pages 55–56). Verses 4–8 see marriage as grounded in the will of the Creator. This is in every sense prior to the permission given by Moses for the writing of a bill of divorce. Marriage is part of the original purpose of God for humanity; divorce was merely permitted and should be allowed only on the grounds of unchastity, and only because human hard-heartedness made the permission necessary.

The grounding of marriage in the will of the Creator means that the renunciation of marriage has to be a vocation (v. 11). Some renounce marriage and for many different reasons (v. 12), including the demands upon them of entry into the kingdom. But such renunciation is only for those called to that state by God.

Matthew goes on to present two pictures of the kingdom of heaven. In the first, children are welcomed and blessed by Jesus as those to whom the kingdom belongs (vv. 13–15; compare 18:1–4). In the second, a rich young ruler discovers that the demands of the kingdom are way beyond anything he anticipates. That is probably what the Matthean version of the conversation between this man and Jesus is about. The young man wants to know what to do so as to gain entrance to the kingdom. Jesus suggest that this is to oversimplify matters. There is all manner of good that might be required of him, for there is a single source who is the initiator of all good. Nevertheless, if he keeps the commandments he will have made a good start. The young man claims to have made a very good start. But the range of good required of him in the use of his possessions is a different issue, and one that defeats him completely. He cannot live up to those kinds of demands.

There is in fact only one way into the kingdom. It is the way that God makes possible: God chooses to make the last first (v. 30). We have of course a part to play. This might involve renouncing all our ties and responsibilities. In the case of marriage, as we have seen, such a renunciation follows a specific vocation from God. But the way into the kingdom still depends on divine help and encouragement (v. 26).

Divine grace and human resentfulness   *Matthew 20:1–16*

The parable of the labourers in the vineyard also concerns money, as do several other parables in Matthew. The landowner in this story gives a day's wages to all who on that particular day have worked for him. They all receive the same, irrespective of the number of hours they have worked. They are also paid in the order everyone least expected; it is a case of 'last come, first served'. The landowner regards this as 'generosity', and whatever we may think of him it might well have appeared so to an ancient economist. Anything less for the labourers enrolled late on in the day would hardly have been worth their while. The ancient economist would have regarded everything as done properly. The landowner pays them all on the spot, including those with whom he agreed a contract. It is the *order* that is unexpected; the first are last and the last first. The parable repeats what the previous chapter hinted about God. God makes the unexpected possible; he chooses the last to be first.

The inclusion in the story of disgruntled workers is hardly accidental. If the story is about unexpected generosity, then it will also be about observant eyes. Generosity is greeted by different reactions, and jealousy is often one of them. That is the case here. Parables used to be treated as having only a single point of interest. Matthew's parables can rarely be reduced to just one focus. They reflect typical situations in ordinary life, and ordinary life is full of varying reactions and troubled relationships. We found the same in the parable of the unforgiving servant (18:23–35). There his colleagues reacted unfavourably to his behaviour. Here the disgruntled workers react unfavourably to their employer. They are like people who see the gracious goodness of God expended on the undeserving and feel that it is all wrong. As Jesus reminded other listeners, God causes the sun to rise on good and bad alike and sends the rain on the just and unjust (5:45). There is a freedom about the activity of God which defies human calculations, and predictably human reactions to God can be puzzled and confused. New styles of reactions need to be developed, matching and not resenting the divine graciousness.

Questions of status   *Matthew 20:17–34*

The third prediction of Jesus' passion and resurrection is a private communication to the disciples, as he and his disciples prepare to go to Jerusalem. 'Son of Man' in verse 18 designates a way of looking at the life and work of Jesus. It pictures him as the victim of injustice and cruelty but also as the one to be raised 'on the third day'. Here it presents his life and work as a contrast between humiliation and vindication. In the final chapters of the Matthean narrative, it is developed further in the crucial contrast between the one who is judged and the one who will judge.

Like the first two predictions of the passion and resurrection, the third is followed by a conversation between Jesus and his disciples. The first concerned Peter's lack of understanding of the Son of Man's mission (16:22–28), and the second concerned freedom from the demands of earthly rulers (17:24–27). The third—the narrative of the mother's request on behalf of her son Zebedee in verses 20–28—is about those who seek status because of their association with the Son of Man. In Matthew the position of this account is significant not only because it follows the third prediction, but also because it comes so soon after the parable of the labourers in the vineyard. It picks up features of that preceding story. As in the parable, the request to Jesus concerns privilege and status: who is first and who is lowest (v. 27). It also contains a vigorous argument between those who are aggrieved at the turn of events. The ten disciples turn on the two brothers and Jesus has to remind them of the values in his kingdom. The way in which earthly rulers make demands on their subjects is the opposite of the Son of Man's pattern of life and work. The Son of Man does not bind people to serve an élite; he suffers in order to deliver people from what enslaves them.

Even the position that the Son of Man enjoys by virtue of his Davidic or messianic status is seen as the role of a servant. The appeal to him as 'Son of David' in verse 30 is answered by a merciful act of healing. There is nothing here of the conquering, warlike picture of some contemporary messianic expectations.

— THE MESSIAH IN JERUSALEM —

Hope for the future of Judaism *Matthew 21:1–17*

Chapter 21 introduces an interesting set of rearrangements of order in Matthew over against Mark. Matthew has the entry into Jerusalem (vv. 1–9), the cleansing of the temple and the messianic healings in the temple (vv. 10–16), followed by the return to Bethany (v. 17). Mark has the entry into Jerusalem (11:1–10), the return to Bethany (11:11), the cursing of the fig-tree (11:12–14), the cleansing of the temple (11:15–19), and the message of the fig-tree (11:20–25). The change of order may not seem particularly significant. But the result of the reordering in Matthew could be quite fundamental. In Mark the impression is given that a prophetic proclamation of punishment on Jerusalem has begun. The fig-tree has been cursed and has already begun to wither. In Matthew, the addition of the messianic healings after the cleansings of the temple introduces a new factor, which changes the prophecy of destruction into a prophecy of reconstruction. The Messiah has brought a new hope of healing for Judaism.

Another feature of Matthew which differs from Mark's account is to be found within the narrative of the entry into Jerusalem. In Mark, the Old Testament background to the triumphal entry is implicit. In Matthew it is explicit; Matthew quotes directly from Zechariah 9:9 in verse 5. The quotation contains the key word 'lowly' (some translate the word 'humble', others 'gentle'). It is the lowly Messiah who enters the royal city. Lowly the Messiah may be, but the prophetic drama of his entry into Jerusalem culminates in an act of violence. He cleanses the temple. There is again a significant difference between Mark's account and the accounts of Matthew and Luke. In quoting from Isaiah 56:7, Jesus in Mark 11:17 refers to the temple as a 'place of prayer for all nations'. Here in verse 13, and in Luke 19:46, 'for all nations' is omitted. The temple is for Judaism; and the one who cleanses the temple offers cleansing for Judaism.

The healings in the temple are greeted by children's hosannas. The children at least grasp the importance of what is happening there. The Messiah has come to offer cleansing and healing to the people. In Matthew's narrative the children in the temple, like the 'little ones' of chapter 18, are especially open to divine truth.

Facing up to truth   *Matthew 21:18–32*

The cursing of the fig-tree in verses 18–22 becomes an illustration of the power of faith. The issue of faith, particularly the role of faith in miracles of healing, has played a key role in earlier Matthean narratives. Even if faith is as small as a mustard seed it can have extraordinary results. There the fallibility of the disciples was recognized. Here the results promised are extraordinary indeed: mountains hurled into the sea (v. 21). Jesus as usual is using extreme pictures to make his point. It is also significant that here there is no mention of 'little faith' here. Faith in this case is qualified by 'and have no doubts'. Jesus' extreme language does not only make a point about the performance of miracles—the mountains being thrown into the sea; he also refers to faith in the same way. He challenges us to a faith which seems way beyond us.

At this moment in the narrative, when Jesus has entered the city and purified the temple, the question is raised about the authority by which Jesus acts (v. 23). At first sight it seems that Jesus evades the question (v. 27b). The reality is in fact somewhat different. Even the apparent evasion contains an implied answer, and the subsequent controversies all seem to centre on that same subject: by what authority does Jesus teach and act as he does? Earlier in the Gospel, Jesus has associated himself closely with John the Baptist. They shared the same message, the same senseless treatment from Jewish leaders, the same positive responses from sinners and the same vocation as representatives of the divine wisdom. Now Jesus makes use of that association to suggest how the question of authority can be understood. The question was born of an unwillingness to face the question as to whether God is at work in the words and deeds of Jesus.

The parable of the two sons in verses 28–31 is a puzzle, perhaps intentionally so. We might as well ask: 'Which of the two did what the father wanted?' The solution proposed in verses 31b–32 is unexpected: the one who could make a mistake and correct it! That is something which the Jewish leaders (and by no means only the Jewish leaders) could not do.

Judgment on the leaders   *Matthew 21:33–46*

The question concerning the authority of Jesus in verse 23 governs the material up to 22:46. It is answered in surprising ways. The first apparent evasion of the question turns out to be a powerful reply. Then three following parables and four conflict-stories reveal further answers of great depth and intensity. The three parables (21:28–22:14) contribute to that answer with a common theme: there will be unexpected entrants into the kingdom who will replace those who expected to be there. The parable of the wicked tenants (vv. 33–43) is the second of the three parables. Its conclusion warns that a new, obedient people will take the place of those who revolt against God and his Son. The parable itself is about a vineyard on which an owner has lavished great care, and about tenants who go to extreme lengths in denying the owner his lawful rights; as a result they are themselves displaced. Those three features of the parable all correspond to elements in the story of Jesus. God has lavished great care on Israel; the Jewish leaders have rejected all God's representatives including, finally, Jesus himself (the son in the parable); they will therefore be displaced in favour of 'those who will produce fruit for him at the right times'.

The quotation from Psalm 118 was used by the early Church to underline the seriousness of rejecting Christ (1 Peter 2:7). Both Matthew and Luke highlight this in their own way. Verse 44— 'Anyone who falls on this stone will be dashed to pieces; and if it falls on a man he will be crushed by it'—is often placed in the margin because some editors are uncertain whether or not it belongs to the original text of Matthew, though it is found at Luke 20:18 (though not in Mark 12).

Whatever may be the judgment of the editors, the verse agrees with the tenor of the whole passage.

Invited guests   *Matthew 22:1–14*

The parable of the feast continues the theme of replacement. The royal wedding feast is ready, but none of the invited guests is willing to attend. A second reminder to the guests produces an even stronger reaction (the parallels with the wicked tenants in 21:35–39 are interesting here); they react violently and their violence brings down the wrath of the king. So servants are sent out to invite anyone who will come, good and bad alike, and these fill the banquet hall.

The significance of the parable is clarified by the meals which Jesus shared with his friends. It is a characteristic of these meals that he ate with publicans and sinners. It was his way of demonstrating acceptance of them. The meal made them welcome, whoever they were. So it is entirely appropriate that in the parable of the feast the newly invited guests should include the bad as well as the good. All were welcome at the feast. The final meal which Jesus ate with his disciples also clarifies another feature of the parable. That meal pointed forward to the messianic banquet. It was an anticipation of the future celebration of God's final victory (see Isaiah 25:6–8). The parable of the feast shared the same kind of expectation. The wedding of the king's son was a parable of the last days, of the gathering together of God's people to share in his joy.

The final section of the parable comes therefore as something of a surprise. All have been made welcome; the feast is ready; the hall is full; the celebration begins. Then the host discovers someone without a wedding garment; and when the offender is discovered he is punished not just by expulsion from the feast but by imprisonment in a dungeon. The traditional explanation is that the wedding garment stands for good works. The clue to the parable is therefore that the king's welcome carries with it responsibilities, which if they are not fulfilled can result in disaster.

Four confrontations   *Matthew 22:15–46*

The four Matthean conflict stories are similar to those in Mark 12 but differ from Mark in their emphases. In the first, the question is raised about the tax payable to the Roman emperor (vv. 15–22). In the Matthean narrative, the coin is presented and its significance is discussed, with two main emphases—the wickedness of the questioners (v. 18 refers to their 'malicious intention'), and the compatibility between what Jesus says here and the previous discussion of taxation in 17:24–27. The response of Jesus is strikingly ambiguous: 'Pay to Caesar what is Caesar's and to God what is God's.' That can mean either that payment to Caesar includes a proper recognition of God or that Caesar and God control separate unrelated realms. Both of these elements correspond with 17:24–27: Jesus pays the tax to avoid offence but in principle claims the exemption for all God's people. In Matthew's Gospel there is no incitement to revolt. The result of the discussion in verses 15–22 about taxation is that his questioners back off. They have no immediate cause for complaint. On the other hand Matthew's material has a cutting edge. It consistently paints the great rulers of the world as tyrannical and oppressive. The emperor is no exception, and God sets a clear limit to such exercise of power. One such limit is the freedom enjoyed by those who are 'children of the kingdom'.

The second confrontation is with the Sadducees (vv. 23–33). The Sadducees deny that there is an afterlife and make their case by means of contemporary marriage law. Jesus answers them with a quotation from Exodus 3:6. At first sight his answer appears to be innocuous. It seems to rest solely on an association of Abraham, Isaac and Jacob with the verb 'I am': 'I am [now as well as I was long ago] the God of Abraham, Isaac and Jacob.' But the quotation does not stand alone. It is accompanied by the basic principle stated in verse 32b: 'God is not God of the dead but of the living.' That is where the argument rests; God is a God of power (v. 29) and that power is able to make alive and sustain life. It is on account of this power that God is and remains God of Abraham, Isaac, and Jacob. He is the one who ensures their continued existence.

The third confrontation is between Jesus and a scribe, over what is the most important commandment. According to him (vv. 37–40) it is Deuteronomy 6:5 accompanied by Leviticus 19:18—the injunctions to love God and to love one's neighbour. In verse 40 these two passages are given a central place in the understanding of all the Law and the prophets. But this verse may mean that these two commands provide firm pegs on which the Law and the prophets can hang; they provide the Law and the prophets with a secure position. Or alternatively verse 40 could mean that they provide the fixed point from which all the Law and prophets can be drawn out; all the Law and the prophets can be deduced from them or traced to them. Probably both interpretations are helpful.

The Law and the prophets indicate all that God requires and the means for interpreting those commandments. The two injunctions are statements of a basic morality, fundamental in every respect to God's requirements. They are foundational, a focus, a summary; they are maxims of a deeper significance than all others, going to the heart of what God requires. In this respect, as in other respects also, they are parallel to the 'golden rule' in 7:12: 'whatever you wish that people would do to you, do so to them; for this is the Law and the prophets'.

In the last of the confrontations Jesus takes the initiative. In Matthew's version, Jesus confronts the Pharisees. He asks them about the Messiah, and they provide a clear statement of the Davidic origin for the Messiah. It is as if Matthew wishes that statement to be clear and unquestioned. In the parallel passage in Mark 12:35–37 the issue is left to inference. Not so in Matthew. Here the Pharisees themselves affirm it. But side by side with that affirmation Jesus places a quotation from Psalm 110:1. The quotation is understood as from the mouth of David, who records a promise given by the Lord (i.e. God) to David's Lord (i.e. the Messiah). The Messiah is to be made Lord over all. From the quotation the inference is drawn that the Messiah must be superior to David. Jesus then asks how in that case the Messiah could be David's son. This conclusion to the discussion between Jesus and the Pharisees is not spelt out. There is no need, since it silences his hearers. Perhaps Matthew implies that there is a richness to the messianic hope which defies political and nationalistic categories. Jesus is not to be restricted to those. He may be a Messiah in the line of David, but there is much more to be said about him than that.

THE FIFTH DISCOURSE:
— FINAL AND ABIDING WARNINGS —

Religious honours   *Matthew 23:1–12*

We cannot be sure where the fifth and final discourse begins. Perhaps chapter 23 is already a part of it, making a long section from chapter 23–25. Certainly if Matthew is based upon Mark, Mark provides the key structural elements for all three chapters. But then again perhaps the final discourse only begins at 24:1, and this chapter is a separate unit.

Whatever the answer to that particular structural problem, chapter 23 begins with an unexpected comment. Jesus compliments the scribes. They carry the authority of Moses as instructor and guide, and they are reliable interpreters of the Law. The trouble is that the Pharisaic scribes do not illustrate in the way they live the quality of their teaching. So on the one hand the scribes are spoken about warmly and positively; on the other the chapter mounts an attack of great ferocity on the Pharisaic scribes because they fail to live out the truth.

The hearers are to distance themselves from their kind of behaviour (v. 8). The avoidance of honorific titles is given as an example of this. Three titles are specifically mentioned: Rabbi, Father, Teacher (some translations prefer the title Leader as the third of these). The reasons why these titles are to be rejected are noteworthy: 'All we are brethren'; 'You have only one Father in heaven'; and 'Your one and only teacher is the Christ' (vv. 8–10). These reasons imply a community all of whom are equally dependent on divine instruction and interpretation. No one has the right to claim precedence over the other. Little wonder that honorific titles are inappropriate. It is those who serve and who undertake the unimportant roles who carry the mark of greatness.

It is interesting to speculate how the Christian communities for whom Matthew wrote would have heard this warning against honorific titles and the reasons for the warning. No doubt they had leaders, interpreters, scribes, instructors, perhaps even bishops. Undoubtedly they valued those who fulfilled such functions. The development of the community depended on them. But to fulfil the function was one thing, to allow the function to become a means to personal prestige was quite another. The function needed to be fulfilled in humility and dependence on God.

Strong language   Matthew 23:13–33

The ferocity of the attack which follows is almost without parallel in the Gospels. Seven sections open with the word 'Woe!'—that is, 'How tragic it would be if . . .'—and in some of them the language is abusive. The first is an attack on leaders who use the keys intended for aiding entry into the kingdom to lock people out. It is not clear how this can be reconciled with approval of Peter's powers in 16:19. He can exclude some by the power of the keys. It can be argued that Peter is authorized to exclude some and would of course be entering the kingdom himself. But the problem still remains of using the power of the keys to lock the gates instead of unlocking them. Peter is permitted to do that for which the Jewish leaders are criticized. Perhaps the 'Woe' is an example of picturesque speech, or maybe it is one of many different approaches in Matthew to entry into the kingdom.

Several of the 'Woes' warn against false perspectives. Unimportant details of practice are given a high profile, whereas major concerns such as justice, mercy and good faith are overlooked. The picture which drives this particular shaft home is unforgettable: these are people who would strain off a midge and swallow a camel! One of the 'Woes' goes further. It accuses the scribes and Pharisees of lawlessness. Externally they have the appearance of being righteous people; internally they have no respect for the law they claim to uphold.

The biting sarcasm of the final 'Woe' brings the sequence to a close. It resembles the language and style of John the Baptist (3:7ff). Like the Baptist, Jesus mocks his opponents and calls them a 'viper's brood'. The 'Woe' is also about prophets. The current generation might as well get on with the task left unfinished by their predecessors and kill off all the prophets. The sarcasm of this passage might seem out character with the Jesus of our traditional reconstructions. But before we ascribe the material to Matthew's attitudes to Judaism and its leaders, we should note the equally sharp irony of the parallel passage in Luke 11:47–48. That does not of course mean that the ferocity of language must go back to Jesus. It could belong to a tradition shared by Matthew and Luke. But may not Jesus and John the Baptist have spoken in the same violent terms of the inevitability of judgment?

Divine provocation and promise   *Matthew 23:34–39*

The opening words of this section could be taken in a weak or strong sense. If their meaning is 'and so . . .', the promise of the prophets, wise men and scribes signals the beginning of a fresh wave of violence. If the opening words are intended to be strong, and they have their frequent sense of 'therefore', then the sentence has a more sinister ring. Not only does the sending of God's messengers signal an outbreak of violence, it provokes that outbreak and the judgment that must follow. 'Therefore' indicates that the decision to send the fresh wave of messengers is consequent on their earlier murders and is intended to implicate the current generation also. This is hostile language, of a piece with the earlier 'Woes'.

Even more striking is the use of 'I' in the opening verse: 'Therefore I send to you . . .' In Luke the parallel names Wisdom as the one who sends: 'So God's Wisdom says: I will send to them prophets and apostles' (Luke 11:49). In Matthew, the one who takes on Wisdom's role in the sad history of successive persecutions is none other than Jesus. It is Jesus who provokes the outbreak of violence so that (some translators again choose the weaker phrase 'with the result that') the current generation may reap its due reward (v. 35). Its atrocities, matching the most appalling persecutions in Jewish history (crucifixion was rare in Jewish circles), will not escape retribution. Moreover, by persecuting God's messengers, it admits its share in the inheritance of all the violence and murder of Israel's history. That is the point of the reference to Abel and Zechariah, the first and the last murders in the Hebrew Bible.

The ferocity of the language in this earlier part of the chapter is in marked contrast with the poignancy of what follows. Israel would not respond; yet Jesus was longing to shelter Jerusalem as a hen shelters her chicks. All to no avail, it seems. And yet the chapter ends not with a threat but with a promise, one which is associated with another triumphant entry of Jesus.

The task of establishing firm, just policies but remaining compassionate and honest is hard in any walk of life. The task of communicating what we stand for in words and actions is even harder. There is no pretence in Matthew that Christ simplifies either task—though he does transform the context of our life, decisions and relationships.

A Maori leader asked an international conference how it could respond to fragility, isolation and modest circumstances wherever they are found. Pray for those who every day struggle with such imbalances of resources and power.

The end is not yet   *Matthew 24:1—31*

Like its parallels in Mark 13 and Luke 21, this passage is a long discourse on the future, triggered off by Jesus' announcement of the destruction of the temple. Matthew has used Mark as his model (you might like to read the comments on Mark 13 on pages 172—75). But to a greater extent than in those parallels it concentrates on how much must happen before the end. Not least must the gospel be proclaimed throughout the earth as a testimony to all nations (v. 14). This anticipates the ending of the Gospel, where the disciples are sent out to make disciples of all nations, baptizing them in the name of the Father, Son and Holy Spirit and teaching them all that Christ commanded (28:19–20). Mark has a similar interest (Mark 13:10) but in Matthew the emphasis is very much greater. In the Matthean context verse 14 seems to be saying that between the present and the end are many challenges to be met and responsibilities to be fulfilled; that should be the force of believers' interests for the time being. Chapter 25 has three parables, all of which sustain that focus, and warn that the time we have has to be used well. There will be plenty of opportunities, and many mistakes to be made.

One of those mistakes is to listen to false prophets. That was made clear at the end of the Sermon on the Mount (7:21ff), and this fifth and final discourse picks up the conclusion of that first discourse and draws out its importance. The warning about false messages is given twice in this passage. First there is the reference to those who will try to mislead Christ's disciples. In a section which is closely paralleled in Mark 13:5–8 and Luke 21:8–9 the false teaching is concerned with the coming of the Messiah and the rumours about various kinds of conflicts. Not that the disciples will be spared these. It is inevitable that they will happen. But not in the time scale suggested by the false teachers. 'The end is not yet' (v. 6). These represent only a beginning (v. 8). Second there is the warning of treachery. Accompanying and in part caused by the false teaching, there will be a loss of mutual trust and care among the disciples. Matthew again uses the word 'lawlessness' (v. 12). It indicates the seriousness of this stage in the pattern of future events.

There is plenty of time for this to happen. The end is not yet. That should not, however, lull the disciples into a false sense of security. Verses 29–31 indicate that the end will be self-evident when it finally arrives. It will be like lightning (v. 27), or like circling eagles announcing a death (v. 28).

Readiness for the end   *Matthew 24:32–35*

The end will be a long time coming. But the disciples should not be lulled into a sense that decisions and responsibilities are unimportant. That concern is reiterated by Matthew in various ways. There is for example the fig-tree parable (vv. 32–33). This could simply be drawing on the traditional imagery of new growth pointing to the summer season. But why is the picture of the summer season chosen and why the choice of the fig-tree? The closest association with the subject matter of the end of time would be summer growth pointing toward harvest, rather than early growth pointing toward the summer season. However the word used for 'summer' at this point in each of the Gospels is used metaphorically of the heavenly paradise. And the choice of 'fig-tree' might symbolize blessings in the end-time for the obedient. This would give the passage a meaning which throws a different light on the subject of the end-time. Long-term responsibilities are important; but they are important not only for fear of a judgment but in expectation of great promise. The parable points to the coming consummation: 'the end is near; at the very door'. But the end-time holds out the possibilities of reward and bliss, as well as of judgment and punishment.

It is maintained several times in Matthew that the disciples do not know the timing of the final hour. Here in verse 36, in a saying shared with Mark (13:32), it is maintained that the Son himself does not know it. It is difficult to know how to take such a saying. It could well be a form of the statement that the timing of the final hour is not known, but couched of course in exaggerated and extreme language. The timing is known only to God.

Before the end comes, watch! *Matthew 24:36—25:13*

The next three parables are a trilogy on the sustaining of concentration and attention, or as Jesus calls it, 'watching'. 'Watching' means obedient readiness for the end, sustained as if through a night watch. There is the illustration from the time of Noah of the all-too-ordinary carelessness and unthinking security evidenced by the patriarch's contemporaries (vv. 37–39). People will be going about their common concerns (vv. 40–41), but the metaphor of the flood awakens memories of 7:27: the foolish will be caught unready and swept away by the disaster. The parable of the burglar follows in verses 42–44. When the burglar might come is an unknown factor. It could be at any time. When the Son of Man will come is similarly unknown. No one can predict it. It is not revealed to anyone in advance. The message delivered in the exaggerated statement of verse 36 is given now in the form of the parable. No one can know the time (v. 44). A consequence is drawn from this. Since no one can know when the burglar or the Son of Man will come, there is only one way: to keep awake and 'watch'! Only in this way can disaster be averted, either damage to house and property, or the disaster of being caught unprepared by the Son of Man.

But what exactly is meant by 'watching'? The next parable (vv. 45–51) offers one answer. The contrast in the parable of the two servants between the faithful and wise on the one hand and the wicked on the other will occur in similar terms in the next chapter. Using parallel language, Matthew and Luke (12:42–48) depict two different states: promotion to full control of a household for a servant who is wise enough to be found trustworthy, contrasted with demotion and worse for a bully and a glutton. 'Watching' here implies a quality of obedience. It means caring for the members of the household, supplying them with food at the proper time, as distinct from using responsibility for one's own advantage, guided by whim and fancy. The pictures of the parable and the life of the disciples can be described in corresponding terms. 'Watching' has those kinds of practical implications.

The oil of watching
Matthew 25:1–13

The parable of the ten virgins continues the theme of 'watching' and the warning that no one knows the day or hour. But the main point of the parable introduces a new factor, that of death. If as seems likely the 'dozing off to sleep' of the virgins hints at the intervention of death, limiting our time for obedience, then the issue of 'watching' becomes even more important. We must watch while we can. Death may intervene and end our efforts to fulfil the divine will. Paul confronted a related problem in 1 Thessalonians 4:15–17: some Christians will be alive at the second coming, some will be dead. Death, presented as sleep, may intervene between now and the bridegroom's call. In that case, 'oil' in the parable stands for acts of obedience. In the parable of the feast it was not sufficient to be there; it was necessary to have the appropriate wedding garment, and the wedding garment stood for good works (22:11ff). So in the parable of the ten virgins it is essential for those who wait for the bridegroom to have oil, and 'oil' stands for good works. The wise have plenty; the foolish have not. 'Watching' and being ready for the coming of the bridegroom means using well the time given to us, particularly for good works.

Is then the message of the parable exactly the same as the message of the parable of the feast? Not altogether. They are similar in their emphasis on the good works which are part of 'being ready' for the kingdom. But in the parable of the ten virgins there is a conversation between the wise and the foolish which introduces quite a new dimension. The wise have enough oil for themselves to get their own torches going, but not enough to share with the foolish. They advise the foolish to buy more, but this proves to be more easily said than done. Buying oil during the night is out of the question, as they discover to their cost. So if the parable is about death intervening to shorten the time available for good works, and oil in the parable is symbolic of good works, then in terms of the overall message of the parable the conversation between the wise and foolish virgins raises and answers a question: can the good works of other people help us to gain entry into the kingdom? They can inspire and encourage us. But they can never take the place of our own. The answer is clearly 'No!'

Responses to opportunity   *Matthew 25:14–30*

This parable is also found in Luke 19:12–27. Its Matthean form has some distinctive features. When the master goes abroad he distributes to his servants 'to each according to his ability' (v. 15). The phrase evokes a 'harvest' passage from Deuteronomy 16:17, which includes the promise that a good farmer will benefit both from divine generosity and from his own God-given ability. The richness of the harvest is the result of both. The parable seems to point in the same direction. The master shows considerable generosity to his servants; the ability of the servants also plays its part. The two together can produce a substantial profit.

We have already noted earlier a second distinctive element in the Matthean form of the parable: the response of the third servant was one of fear. This reaction to his master's generosity inhibits him and distorts his understanding of the master's motives. The servant makes him out to be hard-hearted and grasping. The result is catastrophic. Fear turns the episode sour and the third servant is expelled empty-handed and punished as lazy and unprofitable. Fear is a disabler.

The parable belongs with the parables of the feast and the ten virgins. Like them it is about human responses to divinely-given opportunities. These responses are sometimes positive, and sometimes grudging and fearful. But to what context do they belong? What are these divinely-given opportunities? Are they opportunities of service within the Christian community? Or is at least one level of interpretation the practical level of the narrative itself? The parable would then be a probing of practical attitudes to the use of money. It is about day-to-day matters and decisions and the attitudes which inform them. The kingdom of heaven is about these. It is about finance and the handling of what is entrusted to us. And success and failure have surprising consequences out of all proportion to the tasks described. For the one there is the joy of sharing in the master's work; for the other there is pain and rejection.

Before the judgment seat   *Matthew 25:31–45*

In this final parable of Matthew about the sheep and the goats, daily behaviour comes under the scrutiny of the Son of Man, as king and judge of all. In a vision, the far-off final moment of reckoning becomes a present reality. Sometimes the interpretation of this parable has been restricted to the question of how Christians have been helped or rejected. The 'little ones' are identified as Christian missionaries arriving in some town or village. But the standards of judgment—feeding the hungry, giving water to the thirsty, caring for the stranger, clothing the naked, visiting the sick and caring for the imprisoned—suggest that this is too narrow an interpretation. For all the criteria can be supported from Gentile as well as Jewish sources. It is all the nations that are here before the judgment seat and the verdict hangs on their treatment of their needy neighbours.

The extraordinary feature of the vision is that neither those who had cared nor those who had not cared were aware of what they had done. This stress on their ignorance is bewildering. Surely so much of Matthew's Gospel has been concerned with good works done with clear and obvious intention. How then can the final judgment appear to take account only of the action itself? The answer could be that we are not being asked to take account only of the action in itself. We are being asked to see the simplicity and complexity of loving actions. Throughout the Gospel, Matthew has been interested in Jesus as the teacher who asked for a new awareness of what it means to do what is right. Here in the final discourse the most difficult issue of all is exposed: we cannot always know when we do what is right. God's will in each particular circumstance may not be evident. Often we have to act in faith. That may not be what we expected to find in Matthew's Gospel. We are accustomed to thinking of Paul as the one who commends faith, and

Matthew as the one who commends law. But Matthew's Gospel is not so easily summarized. The final parable has made us face our inadequacies of understanding and awareness.

We cannot always know what is God's will. And hidden within the uncertainties of daily behaviour is a further mystery. We are given the promise: to risk yourself for those in need is to meet Christ and to meet Christ is to find God in our midst. Matthew's Gospel offers this promise in various different circumstances. The presence of the living Christ is with us: he is present where two or three are gathered in his name (18:20); he is present wherever and whenever his disciples baptize and teach (28:20); he is also present in the daily encounter with those in need. This is a promise for every day, in the middle of all our uncertainties and questions: God in Christ is with us.

John Chrysostom, who wrote extensively about Matthew's Gospel, found that this final parable provided a centre for his theology as a preacher, as a citizen and as an early Christian bishop in Antioch. He sensed in the parable of the sheep and the goats a proclamation of Christ suffering not only yesterday but every day, crucified not only once for all but wherever people suffer—a continual, redemptive passion with and for the world.

In a world where suffering is beyond
our strength to remedy, what hope is there,
if not in the One who suffers eternally?

THE SON OF MAN IS DELIVERED — UP TO BE CRUCIFIED —

Prophetic actions   *Matthew 26:1–29*

The final discourse in Matthew ends with the Son of Man in glory, judging all the nations of the world. The passion narrative begins with the same Son of Man unjustly condemned by a human court and handed over to be crucified (v. 2). The reversal of roles is poignant and dramatic. We see the judge of all as the one who is unjustly judged, whose suffering is for the world; we see the one who is crucified as one who will ultimately be vindicated. The reversal of roles is an essential feature of Matthew's good news.

Another feature of the good news is Jesus' anointing by a woman in Bethany (vv. 6–13). It is a costly act, resented by the disciples as a wicked waste, but regarded by Jesus as his preparation for burial (v. 12). Following the commendation in the previous chapters of those who feed the poor, such an extravagance might seem incongruous: verse 9 implies as much. But seen as a prophetic act, deeply personal in its generosity, it is far from incongruous. It has an inner consistency with the good news, which apart from all its other rich associations, celebrates the historic place of women within the Jesus story. What follows presents several contrasts between anointing and betrayal. For the woman in Bethany, nothing is too much; for Judas, Jesus is worth no more than a dead slave (see Exodus 21:32). For the one a meal with Jesus is an opportunity for devotion; for the other it is a time for treachery.

The last supper too is a prophetic act, performed by Jesus as a self-commitment to seal God's covenant with his own death. Shared with his disciples, the meal points beyond that immediate time and place in two specific respects. It is, according to Matthew, 'for many for the forgiveness of sins' (v. 28). Some regard this as an unexpected emphasis in Matthew, arguing from the contrasts between Matthew 3:2 and Mark 1:4. But we have seen a number of places in Matthew where forgiveness is available for all who repent. Jesus' self-commitment concerns not only the disciples but the wider world as well. Jesus also points toward a future banquet 'in my Father's kingdom' (v. 29), either by renouncing the cup (as some suggest) or by warning that this cup will be the last he shares with them until then.

Gethsemane   *Matthew 26:30–56*

The quotation from Zechariah (v. 31) declares the coming crisis as being divinely caused. For Jesus this raises the issue of obedience in its most testing form. It is this issue which is underlined in the Gethsemane narrative. 'My Father,' he prays: what he does now is in his unique role as God's Son. Twice Matthew records his prayer of obedience, the second time using the very words which Jesus taught his disciples (6:9–13). He taught them to say, 'Your will be done'. Now in this critical moment Jesus shows what that means and how costly it is to pray that prayer. The moment is unique, coming before his betrayal, trial and crucifixion. But it is a pattern for all his disciples to follow in every crisis of obedience to God. It is an example of what 'watching' involves. The disciples sleep on; the Son of Man prays.

The Gethsemane scene is interrupted by the arrival of Judas with a large crowd. On the whole in these accounts Matthew's Gospel follows Mark. There are slight deviations in the conversation between Jesus and Judas, and these make even more intense in Matthew the transformation of traditional acts of affection into the means of betrayal. Judas greets Jesus, thus making it certain that it is Jesus they apprehend. The response of Jesus (v. 50) is found only in Matthew and Luke, and in Matthew it is given with variant translations. Some translations understand the verse as a question: 'Friend, what are you here for?' Others suggest that Jesus' reply shows that he knew what Judas intended to do and that he himself could take the initiative: 'Friend, what you have to do, do quickly!' The latter is certainly more in keeping with the control over events which Jesus seems to exercise throughout the Passion narratives.

The requirement that the Scriptures should be fulfilled is twice emphasized in Matthew, once in the words of Jesus and once as a comment by the evangelist. There is no need for the disciples to take action to defend him; the arrest must take its course. To the cutting off of the servant's ear Jesus responds with a comment which is unique to Matthew. It renounces physical force; those who use force will die by it. He renounces in this case the use of spiritual powers also (v. 53); the arrest must run its course as the prophets foretold.

More prophecies   Matthew 26:57–75

Three different references to prophecy occur in this section. First there is the fulfilment of Christ's own prophecy that Peter would deny him three times. The story of Peter's entrance into the high priest's courtyard and the three subsequent denials provides a framework for this portion of the trial narrative. Peter survives and remains a disciple, becoming a major leader in the history of the early Church. That he could survive as a disciple despite a threefold denial of Christ is a witness to the power of forgiveness exercised by and in the name of Christ. That is how Matthew understood the situation. The story is told without any attempt to suggest mitigating circumstances. Peter failed, as Jesus had prophesied that he would. Nowhere is the record challenged. It is very hard to imagine circumstances in which anyone could have invented such an astonishing story of the fall and restitution of a leading disciple to whom the greatest possible promises had been made.

The trial before the Council takes up two other prophecies of Jesus. The first, said in Mark (14:56–59) but not in Matthew to involve false witnesses, concerned the destruction and rebuilding of the temple. It is strange that Mark and Matthew should differ as to whether or not this constituted false evidence. Both record prophetic words of Jesus about the destruction of the temple (Mark 13:2; Matthew 24:2), although neither gives such a prophecy in the precise wording used in the trial. The second prophecy concerns the coming of the Son of Man, given in Matthew partly in response to the question, 'Are you the Christ, the Son of God?' The other part of Jesus' response differs from Mark. In place of Mark's affirmation, 'I am' (Mark 14:62), Matthew has the more ambiguous 'The words are yours' (v. 64). But there is no ambiguity about the high priest's reaction to what he heard: 'He has uttered blasphemy.'

The last case of prophecy in this section belongs to the mocking of Jesus (v. 68). Jesus was, as Mark says, blindfolded at the time, so that either the mockery was a further test of his claims, or the chief priests were officially dissociating themselves from a blasphemer. Ironically— and Matthew would have appreciated the irony—what they achieved by mocking Christ was further evidence that in the history of Jesus the prophets were being fulfilled.

Innocence and responsibility   *Matthew 27:1–32*

The next prophecy to be fulfilled provides a test of ingenuity for anyone. Judas seeks out the priests and elders (presumably on their way to the governor's court), returns the thirty pieces of silver and hangs himself. In Acts 1:18–19 the final action takes place in a 'field of blood' which Judas has bought; in Matthew the name 'field of blood' is associated with 'blood money' and it is the chief priests who designate the silver for the purpose of a cemetery for strangers in the 'potter's field'. This, according to Matthew, fulfils a prophecy which he then cites. But where does the citation come from? It recalls elements from Jeremiah (18:2; 32:9) and Zechariah (11:13), but allows no exact identification.

Jesus is brought before Pilate, who declares him to be innocent and refuses to accept responsibility for a death sentence. No part of

Matthew's Gospel is quite so open to the charge of anti-semitism as this. Verse 25 appears to involve the whole Jewish community in the condemnation of Jesus: 'His blood be upon us and upon our children.' But this was not intended as a curse nor as a signing of a nation's eternal fate. In Matthew's account it was neither of these. The narrative suggests no more than that a particular community accepted a responsibility of which Pilate tried to wash his hands. Granted it was a responsibility for themselves and the following generations, but there is nothing to suggest that Matthew heard or intended this as the acceptance of a curse on the people for all perpetuity.

What happens in Luke 23:11 in Herod Antipas' residence happens in verses 28–31 in the praetorium, and after Pilate's judgment, not before it as in John 19:2–3. Jesus is decked out as a king with royal robe, sceptre and crown for further mockery and abuse. It is difficult to provide a consecutive account of the trial which harmonizes the details from all the Gospels. However archaeological finds in Jerusalem give some support to the Johannine and Matthean narrative here. Rather than possessing a consecutive narrative we have a series of deftly portrayed scenes, like the conscripting of Simon of Cyrene to carry the cross.

The obedient Son   *Matthew 27:33–54*

At three places in the story of the crucifixion reference is made to the 'Son of God'. The first two of these appear only in Matthew. The third has a context unique to Matthew. The first (v. 40) recalls the temptations: '. . . if you are God's Son' (4:1–11). The context is like that of the second temptation: 'save yourself and come down from the cross.' Sonship, as in Gethsemane, has its bitter side, symbolized in the drink given to Jesus on the cross in verse 34, 'wine mixed with gall'. As in Gethsemane there is no way for the Son of God except that of obedience to the bitter end.

The second reference is added to a quotation which closely resembles Psalm 22:8. After reading verses 33–54 it would be helpful to compare the narrative with Psalm 22. There are so many links between the two passages. Those who 'wagged their heads and jeered at him' (v. 39) are an echo of Psalm 22:7. It is true that there is no reference to the Son of God in Psalm 22. For that we have to turn to the Wisdom of Solomon 2:16–18, where the righteous man endures the taunts of his enemies:

He boasts that God is his father.
Let us see if his words are true,
and let us test what will happen at the end of his life;
for if the righteous man is God's child, he will help him,
and will deliver him from the hand of his adversaries.

Wisdom of Solomon 2:16–18 (NRSV)

One who is God's son can expect God to save him. But whatever Old Testament parallel we examine, our understanding of the agony of the Son of God on the cross is deepened. There is no avoidance of death for him. The cry from cross *'Eli, Eli'*—'My God, my God'—may carry its own note of hope. Misunderstood as a call to Elijah (a misunderstanding easier to comprehend in the Matthean text) it quotes the opening of Psalm 22 and carries with it an expectation of deliverance even in the darkness of death.

The third and final reference to the Son of God follows the splitting of the temple veil, the earthquake, the opening of the graves and the rising of saints. Although the detail of these events does not harmonize easily with the later Matthean resurrection narrative, the impact is clear. The death of the Son of God is a cosmic happening. All that occurs marks it as a momentous event. When the Roman centurion gives his testimony to Jesus as Son of God in verse 54 it is not because of the noble character of his death; it is because of its shattering associations. This is the Son of God of the walking on water. There, and at his death and his rising from the dead, the signs of divine activity are present for all to see.

Preparations   *Matthew 27:55–66*

Although women have not occupied a central place in the Matthean story of Jesus, they have an important role. Here, immediately after the death of Christ, the first of his followers to be mentioned are women. During his lifetime they had looked after him. Now Zebedee's wife, who had brought her sons to Jesus asking for a special place for them and who had been told that their cup would be a cup of suffering, has witnessed the full cost of following Jesus. The two others, Mary of Magdala and Mary the mother of James and Joseph, also have a part to play. Joseph of Arimathea, who in Matthew is given the designation 'discipled to Jesus', had asked for the body of Jesus and placed it in his own unused tomb. It is there that the women sit. In this way the narrator has prepared the reader for two subsequent events. The speed with which Joseph had the body of Jesus released for burial might, in Matthew's narrative, have given rise to questions about his motives: had he planned that the body should be stolen, or attempts made to revive it? So there will be the story of how the chief priests and the Pharisees secured the tomb against theft. And much more important for the resurrection narratives, the women know where to go to visit the tomb.

Matthew's version of the burial of Jesus leads logically to the final narrative, the story of the securing of the tomb. But where did the account come from? Almost certainly in the form in which we have it the story is a fiction. The Pharisees appear here for the first time in the Passion narrative. The next morning was a sabbath—which Jews would have organized a deputation on a sabbath morning? In any case initiating this course of action the next morning would be like locking the stable door after the horse had bolted. And if the disciples had temporarily forgotten the promise of resurrection, how likely is it that their enemies would have remembered it? This must surely have been a story answering the charge that the disciples stole the corpse. It was not Matthew's story; it would not answer a charge that they had revived the corpse. In Mark 15:44–45 Pilate checked that Jesus was already dead; not so in Matthew. Mark's narrative was the stronger. But in one way that did not matter. What mattered was not charge and counter-charge, but that Jesus was alive, a living Lord among his people.

What Matthew did in his generation, Hans Urs von Balthasar— one of the great theologians of the last generation—has done in his. Each in his own way has brought together in his understanding of the cross the doctrine of God and the darkest realities of human history. The authority to judge the world is given to Christ as Son of Man; yet in his passion the world passes sentence on him.

You so loved the world that you gave your only Son.
Grant that through our meditation on the passion of your Son
we may come to know you in the reality of your love.

THE CRUCIFIED MESSIAH IS RAISED
— TO UNIVERSAL AUTHORITY —

Dawn
Matthew 28:1–7

In Matthew's Gospel the resurrection narrative begins as dawn breaks. That is probably the best way to interpret the somewhat confusing time reference in verse 1. Matthew follows Mark in recording the coming of the two women to the Jerusalem tomb. They knew where the tomb was and they went to see it. The Marcan details about what the women intended to do are missing. There is no mention of buying in spices, of preparing them as in Luke, or of intending to anoint the corpse. Matthew's account suggests a return to the graveside in order to grieve.

But at that point the story takes a decisively new turn. In Mark the women are concerned about the size of the stone at the mouth of the tomb. How are they to roll it aside? If they are to anoint the body they must have help and help may not be available. In Matthew there are no such worries. There is a miraculous removal of the stone that seals the tomb; there is a supernatural vision of the shining angel who has removed the stone; and the guards lie prostrate, paralysed with fear.

Just as in the narrative of the crucifixion the cosmic significance of Christ's death is conveyed in the lurid colours of an earthquake and opening graves, so the heightened description of the resurrection morning awakens a sense of elation and wonder at what has happened. The language of light and brilliance stirs the emotions and provides a sense of victory. As the angelic figure is described, symbolic expression is given to the power implied in the claim that Christ is risen.

The message given by the angelic figure is that there is no need to fear. The prophecies by Jesus of his own rising have been fulfilled. Furthermore the disciples are to be told that he is risen and will await them in Galilee. In Matthew that meeting will signal the beginning of a long history of mission and the new responsibilities of teaching and baptizing. The story which began with angelic messengers quelling the fears of Joseph and making preparation for Emmanuel, 'God with us', ends with angelic messengers quelling the fears of the women and making preparation for work in the presence of Emmanuel to the end of time.

Recognition Matthew 28:8–10

According to the generally accepted ending of Mark's Gospel (16:8), the women fail to carry out their commission. Apparently from fear and terror they remained silent. We do not hear how the disciples received the message about Jesus meeting them in Galilee. In Matthew elation and wonder have taken place of fear. The angelic messenger has soothed their fears; the associations of the angelic presence are joy and wonder. With no inhibitions the women run to give the disciples a full report, as in Luke's Gospel (Luke 24:9ff).

What follows in Matthew is similar to the vision of the angel: it is an 'appearance' narrative. But what is different is that it is Jesus who meets them. Otherwise the pattern is similar to the angelic vision. The women are not expecting to see Jesus; he greets them, says to them, 'Do not be afraid', and gives them a commission. These are all features which we have noticed in the angelic vision. The appearance of Jesus does, however, add something quite new. There is the devotion of the women who kneel before Jesus, and there is the personal relationship emphasized particularly through the phrase in verse 10, 'Tell my brothers'. This is not simply the story of an 'appearance'; it is a recognition narrative. The one who appears is recognized as the one whom they have known before. The larger context of the 'recognition' story gives this feature even more significance, for those whom Jesus calls 'brothers' are the very disciples who had fled at his arrest (26:56). Their identity is re-established without any hint of rebuke. There are no conditions for their relationship with Jesus except what he himself has established.

The angelic commission is confirmed as Jesus repeats what the angel said about the meeting in Galilee (compare vv. 7 and 10). But it is much more than a repetition. It is a confirmation that their relationship and their hopes are now to be renewed. The promises made are in process of being fulfilled. It is not merely a confirmation of the single commission telling them to leave for Galilee. It is an opening of the door for the confirmation of the lifetime commission which he gave them when he called them to be his disciples.

A final irony Matthew 28:11–15

The Gospel has almost reached its final climax. Jesus has appeared to the women alive from the dead and is about to give the disciples their great

commission and the promise of his continued presence. Between these comes a story of bribery in high places. The guards at the tomb have to be bribed to ensure their silence over what has happened. The irony of the situation is apparent. The chief priests had feared a plot by the disciples to subvert the truth by stealing the body of Jesus and claiming that Jesus had risen. Now, caught in their own machinations, they are having to suppress the truth themselves by bribing the guard to claim that such a plot had succeeded.

These strange interludes have a dramatic function. Like interludes in classical drama they mark the passage of time. They enable the reader to place events in a sequence and imagine the movement of characters and changes of scene. The earlier discussion of the chief priests with Pilate in 27:62–66, unlikely though it may have been historically, marked the dramatic passage of time from the Friday of the crucifixion towards the second of the three days of the resurrection prophecy. Now in this final section the bribing of the guards affords the dramatic space for the news to reach the disciples and the disciples to set off for Galilee.

There is more here than dramatic interest, however. The Gospel writer allows us a fleeting image of contemporary life. A rumour was circulating among the Jews of the day that the disciples were guilty of a hoax. They had stolen the body of Jesus and claimed that he had risen. We know that the rumour was still in circulation well over a century after Matthew's time, and so there is no difficulty in believing the Gospel writer's comment. The Matthean story of the hiring and the bribing of the guard provides a witty response to such a rumour. Even if it was no more convincing as evidence against a hoax than the original rumour itself, it served its purpose not only dramatically, nor only as a reminder of how those in high places wheel and deal. It allowed the witness of the early Church to be heard unencumbered by rumour: the appearances which took place after the first Easter were recorded as events of recognition. The disciples met Jesus again.

The great commission   *Matthew 28:16–20*

The climax to the Gospel directs the reader back to the story itself. The disciples are given a world-wide commission by the Lord of all. Part of that commission is to teach what Jesus taught. The story is not outdated by its finale; rather the finale makes clear the story's continuing significance. What Jesus taught must continue to be the content of the proclamation to the end of time.

Not that the disciples are any different, having reached the finale. Whether they are different after the commission is a matter of conjecture. As they rejoin their Lord, the text gives the impression that they remain the kind of muddled community which we have become acquainted with throughout the whole story. In fact the text of verse 17 bequeaths a final mystery to the reader. Was it just a few of the eleven who were in a state of doubt, or were the doubtful a separate group altogether? The original text hardly makes it crystal clear.

The task of making disciples includes two particular responsibilities. One is, as we have seen, teaching what Jesus taught. The other, given pride of place, is that of baptizing in the name of the Father, Son and Holy Spirit. Recalling the parallelism between John the Baptist and Jesus in Matthew's Gospel, we might consider if this includes John's baptism and Christian baptism. The context is to make disciples of all nations. John's baptism was also apparently available for all. Baptism in the threefold name is only known in the early Church in oriental, especially Syrian, sources. In comparison with the baptismal formulae in the Acts of the Apostles, the use of the threefold name illustrates what we have discovered throughout Matthew's Gospel—an emphasis on the transcendent dimensions of divinity and the humility and suffering of the obedient Son.

The concluding promise confirms the continuity of the story of Jesus with the story of the Church. His divine presence ensures that continuity, as also does the teaching of what he taught. Since what he taught, according to Matthew's Gospel, was a perpetual challenge always to be seeking God's will afresh, studying Matthew's Gospel remains a disturbing and illuminating task.

Matthew's Gospel ends by tracing some of the continuities which God has established across history. To these the written Gospel continues to provide a testimony across the fractures of national, social and religious life.

Dear Lord, may this conclusion be for us a new beginning, and the new beginning a continual unfolding of your eternal grace, through Jesus Christ our Lord.

MARK

Mark's Gospel is the most important in the New Testament, for a number of reasons. It is now widely agreed that it was the first to be written (probably in the years just before the first Jewish revolt in AD66–70). It is the only one of the canonical Gospels which actually describes itself as such: Mark is explicitly evangelical in describing his account from the outset as the 'good news of Jesus Christ'. According to an early second-century writer, Papias of Hierapolis, the Gospel contains the reminiscence of Peter which Mark put together in the most coherent way he could (the details are in J. Stevenson, *A New Eusebius*, SPCK). As nearly all of Mark is found in either Matthew or Luke, we can see how important it was for them that they based their stories of Jesus on Mark. Whatever slight changes they may have made to Mark, it was that account which offered a model and guide for them as to the character of the gospel of Jesus. Of course, the forms in which that common story was told by the four Gospels differ. For example, the ways in which the four Gospels begin and end indicate different emphases. Matthew starts his story of Jesus with a long genealogy, whereas Luke wants to persuade Theophilus that he is being offered an accurate account of the story. John's prologue, on the other hand, takes the story back behind the birth of Jesus to set it within the framework of God's saving purposes. Mark is not concerned about the early part of Jesus' life and is content to begin the Gospel with the critical moment of Jesus' call to his mission to proclaim the reign of God. Mark can claim to be the basis of the good news and as such the starting-place for all subsequent Christian attempts to answer the question: What is the heart of the gospel?

How do we read Mark? Are we in direct touch with the life of Jesus or does this story of Jesus tell us more about the life of the author and the community for which it was written? Those are large questions which cannot be treated in detail here. It can be argued that the synoptic

129

Gospels do at least allow us to see something of the character of Jesus' messianic career (see pages 11–16). But at the same time we do well to concentrate in our reading on the *story* with all the detail that Mark includes, without getting bogged down in whether this or that event actually happened in precisely the way set out in the text. If we stay with the story, we shall find ourselves entering a powerful drama which is likely to capture our imaginations as it has done for many other generations who have sought in it good news for God's world.

Mark's story of the mission of the Messiah starts in the obscurity of a reform movement in the desert before moving into Galilee with demonstrations of divine sovereignty in the healing of broken lives. It is a powerful and urgent story in which we can be left breathless at the pace of events and the dramatic incidents which attend the emergence of the Messiah. As Jesus attracts popular support we are given the impression that the sudden manifestation of divine sovereignty in human affairs will pursue its inexorable path over the whole of the earth. Quickly the storm-clouds gather, however. There is misunderstanding of Jesus' method and suspicion of his claims, leading to a complete mistrust and rejection. The hoped-for acceptance of the Messiah and his kingdom is complicated by a growing division between the official opposition and the small circle of disciples, whose representative Peter confesses Jesus as Messiah without really understanding what this means. The crowds hover between opponents and disciples broadly sympathetic to Jesus.

In the second half of the Gospel (from chapter 9) the separation becomes much clearer, with the disciples round Jesus—although still uncomprehending and finally unfaithful—receiving his teaching about the need for an alternative way. The crowd too oscillates between glad acceptance of the Messiah at the triumphal entry into Jerusalem and rejection when Pilate presents Jesus to them. Meanwhile the machinations of the politically powerful which had already started during Jesus' time in Galilee come to a head in Jerusalem when a different group find themselves threatened by this subversive teaching and life, so that, once in Jerusalem, there seems little opportunity for Jesus to escape the inevitable. His unflinching commitment to the proclamation and demonstration of the reign of God fully recognizes the obstacles which now stand it its way, and he goes to the cross out of faithfulness to his messianic calling. But there a new community is born: the Gentile centurion echoes the words of Mark's title in his confession of faith before the dying Jesus; and the women are told to take the message of the resurrection to the scattered disciples, who can expect to meet Jesus once again in Galilee. So the Gospel ends on a note of promise—the mission of the Messiah Jesus is vindicated; there is healing for a broken world.

The translation used is the Revised Standard Version.

Further reading

M. Clevenot, *Materialist Approaches to the Bible*, Orbis Books

John Davies and John Vincent, *Mark at Work*, Bible Reading Fellowship

Morna Hooker, *The Message of Mark*, Epworth Press

Christopher Rowland, *Radical Christianity*, Polity Press

Outline to Mark's Gospel

Messianic beginnings: Scriptures and the desert	1:1—13
The Messiah's mission in Galilee	1:14—3:35
The impact of the Messiah's message	4:1–41
From one side of the lake to the other	5:1—8:21
The way to the Messiah's Passion	8:22—10:52
The Messiah in the holy city	11:1—12:44
Enduring words for a time of trial	13:1–37
The Passion and vindication of the Son of Man	14:1—16:8

MESSIANIC BEGINNINGS:
— SCRIPTURES AND THE DESERT —

Word and Spirit

Mark 1:1—10

The beginning of the Christian gospel lies not with Jesus but with a quotation from the Old Testament. That is a reminder that the Christian religion takes its meaning from the Jewish Scriptures; indeed, Christianity could be said to be a rereading of the Jewish Scriptures in the light of the conviction that Jesus of Nazareth was the Messiah. The first Christians believed that they now had the key to the story of the people of God in the Jewish Scriptures. It hung together for them because these Scriptures pointed forward to the fulfilment in the coming of the Messiah whom they believed to be Jesus of Nazareth. That point is reinforced by the recognition that the prophetic hope was now being fulfilled: hence the allusion to the Scriptures. Mark, like all the evangelists, wants to start the story with John the Baptist, something which has its roots within early Christian preaching (for example, Acts 10:37) and in the importance Jesus attached to John's ministry (Mark 11:27f, Luke 16:16).

John appears on the scene not, as Jesus elsewhere reminds his hearers (Luke 7:25) in the palaces of kings and princes (who as we shall see in 6:14ff are the ones who destroy John), but in the wilderness. Dressed in the garb of the prophet (compare 2 Kings 1:8; Zechariah 13:3), John preaches a disturbing message, offering members of the people of God a renewed commitment to God's justice in the face of the wrath to come. There was also a promise of the spirit of God which prophets had seen as the mark of a new age, when the spirit would cleanse and enable the people to keep God's word (Jeremiah 31:31; Ezekiel 36:26). It was a message that struck a chord with his contemporaries as many went out into the desert, a reminder that these were turbulent times in which hopes for a deliverance were high and mass movements seeking change were common (see D. Rhoads, *Israel in Revolution*, Fortress Press). It is in the wilderness, on the very margins of society, that John makes his appearance; and it is there that God meets Jesus, at the moment of his identification with the Baptist and his message of God's judgment and the promise for a better future. Like the prophet Ezekiel, who saw

God's glory in a foreign land far away from the glory of the temple in Jerusalem, Jesus saw the heavens opened (compare Ezekiel 1:1) and God's spirit descending upon him far away from the centre of religion. It was a fulfilment of that despairing cry of the prophet in Isaiah 64:1, 'O that thou wouldst rend the heavens and come down'.

Struggle   *Mark 1:12–13*

Mark tells us little about the temptation of Jesus, though it is important to recognize that the testing which is described here does not end in verse 13. Elsewhere in the Gospel Jesus is said to have been tested (12:15, by the Pharisees and Herodians). What takes place here is the beginning of a conflict with Satan which continues throughout the Gospel as Jesus confronts the marks of disorder and disease and brings them to an end: ' If Satan has risen up against himself and is divided, he cannot stand, but is coming to an end. But no one can enter a strong man's house and plunder his goods, unless he first binds the strong man; then indeed he may plunder his house' (3:26). Satan and the forces opposed to God should not be seen as somehow separate from the world of flesh and blood. The agents and victims of injustice and oppression are all part of the human family. Mark's story is about the way in which the Messiah begins the process of overcoming those forces opposed to God. So it is inadequate to see the Gospel as being merely about a kindly teacher who does things to make people better. Rather, it is a bitter struggle against forces which enmesh human beings in their grip and prevent them being truly what God intended: men and women created in God's image. As Jesus tells his hearers in Mark 10:6, he comes to remind them of, and to restore, the situation as it was in 'the beginning'.

— THE MESSIAH'S MISSION IN GALILEE —

The reign of God   *Mark 1:14–15*

The first words of Jesus concern the purpose of his mission, which is to proclaim the reign of God. Most commentators are agreed that we should see in the allusions to God's reign a reference to the fulfilment of Jewish hopes for the future, expressed in Scriptures such as Isaiah 11, though the phrase 'kingdom' or 'reign' of God is only occasionally used in contemporary Jewish texts. It refers to the fulfilment of what had been promised in the Scriptures concerning the demonstration of the sovereignty of God in the affairs of humanity. We know from Jewish texts roughly contemporary with the New Testament that Jews were looking forward to a new era of God's activity when the powers of the world would be subjugated to the divine sovereignty. Jesus declares the end of the times when this has not been apparent: the critical moment when things begin to change has drawn near.

Note that Jesus does not say that the kingdom has arrived; the Greek word indicates that what begins in his ministry is the sign of the dawning of a new age. The Gospels portray Jesus as refusing to offer precise details about what the reign of God would involve and when it would come (Mark 13:32; compare Acts 1:7). Instead of a definite blueprint of the future reign of God, Jesus prefers to get his hearers to use their imaginations to work out for themselves the demands and character of God's reign. He uses images such as those in 2:18–22 to stress the critical nature of the present. And he tells stories (parables) by way of illustration, in which God's reign is likened to events in the natural world, or to a festal meal to which many are invited even if few respond. Some of this is spelt out in more detail in some of the parables in chapter 4. There the reign of God is compared to the growth of seeds with apparently unpromising and small beginnings.

It is a mark of Jesus' concern to engage with responsible and adult human beings that he continually gets them to think about the reign of God by the use of parables. There is no spoonfeeding here. Jesus' authority or power (1:22) is not marked by clearly defined teaching to be received by dependent listeners, but a taxing and searching message which demands a responsive ear and insists that the hearers (or readers) take responsibility for their own response to this critical moment in history.

Challenging disciples   *Mark 1:16–20*

The first action of Jesus is the call of the disciples. The great cost of discipleship is borne out by other sayings in the Gospel (Mark 8:34f; 10:25ff). According to Mark the first disciples left secure jobs and a degree of prosperity. They were certainly not among the landless poor of their area, as Zebedee was wealthy enough to have hired servants (v. 20). Those who were called were not merely to be disciples of another rabbi. Jesus certainly taught them (as chapter 4 in particular makes clear), but those he called were themselves to share in the task of proclaiming the reign of God. Theirs was to be apostolic activity (see Mark 6:7ff) in which a part-time ministry was excluded. It has been suggested that there were for some time disciples of Jesus who sat loose to the social conventions of their day and, like him, lived the lives of wandering prophets who depended on the support of sympathizers (officials like Joseph of Arimathea and Nicodemus seem to have been part of a penumbra of support rather than an inner circle of committed and enthusiastic followers). These disciples challenged the values of contemporary society. There is something of a contrast between the demands laid upon these first disciples called to share in Jesus' mission and the first converts who came to faith as a result of Paul's preaching. They were not expected to give up everything, and as far as we can see Paul encouraged them to remain in the state they were in at the time of their conversion (1 Corinthians 7:17). It is worth asking ourselves whether already in the story of Jesus we have evidence of different levels of support and commitment, between the role of disciple/apostle and that of sympathizer/supporter. The former was to assume a greater importance when a professional ministerial élite evolved in the Church.

Confrontation   *Mark 1:21–28*

It is typical of the good news which Jesus proclaims that it demands action. We have seen how it had led to the call of the first disciples to share in the mission of Jesus and the abandonment of their former way of life. In this second example of the good news we see its challenge to the powers of darkness, when Jesus casts out an unclean spirit in the synagogue. Exorcism and spirit-possession seem to us bizarre and primitive, characteristics of the religion of a bygone age. Even if we want to resist direct imitation of the practice of exorcism, our generation should in fact be well equipped to understand the significance of Jesus' action in dealing with demons and the unclean spirits. Bourgeois life in the First World has for good or ill become fascinated with psychotherapy in all its various manifestations. It recognizes that health must involve the totality of the individual, mind as well as body.

Jesus here begins to confront those powers which isolate individuals, debilitate them mentally and subjugate them to a way of life which brings about ostracism and disintegration. The demon recognizes that in Jesus there is a superior way which it seeks to neutralize. But by the power of that superior way the demon is rebuked and then excluded. (For further reading on this see Charles Elliott's *Comfortable Compassion*, DLT, pages 126ff.)

Action   *Mark 1:29–39*

The reaction of those in the synagogue indicates that they believed that they were confronted with a different kind of power or authority from that of the scribes. The forum for teaching and research, the synagogue, had now become a place for confrontation with the powers of darkness. It is worth reflecting that the pursuit of truth about ourselves and about our world in the light of Jesus and his proclamation of the reign of God will lead us to confront the powers which undergird our world and its powerful interests which enslave us. However, we should take care not to assume that Mark rejects the authority of the scribes, as it is easy for us to set up a contrast between Jesus and his Jewish contemporaries, thus perpetuating the unfavourable assessment of Judaism which is so deeply rooted within Christianity. It was not the authority of the scribes, manifested in the careful study of Scripture, that was wrong. The reign of God offered more than mere words and reflection, but *action* in confronting and overcoming the powers of darkness.

Jesus' first action was to deal with dark powers which affect the lives of individuals and societies. In the healing of Peter's mother-in-law we are reminded that the manifestation of the reign of God demands action to heal the body as well as destroying the powers which enslave and destroy the mind. It is not just in the arena of teaching and religion but in the domestic scene that the transforming power of the kingdom must intrude. The conclusion of the story is a scene where Peter's mother-in-law becomes part of the fellowship, rather than being excluded and confined to her bed of sickness. She exercises a ministry of *service* and so fulfils that important role which Jesus sees as being at the heart of true discipleship: 'the Son of Man came not to be served but to serve, and to give his life as a ransom for many' (10:45).

Is it not the case that the voice of God is often heard in the wilderness, in the least likely places? For example, in our day it is the poor and downtrodden of the Third World who hear God's message of hope, peace and justice in ways which we in the affluent so-called First World are often too deaf to understand. Do movements like those of the women at Greenham Common and people seeking an alternative lifestyle represent a parallel kind of protest against society and its values to that which those first disciples of Jesus were called? How do we deal with the harsh demands of Jesus and their effect on the family? Zebedee was left in the lurch and Jesus himself has harsh words to say about his mother and family later on in 3:31ff (compare Luke 14:26).

Integrated

Mark 1:40–45

Just as Jesus deals with the evil powers that cause the disintegration of human life and the exclusion of those whose lives exhibit the hold of injustice on the world, so in the cleansing of the leper Jesus offers hope to one who was excluded from the fellowship of Israel because of that wasting disease (see Leviticus 13). It is interesting to note how Jesus touches the leper. One recalls the importance attached to the touching of Aids victims by distinguished persons, as a symbol of acceptance and concern. The simple action of touching is a practical demonstration of concern which gives substance to the words 'I will; be clean'. Jesus recognizes the importance of carrying out the normal process of investigation by the priest to ensure that the leper is properly integrated into society. However real the healing was, it was no use unless it was accepted as such by society. Jesus' injunction to silence (a feature which recurs throughout the early chapters of Mark's Gospel) may be related to the need to avoid giving the impression that he was merely a miracle worker or a revolutionary pursuing a military strategy of violent revolution. In every age people are attracted to those with the charisma that can get things done and change the world, merely to satisfy immediate need. Clearly, Jesus as the Messiah is offering a new start and the overcoming of a disordered world. His disciples will soon discover that this is a costly business demanding total change, both individual and social (8:34ff).

All together
Mark 2:1–12

In the story of the paralytic the setting for Jesus' teaching has moved from the synagogue to a home—an indication that the concerns of the kingdom and its teaching must not be confined merely to places set apart for specifically religious activities. The interest was so great that those in need could not get to Jesus. I remember once hearing a Bahian woman from North-East Brazil saying why this story was so important for her. She pointed out that the barriers which stood in the way of the paralytic man reaching Jesus could only be overcome by co-operation and the struggle to use all available ingenuity, even to the extent of removing the roof to get to Jesus. She compared this with the struggle of the local community, which could only achieve its goals by *sharing* in the struggle for justice and not merely pursuing their individual ends.

Discussion centres on Jesus' right to forgive sins. That raises difficult questions about why the paralytic should be regarded as a sinner (an issue which is not taken up here, though touched on briefly in John 9:1ff). There is little doubt that illness, disease and suffering are linked with sin in the Bible, but what is certainly not enunciated here or elsewhere is the belief that disease or handicap is the direct result of an *individual's* sin. Rather, sin manifested in lives which cannot be lived in the fullness that God intends is part and parcel of a fallen world, which Jesus' messianic preaching of the reign of God has begun to deal with. The claim by Jesus to forgive sins is regarded as presumptuous and arrogant (v. 7). The issue of Jesus' authority comes up time and again in the Gospels (compare Mark 11:27ff). It lies at the heart of the difference of opinion between Jesus and his followers on the one hand, and on the other those Jews who rejected Jesus and the claims of those who, like Paul, wanted to read the Jewish Scriptures in the light of him.

On the edge
Mark 2:13–17

Jesus is here once again 'beside the sea', a location frequently reported in Mark, and one which picks up the theme we noticed in the account of the ministry of John the Baptist and the baptism of Jesus, which took place on the margins. In Mark Jesus is not naturally to be found in the synagogue, the temple or the cities and towns; more often than not he is by the sea or in the desert. The call of Levi, a tax-collector who benefited from the political settlement of the day, provides an opportunity to describe Jesus' fellowship with the marginal characters of his day. This provokes criticism from 'the scribes of the Pharisees' (the scribes in this instance being interpreters of the Jewish Law who have a Pharisaic rather than, say, a Sadducean persuasion). Jesus' response at this stage is eirenic (v. 17). His mission is to be seen as complementing the activities of the righteous who have no need of the special teaching which will enable them to understand the mystery of the kingdom. Of course, the irony is that those whose expertise makes them best equipped to understand Jesus' message are precisely the ones who will reject him (3:22; 11:18).

New and old   Mark 2:18—27

Differences of approach and the widening circle of people touched by Jesus inevitably lead to comparisons not only between Jesus and the Pharisees but also between Jesus and his mentor John the Baptist. There can be no escaping the need to recognize and explain the contrast which the drawing near of the reign of God has brought about. Here parables are used for the first time to explain this difference. Just as old wineskins cannot adequately hold new wine, so also the arrival of a new era of the Spirit and the reign of God which overcomes the powers that prevent wholeness need a new set of values. The emphasis on newness does not mean that there is discontinuity with the past, as we saw in Mark 1:2. In the discussion about the sabbath provoked by the plucking of grain, and the infringement of current sabbath conventions, Jesus' justification does not move beyond the interpretative methods and advice of some contemporary teachers, who were quite clear that exceptions had to be made to rigid sabbath observance for humanitarian reasons. Thus a second-century AD teacher called Rabbi Simeon ben Menasiah said, 'The sabbath is given to you; you are not given over to the sabbath'.

Threatened   Mark 3:1—6

The sabbath infringement leads into the next confrontation over what constitutes acceptable behaviour on the sabbath. This takes place in the synagogue and is explicitly concerned with acts of a humanitarian nature which might infringe strict sabbath observance. Although Jesus is not himself reported as doing anything which would have infringed the sabbath in this story, he claimed the right to be the agent of divine action in restoring the man to wholeness. Does this mean that God is infringing his own sabbath laws? The issue is explored further in John 5:1–18: note especially verses 16–18, where Jesus claims to be doing the life-sustaining work of God, which is not prevented by the sabbath. This is taken as tantamount to claiming equality with God. Jesus' Jewish opponents in Jerusalem and their Galilean counterparts in Mark's Gospel are one in their desire to destroy him.

The consequence of these differences of opinion is the coming together of the Herodians and the Pharisees in the desire to destroy Jesus (v. 6). This was an unholy alliance between those who supported the puppet regime of Herod Antipas—son of Herod the Great, murderer of John the Baptist, and tolerated by the Romans—and the religious enthusiasts who wanted to maintain a widespread observance of holiness in everyday life. Ordinarily these two groups would have had little in common. We have seen reasons why Pharisees would have felt threatened by Jesus: he spoke with authority and challenged conventional patterns of behaviour. We may suspect that the Herodians would have viewed Jesus with suspicion as a revolutionary dissident and rabble-rouser, because of the popular following he had encouraged (1:28, 32; 2:1f, 13; 3:7). John the Baptist, who prepared the way for the coming of God's kingdom and also attracted the crowds, fell foul of Herod (1:14, 6:14ff).

Wrong Spirit   Mark 3:7–30

The opposition is matched by a strengthening of the group of supporters who are sent out to share in the same activity as Jesus (v. 14). We shall see in the next chapter how Jesus explains by means of parables something of what has been happening in his ministry. But already the lines are being drawn between sympathizers and opponents as the road to Jerusalem and execution begins to cast its shadow over the good news of the reign of God in Galilee.

Jesus' opponents recognize his power and authority. Because the Jerusalem scribes interpret the Law of Moses, and therefore believe that their authority comes from God, they conclude that Jesus' power must in fact be derived from a source different from God: 'He is possessed by Beelzebub and by the prince of demons he casts our demons' (v. 22). That proposition is ridiculed by Jesus. His extensive overthrow of the powers of darkness (summarized in verse 12) made a nonsense of the claim that he was an agent of those powers with whom he was in conflict. For the first time the gap between Jesus and his opponents begins to widen, as Jesus' eirenic statement of 2:17 gives way to the much harsher assertion that the attempt to link his work with the powers of the Devil is a blasphemy against the Holy Spirit. The readers of Mark's Gospel can easily endorse Jesus' remarks, given that we have been told that the Spirit descended on Jesus at his baptism (1:10).

One of the major issues separating Jews who believed in Jesus from those who did not was that of authority. The Beelzebub controversy raises the question as to how one is to know whether or not a person speaks and acts on behalf of God. On what basis were the scribes able to make their judgment? Were they justified in questioning the basis of Jesus' authority when his claim was made without apparent reference to the religious authority of his day?

Jesus' conflict with the powers of evil asks us to question whether or not we are willing to recognize the importance of naming and confronting these powers, so that we are in a better position to recognize what binds us all, and prevents our liberation to be the children of the living God. We may feel that the language about Satan and evil is too difficult to contemplate. Is this because we have become used to thinking of Satan in supernatural terms, whereas in the Bible Satan and demons are almost always seen controlling and distorting human lives and societies (2 Thessalonians 2:3ff; 1 John 2:18ff)?

New family
Mark 3:31-35

Division does not merely characterize Jesus' relationship with his opponents, for his family are also found to be outsiders. They come to Jesus and seek to break into the circle—but not as disciples, for they stand outside. Jesus' response to them indicates a new understanding of family which is based not on blood relationship but on common cause: 'Whoever does the will of God is my brother, and sister, and mother' (v. 35). To be in the Church is to be part of a larger and more important family, as the disciples themselves are later helped to recognize (10:29ff).

141

> *How do we deal with the harsh sayings of Jesus about the family? How did it come about that the Church came to place the family at the centre of its life, when there are so many other strands in the New Testament which subordinate the family of flesh and blood to wider communal responsibility in the family of God's people?*

THE IMPACT OF THE MESSIAH'S MESSAGE

Growing opposition and division leads into this Gospel's first stretch of teaching—which consists of the parable of the sower and its interpretation, together with two other 'seed' parables—and climaxes in the stilling of the storm. The setting for Jesus' teaching is in the open air by the sea, away from the normal arenas of religious teaching like the synagogue and the temple. The teaching itself takes the form of story-telling rather than the pronouncement of precise dogmas and laws. It is directed to the crowd and uses familiar features of everyday life. In using this illustrative method Jesus relies on his hearers to use their own imagination to come to an understanding of his work. The hearers are expected to listen carefully, not because the answers to their questions are going to be given to them on a plate but because they have to understand for themselves the significance of what is confronting them in the ministry of Jesus.

The story   *Mark 4:1–9, 14–20*

In the Parable of the Sower an everyday occurrence is used as the basis for a significant reflection on the character of the reign of God and the opposition and division it has provoked. The story is unusually followed by an interpretation offered to an inner circle of disciples. From the interpretation Jesus helps his disciples to understand the varied fortunes of the proclamation of the reign of God. It is far from being an unqualified success. Indeed, most of the time it seems to be a failure. Even in those instances where there is a response, this can be short-lived. But appearances are in fact deceptive and the fruit of the reign of God will not be manifest until the future.

142

The parable is told as a reflection on the varied, and often poor, response to the proclamation of the reign of God, as well as an illustration of the cost of taking it seriously. As the interpretation in verse 17 makes clear, there is a price to be paid for discipleship, which the disciples will need to hear more about in the future (10:29ff, 39ff). For those who respond the resources will be given to persist in their discipleship; they will be given more, precisely because they have responded. Those who have not allowed the seed to dwell in them and grow—thereby transforming patterns of existence—cannot hope to be true disciples. This is probably the way we should understand the enigmatic statement in 4:24, which seems to be particularly biased in favour of the 'haves' and against the 'have nots'.

The mystery   *Mark 4:10–13*

In the middle of the parable there is an enigmatic discussion about the mystery of the kingdom and the function of parables in which Jesus seems to suggest that parables are told to *provoke* incomprehension (see v. 12). The earliest interpreters of Mark—Matthew and Luke—found problems with this and softened Mark's harsh wording to make the incomprehension appear to be a consequence of unperceptive hearing rather than the result of the teaching method of Jesus. But there is a sense in which the use of illustration after illustration not only leads to further bewilderment but also contributes by its continued use to incomprehension. The parabolic method demands an assent from the hearer to participate in the process of coming to new understanding. The hearer has to want to make connections between the story and the issue being explained. Thus, it is no use expecting someone who perversely persists in taking literally the metaphor 'as stubborn as a mule' to understand the point that is being made about a particular aspect of a person's character. In a situation where there is hostility and division, that consent which necessarily assists the educative process is often not there. To persist in the use of parables, therefore, will only *lead* to further incomprehension and hostility when this way of teaching is met by anger on the part of the hearers. Why Jesus chose to continue to use this method is unclear. Perhaps it reflects the conviction that the understanding of God's reign must involve the hearer in a transformation of his or her own mind and, therefore, any turning aside from that method of teaching represented a retreat from taking seriously the maturity and integrity of the hearers as men and women created in God's image. People want answers, but Jesus demands that his hearers work out solutions for themselves.

The kingdom manifest   *Mark 4:21—41*

Other parables in the chapter pick up themes from the sower. Both the seed parables promise a future recognition of the most present hidden character of God's reign. It is a small and almost imperceptible beginning in the life of Jesus and his circle which will extend over the whole of creation in the future (compare Daniel 4:12). This point is made in the parables about the light in verse 21; what is at present dark and uncertain will be made manifest. These vague statements should make us pause if we are tempted to consign religion to the interior world only. God's reign is to come to be seen by the whole universe: 'every eye will see him' (Revelation 1:7).

The stilling of the storm is the first of Jesus' so-called 'nature miracles'. Up to this point, Mark has shown the reign of God confronting the powers of sickness, evil and even religion. Here we see how the power at work in Jesus affects the world at large and not merely the individual. The story reflects the biblical imagery of God's rule over the sea: it is God who 'stills the roaring of the seas, the roaring of their waves' (Psalm 65:7). Wind and waves symbolize the hostile forces that rage against life itself, and threaten to return it to primeval chaos. As with the demonic powers earlier in the Gospel (1:26, 3:11), here the life-threatening forces of nature bow before the authority of Jesus, in whom God's will for the harmony of the created order is being restored (see Isaiah 11:6-9). The Messiah and his way cannot easily be encapsulated in some private therapy, a medicine of the soul. The reaction of the disciples to this display of divine power is not surprising: ' Who is this that even the wind and the waves obey him?'

In Mark 4 Jesus teaches not by explaining what the kingdom of God is about in all its detail but by using stories from everyday life. What does that tell us about the way in which we should be communicating the good news? Helping people to understand depends on co-operation and consensus not on simplistic and prescriptive indoctrination. But what happens if the more we try to explain the more our attempts are frustrated? Do we go on doing the same, or change our tactics? What place do pragmatism, strategy and compromise have in the proclamation of the gospel?

FROM ONE SIDE OF THE
— LAKE TO THE OTHER —

In this section of the Gospel, Jesus and his disciples often cross from one side of the sea of Galilee to the other. Their travels take them across some important boundaries—between Jewish and Gentile territory, between what is thought to be 'clean' and 'unclean', between popular acclaim and rejection. The progress of his mission is marked by a growing division between the official opposition and the small circle of disciples, with the crowd hovering between the two, broadly sympathetic to Jesus.

Tell it   Mark 5:1—20

After the stilling of the storm Jesus crosses to the other side of the sea. He is once again away from the mainstream of life, in territory occupied by a man with an unclean spirit living in an unclean place, a burial ground (see Numbers 19:11). The man is possessed and uncontrollable, a threat to others as well as himself. Yet it is 'Legion' who perceives who Jesus is and beseeches him to go away and not torment him. The unclean spirits are cast out of 'Legion' into a herd of swine and perish in the sea, leaving the herdsmen who tended the swine dumbfounded and the man who had once been possessed whole and sitting with Jesus.

This powerful and complex story continues the theme of the stilling of the storm. In an area of uncleanness where pigs were tended, Jesus challenged the spirit of Legion. Why 'Legion'? The link with the military forces of the Roman occupying power is no coincidence. The man embodied the dislocation of life and hope caused by the military presence. Like many sensitive souls throughout the ages the disintegration of his life was a sign of the disintegration of the world. He embodied and acted as scapegoat for the evil pressures and powers which dislocated the world of the people of God—their life and land. His disturbed psyche was the measure of a disordered creation which most people thought was normal. That same sensitivity enabled him to recognize who Jesus was, and to see the upheaval that the Son of God was to bring to his own life and people. The destruction of Legion took place when the unclean spirits entered the swine and perished in the sea. It is difficult to resist making the link with the imagery of the Book of Revelation, where the judgment on the unjust powers and institutions before the reign of God can finally come involves their end in the lake of fire (Revelation 19:20).

Unlike others whom Jesus healed, the man who had been possessed by Legion was instructed by Jesus to go and tell his friends what had happened to him, even though he himself wished to accompany Jesus (v. 18). It is a mark of the importance that Jesus attached to such areas on the margins of Jewish life that he insisted that the man should proclaim the good news. There are interesting comments on this passage in K. Wengst, *Pax Romana and the Peace of Jesus Christ* (SCM Press).

> Do we find it at times difficult to live with the hostility which change provokes? Has Christianity become too much aligned with maintenance of the status quo? How does this coincide with the story of Jesus presented in Mark's Gospel?

Not cut off   *Mark 5:21–43*

The contact with the unclean continues in the story of the raising of Jairus' daughter and the healing of the woman with a haemorrhage. By the time Jesus reaches Jairus' house the young woman is dead, and thus Jesus contracts uncleanness by his contact with her (v. 41), as he had earlier with the leper (1:41). This continued overcoming of the taboos of society in the cause of the reign of God is found also in the healing of the woman with the haemorrhage, who because of her illness would have been in a state of perpetual uncleanness (see Leviticus 15:25). In these two stories, one of which is sandwiched in the telling of the other, the role of women in the Gospel story makes another appearance. In 1:31, the healed mother-in-law of Peter had been the first to demonstrate the act of service (*diakonia*), and now two women who had been cut off from life—one by death, the other by reason of social stigma—are restored to life again. These healings offer an important indication of Jesus' significant attitude to women (see E. Schüssler Fiorenza, *In Memory of Her*, SCM Press).

Not acceptable   *Mark 6:1—5*

Christians are often surprised that Jesus was not accepted among his own people. They feel that faith in him would be much easier if they could have the same living experience of him as his contemporaries had. His visit to his home town, Nazareth, contradicts this. The people there can recognize Jesus' wisdom, but they will not take the next step of accepting his message of the kingdom. They were not expecting this sort of Messiah. Jesus is too familiar, as one who worked like them and whose family they know. They were anticipating something more spectacular. We should not be surprised at the response to Jesus here, because the history of Israel was full of examples of prophets who were rejected because their message challenged the acceptable understanding of God. In Nazareth, people refuse to see God working through one of their own townspeople. In all this it is important to stress the humanity of Jesus. He belonged to a human family and God's kingdom was working through him. In the face of unbelief, any display of divine transcendence through miracles is useless (v. 5).

Jesus does not force the kingdom upon us; he needs our trust, our openness to be willing to recognize in his signs the presence of God. We will not hear the good news of Mark in the right way unless we can identify with Jesus' acquaintances in Nazareth who rejected him when he preached to them. Why might *we* reject Jesus today if he preached in our local congregation or home?

Twelve sent   *Mark 6:6—13*

This rejection in his home town once again points forward to Jesus' final rejection in Jerusalem. But he is not deterred. He has a mission to preach, and now he sets off on his campaign trail. But this is not a one-man show.

He summons the Twelve and this makes clear the nature of his mission. He has come to call the nation to its true vocation. 'The twelve' would evoke the twelve tribes of Israel. The restoration of the twelve-tribe people was expected at the time of Israel's salvation. The book of Ezekiel even pointed to that time when the twelve tribes would be brought to life and be given a permanent share of the land (Ezekiel 34:13; 39:28). So Jesus the prophet performs this symbolic act which is a summons to Israel to awake, to see in Jesus' proclamation of the kingdom the beginning of the gathering of the lost sheep of Israel. In fact Matthew tells us that Jesus told his disciples to go specifically to the 'lost sheep' of Israel (see Matthew 10:6). And so the Twelve are sent out in pairs to prepare the way for Jesus' proclamation of the kingdom. They are to preach repentance— that turning towards God, that openness to being changed, which his townspeople had refused. And they are to travel light.

This is a text that has inspired great missionaries, like Francis and Dominic, and it can help us to see the value of evangelical poverty. It allows freedom from too much that can weigh us down and obscure the point of the message. The purpose of this kind of poverty, as Thomas Merton has said, is to promote clarity, so that those listening to the message can see that the messenger is dependent on God, and not putting faith in a lot of unnecessary clutter. There is an urgency and clarity about the disciples' mission. It is easy for the good news to be so compromised that it loses all its force and power. The lack of unnecessary possessions is the way that the disciples will be able to be seen as representatives of Jesus himself, thereby enabling their hearers to make a clear choice. Jews shook the dust off their feet when they re-entered Palestine after a trip into pagan territory. Jesus recommends this gesture as a way of making the disciples' audience think and repent.

Shadow   *Mark 6:14–31*

The disciples may have set off on their mission with fervour but they will need clear-sighted vision to realize what the mission involves. Mark immediately shows us something of this, in the story of the beheading of John the Baptist. At first we may wonder why this story appears at this point. Mark has inserted it between the sending of the Twelve and their return (vv. 30–31). What is the connection? The disciples should know that their mission for the kingdom of God will arouse the opposition of other kingdoms who feel challenged by it. Herod wants to put a name on this new preacher of another kingdom. He is told, 'He is a prophet like the prophets we used to have', so once again we are alerted to look to the political history of Israel. God established his rule in the face of the claim to absolute power of Pharaoh, and he gave his Law as a guarantee of the freedom which his rule gave to Israel. The history of Israel is a story of the struggles of the prophets against the absolute claims of kings who wished to take the place of God. The very reference to Elijah recalls his struggle with Ahab and Jezebel (1 Kings 21).

With Herod and John we have yet another clash between kingdoms. This Herod is Antipas, the son of Herod the Great, ruler in Galilee and Perea between 4BC and AD39. He married Herodias despite the fact that she was his niece and the wife of his half-brother, Philip, thereby breaking the biblical law. John interfered in this politically charged situation, and as a result was imprisoned. What follows is a story worth any tabloid newspaper specializing in power and sex. Here is the politician surrounded by the military and his cronies, allowing himself to be manipulated by Herodias. What he lacks is clarity of insight. Like David of old he lets himself be led step by step into a situation where his opponent is killed (2 Samuel 11–12).

We are told in verse 29 that John's disciples came and took the body 'and laid it in a tomb'. This sordid story is a reminder to the disciples of the sort of opposition they will face when they attempt to bring about God's kingdom. More particularly, we see here John continuing the work he started early in the Gospel as the precursor of Jesus (1:2–8). Now he serves a model of what will happen to Jesus. As John is 'delivered up', so Jesus will be 'delivered up' (9:31; 10:33). John's passion story is an anticipation of Jesus' death, and just as the disciples' mission in Israel begins with John's death, so will their fuller mission begin with Jesus' death.

John the Baptist interfered in the affairs of a leading politician like Herod. Today people will often say that the Church should not interfere in politics. Herbert McCabe wrote, 'There are plenty of Christians who have no interest in politics; but if their Christianity is real, the politicians are going to have to be interested in them.' John the Baptist was teaching the law of God. If the Church does the same today, will not politicians want to interfere in it?

Feeding

If we want to know what brings about the kingdom, then we need look no further than the accounts of what Jesus does and what he expects from his followers. It is not just a question of activity, but rather the *kind* of activity that arises out of Jesus' teaching. Now he takes his disciples to a desert place where they can be 'by themselves'. This expression occurs seven times in Mark (4:34; 6:31, 32; 7:33; 9:2, 28; 13:3), and in each case it refers to a special instruction given to the disciples. They are alone, but not for long. The crowd sense that whereas the outcome of Herod's kingdom is death, Jesus is the source of life. The references to the desert place bring to mind the feeding with manna with which God kept his people alive in the exodus. The note in verse 34 that Jesus took pity on the crowds 'because they were like sheep without a shepherd' recalls the prophetic criticism of Israel's leaders in a former age (see Ezekiel 34): they were like shepherds who had looked to their own interests and neglected the flock. Jesus is the messianic shepherd who will feed his sheep.

He begins by teaching the crowds, but with the lateness of the hour the crowd is getting hungry. The disciples are willing to be fed by Jesus' words but what do they do when they are faced with the hunger of the crowd? *Their* solution is to send them away and let them fend for themselves by buying food. But Jesus does not accept their solution: 'Give them something to eat yourselves.' The disciples can only think in terms of money and they do not have enough for the needs of the hungry people. But Jesus does not talk in terms of money; he asks them what they have that can be *shared* with others. They have five loaves and two fishes. That is enough. But they have to be organized; they are made to sit down in groups of hundreds and fifties. As one commentator working among the poor in Latin America and reading the text from that situation says, ' In order to help solve the problem, the crowd is organized. Without organization, groups, unions, political parties, the people will not find solutions to their problems'.

Jesus then responds to the needs of the people and satisfies their hunger. He acts as the host of the messianic feast, but he also teaches his disciples how to serve at this meal. As he presides over this meal the obvious connections with the Eucharist are brought out. The way he 'took . . . blessed . . . broke . . .' the bread points forward to the last supper (14:22). So Jesus gives life in the desert. He nourishes with his teaching, he responds to human hunger by giving food, and he feeds us spiritually in the eucharist. Christians often separate these different aspects. We need to be alert to the danger of spiritualizing stories like this one too quickly. Is the feeding of the thousands *principally* a symbol of the Eucharist? First of all, it is the feeding of hungry people. Jesus gives food so that people may live. And he calls on his disciples to be involved in his work by sharing what they have. The story does have eucharistic associations. But do Christians in their celebration of the Eucharist bring out the fact that it is a meal by which Christ shares himself as food and is a symbol of how they must share what they have to bring life to those in need? Jesus satisfies both material and spiritual hunger and teaches by his actions what he expects his disciples to do to bring about the kingdom.

Disturbing presence   *Mark 6:45–52*

The essential unity between prayer and action, the spiritual and the material, is seen in this next incident. Jesus escapes from the crowd and goes off alone to pray. He has fed the people. We know from Matthew and Luke that one of his temptations was to offer bread *alone* (see Matthew 4:3–4; Luke 4:3–4). Prayer clarifies the nature of the mission. The disciple is also tempted to see Jesus as one who only fills empty stomachs. Throughout the feeding story the disciples misunderstood Jesus' true nature. Now he comes mysteriously walking upon the water. Once again he shows his power over the elements of creation, and the word which he speaks in the face of their terror—'It is I'— recalls the divine presence in John's Gospel (John 8:58). The disciples respond with characteristic fear (compare 4:40). They cannot understand Jesus' presence here; they are dumbfounded because the deeper meaning of the multiplication of the loaves eludes them. 'Their hearts were hardened' (v. 52), which is the ominous phrase used of Jesus' opponents in 3:5. The story reflects the fears of Jesus' disciples, who are forever faced with the challenge of deepening their understanding of Christ and the implications of following him.

An alternative culture   *Mark 6:53–56*

Once again Jesus crosses from one side of the lake to the other. It has been suggested that one side is Jewish and the other Gentile. This movement raises a question about the kingdom Jesus is proclaiming. We have seen him as Lord of the forces of creation, but how inclusive is his kingdom? Jesus preaches first to his own people, Israel, for they were to be the God's instrument in bringing his light and justice to the nations (Isaiah 49:6). They are a people set apart; they must maintain a clear identity or they will be assimilated into the surrounding Gentile environment. This is the essence of holiness. (You might like to explore its implications in Alan Kreider's book, *Journey towards Holiness*, Marshall Pickering.) Every religion has laws and rituals which help to remind its followers of their identity; the Jews had their laws of ritual purity to make them aware of what was clean and unclean, and gave them their sense of identity as God's people. In the Book of Jubilees, dated to the second century BC there is the following passage in which Isaac says to Jacob,

> *'Separate thyself from the nations,*
> *And eat not with them…*
> *for their works are unclean,*
> *And all their ways are a pollution and an abomination and*
> *uncleanness.'*

Mark's community, which included both Jew and Gentile, would have been especially interested in what Jesus said about these issues of purity and ritual cleanness which might compromise the universality of the kingdom. Was the kingdom to be limited by racial distinctions? Could Jew and Gentile sit down together and share a meal (a matter taken up in Galatians 2:11ff)?

Obscuring God's demand   *Mark 7:1—23*

The Pharisees and some of the scribes are checking up on the behaviour of Jesus' disciples here, and once again there is conflict. Jesus does not seem to have any objection to ritual in itself, but he criticizes what happens when people—whether Jewish or Christian, we might add—make their religion an end and not a means. Again he stands in a long line of prophets who attack religious practices and traditions which are observed at the expense of the justice which the Law demands (see Isaiah 1:12ff; Jeremiah 7; Amos 5:21). He gives the example of 'Corban', which is a transliteration of an Aramaic word which means an 'offering', a gift devoted to God. Money which should go to the support of parents might be declared 'Corban' and given to the temple treasury. So the basic obligation of justice which the Law demanded—to care for those in need, and honour father and mother—was set aside. We may presume that this was but one example of a universal attitude which uses religion to create the kind of endless ritual which obscures God's basic desire for justice.

Jesus, as we have seen, concentrated his attention for the most part on Israel, but when he goes back to the house (v. 17), he teaches his disciples a principle which undermines some of the Law that keeps Israel distinct. The kingdom, after all, initiates a new order (2:21) and the new wine will burst the old skins. But the challenge of that new order will always arouse fear and antagonism on the part of those who benefit from the old way of doing things. Jesus states that it is not what goes into people from outside which makes them clean or unclean; it is what comes from the heart that causes uncleanness. Mark sees a clear principle in Jesus' teaching here—'Thus he pronounced all foods clean'. This will lead to conflict and to Jesus' death—but it will be taken up after the resurrection, when the new creation will be seen in communities which embody this principle (see Galatians 3:28 for another way of expressing it). It will be invoked by Peter the Jew when he eats with Cornelius the Gentile soldier (Acts 10).

Rituals in religion can be used for good or ill; they help us know who we are. Ritual purity helped to confirm Jewish identity at the time of Jesus. But by declaring all food 'clean', he disallowed its ritual use as an identity marker. The early Christians broke down the barriers between different races and nations—one way they did this was by sharing table fellowship. The overcoming of the deep fear of eating together is a very obvious way in which the power of the resurrection can be seen at work. After two thousand years, some Christians still invoke religious traditions to keep people apart on racial grounds, and so make void the principle which Peter laid down: 'What God has cleansed, you must not call common' (Acts 10:15).

> In Mark's Gospel, Jesus is involved in many situations of conflict. Does following Christ bring you into conflict in your daily life? Are we tempted to suppose that reconciliation *always* characterizes the life of a disciple, that Christians must always eschew situations of conflict?

'Eating the children's scraps' *Mark 7:24—37*

Jesus seeks the lost sheep of Israel but in this next section he reaches out to the Gentiles; he moves beyond the borders of Galilee into the territory of Tyre. Here are two incidents which anticipate that unity of Jew and Gentile which Israel should now appreciate but will come into existence after the resurrection. The Syrophoenician woman would be regarded as doubly handicapped, first as a Gentile and secondly as a woman. She is forced by need to break the normal conventions. Her daughter is under the power of the kingdom of the devil and she has recognized in this foreigner a power that can free her child. She begs him for his help. Jesus' offensive reply reflects his strategy in proclaiming the kingdom of God. It is first for the children, the Jews—they should be fed first. It would be wrong to take their food and throw it to Gentile dogs. As so often in the Gospels, it is the outsider who shows more wit and more faith: ' but the housedogs under the table can eat the children's scraps' (v. 28). Jesus recognizes such faith and casts out the demon. The outsider has shown a good deal more perception than those who are constantly in Jesus' company.

Jesus' response to suffering, whether it is in Jew or Gentile, is seen in the next miracle. Here, still in Gentile territory, a deaf man is brought whose speech is also impaired. There is a meticulous description of the method Jesus employs, like any Greek or Jewish healer: he 'put his fingers into the man's ears and touched his tongue with spittle' (v. 33). Through this very human contact the divine power is at work, symbolized by Jesus' upward look into heaven. The word *'ephphatha'* is another reminder of the exact Aramaic word which was used for the freeing of this creature of God who had been unable to praise his own maker. Those who were witnesses could recognize in this sign the breaking in of God's kingdom in the healing of God's creatures, and 'their admiration was unbounded' (v. 37). Isaiah 35:5—6 looked forward to this moment, and is surely in Mark's mind when he reports, 'He has done all things well; he makes the deaf hear and the dumb speak.'

Boundless hope *Mark 8:1—10*

The next two signs also bear witness to the fact that Jesus is extending his kingdom towards the world of the Gentiles. He allowed the foreign woman to share in the crumbs, but now we are given another feast where the Gentiles receive not just crumbs but the fullness of a meal where there is an abundance of scraps left over. Why are there two miracles of the loaves? Would not one be enough? That might be the reaction of one who, reading the Gospels for the first time, said that he liked Jesus but found the Gospels rather repetitive! This story of the loaves obviously has great importance for Mark and within the context of the whole Gospel he wants to repeat its message. There are differences between the account here and in 6:30–44, but both emphasize Jesus' compassion for the hungry crowd.

Throughout the Gospel Jesus is the source of life. How better can we see this than in terms of food! Hungry people die without food. Jesus this time takes the initiative. He is the source of life here as the one who provides food, and because the life he supplies is superabundant it overflows to meet the needs of the people. Mark has an eye for the details of the baskets and what they contained. In the first account we had *twelve* baskets of scraps at the Jewish feeding, here on the Gentile side we have *seven*, signifying the universal outreach of God's kingdom. Jesus' gift of life bursts through the boundaries; it feeds both Jew and Gentile. Again there is the reminder of the eucharist, so a link between the material and the spiritual sharing is made. Jesus shares his life with hungry people by giving them bread. So the Eucharist is a constant reminder in the middle of a starving world that his followers must show the same concern to share the food that they have with anyone in need, whatever their gender, race, creed or colour.

Discerning the signs   *Mark 8:11–21*

After these life-giving signs, which both point back to the experience of Israel in the desert and look forward to that final messianic feast, the Pharisees re-enact the stubborn refusal to believe demonstrated by the generation at the time of Moses (see Exodus 16). They want a sign from heaven, when in fact they have been given overwhelming evidence in what Jesus has just done. Signs are not given to force belief but to evoke trust and faith in the person of Jesus. The Pharisees reveal a certain blindness in the face of Jesus' signs. However if we are not careful we can read this passage with a similar blindness, presuming that the Pharisees were blind while we are not. In interpreting a passage such as this one, a safe rule to follow is to avoid identifying with those characters who may give *us* a feeling of self-righteousness. We tend to identify with Jesus or the disciples and not the Pharisees. But in fact Mark does not allow us to escape God's judgment by turning to the disciples, for they seem just as blind as the Pharisees. Jesus warns them about the yeast—the blindness of the Pharisees (v. 15)—and yet in their response to Jesus' signs they show the same blindness. They think that Jesus is talking about the bread which they have forgotten to bring with them (v. 16). They cannot see any deeper significance in the sign Jesus performed. If Jesus' opponents want more signs, his followers do not understand the sign he has given. There follows an extraordinary series of questions which express the frustration of Jesus in the face of this blindness. Can they not go more deeply beneath the surface and see in the twelve baskets and then the seven baskets the unity Jesus is to bring between Jew and Gentile? Mark may have had special cause to emphasize this point if in his own community the Jewish and Gentile Christians were failing to live out the implication of Jesus' practice by refusing to share the one loaf in table fellowship.

THE WAY TO THE —— MESSIAH'S PASSION ——

Mark's story of Jesus challenges every generation of disciples to recognize their lack of spiritual perception and their need to heal the blindness that keeps them from seeing the demands of following Jesus. In order to make these crystal clear, Mark has carefully constructed this section of the Gospel by framing it with two stories about blindness. In 8:22–26 he relates the healing of the blind man at Bethsaida, and in 10:46–52 he has the story of the healing of blind Bartimaeus, who follows Jesus 'on the way' to Jerusalem (10:52). Mark uses this phrase in 8:27, 9:33 and 10:32 as a motif to link together the stages of the journey to the outskirts of Jerusalem. On the way, Jesus seeks to alert the disciples to the significance of his ministry and the nature of his messiahship, so that like Bartimaeus they too may follow him into Jerusalem with their eyes open. The same pattern of instruction occurs three times. First, Jesus explains what kind of Messiah he is and what that involves—he 'will be put to death and after three days he will rise again' (8:31; 9:31; 10:33). This is met, secondly, by incomprehension and resistance which, thirdly, gives Jesus the opportunity to explain what is involved in following him as a disciple. Each time, the location changes as the narrative moves on towards Jerusalem and the final confrontation with the hostile powers—from Caesarea Philippi in 8:27 to Galilee in 9:30 and the road to Jerusalem in 10:32.

Moving on   8:22–33

By the time we have reached this stage of the story, Jesus has demonstrated his authority and power but his disciples are still unable to perceive who he really is. At the beginning of the journey that will culminate in Jerusalem, Jesus asks the disciples who he is thought to be (v. 27). Peter confesses that he is the Messiah. But coming to see what this really means turns out to be painful for Peter, who resists losing some of his more comfortable images of Jesus' messiahship. So Jesus has to set about the task of asserting his true identity. 'Who do people say I am?' Peter acknowledges him as the Christ, the Messiah expected by the Jews, but while Jesus does not deny this answer, he immediately qualifies it by claiming another title, Son of Man, whose mission will involve suffering. Peter resists this new teaching and Jesus identifies Peter with the kingdom of Satan. It is salutary to note that the same word which was used for rebuking the unclean spirit in 1:25 is here used of Jesus' rebuke to Peter.

The struggle of discipleship   Mark 8:34—9:1

If Peter, the leading disciple, could not, or would not, understand Jesus, it is unlikely that we latter-day disciples will do any better. Why then do we still go on resisting? Why does Jesus meet such resistance? First, as we have seen throughout the Gospel, there is a violent conflict between the two kingdoms of God and Satan (3:23ff). If Jesus is to be victorious, he will have to struggle unremittingly to dislodge his enemy. And Satan has captured ground in some powerful places. He has control of much that is religious—believers who want a Christ who will bless their firmly held positions and uphold 'what comes naturally' (8:33). He will not disturb worship of the idols of sex, power and money, all three of which are mentioned in this section ('gaining the whole world', v. 36; 'adulterous generation', v. 38).

Resistance to Jesus comes from the gathering of those forces who feel threatened (11:18). Jesus will suffer, not because there is any virtue in suffering in itself, but because it follows inevitably if he is to fight against those forces which have possession of the territory that he claims (3:25). But Jesus also experiences the resistance that comes from within the disciples. In 9:32 Mark tells us that the disciples 'did not understand what he said and were afraid to ask him'. They are afraid that they will lose the props that give them their identity, of losing status and being nothing. Jesus knows this, for an attack on such fear lies at the heart of his definition of what makes a disciple. To be a follower of his is a matter of letting go and allowing God to give us our identity: 'whoever loses life for my sake, and for the sake of the gospel, will save it' (v. 35).

Messiah revealed: contemplation and action   Mark 9:2–29

The story of the transfiguration follows on from the first true explanation of Jesus' identity, and comes as a divine confirmation of his role as suffering Messiah. But it also confirms his glory as the Son of God after the resurrection.

Peter, James and John experience the divine presence on the mountain; they see the glory of God transfiguring Jesus. This is what is promised for all the just, and they want to capture this religious experience, to do the right liturgical thing and erect tents as on the Feast of Tabernacles. But they still do not understand fully what is happening, because 'they were so frightened'. The voice confirms that Jesus is greater than Moses and Elijah: 'This is my Son, the Beloved'. If they are to understand who Jesus is, then they must ' listen to him' as they come down the mountain; there will be teaching in words and actions.

It would be easy to treat the transfiguration in isolation, but it is important to connect it with what follows in the story. It is tempting, as Peter found, to stay on the mountain with this profound religious experience. But it leads immediately back into the needs and sufferings of the crowd. Jesus teaches his disciples that he is greater than Elijah and Moses. He still resembles them, for they too experienced God on the mountain but were then sent back into the political arena. The task of the Messiah and his forerunner will be to 'restore all things' (v. 12). He has to heal the wounds in God's creation, and as he comes from his prayer on the mountain he meets an epileptic child and his anxious father. It is the experience of prayer and contemplation which will give the disciples the power they need to share in the Messiah's work of healing, but once again they show a lack of faith (v. 19), and it is the father, driven by need, who recognizes his total dependence on Jesus: 'I do have faith. Help the little faith I have' (v. 24). Jesus once again shows that he has the power to give life to what appears dead. The incident ends where the story of the transfiguration began, with the need for the experience of God in prayer. The Bible tells us over and over again that prayer and action can never be divorced from one another: 'This is the kind that can only be driven out by prayer' (v. 29).

The way we read the Gospels can often determine the way we understand them, particularly if we isolate incidents instead of seeing one in the light of another. Jesus goes to the mountain top and experiences the glory of God. But he then comes down from the mountain and enters again the difficult world of the sick and suffering. Do we find that our experience of God in prayer leads us back into the world of human need? Does our prayer lead us into social action and our social action into prayer? Or do we separate the two or only specialize in one? Mark suggests that liturgy and social welfare, mysticism and politics must be held together.

The alternative vision   *Mark 9:30–50*

The journey towards Jerusalem continues, and with it Jesus' teaching about what kind of Messiah he is to be. Going through Galilee he repeats the message, 'The Son of Man will be delivered into the hands of men' (v. 31). Jesus will not be in total control and that is what the disciples cannot accept. For them the structures of the world in which they live, the world of Herod and Caesar, are the measure of what the rule of God should be. Their worldly understanding of power has such a grip on their minds that Jesus will need to return to the same point in 10:42f, 'You know among the Gentiles, their so-called rulers lord it over them, and their great men make their authority felt. This is not to happen with you.' Jesus directly opposed the kind of rule based on the oppression which made the *Pax Romana* possible. The disciples in the Church are to provide an alternative vision of the use of power; it is the power to serve one another, to break the pattern of domination by giving precedence to unimportant people like children who have no status (9:36; compare 10:15). Jesus identifies with those who do not have control over their lives. One of the major obstacles to true discipleship is the wish to be

159

with the 'great', to seek positions of status, 'to be one at your right and one at your left in your glory' (10:37). Jesus in fact will come into his glory when he has fully identified with the 'little ones' (Matthew 25:45)—the poor who have been deprived of justice—and when he is raised on the cross between two robbers.

The kingdom of God is meant just for those defenceless ones of whom we are reminded in the Beatitudes in Matthew 5:3ff and Luke 6:20ff. But this is not an easy message, and no doubt in Mark's congregation there were those who ignored the poor in their search for status. Jesus' vivid and extravagant language was needed to shake them out of their complacency. Better to suffer the terrible Roman punishment of drowning with a 'great millstone' than to harm 'one of these little ones' (v. 42).

Human relationships in the kingdom   *Mark 10:1–12*

Jesus moves closer to Jerusalem as he enters Judea. The tension mounts as the crowds gather again. But there is no let-up in the demands of his teaching about entering the kingdom. In order to test him, the Pharisees ask whether he is in favour of divorce. He confronts them with teaching that goes behind the ruling of Moses (Deuteronomy 24:1–4). Moses had allowed divorce because of human 'hardness of heart', the refusal to allow the demands of God to control Israel's life. Jesus sees the wrong sort of human relationship as an obstacle to entering the kingdom, and this includes that between man and woman within marriage. The new order of the kingdom demands a return to that original order of justice which God created at the beginning (v. 6). Marriage should be characterized by the mutual service in love which is the hallmark of the life of discipleship. This is what was intended from the beginning when God made them male and female: 'They are no longer two, therefore, but one body. So then, what God has united, man must not divide' (vv. 7–9; compare Genesis 2:24). Ephesians 5:32 sees Jesus' demand for faithfulness between husband and wife in the kingdom as a sign of his own faithfulness towards his Church. This reminds us that Jesus' hard saying is set in the context of explaining his messiahship in terms of suffering which leads to resurrection.

The way to eternal life   *Mark 10:13—22*

Jesus continues to challenge the mentality of the disciples that will prevent them entering the kingdom, in his conflict with them over status and money. The disciples prefer to turn away the children who have no status. Jesus' anger here shows the preference of God for those who are pushed to the margins of society. So the disciples are to receive the kingdom of God as they would receive a child, by identifying with those on the edges of life.

The same preference is seen in the next scene where a rich man approaches him. The disciples must be relieved that a person of higher status asks Jesus for guidance; he is not only rich but religious too. He wants to know what will give him the eternal life which is the 'entrance ticket' to the kingdom. Perhaps he thinks he can pay the price. In fact he has paid it, by fulfilling all the requirements that Jesus lays down: he has kept the commandments. Jesus challenges him: if he is concerned with life, but not only his own, then let him change his social standing, for in his present situation he cannot really 'hear' the word of God. Jesus has already said that the word can be choked by riches (4:19). If the man wants to love his neighbour, he must share what he has so that the poor might live—just as Jesus is prepared to share what he has so that others might live (10:45; 14:22). Poverty then is not something that is to be cultivated as a condition for following Christ; it is the simple consequence of sharing oneself so that the poor may live. The man faces a choice: he must decide what he finally puts his trust in, whether it is the security that money gives or the security that God promises in faith. He chooses money, and as a result 'he went away sad, for he was a man of great wealth' (v. 22).

God and Mammon   *Mark 10:23—31*

Faith in money is so deep, its hold on the minds of the disciples, then as now, so tenacious, that Jesus has to insist on the danger of making money into a god. But it is a lesson the disciples do not want to hear (v. 24). Conventional wisdom sees riches as a sign of God's blessing. But Jesus sees wealth as a major obstacle to entering the kingdom. However, willingness to let go of riches is a sign of love for God and neighbour, for this demonstrates the same preference for the poor that God has shown.

161

It is hard to enter the kingdom, especially for the rich who think they can pay the entrance fee as a result of their wealth. There is no way of fixing the price, for the demands that Jesus makes on his followers go beyond what they can calculate. The contrast between the huge camel and the tiny hole in the needle points to the impossibility of trying to achieve one's own salvation. It is a gift which only God can give. All the disciple needs is a readiness to accept it, which is symbolized by the readiness to give up, when asked, all those forms of security, like money, that prevent us from hearing God's demands.

Peter and the other disciples have in fact chosen the insecurity of following Jesus (v. 28). So is there a reward for them? There is the promise of plenty but not on the model of the rich man who looks after himself first. The reward is based on the values of the kingdom, which are now being realized in the way the disciples share their riches in common. As if to emphasize further the contrast between God and Mammon, Mark adds the reference to persecutions in verse 30. However much the kingdom's rewards may anticipate the way things will be finally in the world to come, when 'the first will be last and the last first' (v. 31), the style of life Jesus looks for inevitably undermines the self-centred grabbing of the rich.

The way of the Messiah   *Mark 10:32—52*

In verse 32 we are reminded once again that Jesus is 'on the way' to Jerusalem, the centre of power in Israel. Jesus is separated from his disciples—the gap symbolizes the lack of understanding between them over his mission. Perhaps they have begun to fathom the mystery of this journey, but they do not want to know more: 'they were in a daze' (v. 32). Jesus' words about his fate are repeated, for the third time. He has to make clear what sort of salvation is going to be achieved in Jerusalem. Clearly the disciples were still hoping for a Messiah who would come into his kingdom by means of violent power and give them places of glory. But this would be too much like the attempts to 'save' people made by the so-called rulers of the Gentiles, and found throughout history. During his ministry, Jesus has been conscious of those members of God's creation who have been pushed to the edges of the community by sickness, poverty or injustice. They have no claim on the centre of power; they are powerless on the margins of society. His disciples want their leader to come into his glory by assuming power at the centre in Jerusalem

162

(compare John 7:3). They expect Jesus to act as a mighty leader, perhaps in the style of Julius Caesar, who spoke like this when addressing some mutinous soldiers: 'Do you believe that you were of crucial importance to me? Divine providence will never stoop so low that fate troubles itself whether the like of you live or die: as the great ordain, so the affairs of the world are directed—the life of humanity is determined by a few.'

According to Jesus, this is not God's way of acting. Jesus undermines the 'Caesar' style of leadership: 'this is not to happen among you' (v. 43). He will save by working 'from below', not at the centre but at the periphery, among the outcasts. Against the disciples' ideas and plans, he tells them that he will be handed over into the hands of the powerful, to be scourged and put to death (v. 34). This is how he will redeem his people, by giving his life as a *ransom* (in the Greek Old Testament, the word is used for God's historical acts of liberation from oppression). Jesus will come into his glory by drinking the chalice of suffering (see Psalm 42:7; Isaiah 43:2). He will identify with those who suffer under the rule of oppression, and trust himself to the power of God who alone can save: 'after three days he will rise again.' Jesus' death will save, because 'in the power of the resurrection (God) brings out the separation of margin and centre . . . to endorse the death of Jesus as a permanent and effective protest against those structures which continually bring about the separation at the centre and at the margin' (Klaus Wengst, *Pax Romana and the Peace of Jesus Christ*, SCM Press).

So this section of the Gospel ends as it began, with a story of someone coming to sight. According to Jesus in John 9:41, the main problem about seeing (understood here as a metaphor for spiritual insight) is that those who say they can see are in fact blind. Mark shows us a blind man who obviously cannot see but he has the right approach to Jesus. In his need he cries out, 'Jesus, Son of David, have pity on me' (v. 47). He wants to be a follower of Jesus but encounters resistance from the crowds who tell him to keep quiet. In the last few chapters we have seen the nature of that resistance, the powerful obstacles that prevent access to the kingdom of God. The blind man shows the persistence in asking that Jesus says is needed in prayer (9:29), and his prayer for help is answered. He has the faith that is demanded of a disciple, and so he comes to sight. 'And immediately his sight returned and he followed him along the road' (v. 52). We are reminded of what is needed to follow Jesus on the road to Jerusalem where, if we have the eyes to see, we will realize what kind of Messiah he is.

> Jesus tells his followers that his peace is different from the peace of the world. He does not accept a peace based on the way the Gentiles rule. He says to his followers: 'This is not to happen among you.' When you think of Church structures and behaviour, do you think his command is observed?
>
> Why do many preachers avoid the subject of peace and nuclear arms? Is it because it threatens Christians' security? Is this security based finally on status, power, and money? Jesus attacked this sort of security. Are we afraid to end up as vulnerable as he was?

— THE MESSIAH IN THE HOLY CITY —

The journey that effectively began in the villages of Caesarea Philippi, where Jesus announced that he would be rejected by the Jewish leadership in Jerusalem, culminates in his arrival in the Holy City. In the events that are about to unfold, the true nature of his Messiahship and the real power of God's reign will be revealed to those who have the eyes of faith.

The Messiah acknowledged   *Mark 11:1–14*

Jesus eventually arrives on the outskirts of Jerusalem. Expectation and tension are high. It is the time of the Passover, when the Jews were remembering God's deliverance of their ancestors from oppressive slavery and the beginning of the journey into the Promised Land. Hopes would be high for deliverance from the oppressions of the present. Religious fervour and politics were inextricably mixed to produce situations which frequently boiled over into unrest and turmoil. Jesus does not avoid all this. Indeed, in Mark's account of his entry into Jerusalem, his action seems designed to raise hopes and inflame passions. The reaction of the crowd indicates as much (see v. 9). We may be tempted to imagine that Jesus explicitly repudiated violence and political involvement by fulfilling Zechariah 9:9. That may have been in his mind—his action seems to have been deliberately organized (see vv. 2ff)—although (unlike Matthew and John) Mark does not refer to the prophetic text. The sign prompts the enthusiastic response that the

Messiah has arrived. However he came, his arrival meant the end of the unjust order and the beginning of something new. At the very least, Jesus prompts the the crowds of pilgrims to draw that conclusion. It was not a very prudent thing to do, though, particularly when Jesus followed it with an even more provocative act in the temple.

After entering Jerusalem Jesus reconnoitres the situation (v. 11), possibly making an assessment for the demonstration in the temple that would take place on the next day (v. 12). On his way back to the holy city from his lodging in Bethany, he finds a barren fig-tree, not surprisingly so, for we are told that it was not the season for figs. Jesus' apparently unreasonable reaction in cursing the tree can best be understood as a pronouncement by the Messiah of the refusal of the created order to acknowledge his presence. There was a widespread belief that the messianic age would be characterized by a time of plenty and productivity, when the natural world would return to pristine perfection (Isaiah 11). The tree is alluded to again in verses 20ff. The sandwiching of the incident in the temple in between the account of the cursing of the tree and the disciples' remark probably signals that we should see the barren fig-tree and its cursing as a sign of the barrenness of the temple and the demise that Jesus' demonstration points to. Instead of welcoming their Messiah and acknowledging his right to rule in Zion, those responsible for the temple demonstrate hostility to his cause and reject him.

Juxtaposed, then, with the enthusiastic reception for Jesus' entry into Jerusalem is a recalcitrant institution and a blindness to the way of the Messiah. That response is barren and destined to destruction. As we shall see, the moment of the destruction of the Messiah in 15:37f also marks the moment of the destruction of the mystique and authority of the temple and its supporters. The fragile protest in the temple and the sign of the withered fig-tree are to the eyes of faith symbols of judgment. The disciples are told that such little signs made out of faith and conviction, puny though they might be, can in the providence of God point forward to that judgment and dramatic upheaval (v. 23, where the mountain probably refers to Mount Zion: compare Zechariah 14:4ff).

The barrenness of worship without justice   *Mark 11:15—26*

To refer to Jesus' action as the 'cleansing' of the temple is probably not an accurate description. There were many Jews of Jesus' day who thought that the temple needed reform so that a true worship could be offered. Jesus, however, seems to be interested in more than reformation. His action is a brief interruption of the sacrificial system which most Jews believed had been ordained by God. As well as the explicit allusions to Isaiah 56:7 and Jeremiah 7:11, there is probably an allusion to the eschatological prophecy of the last verse of Zechariah: 'And there shall no longer be a trader in the house of the Lord of hosts on that day' (14:21). One of Jesus' more outspoken followers, Stephen, voiced his rejection of the temple (Acts 6:13; 7:48). No doubt there were those who wondered whether the institution of the temple, linked as it was to the dynasty of Solomon, could be a legitimate expression of the ritual connected with the tabernacle as set out in the Law of Moses. By quoting the passage from Isaiah about the house of prayer, Jesus emphasizes activity which, while not incompatible with the sacrificial system, plays down its importance. In the later chapters of Isaiah we have a picture of Israel as a light to the nations (Isaiah 49:6), a hope which was to be fulfilled when the Messiah came and the nations themselves began to return to Zion. Prayer was an important part of the worship of the synagogue, where no sacrifice took place. Jesus points forward to the kind of worship that would characterize both Judaism and Christianity after the destruction of the temple.

There is also a reference to Jeremiah 7. This is the famous and outspoken denunciation of the temple and its worship by Jeremiah. That hint may remind us of the importance placed in that chapter on the integration of worship and social justice. It is that totality which Jesus' proclamation of the kingdom holds together. He believed that the temple and its upkeep were driving worship and justice apart, as had so often been the case in the past (Isaiah 1:11; Amos 5:21ff). Jesus here allies himself with the prophetic critique of a religion which supposes that it is possible to keep devotion to God separate from the struggle for justice and peace.

By what authority?   *Mark 11:27–33*

Following Jesus' attack on the temple, the issue of authority emerges once more. This has already been addressed, at least indirectly, earlier in the Gospel (3:22ff). As in the later discussion of paying taxes to Rome (12:13–17), it is quite clear that Jesus is put on the spot here by an awkward question. He deals with this by posing a counter-question and thereby avoids having to offer a direct answer to his opponents' question. In so doing it is interesting to note that he does raise the issue of the authority of another prophetic figure, John the Baptist, whose role some might have questioned (Luke 7:31ff). Jesus' action in the temple had already led the authorities to seek to execute him (11:18). Here he refuses to offer unnecessarily incriminating evidence to those whose questioning is geared only to finding information to secure his downfall. It is worth noting that the issue of authority and an authenticating sign also arises in the differently positioned account of the 'cleansing' of the temple in John 2:18f.

The fate of God's envoy   Mark 12:1–12

Hostility has cast a shadow over Mark's story ever since the end of chapter 3. In the parable of the sower Jesus explained to his disciples something of the struggle involved in proclaiming the reign of God and the opposition it faced. Now he tells a parable which is directed to opponents. The authorities recognize that he is using the story of the wicked tenants to illustrate their reaction to him. By now he would have perceived something of their intentions, and this may explain the way that he had moved in and out of Jerusalem to avoid arrest (11:12). The authorities are challenged by the story with its allusions to Israel as the vineyard of God in Isaiah 5:1ff. Stephen's speech also alludes to the way in which there is an uncompromising rejection of those whom God sent to Israel (Acts 7:51ff; compare Luke 11:49ff). The reference to the 'beloved son' reminds the reader of the heavenly voice at Jesus' baptism and the transfiguration (Mark 1:11; 9:7; in the Greek version of Genesis 22:2, Isaac is referred to as Abraham's 'beloved son', and Ephesians 1:6 refers to Jesus as 'the Beloved'). The promise of judgment is spelt out to the disciples in chapter 13. Meanwhile by quoting Psalm 118 in verse 10, Jesus asserts his conviction that the way of the Messiah will ultimately be vindicated, whatever the men of power may do to him.

God or Caesar?   Mark 12:13–17

No passage has been subject to more detailed scrutiny than the discussion of the tribute money. The way it was read both by Matthew and Paul indicates that it *was* taken as an injunction to pay taxes to Caesar and to recognize the demands of the state as legitimate (Matthew

22:15ff; Romans 13:7). But Luke tells us (Luke 23:2) that it was included as part of the basis for the case against Jesus before the Roman prefect. This should make us pause before assuming that the meaning of the saying is entirely transparent.

Once again, the context of the saying is one in which Jesus is being put to the test by his opponents. In such a situation it is unlikely that Jesus would have given an answer that would have implicated himself either with the rejection of Roman power by the Jewish freedom-fighters, the Zealots, or those collaborators who had come to some accommodation with the occupying power. Jesus makes his opponents show them a coin, which suggests that he himself does not possess one, and asks them to identify the image engraved on it. Perhaps he wishes to point out that the possession of the coin by Jews is evidence that they are already contaminated by an alien ideology which in direct contradiction to Jewish law allowed images of human beings to be engraved (see Deuteronomy 5:8ff). Those who possess such objects of an alien system might expect, therefore, to have to abide by the rules of that system. So Jesus' response may indicate that participants in the Roman economic system, based as it is on slavery and conquest, are bound to pay the tax. But those who recognize the supremacy of God over the universe maintain their distance from Rome and its exploitative and idolatrous practices.

Jesus' words do not involve acceptance of a separation between the sacred and secular spheres, a feature of some aspects of contemporary Christianity but certainly not typical of Judaism of Jesus' day. Jews regarded God as the creator of the world. The whole universe was regarded as God's domain, and no earthly ruler had any absolute right of possession or authority. Thus, giving God his due meant offering to the supreme ruler of the whole world all that belonged to him. Why then does Jesus not say this clearly and unambiguously? More than likely, it was because the situation demanded circumspection. Jesus is not here offering a definitive ruling on relations between his followers and the state, but a clever, if ambiguous, answer from the tight corner into which his opponents had put him.

Resurrection: a common hope
for Jews and Christians   *Mark 12:18—27*

We have a glimpse in this chapter of the contrasting views of the different groups in Judaism of Jesus' day. Whereas the Pharisees and

Herodians had combined (as in 3:6) to test Jesus on the tribute money, now another group poses a different question about the significance of resurrection. Belief in the resurrection had become something of a test-case for the Pharisees, as Paul was to demonstrate in Acts 23:6. The Sadducees refused to accept it, probably on the basis that it was not found unequivocally in the bulk of the Old Testament (Daniel 12:2 is the only unambiguous reference, and this dates from the second century BC). The Sadducees attempt to ridicule the resurrection belief by posing the hypothetical situation in the age to come when a woman had been married to seven men as a result of levirate marriage (see Deuteronomy 25:5). Jesus appears to be saying that marriage is an ordinance for the old age which is passing away, not for the new. He also claims that the idea of resurrection is consistent with the teaching of Moses, interpreting Exodus 3:6 in a way that would be familiar to the rabbis if not to us.

There are hints elsewhere in the New Testament that some early Christians thought that the values of the new world should apply in the old one. 1 Corinthians 7 suggests that marriage and family ties were repudiated in some quarters, something Jesus himself seems to recommend (Mark 3:31ff; 10:29ff). There is a fascinating discussion of this issue in the chapter 'Living like Angels' in Robin Lane Fox's book, *Pagans and Christians* (Penguin).

The essence of religion   *Mark 12:28–34*

Among all those who put questions to Jesus in this section of the Gospel, one scribe appears to be more perceptive in his apparently innocent question about the greatest commandment. However, there may be more to this than meets the eye, as a definite answer to this particular question might have landed Jesus in the quandary of having to assert that some parts of the Law of God were more important than others (compare Luke 11:42). Had he done this, he would immediately have been asked about his authority to determine the more and less weighty matters of the Law. Jesus summarises the teaching of the Law by quoting part of the *Shema* (the Hebrew word for ' hear', the first word of Deuteronomy 6:4—'Hear O Israel . . .'), and adding words from Leviticus 19:18. The verses from Deuteronomy 6 were the corner-stone of Jewish piety and were uttered regularly by Jews. Jesus' answer affirms the belief in one God and the responsibility to love him and the neighbour (another expert wanted to pursue the identity of the neighbour in Luke 10:29ff). The scribe is sufficiently wise (v. 34) to note that these are more important than the offering of sacrifices. This picks up a theme to which we have alluded before. Religious practice uncoupled from the pursuit of social justice is an abomination to God and roundly condemned by Jesus and the prophets.

The Messiah and true devotion   *Mark 12:35–44*

Jesus' entry into Jerusalem has raised the question of messiahship. There was much discussion at the time of Jesus over the character of the Messiah: would he be a prophet, priest, king or a little of all? Would he use force to deliver Israel from the oppressor? Jesus seems here to be questioning an exclusive link with the Davidic line and perhaps opening up the possibility of seeing the Messiah or anointed one as a prophet figure (as in Isaiah 61:1, 'The spirit of the Lord is upon me because God has *anointed* me . . .'). He does this by using Psalm 110 to suggest that this passage implies a more exalted status for the Lord's anointed than merely a descendant of David. In the history of Christian thought we see such ideas taken up. While Jesus continued to be called the Messiah (or 'Christ' in Greek), other more honorific titles were used, like 'Son of God' and 'Lord'. There is a good discussion of Jesus' messiahship in Anthony Harvey's *Jesus and the Constraints of History* (Duckworth).

Jesus' disputations with the scribes prompt him to go on to castigate them and their practices. There are longer versions of the kind of denunciation we find in verses 38–40 in Luke 11:39–52 and Matthew 23. Throughout the teaching of Jesus we are left with the clear impression that there is no substitute in true religion for practice. Unless this matches rhetoric, devotion to God is null and void (Matthew 7:21; 1 John 3:15ff; Micah 6:6–8), a point noted by the scribe in his answer to Jesus in verse 33.

Whereas the priests made great profit from their religion, Jesus finds true religion best exemplified in the devotion of the poor widow. Jesus' society, like every other, considers the rich and powerful to be great benefactors whose names are remembered. Jesus will have none of this and has already told his disciples so (10:44). As we saw in 12:15, Jesus himself did not possess a coin. Elsewhere in the Gospels he is reported to have questioned the monetary system: the disciples are sent out without money (6:8); the food for the multitude is to be given not bought (6:37ff); the moneychangers' tables are overturned (11:15). In contrast, the Messiah is betrayed for money (14:11). As 10:25 indicates, money is a commodity which interferes with discipleship (compare Matthew 6:24). It is the little people of the world, those who trust in the God who sides with the poor and the outcast, who can perceive a proper order of values. Sacrificial giving is a symbol of the saying in Matthew 6:21: 'Where your treasure is, there will your heart be also'. This is something that Paul had to remind the Corinthian church about, as they were tempted to suppose that religion was just a matter of having peace with God. Practical service and the sharing of resources are an integral part of Christianity (2 Corinthians 8:8–15).

A feature of the second half of Mark's Gospel is the pervasive criticism of the temple and the hostility of those in authority in Jerusalem. It is worth reflecting that the ritual institutions of the Christian Church are deeply indebted to the temple in Jerusalem. What does Jesus' stinging criticism and prediction of destruction say to those of us who find ourselves understanding mission and ministry so much in terms of what goes on in holy buildings?

ENDURING WORDS FOR — A TIME OF TRIAL —

The message of doom on the temple and the foreboding of a terrible abomination of desolation come at the end of Jesus' career, if the chronology of the synoptics is followed. By that time opposition was widespread; the journey to Jerusalem had not led to national repentance, but to a plot by the hierarchy to kill Jesus. In such circumstances it was no surprise that Jesus should predict judgment. After all, the one who believed himself to be the Messiah was rejected by those who administered the shrine of God's presence. There were parallels with Ezekiel's day, when the glory of God left a temple destined to destruction (Ezekiel 10). Now, the divine glory had been glimpsed elsewhere, manifested outside Jerusalem, in Jesus' message of the good news of the reign of God and his conquest of the powers. As we shall see, at the moment of the death of the Messiah the veil which shrouded the holiest part of the temple in the mystery and awe was rent in two. It had become an empty shell; the glory had been removed. Jesus announces that a decisive shift is to take place in the location of the divine glory, away from the centre of economic and ideological power towards the weak and poor (embodied in the crucified messianic pretender), to those who identify with him and to the poor with whom he chooses to identify.

No stone upon another will be left   *Mark 13:1–2*

The temple was the focus of Jewish life, and as such elicited great affection from Jews in many parts of the Roman world. Its place at the centre of religious life in Jerusalem should not mask its political and economic significance. The prominent position occupied by the high priest depended on his role in the temple. Caiaphas' remark in John 11:48 about Jesus' threat to the temple would have been typical of the fear of those whose position was dependent on the continued well-being of the temple. The daily round of sacrifices created a lively industry in Jerusalem and its environs. Threats against the temple, for whatever reason, would have been threats against the economy of Jerusalem and powerful vested interests. That is precisely what Jesus appeared to be doing in his action against the temple and its authorities. How often in history have the interests of the powerful been the reason for silencing voices of opposition! One thinks of Archbishop Oscar Romero in El Salvador, who dared to raise his voice against the economic interests of the powerful élite in the country and paid for it with his life. Jesus is well aware that the stand he is taking will lead to a similar consequence (12:7f). As the threat to his life draws closer, he now takes the opportunity to warn his disciples of what lies ahead.

The uncertainty of the life of faith   *Mark 13:3–13*

In the eschatological discourse in Mark 13 the uncertainties and frustrations of the present age—the messianic fulfilment and its rejection—lead to an upheaval of cosmic proportions which shakes the foundations of the established order (vv. 19, 24, 28f). That upheaval will leave little left of what now seems to be permanent (v. 31). It is the words of the Messiah which will endure for ever, and his way and its followers will be vindicated (v. 26).

The comment about the beauty of the temple prompts a prediction from Jesus about its demise (fulfilled in AD70 when the temple was destroyed by fire by Roman legionaries; this is also alluded to in Luke 19:41ff). This prediction is accompanied by a series of warnings (vv. 5ff) in which Jesus speaks about the difficult road ahead for his followers and the way in which the end of the temple marks an end to the world as the disciples know it. Society was facing an enormous upheaval in which the complacent would find themselves overtaken by events they could not understand, while those who could read the signs of the times would need to be alert and watchful in the face of disaster. We may want to know whether 'wars and rumours of wars' (vv. 7ff) might indicate the end of the world (and there are many books which confidently identify these prophecies with persons and events in the contemporary world). Jesus' words are specifically directed to the world order of his day, though that should not prevent their being used by us for our under-standing of an appropriate response to decaying structures and vested interests in our society. What is above all necessary for the disciple is not precise interpretation of the meaning of the passage but, in the face of signs of evil and false understandings of the way of the Messiah, to remain committed to the goal of seeking first God's kingdom and God's justice.

Jesus' words are not so much preoccupied with the attempt to satisfy curiosity about the details of the 'times and seasons' as to provide dire warnings of the threat of being led astray, of failing at the last, and of the need to be ready and watchful so as to avoid the worst of the disasters to come. In the bleak moments of the last days there is little attempt to dwell on the privileges of discipleship. The future is not without hope, but the hearers are made to dwell on their responsibilities in the short and medium term, as the essential prerequisite of achieving eternal life. Jesus refuses to offer any other reassurance than that the disciple on trial will find the support of the same Spirit which empowered Jesus' proclamation of the kingdom of God (v. 11). Commitment to the proclamation of the kingdom without fear and favour, in whatever forum, would ensure the presence of God's Spirit and would be continuing testimony to the way of Jesus of Nazareth. The task of bearing witness to the kingdom is no hole-in-the-corner affair but involves very public and vulnerable exposure before the powerful (vv. 9f).

Discerning the abomination of desolation   *Mark 13:14–37*

In verse 14 there is the enigmatic reference to the 'abomination of desolation'. This phrase has its origin in the Book of Daniel where it refers to the desecration of the temple in the middle of the second century BC (Daniel 9:27). Matthew makes the connection explicitly (in 24:14) and Luke's version has the passage refer to the destruction of Jerusalem as a whole (Luke 21:20). What Mark understands by this is by no means clear. His aside to the readers ('let the reader understand') suggests that he supposes that they would have had some event or person (the participle 'standing' seems to indicate a person rather than a thing) in mind. What that may have been we have no way of knowing, though suggestions have included the attempt by the Roman emperor Gaius Caligula to set up a statue of himself in the temple ten years after Jesus' death, and the desecration of the temple by the Roman legionaries in AD70.

The Gospel also addresses *us* as readers: 'Let the reader understand'. If only we have eyes to see, we can make sense. Many throughout history have been attentive to that summons as they have sought to see the abomination of desolation around them. They have perceived that their own generation has been faced with a challenge which it could only ignore at its peril. May it not be that for our generation our critical moment has come? Some of our brothers and sisters in South Africa have recently answered this question with regard to their own situation in the affirmative. In the Kairos Document they challenge their countrymen and women to read the signs of the times, to seek the things which make for *real* peace; and they predict disaster if there is a failure to recognize the time of the visitation. For them, the Kairos, the critical moment, has assuredly arrived. The historical purist may retort: 'Jesus could not have this in mind'. But the question is: what *did* he have in mind? Are we in a position to be sure that the canonical text cannot be put to this kind of use as none of us has, or ever will have, any access to the mind of Jesus? Surely, a mistaken exegesis would be one which reduced the meaning of the abomination of desolation solely to contemporary events and institutions. What is spoken of here is the manifestation of an ultimate incarnation of wickedness. But even if we cannot identify the abomination of desolation *totally* with these contemporary manifestations of evil, we should not refrain from linking situations where power is being used to limit, suppress and destroy with the symbol of sacrilege and desolation spoken of in the Gospel. As we seek to follow the pattern of Jesus' life, there will be occasions when manifestations of that kind of wickedness, which is an affront to God's purposes, may confront us, and the abomination of desolation cast its shadow on our lives. We should recognize that institutions created by fallible men and women in the interests of power are all to a greater or lesser extent demonic and can assume sub-human proportions when that power is abused and humanity threatened. What is being condemned here is not merely an individual but a symbol of the distorting power of evil. Followers of Jesus in every generation should learn to see and to name it, for there can be no accommodation with that which promotes the opposite of all that Jesus and the way of the cross stand for.

The consequence of the manifestation of evil is the avoidance of compromise and the need to create distance so as to maintain holiness and distinctiveness of witness to the kingdom. The disciples can expect to maintain a critical distance from the institutions of the old order (vv. 14ff). Life along the usual lines is no longer a realistic option for the disciple, who must be ready to flee to the mountains. The consequence is social separation and a refusal to join in the normal pattern of society. So, by contradicting and resisting, the disciples dispute that the world belongs to those who claim to rule over it. That is not to escape, however, because the reality of life in the time of great evil is particularly difficult for those who resist. Here in verses 13 and 22, as in the Book of Revelation, there is the call for endurance.

The picture is not entirely hopeless. The certainty of vindication is there (v. 26), but what precisely will happen to the elect when they have been gathered from the four corners of the earth is not touched on at all in Mark. The element of judgment at the Parousia of the Son of Man is not developed here, though at the climax of Matthew's version (25:31ff) there is the final assize with the Son of Man sitting on God's throne separating the sheep from the goats.

THE PASSION AND VINDICATION —— OF THE SON OF MAN ——

The machinations of the politically powerful which had already started during Jesus' time in Galilee have now come to a head. We have seen how Jesus' presence in Jerusalem has led to another group of Jewish leaders finding themselves threatened by his subversive teaching and life. There seems little opportunity for Jesus to escape the inevitable: his earlier words about the destiny of the Son of Man (8:31ff) now await their fulfilment.

In memory of her   *Mark 14:1–11*

From warnings about the future prompted by a disciple's admiration of the temple buildings, Mark returns us to the matter in hand, Jesus' presence in Jerusalem. He presents this period as something of a personal triumph for Jesus, who outmanoeuvres his opponents, demonstrates his messianic teaching and authority and challenges the people of God. There seems to be a return to the optimism of the opening chapters of the Gospel when the conflict with the forces opposed to God's reign are overcome. The shadows of opposition and persecution seem for a moment to be blown away. Yet behind the scenes the determination of the political authorities to destroy Jesus is moving on apace (v. 2), prevented only by the impression they have of his popularity and the unrest that could be the consequence of his arrest and execution. The opportunity to 'neutralize' Jesus is offered by the defection of Judas, one of Jesus' circle. Mark does not tell us the reasons for this, though we may imagine that a number of his circle may have been dissatisfied with Jesus' messianic strategy, as exemplified by another leading follower, Peter (8:33). The authorities can now see that the support for Jesus appears to be less solid. In verse 11 we see them using their power vested in wealth to reward the one who has passed from the side of the new age (God) to the old (Mammon).

Sandwiched in between the description of the way that the authorities deal with their problem is the account of the anointing at Bethany. Once again we note that Jesus is identified with an outsider, a leper, and that the central figure of the story is a woman. She anoints Jesus and incurs the rebuke of others for the waste involved. What they cannot recognize here is the significance of what is going on. Jesus the Messiah is present and recognized as such by the woman, not in words but in deeds. The supposed waste is in fact a preparation for burial and not an extravagant act. It is difficult not to make the connections with other parts of the Bible here. In the Old Testament it is the priest who anoints the King-Messiah (1 Kings 1:39). Here a woman claims that right and is acknowledged by Jesus to have seen in the one destined to death the true pattern of messiahship (set out in 10:45). Another outsider, the soldier at the foot of the cross in 15:39, will recognize this verbally and publicly. We should take care not to draw conclusions from this passage about our use of resources. Nor should we assume that Jesus is inculcating a fatalistic attitude towards the existence of poverty with his statement in verse 7. The witnesses of the event are reminded that the woman's action is very significant for him and that there will be opportunity enough to feed the poor when he is dead. Jesus is asking them to recognize that there is a terminus to his time on earth with them, a fact marked by the woman.

The other point to note is that Jesus gives a central place in the proclamation of the gospel to the story of this woman. It is quite extraordinary to note that the words 'what she has done will be told in memory of her' are similar to those attributed to Jesus in 1 Corinthians 11:24, when he speaks of the repeated act of sharing bread and wine: 'Do this in remembrance of me.' So the woman's place in Christian memory and story is guaranteed. Not only did she act in a priestly way by anointing the Messiah who was about to suffer and die but also her action was placed on a par with the memorial of the death for which she was preparing. The most priestly moment in the Gospel story, the anointing of the Messiah, is performed by a woman.

We are left with the question as to what we can learn from this incident about the role of women in the life of the people of God. If you want to explore further some of the implications of this story, try reading parts of Elizabeth Schüssler-Fiorenza's book, *In Memory of Her* (SCM Press).

The new covenant   Mark 14:12–25

Jesus now prepares to eat the Passover meal with the disciples (vv. 12ff). At this stage life is carrying on as normal. Perhaps the disciples had been lulled into a false sense of security by the success of Jesus' activity over the previous few days. We may suspect also a growing sense of bewilderment as they were confronted with talk of Jesus' betrayal and death during the Passover meal and the subsequent arrest in the Garden of Gethsemane.

During the meal Jesus takes bread and wine. The symbolic significance of food is very much part of the Passover ritual, so it would come as no surprise to the disciples that food is being interpreted symbolically. However they would be startled by the departure from custom as Jesus links the bread, which is broken and shared, with his body, and the wine with blood which seals the new covenant relationship between God and humanity. The Passover meal offered an opportunity for participants to share in the present realization of

177

God's liberating work in the past. So it was not just a memorial meal. That was why at Passover-time there was always the heightened anticipation that the God who redeemed his people from slavery in the past would act in like manner again. The past, the present and the future were brought together. This is also a feature of the Christian celebration of the Lord's Supper, when we do this 'in remembrance' of the liberation effected by the Son of Man (Mark 10:45 sees Jesus giving up his life for the purpose of liberation).

We may note that Mark's account of the supper, unlike that in 1 Corinthians 11:23ff, contains no reference by Jesus to a repeating of the ritual: Mark has no 'do this in remembrance of me'. Also, the significance of the words should be noted. Unlike Matthew, who has Jesus interpreting the wine as symbolic of the blood which effects the remission of sins, Mark talks of the blood of the new covenant poured out for many. As we see in passages such as Exodus 24, the shedding of blood forges an agreement. This is surely what Jesus intends us to understand by his death. It seals the fact that the reign of God has been demonstrated in his life and ministry, and indicates that, in Paul's words, God was in Christ reconciling the world to himself (2 Corinthians 5:19). This work of God in Christ will be brought to its consummation in the future. The future dimension is stressed by Jesus as he abstains from drinking because he longs to share in the messianic banquet when God's reign comes on earth as in heaven (v. 25).

These images of eating and drinking in the kingdom of God are expressions of the delight of fellowship and sharing in very concrete ways which characterize God's purposes for humanity. We need to be careful not to spiritualize these passages; they are very earthy. We may not be able to describe in detail what the fulfilment of God's purposes will entail, but by using metaphors like these we are able to hint at something of what we may hope for (see also Matthew 8:11).

> Jesus does not speak very often about the meaning of his death, and yet Christian theology has made this the centre of its understanding of salvation. What guidance do the words of Jesus at the last supper and elsewhere in Mark (for example, 10:45) give us about the way we should understand the significance of the cross?

Jesus struggles in Gethsemane *Mark 14:26–42*

After the meal Jesus and the disciples go out to the Mount of Olives, where he predicts that the imminent events will lead to the rout of the disciples, despite their assertions of perseverance (vv. 27f). He also prophesies that he will meet them in Galilee rather than in Jerusalem, something which is echoed by the young man at the tomb in Mark 16:7. The city and its temple have proved to be impervious to the challenge of the Messiah and borne no messianic fruit (11:13). In the garden of Gethsemane we find that the conflict between the hope of the reign of God and the impending reality of arrest and possible death continues to tear Jesus apart inwardly. In a sense that struggle in Gethsemane epitomizes the struggle of the Christian way. It must encapsulate cross and resurrection, failure and victory, hope and despair. In the words of Jesus we find the sorrow (v. 34) and the longing for another way (v. 36). Here for the first time he addresses God with that distinctive and tender parental word 'Abba', which according to Luke 11:2 Jesus taught his disciples to use. It is also found embedded in the Greek writing of Paul in Romans 8:15 and Galatians 4:6.

The disciples sleep, indicating further the emerging gulf between themselves and Jesus. However strong their protestations of loyalty (v. 31), they cannot share in Jesus' inner turmoil and struggle. This will only be exemplified further by the events of the next twenty four hours, as the inner circle of disciples act like sheep when the shepherd is removed (v. 27).

The arrest *Mark 14:43–52*

Jesus' arrest is accompanied by a brief skirmish in which one of his disciples produces a sword (compare Luke 22:36ff and 49), suggesting that some of those who went out to the Mount of Olives with Jesus may have thought that they were about to engage in a decisive messianic struggle (note the place of the Mount of Olives in messianic hope in Zechariah 14:4ff). But the attempt to resist is a misunderstanding of the way of the Messiah. Yes, he is revolutionary; yes, he proceeds by turning the world upside down; but his way is other than that suggested by conventional wisdom (10:44).

The enigmatic reference to the young man in verse 51 has been the subject of much discussion, particularly in view of the mention of another man who appears as a witness to the resurrection in 16:5, this time clothed. The incident is found only in Mark, and this has led some commentators to speculate that the man who ran away naked is the evangelist himself! There is no obvious reason why Mark should have mentioned the young man—it is just possible that we have here a historical reminiscence that was seen as a fulfilment of Amos 2:16.

On trial as a subversive   *Mark 14:53–72*

Jesus' trial before the authorities is sandwiched between the two parts of the story of Peter's betrayal in 14:53–54 and 14:66–72. 'Sandwiching' is one of Mark's literary techniques—we noticed it earlier, in the way that the account of the cleansing of the temple is sandwiched between the story of the fig tree in 11:12–21, and the healing of the woman with the haemorrhage between the raising of Jairus' daughter in 5:21–43. Mark's narrative has the effect of highlighting the difference between Peter and Jesus in the face of testing. Peter, despite his earlier affirmations of loyalty and devotion, denies any connection with Jesus and his cause; by contrast Jesus defiantly maintains his stand in the face of his adversaries.

There has been much debate about the trial of Jesus before the Sanhedrin (vv. 55–64). Scholars have pointed out that the account in Mark seems to infringe every regulation for the trial of a capital offence known to us from Jewish law. Several ways of dealing with these problems have been suggested. Some have argued that Mark's version is an invention by Christians to place the whole blame on the Jews and so make Christianity seem more palatable to the Romans. A more likely explanation is that we should regard the account in Mark as the culmination of a judicial process which may have begun long before (possibly hinted at in passages like Mark 3:22ff). In the light of chapters 11–13 it causes no surprise to find that the issue on which Jesus is first interrogated is his attitude to the temple. Mark indicates that the testimony of the witnesses did not agree. We should not suppose from this that Jesus never spoke against the temple. Rather his exact words were uncertain, which is borne out by the conflicting versions we have in the Gospels (Matthew 26:61; Mark 14:58; 13:2; John 2:19). Whatever Jesus may have said against the temple was seen as treasonable. We can imagine the reaction Jesus may have provoked if we consider how annoyed some people become in Britain when a focus of national life like the monarchy is criticized. Jesus remains silent for part of the interrogation (v. 61). Perhaps it is a measure of his refusal to accept the jurisdiction of this court, particularly as in the divine tribunal he will be vindicated as the Son of Man (compare Daniel 7:9–14, where the 'one like a son of man' is given divine approval over the representatives of the mighty of the nations). Eventually he does speak and accepts the title Messiah unequivocally (but compare Matthew and Luke, where this is less clear), and proclaims his future vindication in the sight of his enemies (compare Revelation 1:7). These words provoke rage in the high priest, who prompts Jesus' condemnation to death.

In reflecting on this narrative it is important that we recognize that it was not the Jewish nation which condemned Jesus to death but the political authorities who viewed him as a threat. After two thousand years of anti-semitism we must read this passage as an account not of Jews persecuting the founder of Christianity but of a Jewish élite persecuting a Jewish prophet (note the command to prophesy in v. 65), much the same as happened to Jeremiah (see Jeremiah 26). There is some truth in the view of the Jewish scholar Ellis Rivkin that the question we should be asking is not 'Who crucified Jesus?' but 'What crucified Jesus?' His answer is: the Roman colonial system and its links with the priestly aristocratic élite, who had a common interest in stability (see Ellis Rivkin, *What Crucified Jesus?*, SCM Press).

The Messiah confronts the representative of the occupying power
Mark 15:1–5

At the beginning of chapter 15 the story suddenly takes an unexpected turn. The Romans have hardly made an appearance in Mark's Gospel, except for the brief reference in the discussion of the tribute in 12:13ff. But now Jesus is taken off to Pilate (thus fulfilling the prediction of Jesus that the Son of Man would be 'handed over' to the Gentiles; see 8:31; 9:31 and 10:33f). Why was this necessary? Could not the Jewish authorities have dealt with the situation themselves? After all, they found Jesus guilty of blasphemy and deserving death. The fact that Mark gives no reasons for this course of action has given rise to suspicion about the historical worth of his account. Why then does Pilate suddenly and inexplicably become involved? Much will depend on the weight we place on the comment in John 18:31 that the Jewish court did not have the right to execute a convicted person. If that is correct, we may be able to understand why Pilate had to become involved.

When Jesus appears before Pilate, the issue of his messianic pretensions is uppermost, though according to verse 3 there were many other charges made against him. A Messiah would offer an alternative to the Roman system, and as such could be considered a threat to the status quo (this is brought out in Luke 23:2f). Jesus remains silent. There may be a hint here of Isaiah 53:7, though once again one should not ignore the power of silence in a situation where a defendant seems to have everything stacked against him. The refusal to answer can suggest non-recognition of the procedures and a refusal to 'play the game' of the accusers and captors. That sense of detachment comes through even in the Johannine account of the interrogation by Pilate. The extended conversation between Jesus and the Roman prefect in John 18:33ff is hardly a dialogue; like ships that pass in the night, there is a confrontation between different systems of value, and a total lack of comprehension on Pilate's part.

Jesus, Barabbas and Pilate   Mark 15:6–20

Pilate's amazement (a reaction found elsewhere among Jesus' opponents, for example 12:17) leads him to resort to a stratagem: he decides to use the custom of the release of a prisoner to deal with the situation. Mark certainly wants us to think that Pilate recognized that Jesus had been hauled before him because of the hostility of the priests (v. 10). To have refused to do anything about Jesus would have put Pilate in a difficult position. He could be seen to be weak with 'terrorists'; though, equally, he must have realized that any punitive action against Jesus and his followers would run the risk of provoking a hostile reaction from sympathetic crowds massed for Passover. He resolves this dilemma by putting the ball very firmly back in the court of the Jewish leaders. By offering to release either Barabbas or Jesus he appears magnanimous, and at the same time the decision is taken out of his hands. The amnesty then functions as a device to avoid a difficult choice. If the crowd choose Jesus for release, all well and good; if they opt for Barabbas, Jesus' death is none of his responsibility. Here is a classic example of the weakness of the men of power who cannot pursue justice. In their different ways the pursuit and the preservation of vested interests dominates the actions of the participants. The Jewish aristocracy fears for the temple; Pilate fears for his career (compare John 19:12f).

There are several intriguing things about this passage, not least the fact that no convincing parallel has been found to the Passover amnesty in non-Christian sources. We should also pause to ask what can possibly be meant by 'the insurrection' in verse 7. Are we (and the original readers of Mark) supposed to have access to accounts of contemporary Jewish history and know what this refers to? Or is the answer to be found in the story that Mark is telling? Could it be that 'the insurrection' is a reference to the disruption sparked by Jesus' entry into Jerusalem and the temple a few days before, in which Barabbas was arrested? Of course, there is no way of knowing. Whatever we decide, the story at this point indicates that Jesus is in the midst of a maelstrom of Jewish politics, a fact of which we have already been aware in Jesus' careful response to the issue of the tribute. It is a reminder that we are reading a realistic story of a man of flesh and blood caught in the webs of political prejudice and the struggles for power. Too often we are tempted to want to see Jesus as somehow floating above this tangled web without realizing the human pain and torment that he felt, as is evident most clearly in Gethsemane.

There is a difference in the reaction of the crowd at the entry into Jerusalem and that which cries for Jesus' execution in verse 13. Mark suggests that the chief priests stirred up the crowd, but there must have been sentiments for the priests to have played on for such a change of heart to have taken place. As we noted earlier, threats to the temple were not only directed to a focus of devotion but to the livelihood of a large sector of the population of Jerusalem. If Barabbas made common cause with those who sought to bring about God's kingdom by force of arms, it is likely that he would have wanted a *reformed* temple and would not have threatened to destroy it or predicted its destruction. No wonder that his release posed less threat to the comfortable life of all concerned, however much oppression and misery may have been caused by those who ruled Judea.

Mark goes on to describe the mocking of Jesus by the soldiers (vv. 16ff) in a passage full of irony. The taunts of those who dress Jesus as a king and hail him as such are known to those of us who read the texts as unconscious expressions of the reality of the situation. At the beginning of the Gospel (1:1) we were informed that Jesus is the 'Messiah, the Son of God'. In the midst of this apparent humiliation the reality is that the way of the kingdom and the way of the cross are precisely the way of the Messiah.

The execution of the Messiah for treason *Mark 15:21-39*

The description of Jesus' execution is full of allusions to the Old Testament—Psalm 22 in verses 24, 31 and 34, and Psalm 69:21 in verse 36. Jesus' death is hardly the death of a typical male hero. Not only can he not carry his own cross (v. 21), but he seems to deny God's presence at the very last (v. 34). In an age when the 'macho' image of powerful men abounds, this picture is a salutary reminder that at the heart of the Christian gospel is a fragile human being, alone and impotent. No more telling a statement could be found than that the God whom we worship for all eternity is, at the moment of crucifixion, identified with the poor and wretched of our world, for that is how Jesus ended his life on earth.

Even at the last Jesus is taunted with the claims he made about the temple (v. 29). Like the Pharisees earlier in the Gospel (8:11), the bystanders want a miracle as proof of Jesus' authority. Practical demonstrations of God's sovereignty have abounded, but these have been attributed to Beelzebub (3:22). Now there is the ultimate sign of the Messiah as an outcast for those who have eyes to recognize it. Only one can see this—the centurion in verse 39—and everyone else reviles Jesus (v. 32). The echo of the opening words of Psalm 22 on the lips of a dying man are heard by the bystanders as a summons to Elijah, the prophet who would come before the great and terrible day of the Lord (Malachi 4:5). Those who stand there do not believe that Elijah or the great and terrible day of the Lord will come. Jesus is just one more messianic fanatic who dies disillusioned. But they are wrong. Mark tells us that the moment of the death of the Messiah marks the destruction of the veil in the temple, the means of preserving the mystery of God (v. 38). The temple is shown to be an empty shell. The institutions of the old order stand condemned and derelict in the face of the radical alternative way of the crucified Messiah. Earlier in the Gospel, Jesus told his disciples that Elijah had come and had been rejected (9:13). Now the day of the Lord has arrived, not as salvation but as darkness and judgment on an unjust society maintained by a narrow-minded élite. They preferred religion to be confined to the activities of a temple whose maintenance had become an end in itself. It is as if the denunciation spoken by an earlier prophet rings out as Jesus dies: 'Woe to you who desire the day of the Lord! Why would you have the day of the Lord? It is darkness and not light . . . Is not the day of the Lord darkness and not light and gloom with no brightness in it? I hate, I despise your feasts, and I take no delight in your solemn assemblies. Even though you offer me your burnt offerings and your fatted beasts I will not look upon you . . . But let justice roll down like waters, and righteousness like an overflowing stream' (Amos 5:18–24).

The women, the tomb and the
message of the resurrection
Mark 15:40—16:8

Earlier in the story Jesus' disciples forsook him and fled (14:50), and Peter betrayed him (14:66ff). By now the men have disappeared from the narrative, and it is the women disciples who view the tragic events from afar. According to verse 41 these were his true followers and ministers in his hour of need. Together with a sympathizer, Joseph of Arimathaea (what had he been doing during the meeting of the Sanhedrin when Jesus was condemned? Had he remained silent for fear of being implicated?) they seek the body of Jesus from Pilate, who confirms Jesus' death from the report of the centurion who confessed him as the Son of God as he watched him die. The women take careful note of the tomb, and return there once the Sabbath is over to anoint Jesus. But their intentions are misplaced, for two reasons. First, this action has already been performed by the unnamed woman whose memory will live on through the telling of the story of Jesus (14:3ff). Secondly, when the women reach the burial place they find not the body of Jesus but an empty tomb.

In all our oldest versions of Mark the account finishes somewhat abruptly with verse 8. The accounts which describe Jesus' meeting with the disciples are almost certainly later additions. We cannot be sure whether Mark intended his version to end here. Alternative explanations are that the evangelist was prevented from completing the Gospel or that the final page was lost at a very early stage. We shall probably never know the answer to these questions. What we can do is to read the text as if it did stop here, as is suggested by our oldest manuscripts. The story is thus not rounded off. We are not told that everyone lived happily ever after; there is none of the feeling of completion and satisfaction that is found at the end of the other Gospels. The women are fearful and other disciples are in disarray. The story ends in utter bewilderment, with their meeting a young man in white who tells them of Jesus' resurrection, instructs them to announce the fact to Peter and the disciples (the singling-out of Peter is significant in view of his failure

185

throughout the Gospel to grasp the meaning of Jesus' messiahship: he is to be rehabilitated), and promises a meeting in Galilee. We are left with the women departing in fear without telling anyone, themselves the central figures in this climax to the story as recipients of the good news of the resurrection.

The promise of a meeting with the risen Jesus in Galilee takes Mark's readers back to the place where the story started. Galilee is where Jesus first announced the dawning of the reign of God, where discipleship began, and where he offered hope to the poor and marginalized. The Easter Jesus is to be encountered 'out there', where we might least expect to find him—not in the temple or the King's palace, not even in heaven. Mark's ending is a pungent reminder that all who long to see the Risen Jesus will be disturbed by his life and devastated by the failure of his ongoing mission, but must learn to find him in the persons and places that are unfashionable and unconventional—among the oppressed minorities and the social lepers: the prisoners of conscience, the victims of AIDS, the racially despised groups, the poor. Mark has left us with a disturbing end to a disturbing story.

Think back over the story you have read. Has it been good news to you? Has the way of the Messiah altered your way of looking at the world? Note the areas where it has offered you hope and consolation and the places it has challenged you.

Jesus told his closest followers in Mark 10:39 that they were to share his cup of suffering. Where do you think the kind of representation he refers to in 10:42–45 of the life of the crucified Messiah takes place? Where does it take place in your life and that of your church or community? Does the life of the people of God reflect the identification of Jesus with the poor, the outcast and those of no account?

LUKE

In the preface to the first of his two volumes, Luke tells us something about the kind of work he is writing, the sources he has used, and his aims in narrating the story which begins with Jesus and reaches into his own time.

Seeing that many others have undertaken to draw up accounts of the events that have reached their fulfilment among us, as these were handed down to us by those who from the outset were eyewitnesses and ministers of the word, I in my turn, after carefully going over the whole story from the beginning, have decided to write an ordered account for you, Theophilus, so that your Excellency may learn how well founded the teaching is that you have received.

Luke 1:1–4 (NJB)

In writing his 'ordered account' Luke is strongly influenced by Jewish and Greek ways of writing history. He wants to set the events surrounding Jesus, in which God's ancient purposes disclosed in the Jewish Scriptures are being fulfilled, on the stage of world history. He acknowledges that his account of them is not the first, and it draws on the memories of those who accompanied Jesus (the 'eyewitnesses') and founded the Church (the 'ministers of the word'). It is very likely that Luke used Mark's Gospel, though his omission of parts of it (particularly Mark 6:45—8:26) has caused some scholars to wonder at what stage in his own writing he actually used Mark. Luke includes some of Jesus' teachings that are found in Matthew but not in Mark, which suggests that Luke, like Matthew, drew on a collection of the sayings of Jesus. Luke also includes material which is found in none of the other Gospels, including some of the best-known parables of Jesus, such as the good Samaritan, the prodigal son and the rich man and Lazarus.

We do not know the identities either of the author or the recipient of this Gospel. Luke is traditionally thought to be the co-worker of Paul mentioned in Philemon 24, Colossians 4:14 and 2 Timothy 4:11, and in some way responsible for those parts of Acts written in the first person plural—the 'we-passages' in Acts 16:10–18, 20:5—21:18 and 27:1—28:16. On his own admission, however, Luke was not an eyewitness of the Gospel events. Theophilus was probably his patron. Yet we do not need to be able to identify the Gospel's author or intended recipient in order to discern its purpose—verse 4 of the Prologue provides the best clue here, though the translations vary. With the New Jerusalem Bible, compare the New Revised Standard Version: ' . . . so that you may know the truth concerning the things about which you have been instructed'. Does Luke write to persuade Theophilus of the true interpretation of what he has heard about, or to show how the teaching he has received can help him to be more confident in his faith? The latter seems more reasonable, because Luke appears to be more concerned with building up the security of people who are already believers, than with instructing someone who knows little or nothing about the faith.

A plausible setting for this Gospel (and its sequel) is to imagine Luke writing maybe ten or twenty years after the fall of Jerusalem in AD70. The movement that began among Palestinian Jews was now becoming increasingly Gentile. The urban Christian congregations round the Mediterranean included people drawn from different religious, political and economic backgrounds. Luke addresses various questions in the minds of his readers:

◇ Where do we, as Jewish or Gentile believers, fit into a movement which is rooted in, though now increasingly separate from, Judaism?

◇ What are we, as Roman citizens, to make of a movement whose founder was crucified by a Roman procurator?

◇ What does it mean for rich and poor people to be part of the same Christian movement?

Questions such as these raise issues of basic trust and confidence in the Christian movement. Luke's 'ordered account' seeks to address them, by writing with one eye on the past and the other on the circumstances of his own day. It is therefore a work of pastoral theology, which addresses the particular problems and opportunities faced by his audience with the story of Jesus' ministry and (in his second volume) an account of the spread of Christianity as far as Rome.

Further reading

G.B. Caird, *St Luke*, Pelican New Testament Commentaries, Penguin, 1963

I.H. Marshall, *The Gospel of Luke*, Paternoster, 1978

C.H. Talbert, *Reading Luke*, SPCK, 1990

Brian Beck, *Christian Character in the Gospel of Luke*, Epworth Press, 1989

Outline to Luke's Gospel

The preface	1:1–4
A new chapter in the story of Israel	1:5—2:52
Preparing for the salvation of God	3:1—4:13
Good news in Galilee	4:14—9:50
The journey to Jerusalem	9:51—19:28
Jerusalem and its temple: The end of Jesus' public ministry	19:41—21:38
From the upper room to the high priest's house	22:1—23:1
From the governor to Golgotha to the grave	23:2–56
Jerusalem: A new day begins	24:1–53

A NEW CHAPTER IN
THE STORY OF ISRAEL

Announcing a great prophet *Luke 1:5–25*

Luke has written his first two chapters in the style of the Jewish Scriptures. They are shot through with allusions to biblical stories. He is saying that in the events he relates, the story of God's people has taken a new turn. These early chapters form an overture to the Gospel, as themes which Luke develops more fully later on are given an initial airing. He begins on the familiar ground of traditional Jewish piety with the childless couple Zechariah and Elizabeth, but soon introduces us to a variety of people: the young Galilean girl Mary, engaged to Joseph (1:26–27); shepherds in the fields around Bethlehem (2:8); the elderly Simeon and Anna in the temple (2:25, 36); and again in the temple teachers of the Jewish faith, astounded by the twelve-year-old Jesus' questions and answers (2:46–47). Already we are being prepared to hear good news for all kinds of people.

In the holiest part of the temple we find Zechariah burning incense. In this atmosphere of prayer and worship, the angel Gabriel appears to him and announces that the spirit of God will bring Elizabeth's barren years to an end. Her son will follow in the footsteps of biblical heroes: he will be dedicated to God like Samson and Samuel, and enlivened by the spirit and power which animated the greatest prophet of them all, Elijah. His life's work will mark the beginning of the new chapter which the Holy Spirit is about to write in Israel's history. He is to prepare the people of God for what is coming.

Elizabeth's barrenness is a sign that Israel is unable to give birth to its own salvation, epitomized perhaps by the ironic lack of faith on the part of the priest praying in Israel's holiest place. Zechariah reminds us of Abraham and Sarah, who also found it hard to believe that they would have a child (Genesis 17:15–22; 18:1–5); now, as then, the word of God does not always find a ready welcome. If the story of God's people is to take a new turn, John's preparation of a people 'fit for the Lord' (v. 17) could not be more urgent.

Announcing the Messiah

The same angel who appeared to Zechariah in the temple now has a message for Elizabeth's cousin Mary. If anything, Mary has more reason for dismissing the angel's words, because his second annunciation is even more breathtaking than his first. Mary's divinely favoured virgin womb will give birth not merely to a prophet but to the Messiah. Her child will be named after Joshua (Hebrew for 'Jesus'), who established the people of Israel in their own land. He will not simply prepare the nation for whatever God has in store, but rule over it for all time as the successor of David. His character will not be modelled on the great men of old, like Samuel or even Elijah, but on God himself. Mary's child is conceived by the Holy Spirit: as God's Son he can be nothing other than holy. In every way, the one promised to Mary surpasses John.

Luke proceeds with great reserve in his account of the annunciation to Mary. He and his first readers were well aware of stories of great men conceived by the intervention of the gods. Luke conveys the true greatness of Jesus by drawing on the imagery of the Jewish Scriptures, which speak of the Spirit of God hovering over the waters in the beginning (Genesis 1:2), and the overshadowing presence of God in the wilderness (Exodus 40:35). God's initiative and creative power are brought to birth in Jesus, who lies at the heart of the Spirit's new work in salvation. Luke is not interested here in biology, but in the fruitful action of life-giving divine grace.

Like Zechariah, Mary too is surprised at what she hears, though her response could not be more different. Mary's natural desire to overcome her puzzlement is a world away from Zechariah's sceptical demand for a sign. The word of God is enough for her, and she shows herself to be a model believer. Hers is the kind of faith God looks for in his people. It is found supremely in her son, even in his darkest hour (22:42).

Praising God for raising the lowly

Luke continues to weave together the lives of John and Jesus, as Mary goes to share her news with her pregnant cousin, Elizabeth. Even her unborn baby is caught up in the joy surrounding the coming of the Messiah! Inspired by the Holy Spirit, Elizabeth echoes the angel's greeting to Mary: she is indeed favoured by God, not least because she has trusted his promise. The older woman's words are marked by humility and generosity towards her young visitor, 'the mother of my Lord', for Mary's child already carries the divine name. If Elizabeth is looking forward to great things from her own son, she can expect even more from the child of her young relative.

Mary's song is reminiscent of Hannah's in 1 Samuel 2:1–10, as her faith expresses itself in praise. She begins with the 'great things' God has done for her, only to extend her vision to the world at large. So confident is she of what God *will* do through her son that her Magnificat speaks of what God *has* done. Her praises have a cutting edge to them. God will keep faith with his promise to Abraham and his descendants, but not without surprising them. The messianic ruler of God's people will re-order society in favour of the disadvantaged. Status and position are to be reversed, as pride of place is given to the lowly and hungry rather than the powerful and rich (this is echoed further in Jesus' beatitudes in 6:20ff).

Luke leaves us with the impression that the work God will do through John and Jesus has already taken root in the lives of their expectant mothers. Elizabeth and Mary are examples of a 'people fit for the Lord', whose status as humiliated and lowly (in those days women were of little account, other than as wives and mothers) has already been altered. As they announce God's coming salvation, they invite the response of faith, joy and praise.

Praising God for freedom and peace   *Luke 1:57–80*

So far, women have dominated Luke's narrative, which has concentrated on their faith in the word of God. Zechariah's dumbness is at last released when he writes down the name of his son, showing that he too now believes the promise made by the angel. Now it is his turn to come under the influence of the Holy Spirit, who inspires the song and prophecy.

Zechariah's *Benedictus* draws on the Jewish Scriptures, and develops many of the themes in Gabriel's earlier words to him, and Mary's song. To her praise for the re-ordering of society is added Zechariah's hope that Israel will at last be freed from its enemies. His week-old son is to be the prophet who will pave the way for the new order, as the angel had said. In the heady events of these days, God is proving himself faithful to his word to Abraham (Genesis 22:16–18) and David (2 Samuel 7:12ff), as he leads his people towards the age of peace which the prophets hoped for (Isaiah 9:6–7; 11:1–10). Characteristically Luke shows that good news is not a private matter. As Mary had shared her joy with Elizabeth, so family, neighbours and people from the surrounding countryside now enter into the excitement and wonder of these events.

The new state of affairs which Gabriel, Mary and Zechariah announce has been described so far only in general terms. As yet we have not been told precisely how John will prepare for the coming age, or what Jesus will do as Messiah. Like those in Judea, we too are left wondering, 'What will this child turn out to be?' How will Israel's society be restructured? Who are the enemies from which the nation is about to be delivered? How will God prove faithful to his ancient promises? Like Luke's characters, his readers too are full of anticipation as the Gospel story unfolds.

The Messiah, the emperor and the shepherds   *Luke 2:1–20*

Uncertainty surrounds the census which takes Joseph and Mary to Bethlehem. We know of one in Palestine when Quirinius was governor, but this was about ten years after the death of Herod the Great, during whose lifetime Jesus was born (1:5; Matthew 2). When the emperor Augustus held a census during the lifetime of Herod, the governor in Palestine was Saturninus. With the present state of knowledge, the historical problems cannot be solved, but Luke's concern is not restricted to providing historical detail. He wants to show that Jesus belongs to the wider history of the known world, and not merely to local and provincial Jewish life. He also wants to contrast Mary and Joseph with Galileans who, according to the Jewish historian Josephus, rebelled against the census at the time of Quirinius (Acts 5:37): unlike them, the family of Jesus is obedient to the Roman rule. Luke also wants to show that God's purposes are worked out not only through people like Mary and Elizabeth who consciously obey his word, but also through those who unwittingly play a part in the drama of salvation. Jesus is only born in the city of David by the good offices of the Emperor! Luke encourages us to have the broadest possible vision of God's salvation; firmly rooted in Jewish soil it may be, but its embrace knows no boundaries.

In his nativity story, Luke movingly sets glory and humility side by side. The skies are full of heaven's messengers, but the first to be told of Mary's child are shepherds, a despised class because of their reputation for dishonesty and their neglect of religious observance—which was an unavoidable occupational hazard. As we have come to expect by now, they too are caught up in joy and praise. Likewise the one born to Mary is heralded by the angels as 'a Saviour, Christ the Lord', but we find him lying in the humblest of places. A passage which starts with the Emperor but has more about the shepherds reminds us that God prefers us to establish his all-encompassing salvation among ordinary 'down to earth' folk, such as we have met in the Gospel so far. This truth is worth all the pondering and treasuring that Mary affords it.

The Messiah and the temple   *Luke 2:21–52*

These two scenes are separated by some twelve years, but linked by the theme of Jesus' being brought to the temple. His first visit, when he is about six weeks old, marks the end of Mary's time of purification after childbirth. According to Leviticus 12:6–8, the offering they make shows that Mary and Joseph are poor people. Like Samuel before him, Jesus is dedicated to the service of God (1 Samuel 1:11, 22, 28). Jesus' second visit occurs at Passover-tide. His words to his anxious parents when they at last find him recall his dedication to God as a young baby: 'my Father's' house is the very place they should expect to find one whom they have handed over to God.

The contrasts in this passage are worth noticing, not least because they recur time and again in Luke's writing. Notice the people who speak well of Jesus: Simeon and Anna praise God for the one in whom they see so much promise, and the Jewish rabbis are astonished at his powers of enquiry and insight. Once more Luke underlines the range of Israelites drawn to Jesus, from the Spirit-led ones who have waited prayerfully and patiently for the coming of Israel's salvation to the institutional guardians of Israel's religious heritage. Look further at those to whom the salvation is directed: Mary, Joseph and Jesus (with verse 51 compare Exodus 20:12) are presented as practising Galilean Jews; Simeon, Anna and the rabbis are at home in the temple in Jerusalem. Yet Simeon's song shows that God's promise extends beyond Judean and Galilean Jews, to the Gentiles. Finally look at the responses to Jesus himself: those around him here may speak well of him, but Simeon hints at a darker side to Jesus' destiny. The salvation which re-orders Israel and embraces the Gentiles will not be established without opposition and pain. In Luke's story Jesus does not journey to Jerusalem again until the days leading up to his crucifixion.

> The gospel is for everyone, but God starts with the humble, the poor, the outcasts, those of little reputation in the rest of the world's eyes. When God comes to remake the world, our values are turned on their heads. In his book The Broken Body (Darton, Longman and Todd, 1988), Jean Vanier, the founder of the world-wide L'Arche communities for the mentally handicapped, writes of the way that following Jesus is not a matter of climbing up the ladder of success and power, but walking down to discover the life of Jesus hidden in the poor, the sick, the old and the disabled.

—— PREPARING FOR THE SALVATION OF GOD ——

The fruit of repentance   *Luke 3:1–14*

If the first two chapters are the overture to the Gospel as a whole, this next section forms the prelude to Jesus' Galilean ministry. In what he writes about the Baptist's work, Luke begins to fill out his understanding of salvation with the familiar gospel language of repentance and forgiveness. But he is careful to convey the breadth of meaning in the message he announces. To do this, he repeats two of the strains we have already heard in the Gospel. He starts by anchoring the work of John and Jesus in the public world of Caesar, the Roman governor, the tetrarchs and the high priests. Then he goes on to show that what God is doing in John and Jesus fulfils the Jewish hope for salvation expressed in the Scriptures. Notice that Luke quotes more of Isaiah 40:3–5 than either Matthew (3:3) or Mark (1:3), in order to underline the message of Simeon's song that God's salvation is for all humankind.

References to politicians, priests and prophets at this point in the Gospel serve to amplify the preaching of John: God is not content merely with outward religious observance, or with repentance which goes no further than inward thoughts and attitudes, or with forgiveness for the children of Abraham alone. The fruit of repentance must show itself in the wider public world. With this in mind, John issues a threefold warning. First, against *complacency*: his Jewish hearers must not think that their identity as Abraham's descendants automatically qualifies them for the coming salvation. God is interested in everyone, and all are called to bear the fruit of repentance. Second, against *economic divisions*: within the people of God, life's essentials—clothing and food—should be shared, not hoarded (a matter which Luke highlights in Acts 2:42–47; 4:32–37). Third, against *greed and extortion*: those who collect too much in taxes or supplement their low pay by intimidation must cease their oppression. A people 'fit for the Lord' and ready to receive his salvation must have no truck with racial and religious superiority, or anything that sets them against one another.

A sense of expectancy   *Luke 3:15–38*

Like the crowds baptized by John, Luke's readers too have a sense of expectancy as we wait for the Messiah's ministry to begin. To prepare us all the more, today's passage contains three sources of testimony to Jesus. First there is the witness of John himself, who sees the Messiah as a baptizer with the Holy Spirit and a winnower: the second image explains the first. The winnower's job was to separate grains of wheat from the chaff. When shovelfuls of mixed grain fell back onto the threshing floor, the chaff was blown away by the wind. The grain was gathered and stored, the chaff collected and burned. So the Messiah will gather together the people of God, but not without division and judgment. He will bring Israel to life through the Holy Spirit (see Ezekiel 37:1–14), and in so doing will separate out and burn the chaff. John looks forward to the birth of the Church at Pentecost, though in picking up the words of Simeon in 2:34, he also points ahead to the conflict and division brought by Jesus and the apostles. Their own rejection by the leaders of Israel is foreshadowed in John's imprisonment by Herod.

The second source of testimony to the Messiah is the heavenly voice: 'You are my Son; today I have fathered you'. Unlike Matthew and Mark, Luke separates the baptism of Jesus from the descent of the Spirit and the voice. What is important here is that Jesus is at prayer, a favourite theme in this Gospel (5:16; 6:12; 9:18, 28–29; 11:1; 22:41). Luke's first readers would understand his reference to the opening of heaven and the voice as a claim to divine revelation: now in the words of Psalm

196

2:7, God adds his testimony to that of the characters who have appeared in the Gospel up to now. God confirms that Jesus is the expected messianic king, and anoints him with the Spirit for his new office. What we have here may well go back to Jesus' own baptismal experience. At the Jordan he became aware of God's call to begin his messianic work, for which the Spirit was given to equip him.

Finally Luke himself testifies to Jesus in his genealogy. Matthew's version (Matthew 1:1–16) traces Jesus' descent from Abraham through David, whereas Luke works back from Jesus, through David and Abraham, to Adam. This is yet another example of Luke's understanding of the universal scope of the gospel. Jesus marks a new beginning, not only for Israel but for all humankind. We can all expect great things of him.

The desert: testing and victory *Luke 4:1–13*

As he prepares to begin his public ministry, Jesus has to choose which path to take: there is more than one way to be Messiah. In his struggle for the will of God, he comes face to face with the devil, the symbol of all that opposes God's way of establishing his salvation. Like Matthew (4:1–11), Luke expands Mark's brief account (1:12–13) into a fuller dramatization of Jesus' struggles. The story here is constructed around verses from Deuteronomy 6:13, 16 and 8:3, and is based on the temptations of other sons of God: Adam is tempted in the garden (Genesis 3:6), and Israel (Hosea 11:1) is tempted in the wilderness (Psalm 106:14f). The devil's threefold refrain brings out the essence of the tempting: 'If you are the Son of God . . .' highlights Jesus' struggle for his vocation. Will he be faithful to his God-given role as Messiah, for which the Spirit empowers him?

The first temptation plays on Jesus' ability to work signs. Not only here, hungry in the desert, but also when he is confronted by opposition and unbelief (11:29–32) does he face this temptation. Will he carry out his ministry by appealing to faith, or try to verify his authority by dazzling displays of power? The second temptation relates to Jesus' confrontation with those who hold political authority. Will he seek power by compromising with the leaders of Israel, or will he challenge them in the name of the kingdom of God? Will he fall in with those who want violent confrontation with Rome? The third temptation asks Jesus to live in some other way than by trusting the one he knew as a father. In the trying situations of conflict and doubt which he will face time and again, will he live by putting God to the test? Or will his be the way of obedient trust seen in Mary, for whom the word of God did not need further proof?

Jesus emerges victorious from his time of trial. The Spirit whose power conceived him, who anointed and filled him in preparation for his public ministry, enables him to use the Scriptures to fight against the devil (compare Ephesians 6:17, where 'the sword of the Spirit' is 'the word of God'). But the battle with evil is not over, and Luke's readers know that they too will need to struggle to remain faithful to the gospel. They can be assured, though, that like Jesus, they too have the resources of the Spirit and the Scriptures to see them through.

— GOOD NEWS IN GALILEE —

Nazareth: approval and rejection *Luke 4:14–30*

At last Jesus appears in public! From 4:14 to 9:50 he is almost exclusively in Galilee where he builds up quite a reputation as a rabbi. So it is not surprising that when he goes to the synagogue in his home town of Nazareth, he should be asked to preach. He chooses a passage from Isaiah 61, reading it first in Hebrew (the language in which the Scriptures were written) and then in Aramaic, so that everyone can understand. Translation into the vernacular tended to be somewhat loose; Jesus combines words from Isaiah 61:1–2 (which no doubt echoed his own experience of the Holy Spirit following his baptism) with others from Isaiah 58:6. The resulting text sets out his understanding of his messianic mission: he is the Spirit-anointed herald of good news to those who are without hope. He brings freedom to the oppressed by inaugurating the 'jubilee year' of release (Leviticus 25). Reading the Gospel further, we see how in healing and exorcism and in his ministry to the poor, tax-collectors and sinners, the victory Jesus won in the desert is established.

Jesus' sermon meets with a mixed response. Initial approval soon gives way to unease and rejection as he uncovers what lies behind the apparently harmless remark about the teaching of 'Joseph's son'. Was hostility lurking just below the surface of the congregation's warm response? Did these Nazarenes think that their local hero should only look after the needs of his own folk? Jesus will have none of this! He points them to other heroes, from Scripture this time—the prophets Elijah and Elisha. Both had a ministry beyond the boundaries of Israel, and Elijah was rejected by his own people. Their experience bears out the proverbial saying about the welcome afforded to a prophet in his own country. Jesus' work will take him beyond Nazareth and Galilee; there is even a hint here of a salvation which includes Gentiles.

So Luke sets out the programme of Jesus' ministry in this opening episode in Galilee. Animated by the power of the Spirit, the salvation he brings touching every level of existence, Jesus fulfils the prophecy of Simeon in 2:34-35. He is rejected because he dares to believe that God's salvation must take him beyond the safety of what is familiar to him. He manages to escape this time with his life, but the controversy he sparks off will dog him from here on.

Capernaum: the authority of Jesus' word   Luke 4:31–44

In Nazareth Jesus had claimed divine authority, only for those who heard the local rabbi's teachings to reject the words of 'Joseph's son'. Twenty miles away in Capernaum, those who are impressed or astonished at his teaching and enquire about the source of his authority are answered, ironically, by the demons: we are hearing the words of the Son of God, the Holy One of Israel. The powers of evil recognize the fulfilment of the angel's promise to Mary in 1:35—Jesus, who was conceived by the power of the Holy Spirit and is now enlivened by that same Spirit, is holy, the Son of God.

The divine authority of Jesus is evident both in his teaching and in the threefold rebuke he utters against the malevolent powers of the demons and the fever. Where evil holds sway, the word of Jesus brings freedom: the man in the synagogue is delivered unharmed from the grip of the unseen spirit, and Peter's mother-in-law is restored to her accustomed role. What is more, Jesus silences the demons, so that they do not raise false hopes about the kind of Messiah he will be.

The references to the devil and demons at the beginning and end of chapter 4 sit uneasily with a modern scientific outlook. 'Mythological' it might be, but no more so than the language of mental illness with which we are more accustomed. The reality referred to is no less real for its being expressed in an ancient form of language. In the name of the kingdom of God, and in the power of the Holy Spirit, Jesus attacks the very forces which bring disorder and disintegration to individuals, institutions and society at large. The victory he won over their assault on him in the desert is here extended throughout Galilee as far as Judea. In the gift of the Holy Spirit made available through his resurrection, that victory will spread still further (see Acts 1:8).

The lakeside: the call of the first helpers   *Luke 5:1–11*

Jesus now starts to enlist the support which the urgency and success of his mission need. He must use the fisherman's boat if he is to teach the crowd by the lakeside. But more than that, he must find helpers to join him in the mission of the kingdom of God. Simon may be faced with an unwelcome suggestion that he and his tired companions return to the lake to make up for their fruitless night's toil, but he does in fact have good reason to believe in the authority of Jesus' words: he has already seen the effectiveness of Jesus' rebuke on his mother-in-law's fever. Now, in the boats full to the point of sinking, the power of Jesus' word touches him personally.

Astonishment and wonder in the face of such awesome power are by now familiar ingredients in the Gospel (1:65; 2:18; 4:36). What is new here is Simon's profession of unworthiness in the presence of Jesus. Despite this, Jesus calls him to strike out into even deeper water, catching people now rather than fish, in the work of the kingdom. Simon's recognition of his own shortcomings is a reminder of things to come in Luke's story: the one who will most forcefully assure Jesus of his support in the hour of greatest need will fail him most signally (see 22:33–34, 54–62). And yet Jesus' faith in him does not falter, and Simon Peter will become one of the trail-blazers of the Church's mission to Jews and Gentiles once the idea that God has no favourites comes home to him personally (see Acts 10–11, especially 10:34 and 11:17).

The call of Simon to the mission of Jesus is very important for Luke. Here we have a companion of Jesus from his days in Galilee, a Galilean Jew himself, who represents both the gospel's roots in Judaism and its embrace of the Gentile world. Jewish and Gentile converts among Luke's first readers would be reassured by a disciple with whom they could identify, not only in his unworthiness and failure, but also in his commitment to a gospel for all people.

Luke's stories of John the Baptist's call to repentance and Jesus'
encounter with Simon can help us towards a richer
understanding of the meaning of repentance. During the
penitential season of Lent, we often trivialize repentance by
seeing it in the rather negative sense of giving something up. But
repentance is more of a turning towards God than a turning
aside from ourselves. Simon showed repentance, not primarily
by facing up to his own unworthiness, but in embracing the call
of the kingdom of God. John invited Israel to find out what God
wanted by turning towards him in the wilderness, which the
prophets saw as a place of new beginnings (Ezekiel 20:36; Hosea
2:14ff). Carlo Carreto is an Italian monk who lived in the desert
for a while. He encourages us to consider creating a 'desert
space' in our lives, turning towards God by giving more time to
prayer (see his Letters from the Desert). That way the fruit of
repentance—which John called for, and Simon lived out as a
disciple and Church leader—may be found in us.

The healing of an outcast   *Luke 5:12—16*

Luke now proceeds to develop further the picture of Jesus as the Spirit-
filled Messiah bringing freedom to the oppressed. This passage brings
him face to face with a leper. The term is used in the Bible of a variety of
skin diseases. What they have in common is their power to mark the
sufferers as outcasts, according to the laws in Leviticus 13 (especially
vv. 45–46). Although these illnesses could be spread through touch, the
main reason for isolation was religious rather than medical. Skin disease
was understood as a sign of religious 'uncleanness'. To touch something
unclean was to make oneself unclean: so to prevent contact between
'clean' and 'unclean', lepers were made to live away from family,
village and worshipping community.

   In healing the leper, Jesus challenges a religious interpretation which
only adds to the burden of this disease. By touching the man, Jesus
abolishes the religious distinction between clean and unclean. Far from
being contaminated by the leper's uncleanness, Jesus makes him clean.
But he goes further than merely curing the man's body. He sends him to
the priest, as the law of Leviticus 13 requires, so that the man can be
brought back into the community.

Jesus' attitude to Jewish Law is worth noticing here. On the one hand, he recognizes that the Law can be oppressive, when it makes hard and fast distinctions between one and another on the basis of the outward state of the body. And yet if the man is to be treated as a whole person, he needs to be seen as a social being, and the separation from his family and community overcome. The only way to do this is by complying with the Law's requirement. Jesus frees the man from the oppressive aspects of the Law, without denying the value of Law where it genuinely serves the well-being of God's people.

The healing of a sinner   *Luke 5:17–26*

In the previous passage the leper believed that Jesus could heal him. Here we meet four men whose faith in God's healing power at work in Jesus is so great that they are undaunted by the crowd which prevents them from getting their paralysed friend to Jesus. Their faith is rewarded, as Jesus first declares that the man is forgiven and then heals him of his paralysis.

In the house listening to Jesus' teaching are Pharisees and teachers of the Law from as far away as Jerusalem. Had these representatives of the official Jewish leadership come to investigate this Galilean rabbi's claim to divine authority, and to check the orthodoxy of his teaching? He was, after all, making a great impression throughout Galilee. Unlike the paralysed man and his friends, they are unable to accept Jesus' declaration of forgiveness without questions. By healing the man, Jesus demonstrates that the source of his own authority to forgive is indeed 'God alone' (vv. 21, 24), and invites his opponents to share the faith of the friends.

Why does Jesus need to assure the paralysed man that he is forgiven? Is his sickness a result of his sin? Elsewhere, Jesus severs the connection made by popular belief (John 9:1–13). It may be that this man's paralysis is the result of some particular sin he had committed, or more likely, that he shares the common belief that his sinfulness is to blame for his sickness. By responding to him as a whole person, Jesus first frees him from the paralysis of guilt, before going on to heal his paralysed body.

As in the synagogue at Nazareth, Jesus provokes division. The faith of the four friends, alongside the sense of awe among those who praise God for the healing of the paralytic, form the perfect foil for the oppressive attitudes of the scribes and Pharisees. They too need the Messiah's liberation, but we shall soon learn that their intentions are quite different (6:11).

The call of Levi, outcast and sinner
Luke 5:27–32

After healing an 'outcast' leper and a paralysed 'sinner', Jesus meets someone who is regarded both as an outcast and a sinner. No self-respecting Jew would do the job of Levi, the tax-collector, whom Jesus calls to be a disciple. In Galilee, tax-collectors could be found in the pay of Herod or the Emperor. They were a despised class: their association with the occupying power of Rome meant they were stigmatized as collaborators, and their work allowed ample opportunity for dishonesty and extortion. Banned from the synagogue, they were treated as the lowest of the low.

Through the good offices of his new disciple, Jesus shares table-fellowship with people of Levi's acquaintance. For the practising Jew, the meal table was the place where social and religious attitudes were rehearsed and reinforced. The Pharisees believed that to eat with those regarded as 'unclean' or 'sinners' was to go against the Jewish Law. Jesus is a mystery to the Pharisees. While he claims divine authority for his teaching and actions, his willingness to mix with the unclean flouts accepted conventions. He appears to have nothing but contempt for the will of God.

Jesus justifies his behaviour by comparing himself with the doctor, who deals with the sick rather than the well. To be concerned for 'sinners' does not mean that he has no interest in the Law or the 'upright', only that he gives priority to liberating 'outcasts' who are deprived of the hope of salvation. Distinctions between 'insiders' and 'outsiders' are abolished in the new people of God Jesus is gathering, a message which Jewish and Gentile Christians among Luke's first readers do well to hear (see Acts 11:3).

Festivity not fasting
Luke 5:33–39

The controversy which has been a feature of Jesus' exchanges with Pharisees and scribes in the last two episodes continues. The point at issue now shifts from the company he keeps to the attitude he and his disciples display to hallowed religious practices. Jesus is hardly negligent when it comes to prayer, as we have already seen in 3:21 and 5:16, but he and his disciples evidently lack the due sense of seriousness which the Pharisees' and others' regular fasting imparts to life. Jesus' answer highlights his understanding of the significance of his ministry. The good news and liberation he brings are cause for celebration, as the references to joy and praise which punctuate the first two chapters of the Gospel lead us to expect. The festivity of a wedding rather than the sombreness of fasting is more characteristic of the salvation he brings.

The parables of the cloak and wineskins make it clear that despite Luke's heavy emphasis on continuity between the older Jewish order and the messianic ministry of Jesus, there is something new here which does not match the old. Indeed the new is so explosive that it threatens to ruin the structures of the old. The traditional ways have become barren, like the womb of Elizabeth, and they need the life-giving power of the Spirit if they are to bring God's salvation to birth. Jesus' critics are still intoxicated by the old wine, and do not see any need for the new. But who can stand in the way of rejoicing when those prevented from even sipping the old wine (the outcasts and sinners we met in the last two readings) are now freely drinking the new?

The needy are more important than religion *Luke 6:1–11*

The controversy over attitudes to religious practice continues, as Jesus and his disciples are censured for their behaviour on the sabbath. The disciples' actions of picking ears of corn and rubbing them between their hands counted as one of the categories of work which was forbidden by the stricter rabbis on the sabbath. Likewise, Jesus' healing of the man with the deformed hand on another Sabbath could be interpreted as work, and therefore violated the Law. Luke's observation in verse 2 that 'some of the Pharisees' questioned the disciples' behaviour is an important reminder that not all of their number would have found these actions offensive. More liberal Pharisees, for example, would have had no difficulty with Jesus' healing on the sabbath.

Jesus justifies his actions by highlighting the intention of scriptural Law. He refers to the story of David in 1 Samuel 21:1–9 to argue that human need overrides legal requirements. He goes on to argue that there can be nothing wrong in doing good by saving life on the sabbath (v. 9). As 'Lord of the sabbath', Jesus is prepared to uphold the Law when it serves the best interests of human beings, as the story of the healing of the leper demonstrates. But he will not allow the interests of the more conservative rabbis to make observance of the Law into an end in itself.

The sabbath was an important institution for the Jews. Together with the regulations about table-fellowship which forbade Jews and Gentiles eating together, the sabbath laws provided a public way of professing and maintaining Jewish identity. Jesus claims to be the Spirit-inspired interpreter of the will of God, but his attitude to the ancient identity-markers of Israel, together with his re-ordering of society in favour of the disadvantaged, presents a real challenge to the official agencies of social and religious control. His earlier reference to the bridegroom being taken away (5:35) is perhaps an indication that he senses the gravity of the issues at stake. Verse 11 makes it clear that his opponents do not doubt this for a moment.

Liberation for all Israel   Luke 6:12–19

The stories of Jesus' healings, and the controversy they generated, have clarified the nature of the salvation announced in the words of the angels, the songs of Mary, Zechariah and Simeon, in the preaching of John the Baptist and in Jesus' sermon at Nazareth. We have seen how Luke depicts the Spirit-endowed prophet proclaiming the good news of the kingdom of God throughout the towns and synagogues of Galilee and Judea, his reputation reaching even as far as Jerusalem. Jesus rules as Israel's messianic king by freeing the oppressed and defeating the powers of evil. His reign is marked by welcome for outcasts, feasting and celebration, satisfaction of human need before religious observance, and prayer. His teaching makes a great impression because his new interpretation of the will of God for Israel carries divine authority.

Jesus' prayerful choice of the Twelve reveals more of the significance of all this activity. He is indeed restoring Israel, as Simeon hoped (see 2:25). Although we know nothing about most of this specially selected band, it is their number which is most important. The Twelve represent the whole nation of Israel, from fishermen (Simon Peter, James and John) to tax-collectors (Levi, here called Matthew) to revolutionary sympathizers (Simon the Zealot). The will of God is to restore Israel as *one family*, as the parables in chapter 15 will demonstrate.

Luke highlights Jesus' appeal to all Israel by noting that people come from all over the country to hear Jesus and to be healed. As we await his teaching we are reminded that he is more than a worker of miracles. Jesus' 'sermon on the plain' will demonstrate that he is as concerned with the healing of social divisions and the development of the human qualities which bring this about, as he is with the healing of the body.

> Jesus often found himself in trouble with those who made the rules in his society. Churches and religious bodies, like any other institution, need rules, but we can very easily confuse the necessary order they bring with the will of God for all time and all places. Sometimes our rules are no more than reflections of our own incomplete understanding of the gospel. They become dangerous when they have us forget that God is more interested in setting the oppressed free than propping up the systems in which we often try to contain him.
>
> Remarkably, God stays faithful to the Church as to Israel, but it does not follow that he is happy with things as they are in the Church. There are always new areas of need in society and the wider world, and the Spirit of God is always trying to draw out our loving response. If we try to take refuge in the safety of our rules and regulations, we may find that God has ways of bursting them open. We need to pray for discernment, so that we may know the difference between faithfulness to the Church and resistance to the Holy Spirit. The way of Jesus demands loyalty to the values of God's kingdom before anything else.

Whose side is God on?   Luke 6:20–26

Luke has referred to the appeal and authority of Jesus the teacher in his narrative, without telling us much about the actual content of his teaching. In the rest of chapter 6 he remedies this by including a collection of Jesus' sayings. The Sermon on the Plain here corresponds with Matthew's Sermon on the Mount (Matthew 5–7). Both Sermons begin and end alike, though Matthew's is longer.

In this opening section, Jesus tells us of those whom God is blessing through his ministry of preaching and liberation. The poor, hungry, weeping and persecuted are not favoured because they are any better than others, but because the situation they live in is deeply offensive to the God who wants Israel's liberation. At best, they just about manage to keep their heads above water. They weep with exasperation because the world is ordered to their disadvantage. Like those who will later spearhead the Christian mission, and whose experience is reflected in the actual wording of verses 22–23, they are publicly resented by those who have power. In Jesus, God shows that he is on their side, as Mary celebrated in her song (Luke 1:51–53). The blessing they receive now will be complete when God's kingdom comes in all its fulness.

If the poor and hard-pressed are not blessed because they are any better in themselves, neither are the rich condemned because they are necessarily any worse. If Israel is to be restored as one family, those who currently have all the advantages cannot afford to be indifferent to the fate of the disadvantaged. Jesus here expects the wealthy to use their power and influence for the benefit of the poor. Should they refuse, they must reckon with God's judgment—a warning which is underlined later in the parable of the rich man and Lazarus (16:19–31).

Words for a divided world   Luke 6:27–39

Jesus began his sermon by addressing a situation that was divided by access to wealth and power. He goes on to argue that in order to overcome social fragmentation, economic re-ordering alone is not enough. Only the energy of love is sufficient—love which overcomes enmity and breaks the vicious circle of violence. Such love is so generous that it overcomes the desire to receive anything in return.

Jesus is not so idealistic as to think people can live without making enemies but he does expect a creative response to those intent on harm and abuse. The words of verse 27 are echoed elsewhere in the New Testament (Romans 12:14–21 and 1 Peter 2:18–25), showing that Jesus' teaching was recognized as fundamental for Christian living. The specific examples in verses 29–30 are designed to provoke the imagination of disciples into making a loving response to whatever kind of violence they receive from their enemies. Jesus wants to see evil overcome, not extended. 'Evil propagates by contagion. It can be contained and defeated only when hatred, insult, and injury are absorbed and neutralized by love' (G.B. Caird).

Jesus looks for a generosity in human affairs which moves beyond the natural desire for mutual gain. His words about doing good and lending to those from whom one can expect nothing in return would have particular force for the wealthier members of Luke's church. How can their practical love for their poorer brothers and sisters be effective if they look for some financial benefit in return? If the advantaged start to live for the disadvantaged, they cannot expect material reward. However undeserving others may appear to be, love expresses itself in mercy and generosity, not judgment and condemnation. Jesus assures those who live according to this teaching that their actions reflect the generosity and mercy of God, from whose abundance they will receive. That reward surely outweighs all other.

Salvation or disaster? *Luke 6:39–49*

Jesus opened his sermon with talk about salvation for those denied access to wealth and power, and went on to advocate love as the power which overcomes barriers in a divided world. So how does love win through and bring salvation, given that living among enemies and the undeserving can so easily ruin even the best of intentions and the highest of motives? According to Jesus' words in verse 47, the generous love which absorbs and neutralizes evil is embodied in the true disciple who listens to and lives by his teaching. This person will not try to view the faults of others without first considering the magnitude of their own shortcomings. Only then can love for the other be effective. According to verse 45, true disciples draw on the reserves of love and goodness which have been formed in their own lives through the generosity and mercy of God. Only then can one speak of the love which transforms hatred and bitterness.

Jesus contrasts true disciples with those who reduce the service of the kingdom to the expression of right belief or true confession of faith— merely calling him 'Lord, Lord' without taking his teaching to heart. These people are like one blind person trying to lead another, or the man who builds a house without first digging foundations. The end is the same: disaster (falling into a hole in the ground), ruin (a collapsed building). Here love is consumed by evil, and salvation is never established, because the task is attempted with insufficient resources.

The true disciple, then, is one who lives in the company of Jesus, listening to and acting upon his words. For Luke, Jesus' teaching has authority because it is of a piece with what he does: he preaches liberty to the captives, and at the same time frees the oppressed. His action to liberate the powerless is driven not by hatred of the powerful, but by a profound sense of the unlimited generosity and mercy of God, even for his enemies. So, if Israel's ruin is to be avoided and its salvation established, it must look to the example of its Messiah.

Crossing the barriers with compassion   *Luke 7:1—17*

After addressing the crowds out in the countryside, Jesus returns to the towns of Galilee. Luke here includes two very different healing stories, the first of which makes much of the Gentile centurion's faith. This wealthy army officer is obviously highly thought of by the leaders of the local Jewish community. Luke alone tells us of his generosity in building the synagogue (compare Matthew 8:5—10). But the officer does not share the high opinion others have of him. Like Peter in an earlier story, he knows he does not deserve to be in the company of Jesus—though like Peter he too recognizes the authority of Jesus' word. The officer has the kind of faith Jesus looks for in Jew and Gentile alike.

The second story makes much of Jesus' compassion. This time he meets great sadness compounded by imminent destitution. The woman has not only lost her son, but her sole means of support. In raising the man and returning him to his mother, Jesus ensures that she too will live. The way Luke tells the story recalls the prophet Elijah, who also restored a son to his widowed mother (1 Kings 17:17—24).

Though these two stories are quite different, they have some common features. In each of them healing comes at the word of Jesus, and they both demonstrate Jesus' power to overcome barriers. He deals with people whose economic circumstances could not be further apart, showing compassion to rich and poor alike. The extravagant way he praises the officer's faith shows that Jew and Gentile can be brought together through faith in him. We are reminded of another important Gentile in Luke's story, Cornelius, who is also well-disposed towards the Jewish community (Acts 10:2), and who also comes to faith in Jesus. Luke, then, uses these two healing stories to assure his readers that their attempts to overcome the barriers between Jew and Gentile and rich and poor in the one Church are firmly rooted in the compassion of Jesus.

Moving beyond doubt   *Luke 7:18—35*

So far in the story, reaction to Jesus has tended to polarize between widespread acceptance and rejection. But these extremes are not the only ways to respond to the ministry of Jesus. It is possible to have honest doubts, as the question of the imprisoned John the Baptist shows. Perhaps John was rather disappointed at the reports of Jesus' healing and teaching. Maybe he expected the Messiah to place a heavier emphasis on divine judgment—John too has heard of Jesus' eating and drinking with sinners. The Baptist's uncertainty allows Luke to put the question of the significance of the story he is telling to its main character: 'Are you the one who is to come, or are we to expect someone else?'

Jesus asks John's disciples (and the readers of the Gospel) to place what they have seen and heard alongside words from passages in Isaiah (26:19; 35:6; 42:7; 61:1) which refer to the time of Israel's renewal. The answer to John's question is that *this* in Jesus' own ministry is what the Scriptures point to. John is being invited to move beyond the doubts of uncertainty and disappointment to the confidence of faith.

Jesus goes on to speak very highly of John's unshakeable honesty and rejection of luxury. He is indeed the greatest man who ever lived until now, and those who accepted his baptism recognized his vocation from God. He may not yet have the confidence that the future he longs for really is arriving in Jesus, but there is more that unites than divides them. They both polarize opinion along the same lines: tax-collectors and sinners for, lawyers and Pharisees against. They both find themselves criticized for refusing to dance to the tune of the powerful. And of course they are both rejected by the representatives of the rulers. But whereas doubt flourished in all the darkness of John's prison cell, faith remains strong all the way to the cross. This is the measure of Jesus' all-surpassing greatness (see the comments on 1:26–38).

Salvation for the doubly-oppressed   Luke 7:36–50

This story picks up the summary words in 7:29–30, by showing how different responses to the baptism of John are reproduced in the ministry of Jesus. We can imagine the scene at the house of Simon the Pharisee. Jesus is reclining at table, opposite his host: the unnamed woman has entered the dining room through the door customarily left open for beggars and admirers of guests. Jesus hardly moves during her weeping and anointing: as he waits for her to finish it is obvious from the host's face what he is thinking. Simon mistakenly believes that if Jesus really knew what sort of woman this was, he would see her exactly as the Pharisees do. To them, she is both a woman in a patriarchal society (which makes her by nature inferior to men), and a prostitute (and so a particularly unclean sinner). She is therefore *doubly* oppressed.

Jesus uses the story of the two debtors to interpret the behaviour of his host and the uninvited guest. She is a great and notorious sinner, who has come to realize through Jesus (either through hearing about his teaching, or by meeting him previously) how much God is willing to forgive her. Her extravagant greeting is a token of her great love for God in return for the mercy lavished on a doubly-oppressed person, now released from her heavy debt to God. Simon is a devoted and upright member of a respected religious group, one who would not dream of putting himself and the woman at the same distance from God. His merely polite way of receiving Jesus says more than words could about how much he thinks he owes God.

The scene at the meal table encapsulates Jesus' offer of salvation. Simply by addressing her in public, Jesus affords the woman the respect and honour due to one whom God loves. His words of forgiveness and peace constitute a powerful liberation for the woman and those like her. But as long as they see their debt in such small terms, Simon and his kind will continue to fulfil the words of verse 30 and deprive themselves of their place in God's purpose—the extravagant joy of salvation which comes through repentance and faith.

> When we read of God's special love for the poor, the disadvantaged and the outcast, we can often feel resentful or guilty if we are none of these. If God has a 'bias to the poor' (to borrow the title of a book by David Sheppard), does this mean that he does not love the rich? And do we have to exchange our advantage for disadvantage in order to receive God's blessing? Jesus shows that there is no virtue in being poor or disadvantaged, because his love is directed towards overcoming them. We need to ask how we can use whatever power we have to co-operate with the ways of divine love in a broken and divided world.
>
> Resentment and guilt can be crippling, but they can be overcome as we allow ourselves to be persuaded of the limitless reach of the love of God, and to be guided in its paths.

Salvation and the hard of hearing   *Luke 8:1–10*

The last chapter showed that even Gentiles are welcome in the restored
Israel Jesus is creating, and women have equal dignity with men. Jesus'
attitude to the unnamed woman in Simon's house is echoed here in the
mention of the women in verses 2–3. If twelve men symbolize the new
community, the women who accompany them are no less significant.
Some obviously provide financial support for the itinerant band. But
their presence reminds us again of Jesus' capacity to unsettle and
disturb, for many in Israel would have taken offence at the woman who
left her home to travel around in the company of a rabbi. Little wonder
that his ministry provokes division.

The parable of the sower takes up the different responses to Jesus. He
told the story originally to assure his disciples that however disappointed
they may be by the rejection of his ministry, it will always bring a rich
harvest when it falls into goods soil. Those who hear the gospel are
challenged about the way they receive 'the secrets of the kingdom of
God' which Jesus is revealing. He is making known the hidden purposes
of God, whose unlimited mercy is proving itself in the community of the
liberated, now appearing in Israel. But some will 'see and not understand': they miss the meaning of what Jesus is doing.

Perhaps we should not be surprised that something as challenging as
Jesus' vision of the kingdom of God meets with a positive response from
relatively few. We have seen that those who oppose Jesus in Luke's
story have much to lose: the self-importance which finds it hard to
accept that God has interests beyond local and national boundaries
(4:28–30), the privileged status which goes with the authority of
religious officialdom (5:21), the security of wealth against the poverty
in which the majority live (6:24–25), the power of gender in a
patriarchal society (7:39), and so on. And even those who stand to
gain most from Jesus will need to struggle if the gospel is to flourish, as
the following passage shows.

Allowing the gospel to flourish   *Luke 8:11–21*

The parable of the sower is the only one of Jesus' stories whose meaning
is explained—we are left to draw our own conclusions about the rest.
Although there is nothing inherently improbable in Jesus' interpreting
his teaching further to his disciples, many scholars think that the

explanation given here comes from the early Church. Certainly there are signs that Luke is interpreting the parable for his own audience. He is concerned that they should respond faithful to 'the word of God', an expression which he often uses in his second volume for the teaching of the apostles (Acts 6:7; 12:24; 13:49; 19:20). The Church's preaching may meet with a response which is strong on enthusiasm but weak on commitment—which suggests that the joy we have met in the story up to now is not enough on its own. The gospel will have to struggle against the pull of wealth and the pleasure this brings. Here is a rival to be reckoned with, if a mature human and Christian community is to grow (16:13).

What is said about the good soil reminds us of the sermon on the plain. The word of God produces a plentiful harvest only if it is allowed to grow in soil of an 'honest and good heart', where generous love overcomes evil and reaches out to the poor and undeserving (compare v. 15 with 6:28–38). In this sense those who have will be given more, and those without will lose even what they think they have. In the encounter between the word of God and the world he loves, nothing can be taken for granted. The power of evil and the struggle to overcome temptation call for that perseverance whose best example is Jesus. In him the word of God has yielded a rich harvest of the Spirit (4:1–13). The word bears fruit in those who are prepared to go on hearing and living by it (compare v. 21 with 6:46–49). In this way the family of Jesus fulfils the prophecy of Simeon, as the light of the gospel is seen by those who come into the Christian community (compare v. 16 with 2:32).

Authority over the power of chaos *Luke 8:22–39*

Since 5:12, the narrative has been interlaced with stories of Jesus' healing and blocks of teaching. Following the material on the parables, the rest of this chapter consists of four healing stories, which focus on the authority of Jesus over life-threatening powers. The first two share a common theme, in the power of Jesus over the forces of chaos. Behind the story of salvation from danger on the lake lie biblical expressions of God's rule over the sea (Psalms 46:3; 65:7; 89:9–10). Wind and waves symbolize those hostile forces which rage against life itself, and threaten it with the rule of chaos. As with demons earlier in the Gospel, these powers too are no match for the word of Jesus. Faith sees the power of God over his creation revealed in Jesus, who not only re-orders the life of Israel but also restores the created order, whose harmony is one of the hallmarks of the age of salvation (Isaiah 11:6–9; 35; 55:12–13).

The yet more dramatic story of the salvation of the Gerasene demoniac has Jesus on Gentile territory for the first time in Luke's Gospel, showing that the power at work in him is not limited by the boundaries of Israel. The distressed man has been forced to live among the tombs by demonic powers which have taken hold of him. His name—'Legion'—suggests that the source of his disorder is the pressure and strain inflicted on his environment by a foreign army of occupation. Four legions of Roman soldiers occupied the province of Syria, of which the man's homeland was a part. He had internalized those forces which threatened his community with chaos, and was now 'possessed' by powers which pushed him into the world of isolation and death. Their destructiveness can best be seen by what they do to the pigs. We should not think that Jesus has scant regard for animal life in liberating the man. It is possible that as Jesus fought to free the demoniac and to bring the calm of salvation to him, the pigs were terrified by the man's bizarre behaviour, and plunged to their death.

Jesus once again provokes division, as the local population ask him to leave, and the man begs him to stay with him. But there is good news for him to announce to Gentiles, just as the disciples are being prepared for their mission to Galilee.

Authority over the powers of death   *Luke 8:40–56*

Luke has been presenting Jesus as one who brings liberation by pitting himself against the various powers—principally religion and wealth—which structure society in Judea and Galilee. As Jesus has moved beyond the boundaries of his own country, so the range of these powers has extended, to include those natural forces which threaten the world with chaos, and the powers of the imperial army which bring distress and disintegration to an occupied people. Today's reading shows Jesus facing the ultimate life-threatening power, death. It has taken hold of the twelve-year-old daughter of Jairus, a prominent official of the synagogue whose publicly acknowledged faith in Jesus at last breaks the pattern of official religious opposition. But before Jesus can struggle through the crowds to reach her, he encounters an example of living death, in the unnamed woman who has been suffering from an incurable continuous bleeding for the same twelve years. To add to her other burdens, she is permanently unclean (see Leviticus 15:19–30), an outcast deprived of normal human contact.

Her desperation—or is it courage?—in publicly seeking out Jesus is met with an apparent attempt to embarrass her before the crowds. His motive is to lead her from the superstition and fear which allow her to touch only his coat, to the faith which openly acknowledges God as the source of her healing. Not only is her illness cured, she is also freed from the excluding power of the death she has carried within her. To this now restored daughter of Israel, faith brings the salvation and peace which another woman in the Gospel also received (7:50).

Meanwhile the daughter of Jairus lingers in the grip of death. Delay in order to deal with one manifestation of death's power only realizes Jairus' worst fears, but Jesus' appeal for faith rests on what Jairus has just seen. His defiant words to the mourners ('she is not dead, but asleep') echo the early Christian faith that the departed are asleep in the Lord (see 1 Thessalonians 4:13), waiting for the full and final revelation of his victory. The power of life over death in Jesus even extends to his encouraging the girl's parents to feed her.

Mission: extending the work of liberation   *Luke 9:1–10*

A certain ambivalence has so far marked Jesus' attitude to spreading the news about him. The demons are silenced (4:35), and the healed are told to keep quiet (5:14; 8:56), but then the former demoniac is positively encouraged to tell of what God has done for him in the Gentile world to which he belongs (8:39). Jesus is understandably anxious to avoid misleading the Galilean crowds about the kind of messianic work he is doing. He does not want the wrong sort of expectations to fasten onto him—though his attempts at silencing people appear to be futile (4:37; 5:15). Now Jesus deliberately sends the twelve disciples out with the express intention of extending his work. Ambivalence is set aside, because the Twelve have been with him for most of the story of the work in Galilee. They, the nucleus of the restored people of God, know the secrets of the kingdom, and can therefore be trusted with the task of extending it. They are aware that Jesus is no mere worker of miracles; neither is his attention directed towards a political struggle against the Roman occupying forces.

'Preaching the kingdom of God' and 'healing' are shorthand expressions for a project of liberation whose goal is the renewal of God's people.

The Twelve are given authority for work which is more than preaching. But the content of the 'more' is not merely supernatural signs and wonders associated with physical cures and exorcism. In the ministry of Jesus, 'healing' extends beyond the body to the re-ordering of relationships, with God and within society. The mission of the Twelve is therefore an extension of the all-embracing salvation which Jesus brings. In their journeys from village to village, they are to live by faith, accepting hospitality where it is offered and travelling light. Those who reject them place themselves outside the people of God, symbolized by the disciples' shaking the dust from their feet.

Herod's reaction to the work of the kingdom once again allows Luke to raise the fundamental question about Jesus: 'Who is this?' Opponents and disciples alike have already asked it (5:2; 8:25), and Luke's hints at a reply (7:16–17, 39) leave us waiting for something more definitive than the hearsay opinion which Herod has heard.

The kingdom of God: feeding the hungry   *Luke 9:11–17*

The return of the Twelve brings the need for rest, but Jesus is willing to talk further about the kingdom and to heal those who have perhaps been drawn to him through the apostles' mission. As the day wears on, the disciples reveal their indifference and powerlessness. By contrast, Jesus is so concerned about the crowd's hunger that he takes steps to alleviate it.

The feeding of the five thousand is the only 'miracle story' common to all four Gospels, although each evangelist tells the story in his own way. In the background is Moses' feeding the people of Israel with manna in the wilderness (Exodus 16), and Elisha's feeding one hundred men with twenty barley loaves, after which some was left over (2 Kings 4:42–44). Luke provides something of an answer to the question about Jesus which immediately precedes this story. Jesus stands in the line of the great leaders and prophets of God's people, a view Luke has expressed earlier in the Gospel in 4:18–19 and 7:16–17.

But Luke sees Jesus as more than a prophet. In the birth stories he is the 'son of God' and 'Christ the Lord'. At his baptism he is anointed by the Spirit of God. In the synagogue he sees himself in the prophetic passage about the work of the messianic agent of God's rule, which extends over Israel and all creation. Jews were fond of picturing the age when God's rule would finally be established as a banquet (Isaiah 25:6–8). Jesus' habit of eating both with the respectable and outcasts is a sign of the coming age of salvation (6:21; 14:16–24). So the feeding of the great crowd that he welcomes, teaches and heals can be interpreted as a foretaste of the coming kingdom of God, which Jesus is beginning to establish.

But there is still more in this feeding. We can hardly miss the connection between Jesus' taking, blessing, breaking and distributing the loaves and fish and his actions at the last supper (22:19–20). If Jesus is the prophet-Messiah who brings about the kingly rule of God, he does so as one whose power is revealed in service (22:27), and who is prepared to give his life for the liberation which God's kingdom brings.

The healing stories in the latter half of chapter 8 continue to make the point that for Jesus, healing was always more than physical cure, because he was concerned to encourage faith in God and communion among people. What is often missing in the Church's rediscovery of the healing ministry is the recognition that illness is not merely to do with sick individuals but with disease in society. To cure the person without challenging the diseased environment is to fall short of the breadth of healing required, a point made in the recent book by Stephen Pattison, Alive and Kicking, SCM Press.

If we are right to attribute his distress to the pressures of an occupying army, the story of the Gerasene demoniac is a good example of the healing of an individual which does not leave the environment from which he came untouched. In sending him back home to declare what God had done for him, Jesus ensured that the challenge of God's kingdom was heard where distress was being caused. Our prayers for healing need to be informed by the wider view of disease. What might it mean to work for healing of those who are most vulnerable in our society? Like the Twelve sent out by Jesus, we too are called to be agents of God's healing kingdom amidst the broken lives and homes, and in a diseased and divided world.

The Messiah: rejection and vindication

The decisive question about Jesus is at last answered, by one of the Twelve. Jesus reveals the path his messianic vocation will follow, and as he directs himself and his followers towards Jerusalem, the urgency of his mission intensifies.

Jesus does not allow his disciples to be content with repeating the popular opinion that had been reported to Herod. Peter's confession echoes the angelic announcements and prophetic responses at the beginning of the Gospel (1:31–35; 1:68–75). But the need for circumspection remains, because Jesus will carry out his messianic work in a surprising way. Although he is prepared to see himself as Messiah, he prefers the enigmatic language of the 'Son of Man', because the association of messiahship with military victory can so easily mislead those whose expectations he raises. In verse 18 Luke implies that Jesus reached his own understanding of his vocation through prayer. We can imagine Jesus' meditating on the course of his ministry in the light of the Scriptures, to determine what *must* happen to the Son of man, according to the will of God.

It may well be that Jesus found Daniel 7 particularly helpful. In the prophet's vision of God's throne (vv. 9–10), 'one like a son of man' comes on the clouds of heaven. The 'Ancient of Days' (God) gives him everlasting rule over the beasts, who represent the enemies of God's people. We later learn that the 'one like a son of man' stands for 'the saints of the Most High God', who have been suffering under the rule of the beasts. But now their enemies are defeated, and they are vindicated (vv. 25–27). Jesus can see himself as this 'son of man' figure, facing suffering and rejection from those who oppose his vision of God's kingdom. But he believes that he and his cause will ultimately triumph, because God is faithful to the anointed one who always obeys his will.

Jesus had earlier given the Twelve a share in his messianic power and authority before sending them out to preach and heal. Here he tells them that as the nucleus of the new people of God they will also be caught up in the suffering of the Son of Man. But if discipleship cannot be equated with triumphalism, neither is it the cause for morbid pessimism. Those who go the way of Jesus 'daily' (Luke adds this in verse 23 to the version of the saying in Mark and Matthew) by abandoning all other sources of security will have the joy of seeing the kingdom of God taking shape around them (17:21), and share in the vindication of Jesus' mission.

The Messiah: listen to God's chosen Son   *Luke 9:28–36*

In the first three Gospels, the story of Jesus' transfiguration is clearly linked with Peter's confession and Jesus' anticipation of his suffering and rejection. Three details in Luke's account are not found elsewhere. First, he has Jesus at prayer. Together with the earlier reference to Jesus' praying in verse 18, this suggests that Luke saw the period of Jesus' ministry as one of intense inner struggle. As at the time of his baptism, he needs to be in prayer because decisive issues which affect the course of his ministry are at stake. Evidently Jesus enters such a depth of prayer that heaven and earth are united: his face and clothes reflect the glory of God's dwelling-place, and he sees two figures whom popular belief held to have gone straight to heaven after death, Moses and Elijah.

Second, Luke has Jesus speaking with Moses and Elijah about what lay ahead of him in Jerusalem. They are discussing his *exodus*, variously translated as 'departure' or 'passing' in verse 31. We have already been warned that the Jerusalem authorities will be instrumental in Jesus' death. Here we are told that in Jerusalem, Jesus will accomplish an act of liberation which will seal the freedom of the people of God and defeat his enemies. What happens in the holy city will bring his whole ministry to fulfilment.

Third, Luke refers to the disciples' sleep. Peter, John and James also fall asleep in Gethsemane (22:45). Here, they wake up just in time to be drawn into Jesus' vision. Their suggestion about building shelters perhaps indicates a desire to prolong the glorious experience they have just begun to enjoy. But the real point of the transfiguration is given by the words of the voice which comes from the cloud and addresses the three tired disciples. They should listen to the 'chosen son' of God, especially what he has been saying about the outcome of his messianic work (Jesus is also referred to as God's 'chosen one' in 23:35, when he is on the cross). In all that lies ahead of them, they will need to be confident that Jesus really is pursing the will of his Father.

The Son of Man: the shock
waves of his destiny   *Luke 9:37–50*

Why could not the disciples drive the unclean spirit out of the boy? They
have, after all, been given power and authority over all devils (see 9:1).
Jesus' impatient outburst suggests that they have lost some of the faith
they once had. But where their ability to channel the power of Jesus is
blocked, the authority of his word is undiminished. It may well be that
what Jesus has been saying about the necessity of his suffering is
responsible for overwhelming the disciples' faith by misunderstanding
and fear. They are no longer able to take in what he says about his destiny;
neither do they feel sufficiently confident to pursue the matter further.

Where Jesus had spoken earlier about renunciation and selfgiving as
the characteristics of the way of the Son of Man and his community, now
the disciples' behaviour begins to display the very opposite, as talk about
greatness and rank intrudes. Jesus has to recall them to the inversion of
worldly values which the kingdom of God announces and realizes (1:46–
55; 6:20–23). By placing a child next to him, he says that to welcome
one like this, who is weak and insignificant in the eyes of the world, is to
welcome him, which is to welcome God. If a child symbolizes the
Messiah, the least can be the greatest, and all ideas of rank are turned on
their head.

When the faith of the disciples is disturbed by the shock waves of
messianic suffering, they can very easily resort to jealousy and self-
protection. The ministry of one who is not part of the 'in-group' ('we
forbade him, because he does not follow with us'—v. 49) is easy prey for
the insecure. Here the disciples behave like Jesus' opponents, and he has
to remind them of what he says repeatedly to scribes and Pharisees: the
action of God is not restricted to what they consider to be the 'proper
channels'.

—— THE JOURNEY TO JERUSALEM ——

Jesus now shifts his attention away from the towns and cities of
Galilee towards Jerusalem. The whole of this section of the Gospel
tells the story as though Jesus were on a journey from Galilee to the
capital city, where the forces of opposition will intensify, and bring
about his death. Problems with geographical detail suggest that

Luke is responsible for a rather artificial construction, in which largely teaching material is placed in the context of Jesus' final journey. On the road to Jerusalem, he instructs his followers about the demands of the kingdom, all the while challenging those who oppose him to respond to the crisis his ministry provokes before it is too late.

Discipleship: the cost of the kingdom   *Luke 9:51–62*

Jesus is heading for the place where he is to be 'taken up'. The Elijah theme surfaces once more (see 2 Kings 2:9–11), but Jesus does not ascend to heaven in a fiery chariot. For him, the journey which culminates in his ascension goes by way of a final confrontation with the powers which govern Jerusalem, as we have already been told. What is at stake is his vision of God's kingly rule, which brings about the liberation of Israel. The opposition he has already met in Galilee (see especially 5:17—6:11) will only intensify as he nears his final destination. But he has already resolved to suffer all that his enemies can do to him, such is his faith in God who has called him and anointed him.

On the way to Jerusalem, Jesus and his disciples pass through Samaria. Perhaps this is yet another instance of his desire to break down barriers (10:29–37; 17:11–19), but this time he is rejected by those to whom he seeks to reach out. The messengers catch something of the age-old enmity between Jew and Samaritan, which was directed especially at Jewish pilgrims to the temple in Jerusalem. Samaritans had their own rival shrine on Mount Gerizim. Where James and John want to emulate Elijah in 2 Kings 1:10, Jesus prefers to live by his own teaching (6:27–35). Disciples with their faces set towards Jerusalem must find ways of overcoming the hatred they will encounter at the journey's end.

More words on discipleship conclude this section. Those who accompany Jesus must renounce their attachments to property and family, even where religious duty weighs heavily upon them (as in the case of burying one's father). Single-minded commitment to the kingdom of God must take priority over everything else for those in Jesus' itinerant band. The message of the sermon on the plain is found in these verses; even disciples who do not follow Jesus to the cross in a literal sense must re-order their whole lives around the values of the kingdom of God.

Discipleship: mission in the wider world *Luke 10:1–16*

The participation of the disciples in Jesus' work has been in the air ever since the promise to Simon Peter in 5:10, that he would be 'catching people'. Jesus has called twelve of his disciples to be 'apostles' (6:13)— the word means 'one who is sent'—and later he sent them to preach and heal in Galilee (9:2). Jesus also sent a missionary into Gentile territory—the Gerasene demoniac whom he healed was told to spread the news of what God has done for him (8:39). And he sent messengers into a Samaritan village, ostensibly to arrange accommodation, though to Luke it may well have been more significant (9:52). As is abundantly clear in the Acts of the Apostles, Luke is intent on giving an account of the Church's worldwide mission, which, according to the account of the appointment of a large number of missionary agents, has its foundation in the ministry of Jesus. In Genesis 10 there are seventy (seventy-two in the Greek Bible) nations in the world. So Jesus' sending the seventy (-two) symbolizes the universal reach of God's salvation: what is happening within the bounds of Israel is God's intention for the whole world.

The instructions here are similar to those in Matthew 10 (addressed to the Twelve), and develop further the material in 9:1–6. The passage reads like a list of guidelines for missionaries. Mission is fed by prayer and dependence on God. The task is urgent, because the harvest is ready. Missionaries represent the one who sends them, so their work will meet with welcome and also rejection. It will bring division between those who are blessed by the peace of the kingdom and those who come under its judgment. It is interesting to observe that the missionaries are to accept hospitality where it is offered, eating whatever is set before them. Luke hints at one of his major concerns in Acts, the place of the Jewish food laws (see the account of the conversion of the gentile Cornelius in Acts 10–11).

Why did Jesus condemn Chorazin, Bethsaida and Capernaum, which were all prosperous lakeside towns? Perhaps he was seen as a threat to the comfortable lifestyle of their people, and the religious attitudes which supported it. The universal mission of the kingdom leaves no part of life untouched.

Discipleship: the gift and privilege of mission

Just as the Twelve gave Jesus a report of what had happened when he sent them out, so here the seventy (-two) tell Jesus of their success over the powers of evil. What they have seen Jesus do they now do in his name. Not surprisingly he is encouraged by their news, and he tells them about a vision he has seen. Talk of 'Satan falling like lightning from heaven' sounds strange to us. It relies on the belief that heaven and earth are two sides of the same reality. Everything on earth has its counterpart in heaven; for all that happens in the sensory world of human history, there is a corresponding event in the heavenly realm. The book of Revelation is shot through with this way of interpreting reality. Jesus speaks, then, of his prophetic vision of the final victory over Satan, whose fall from heaven will surely be matched by his defeat on earth. Jesus' own victory over temptation in 4:1–13, the authority of his word over demons, and now the success of the disciples are the evidence on which his vision rests.

Jesus goes on to guard the disciples against the intoxication caused by power. Like the other forms of power (religious, economic, political) we have met in the Gospel, power over evil can easily be corrupted. The disciples are only human, and they can be tempted to view their power as an end in itself. What is far more important, says Jesus, is that they recognize that they belong to God, because their names are written in heaven. They are unlikely agents of God's universal purposes, because they are more like uneducated children than clever people. What they have participated in has come as a gift to them. They are indeed privileged to see the secret purposes of God finally being revealed. So a proper humility will prevent their success from deluding them about their own status and importance.

If Jesus' vision of victory over evil draws back the curtain which separates earth and heaven, then his joyful utterance in verses 21–22 opens up something of the mystery of his own person. This man of prayer and the Holy Spirit, who announces and establishes liberation in Israel, knows and is known by God, as a son to his father. If Jesus has been given special privilege and responsibility, his disciples are entirely dependent on him and his Father for their place in the work of salvation.

> *Success is intoxicating. Who can blame Jesus' disciples for being so swept along by his ministry that they found talk of his Passion hard to take? It is just as easy for the Church today to conform to a success-oriented society, to measure faithfulness by effectiveness, and to short-circuit the cost of discipleship. The model for our faith is always Jesus' relationship to his Father. Obedience means refusing to live by the indicators of success we find around us, and trusting instead in God's testimony to his own Son.*

Discipleship: the practice of mercy   *Luke 10:25—37*

The parable of the good Samaritan is perhaps the best known of all Jesus' stories. The lawyer wants to test Jesus' ability to interpret Scripture in order to define the will of God. His question could be paraphrased as: 'How can I be sure of having a place in God's people when the new age of the kingdom of God finally arrives?' The reply Jesus draws out of him summarizes the intention of the whole Law as the love of God and neighbour (Deuteronomy 6:5; Leviticus 19:18)—the one is inseparable from the other. According to Jesus, membership of the people of God in the age to come is guaranteed by behaviour now: 'do this and you shall live'. The lawyer pursues the matter further, because he wants to know Jesus' opinion on a hotly-debated issue in legal circles. His second question could be paraphrased as: 'How do I recognize those who are also members of the people of God?' In reply, Jesus tells his now familiar story.

The parable relies on well-worn stereotypes: priest and Levite as devoted observers of the requirements of the Law, the mixed-race Samaritan as one who lies outside the people of God. The behaviour of the priest and Levite is entirely in keeping with the letter of Scripture: the wounded man might be dead for all they know, and touching a corpse brings defilement (Numbers 19:11ff). At the very least, helping the man would interfere with religious duties in Jerusalem. The Samaritan is governed by no such scruples. Ignorant of, or indifferent to, these Scriptures, the nationality of the wounded man is of no concern to him. All that matters is that he is cared for.

By making a Samaritan the hero of this story, Jesus shatters the lawyer's religious and social values. He and his kind are asking the wrong question: not 'Who is my neighbour?' but 'How can I prove myself a neighbour?' would be more appropriate. The answer lies in the practice of mercy, which is not restricted by the barriers of nationality, religious purity, or even friendship (compare 6:28–36). Jesus highlights a paradox: those who are preoccupied with the letter of Scripture may find themselves outside the people of God, because they are deaf to his word.

Discipleship: listening to the word of the Lord
Luke 10:38–42

If the parable of the good Samaritan interprets 'you shall love your neighbour as yourself', then the story of Martha and Mary may well give the sense of 'love the Lord your God with all your heart, soul, strength and mind'. If love of neighbour shows itself in the Samaritan's neighbourliness, love of God is seen in Mary's attentiveness. The Samaritan's love for his neighbour brings him to the body of a half-dead man: Mary's love for God sets her at the feet of Jesus. Here she adopts the characteristic attitude of a disciple before her teacher.

Is Martha's complaint about Mary justified? After all, she is left with a meal to prepare, and Mary selfishly allows her to get on with it. Jesus' reply suggests that this is one of those occasions when serving him by being busy is inappropriate. He is not exalting the contemplative over the activist, neither is he saying that true disciples leave others to do the menial tasks! He does reckon, however, that Martha is being distracted by her understandable anxiety to be hospitable. She who had welcomed Jesus into her home in the first place was now trying to honour him by an excessive amount of preparation for a meal. He seeks to discourage her from going to so much trouble—a simple meal would be quite sufficient. Mary has chosen the 'one thing that is necessary', which is to take advantage of the opportunity to listen to the Lord's teaching. Jesus refuses to deprive her of that by heeding to her sister's complaint.

'Love of God' requires the disciples of Jesus to be attentive to his teaching. Only then can 'love of neighbour' be delivered from 'love of one's own kind', or 'love for those who can love in return' (see 6:28–36 again). Those who serve Jesus by putting love into practice must find the opportunity to be attentive to him within their busy lives. They can only meet God in the needs of others if they also meet him in the words of Jesus and in the place of prayer.

How can we discover the will of God? How do we know what pleases him? The lawyer's question in 10:25 is crucial for all of us. Yet however much we depend on the Bible, Jesus suggests that even this is not enough. Like the rules of religion, the Bible can sometimes deafen us to the word of God, especially when we become preoccupied with the 'letter' of its teaching. According to Jesus there is another way to discover God's will and purpose. It is carried out wherever, and by whoever, compassion is being exercised. Whenever people act as neighbours and cross over to help the needy, God's will is done.

To say this is not to go soft on truth. Living by compassion led Jesus to the place where God's glory is most clearly revealed— the cross. If we want to please God, we need to listen to Jesus and be people of compassion—which means being prepared to follow him on the way to the cross. These words are hard, but at the same time they are radically life-giving and liberating. The will of God brings freedom and hope to the world. To live by compassion is to enter into the joy of Easter.

Discipleship: praying with confidence   *Luke 11:1–13*

The example of Jesus as a man of prayer has by now made such an impression on his disciples that they ask him to teach them to pray. Luke's version of the Lord's Prayer is different from the longer version found in Matthew 6:9–13. In Matthew Jesus offers a crisp and concise prayer as an example of the kind of prayer which contrasts with the verbosity of Gentile prayers: 'pray like this . . .' Luke provides a model prayer for the Christian community to use: 'when you pray, say . . .' Both versions of the prayer start with an intimate address to God as 'Father'. Jesus introduces his disciples into his own intimate relationship with the Father, expressed in 10:21–22. 'Each time of prayer is an attempt to open ourselves more fully to that direct communion with the Father which Jesus knew, and to realize more deeply our relationship to him as adult sons and daughters' (J.V. Taylor, *The Go-Between God*, page 234).

The intimate address is followed immediately by the request that God's name (his nature and purpose) be seen for what it is: God will be reverenced when the kingdom which has begun to appear in Jesus' ministry comes in all its fullness. Three petitions then echo the needs of the Christian community: for the daily gift of no more than enough to eat (note the hostility to accumulated possessions in 12:16–21); for the gift of forgiveness which shows itself in the readiness to forgive debtors (does Luke want his readers to notice the economic nuances of forgiveness? See 6:34–35); and for strength to remain faithful to the gospel by overcoming temptation.

Luke then adds further teaching on prayer. In the parable, the destitute host's friend will supply what he needs, not least because the poor man is not ashamed to ask. If a friend is prepared to overcome his reluctance to disturb his family in order to be generous at midnight, how much more will God be generous to those who pray! The same message is found in verses 11–13. Disciples can therefore be confident in prayer—not that God will always give them what they ask for, but that they will never ask, seek or knock in vain. His most characteristic gift is the Holy Spirit which Jesus received while at prayer (3:21). In the gift of the Spirit to the disciples as to Jesus, the request that 'your kingdom come' begins to be answered.

Resistance: does Jesus work for the devil? *Luke 11:14–28*

Since Jesus began his journey to Jerusalem in 9:51, the talk has all been of discipleship, living according to the demands of God's kingdom. Now Jesus begins to challenge those who oppose him to respond to the crisis provoked by his ministry before it is too late.

In verse 15 we meet people who, while they cannot deny that Jesus teaches and heals with authority, refuse to accept that its source lies in God. They accuse him of casting out demons by the power of black magic, of working for the devil. For his part, Jesus cannot see how their argument can possibly make sense. If the powers of evil were fighting one another, their grip on the world would soon collapse—clearly this has not happened. Though Jesus is convinced that the devil's days are numbered (10:18), the struggle against evil is not yet over. Jesus then claims that his detractors are being inconsistent. After all, he is not the only exorcist they know of—others too ('your sons') draw on the power of God to overcome evil. Why then should *he* be singled out and his work smeared in this way? In his exorcisms, Jesus claims to use the power of the 'finger of God' (Exodus 8:19; Psalm 8:3). His healing work is like an invading army of liberation, attacking the fortress of the evil one with the kingly rule of God, and releasing what the enemy has held captive. In this struggle, no one can remain neutral: one is either for or against Jesus and the work he is doing. But as verses 24–28 make clear, exorcism alone is not enough to establish freedom. Those released from the grip of evil must fill their newly 'swept and tidied' lives with the word of God (like Mary in 10:39) and the Holy Spirit which comes through prayer (11:13).

The imagery of a struggle between God and the devil, good and evil, may suggest a rather black-and-white picture of life. Yet we often find it hard to pinpoint the absolutes of good or evil: we are aware of much that is coloured by the ambiguous shades of grey. Jesus' point here, though, is that the rule of God *does* have real enemies. The powers of evil never abandon their grip without a struggle; so they must be identified and fought, in the name of God's kingdom. In this work of liberation, neutrality is impossible.

Resistance: the demand for unambiguous proof
Luke 11:29–36

Jesus refers those who demand 'signs'—unambiguous proof of the source of his authority (vv. 16, 29)—to the Scriptures. Jonah was called to denounce the wickedness of the great city of Nineveh. When he eventually fulfilled his commission, the (Gentile) Ninevites believed him and repented (Jonah 3). Likewise the (Gentile) Queen of Sheba was drawn to the God-given wisdom of Solomon (1 Kings 10:1–10). Jesus maintains that Gentiles who possess the repentance Israel lacks will condemn them on the day of judgment—which is a complete reversal of traditional Jewish belief. According to verse 30, the only sign Jesus is prepared to give is the Jonah-like sign of the Son of Man. His own call to repentance should be enough, because the Spirit-endowed agent of the kingdom of God is greater than either Jonah or Solomon. If Gentiles turned to God through them, how much more should Israel repent through the Son of Man!

For Jesus, the hallmarks of repentance are faith and love. Faith is prepared to trust in the good intentions of God by living in the dependency of attentiveness (10:39) and prayer (11:1–13). Faith believes in the power of God over evil on the basis of the love which overcomes evil (see once more 6:28–39). Jesus always runs the risk of being misunderstood, because he defies even those ways of checking for validity and truth which his own people have cherished in their religious tradition. For him, the will of the one whose chief quality is generous love for the undeserving (6:35) is the sole benchmark of truth. This suggests that the liberating power of Jesus over evil cannot be subjected to demands for proof. The Spirit which is in Jesus is the spirit of compassion and mercy, which can be neither defined nor confined by legal or religious or family or national obligations. His power is not naked and unambiguous, because it is characterized by love, which seeks to evoke faith without ever being able to compel it. The images in verses 33–36 suggest that the assurance and light sought by demands for unambiguous proof come only by allowing the eye to focus clearly, with faith and love, on the lamp of Jesus and his gospel.

Resistance: the demand
for obedience to rules   *Luke 11:37–54*

Jesus has encountered resistance from unnamed sources in the last two readings. This time we are in no doubt as to his opponents. In 5:30 and 7:39 he has already angered the more conservative Pharisees by his attitudes to those whom they regard with contempt, and in 6:1–11 he has clashed with them over the Sabbath law. Here Jesus finds their attitudes to the Law and their practice of faith petty, burdensome and hypocritical.

Where the Pharisees are more concerned with a washing which merely symbolizes purity, Jesus is more interested in the purity of the heart. The religious are easily submerged by trivialities—such as tithes on garden herbs—at the expense of the more important issues. But then, how can they care about justice and the love of God, when they are so full of greed? They delude themselves into thinking that others should enter into their self-satisfaction. They fail to realize that their unwashed and untithed hearts contaminate those whom they ought to be encouraging in the practice of justice and love.

The Pharisees' lawyers have made religion burdensome, not liberating. They themselves lift not a finger to help those whom they oppress with their religious rules. Their hypocrisy is shown in the honour they pay to the tombs of the very prophets whom they would be the first to condemn—as their attitude to the prophet Jesus reveals. By concentrating so much on what is trivial and secondary, they fail in their responsibility to unlock the meaning of Scripture and bring knowledge

229

of God both to themselves and to the people at large. So Jesus gives the present generation of Israel's religious leaders a choice: they must either break with the past, or face the consequences of former generations' resistance to God's messengers—Scripture's martyrs, beginning with Abel (Genesis 4:8) and ending with Zechariah (2 Chronicles 24:22).

Critical though Jesus is here, he speaks out of a genuine concern to welcome even his opponents into the renewed people of God. In verse 37 we see that he is just as prepared to eat with Pharisees as with tax-collectors and sinners. But those with religious power in Israel find the repentance which Jesus demands virtually impossible. As the passage ends, opposition to him seems to be mounting—which is all the more ominous, because now he is on the road to Jerusalem.

Faith, fear and opposition   *Luke 12:1–12*

The next group of readings, down to 13:21, are intended to encourage the disciples of Jesus to live faithfully and responsibly in the face of various pressures and challenges. In this first passage Luke has brought together a number of Jesus' sayings which occur in other circumstances elsewhere in the Gospels. There is a common thread—how those who live by the gospel are to cope with the opposition it provokes. Jesus begins by warning against the pretence typified by those Pharisees who resist him. Like yeast, its influence is out of all proportion to its size. However attractive it may be for frightened disciples to hide their allegiance to Jesus and his cause when other authorities put pressure on them, such deceptiveness does not fool God. Ultimately it will be exposed for what it is.

According to Jesus, there is a healthy fear of God which serves as a great resource when disciples are afraid of the gospel's opponents: 'He is the one to fear'—but not as one who threatens! If Jesus' followers can entrust their weakness, anxiety and insecurity to the one who remembers the sparrows and counts every strand of hair on the head, they can stand against all who defy the gospel. More than that, they know that the one whom they confess will vindicate them on the day of judgment. Even now, they can rely on the resources of the Holy Spirit (with v. 12 compare 11:13). Jesus' words here would have brought great encouragement to Christian Jews among Luke's first readers. They were having to run the gauntlet of conservative Jewish opposition, as members of a church in which Jews and Gentiles ate together (Acts 11:1–3).

230

There is a sharp challenge, though, in Jesus' words. To deny him and his gospel, or to blaspheme against the Holy Spirit by failing to identify with what God is doing in the mission of Jesus, is to risk ultimate rejection (with vv. 9, 10 compare 9:26). In both cases the repentance (turning to God) which receives God's forgiveness is impossible. So the benevolence of God, the gift of his Spirit and the prospect of judgment encourage the followers of Jesus not to lose their nerve in the face of opposition to the very principles of the gospel.

Faith, fear and wealth   *Luke 12:13–34*

In the previous reading, Jesus addressed disciples who were tempted to retreat from any public expression of the gospel. Here he speaks to those whose search for security leads them either to hoard what wealth they have or to worry about what they lack. Jesus calls his followers to base their attitudes to wealth on faith in God rather than fear. The mistake of the rich man in the parable is not success or enjoyment, but selfishness and greed. Material excess can become a substitute for God, a form of security which invites the trust which should be reserved for him alone. The rich man's greedy faith in possessions discourages him from sharing his surplus. He is a fool, because the object of his faith has no ultimate value.

If the rich are not to allow their anxiety for security to seduce them into greed and selfishness, those who have less must not worry about food and clothing. Jesus' words in verses 22–34 were probably spoken originally to the 'little flock' of disciples who followed him around Palestine and quite literally had to live off the generosity of others (8:3; 9:3–4; 10:4–8). The God whose benevolence feeds the birds and clothes the flowers with a beauty beyond human making has ways of meeting the mundane needs of those who live for his kingdom. Faith, then, overcomes fear, whether it is wealth or lack of it which worries the followers of Jesus.

In giving these words of Jesus a wider airing, Luke has another audience in mind. In his own church there are rich and poor Christians. In the Sermon on the Plain we read of his concern that the rich should be generous towards the poor and undeserving, after the example of divine mercy (6:30–38). The Christian community lives by the values of the kingdom; rich in the sight of God (v. 21), its treasure is in heaven (v. 33). So hard-pressed Christians can be free from anxiety about the basic necessities of life, because their richer brothers and sisters are not so foolish as to hoard what surplus they have. In a world in which there are still rich and poor, and ever more inducements to live by faith in possessions, the teaching of Jesus here has certainly not lost its force.

Motivation for faithful living   Luke 12:35–48

The last two readings have been full of motivation for faithful discipleship, not least in their insistence on trust in the resources of God's kindness and the gift of the Holy Spirit. But there has been another side: God is the judge of all human endeavour (vv. 2–3, 5, 20), and his benevolence must not be taken for granted. Human beings must reckon ultimately with God, and this also motivates life in the present. An open loyalty to Jesus and the values of the kingdom provides the measure against which his followers will be judged.

The judgment theme dominates this passage. Jesus uses the parables of the master and the burglar to speak of the crisis which his ministry provokes for Israel (see further 12:49–59). Will the disciples be on the alert, ready for the coming judgment? As the early Christians reread these stories, they reinterpreted them in terms of another crisis—the coming of Jesus the Son of Man as judge. Though they do not know precisely when he will come, his followers must be ready.

Peter's question in verse 41 draws out the implications of Jesus' injunctions for church leaders, 'stewards whom the master will place over his household' (with v. 42 compare Acts 20:28, 31). In that sacred trust which they have been given, they are to be alert by carrying out the master's will faithfully. Those who shirk their responsibilities will be severely judged. Note the reference to 'food' in verse 42. In their concern for the ordering of the community's affairs, the church's leaders should have a particular interest in the well-being of poor (Acts 4:32–37; 6:1–6).

God's judgment, then, is a force to be reckoned with. It is never arbitrary, because according to verse 47, its yardstick is 'what the master wants'—that is, the vision of the kingdom of God which Jesus has entrusted to his followers. God's judgment is not meant to frighten us into subservience, but to alert us to the responsibility of taking seriously his faith in us.

Understand what is going on!   Luke 12:49–59

The note of judgment in the last passage is intensified in this one. Fire is a common image of judgment in the Bible. In 3:16–17, we were told that John the Baptist had looked forward to one who would 'baptize with the Holy Spirit and fire', judging and purging the people of God. Evidently Jesus also sees his ministry in these terms—the fire of divine judgment is not yet blazing, but it soon will be. It has been kindled in the division which he has provoked in Israel. As God's judgment approaches, so the most basic social relationships are torn apart (with vv. 52–53 compare Micah 7:4–7). Jesus' ministry has a way of bringing out into the open what some would rather keep secret. Luke has often shown us how fragile harmony is shattered as Jesus exposes the thoughts and attitudes of those whose vested interests run counter to God's kingdom.

Jesus calls on the crowds to discern the significance of the times in which they live. They should use the wisdom which enables them to read the weather or keeps them from the debtor's prison to interpret what is happening to the nation. By creating a new order in Israel, Jesus is trying to prevent a headlong rush towards national disaster. Concern for those on the margins of society, renunciation of violence, restoration of Israel as one people, an end to nationalistic pride—all these will be the fruit of listening to Jesus and learning to live humbly before the one whose mercy is without limit. On the basis of his faith, and his own reading of the signs of the times, Jesus believes that if he and his cause are rejected, the nation's doom is assured.

If Jesus' ministry exacts a high price from the nation, it is no less costly for him. As he journeys towards the heart of Jewish life in Jerusalem, he faces the prospect of being swept aside by a torrent of suffering and death. Luke's readers know the outcome of Jesus' ministry. His rejection, execution and resurrection were followed about forty years later by the Romans' destruction of Jerusalem. In the meantime, the fire of the Holy Spirit was freeing the Israel of the Church from nationalistic and racial pride, social and economic division, and hatred of Rome. There can be little doubt that the liberating work of the same Spirit is by no means finished.

Repent while there is still time! *Luke 13:1–9*

In two nearby passages, Jesus has twice warned about hypocrisy (12:1, 56). Though the word is not mentioned here, the attitude is certainly in view. The hypocrite prefers to believe that his or her life really is as it appears to the outside world. It is often difficult, if not impossible, to shatter this illusion, because it entails breaking through what can be a carefully constructed system of defences and deceptions. Sometimes suffering or tragedy manages to pierce the armour, and force the hypocrite to come to terms with the truth about himself. But when disaster befalls others, the illusions on which hypocrisy thrives can only be reinforced. Those whom it avoids have no need to change their ways or attitudes, because they interpret the fact that they have been spared as proof of their moral uprightness.

The strident call of Jesus to repentance—an about-turn in self-understanding, values, way of life—left many of his hearers unmoved. Their view of themselves and their place in the world remained undisturbed by his teaching and activity; from where they stood, nothing could persuade them that he was anything other than misguided. We know nothing of the events referred to in verses 1–5, only that Jesus uses them in an attempt to undermine the misplaced self-confidence of the hypocrite. By disallowing any connection between tragedy and the unworthiness of those it strikes, Jesus tries to shake his hearers out of their complacency. The parable in verses 6–9 gives his appeal a note of urgency. Fig-trees normally mature within three years; if they are still barren, they are unlikely to produce any fruit, and ought to be cut down. The delay procured by the vinedresser suggests that the fruit of repentance has one last chance to appear—if the barrenness of hypocrisy persists, drastic action will be taken.

Rejoice at the power of the kingdom! *Luke 13:10–21*

Another sabbath controversy (compare 6:1–11) provides a clear-cut example of the kind of hypocrisy Jesus has been struggling against. Jesus takes the argument to his opponents. The rabbis allow certain kinds of work to be done on the sabbath: if animals can be watered, surely a woman whose need is much greater can be helped! But Jesus' defence of his action is based on something more than the woman's plight. He believed that it was necessary to release her, because the kingdom of God demands the liberation of all who are held captive (4:18–19). According to Jesus, the work of the kingdom takes precedence over the requirements of the law or the niceties of religious practice. While most of the synagogue congregation are delighted at the woman's new-found freedom, Jesus' critics are left reeling by his assault on their mentality (v. 17). We may find ourselves wondering whether his opponents are in the grip of a much more pernicious form of disability than the woman had been.

The parables of the mustard seed and the yeast give us some indication of the uphill struggle of Jesus' mission, as he saw it. The power of the kingdom of God to overcome evil and re-order the world is pretty small-scale when it is set against the entrenched attitudes and practices which Jesus challenges. And yet the ultimate outcome of Jesus' work is out of all proportion to the way it appears on the road to Jerusalem. The tiny mustard seed grows into a tree twice the height of a man; even a small amount of yeast can raise a whole basin of bread dough. The tree with birds in its branches is an image of the nations of the world in Ezekiel 17:23 and 31:6; the liberating yeast of the kingdom is much more powerful than the debilitating yeast of hypocrisy (see 12:1). So Jesus' cause may appear to be small and insignificant, but its influence will spread beyond the narrow confines of Palestine, as Luke's readers can testify. These parables offer great encouragement to those in danger of being worn out by the struggle to stay faithful to the gospel, a theme which has run through many passages in this section of the Gospel.

In the words of Jesus about anxiety, wealth and poverty, we are reminded that God is benevolent and compassionate, providing the mundane daily needs of all his children. And yet in the parables of chapter 12, he is a severe judge who does not hesitate to exercise his power over life and death. Can the two—compassion and judgment, love and anger—be reconciled?

In his book The Gospel of Anger (SPCK), Alistair Campbell makes the point that anger is part of love. There is such a thing as 'loving anger', which we often experience in ourselves and certainly see in Jesus. In the teaching of Jesus we find a good deal of straight talking and sharp challenge, and yet in all this Jesus maintained an attitude of loving acceptance. If love is real, it will inevitably react when the objects of love abuse one another. How can God's love fail to express itself as the fire of judgment when his chosen people behave towards one another as they do? But his anger is never the last word; fire purifies as well as consumes. Divine indignation is the prelude to a renewed world.

Single-minded pursuit of salvation Luke 13:22–35

The next group of readings say more about the salvation which Jesus offered to Israel, and the demands it made on those who wanted a share in it. On the road to Jerusalem there is no room for speculation as to how many will be saved—a common topic to debate among Jews. Jesus puts the onus on his hearers to make sure *they* are included in the liberation he brings. As we have seen, Jesus does not offer Israel a range of equally valid ways of reaching the redemption they long for. He claims that his vision of the kingdom is the God-given way to restore and renew the life of the people of God. In this sense the door is narrow, and it is open for a limited period of time. But there is considerable breadth to Jesus' vision. Contrary to popular belief, Gentiles will be included in the kingdom. His restoration of Israel is but the first course of a banquet to which all the nations are invited (Isaiah 25:6ff). Salvation is not reserved for an exclusive religious or national club, yet only a decisive response to Jesus' mission will prevent the one seeking salvation being locked out for the night.

Jesus exemplifies the single-mindedness he demands from his hearers. Herod may well be disturbed by his popular appeal, but Jesus will not be frightened into leaving Herod's Galilean territory. He still has work to do there before he goes to Jerusalem for the final show-down. Once again Jesus anticipates the reception he will receive in the holy city. History has taught him well enough what happens to prophets in that place, but he will not be deflected from his messianic work of gathering together the family whose home is in Jerusalem (v. 34; compare Isaiah 60:4; Zechariah 10:6–10). The words of his lament lead us to assume that he has preached in Jerusalem before (as the Gospel of John makes clear), but he will not be seen in the city again until he is hailed as its Messiah (the words quoted in verse 35 are from a messianic psalm). The fact that today's passage begins and ends with more hints of Jesus' destination in Jerusalem reminds us that his salvation is not easily established. And as we have heard earlier (9:23–26), his call to single-minded discipleship suggests that he does not bear the cost of bringing that salvation alone.

Turning the tables

Jesus' concern for the whole family of Israel shows itself once again in his willingness to receive the hospitality of those who do not share his vision of the kingdom of God. He uses the opportunity provided by a Sabbath meal with Pharisees to challenge some of their basic attitudes. During the meal, a man whose body is badly swollen drifts into the house. Will Jesus heal him? Will the host and his friends argue from the Jewish Law that the man should be left to suffer until the Sabbath is over? Jesus fills the silence of the Pharisees with compassion. Having healed the man, he reminds them (as he had in 13:15) that the sabbath would not prevent them from rescuing a stranded son or animal; why then leave the man in his pit of suffering for one more day? Jesus turns the tables on those who relegate response to human need into second place, behind the parading of their own religious observance.

The same reversal of values comes out in Jesus' comments on the social behaviour of those who consider themselves important and powerful. Sitting in the best places at a meal is a way of presenting self-image to the world. Not only is this dubious social etiquette, which could lead to embarrassment if someone more important were to arrive, it also runs counter to the values which God prizes, because, as we saw in the Magnificat and the sermon on the plain, he raises the humble, not the proud. Inviting only those of the same social class or religious outlook may well enable birds of a feather to stick together. But God is interested in those whom this particular attitude overlooks: 'the poor, the crippled, the lame and the blind', regarded by some Jewish groups in Jesus' day as being beyond the pale of salvation. The values of the kingdom run counter to attitudes and behaviour based only on the possibility of mutual benefit (6:27—38). Jesus reveals that God's way of ordering the world turns the tables on so much that it is taken for granted in religious and social life.

Who will be at the banquet?

The advent of fast food has made it much easier for us to eat a ready meal, by removing much of the hard work from food preparation. But we may well have lost our sense of the symbolic value of eating together. A meal is a token of God's gracious provision of the gift of sustenance; a meal eaten with others is a social event which brings people together, often in celebration; a meal to which one is invited conveys the grace of welcome and acceptance. Little wonder that the Jews were fond of picturing the salvation for which they longed as a great banquet, the 'meal in the kingdom of God' (v. 15, and 13:29). But who will be at that meal? Jesus has been challenging cherished assumptions about the guest list throughout his ministry.

The remark made by Jesus' fellow guest in verse 15 raises precisely the question of *who* will eat at the table of salvation and enjoy the blessing of the kingdom of God. The parable here underlines and amplifies the message of the shorter one in 13:25–27 and the saying which follows. Those who hear and read Jesus' story are invited to identify with one or other of the groups in it: the large number initially invited; the poor, crippled, lame and blind from the streets and alleys of the town; and people from the countryside beyond the town. Jesus' critics obviously come into the first category, those Jews whom they consider to be outsiders and no-hopers into the second, and non-Israelites into the third.

The parable interprets Jesus' mission. His teaching and activity reveal the grace of God which recognizes no religious or national boundaries; the divine intention is that we should all be able to celebrate and enjoy his gift of life as one human family. But some exclude themselves from feasting on the rich fare of the kingdom's banquet, because they are not able to stomach a cause which embraces those whom they want to keep at a distance. Accepting the invitation to salvation means rejecting the religious and economic privileges they enjoy. The tragedy is that they prefer these to the joy of God.

Words for would-be disciples   *Luke 14:25–35*

We have seen how throughout his ministry Jesus insisted that the kingdom of God involves a re-ordering of life at every level. Repentance means that no stone should be left unturned—whether attitudes, religious practices, personal relationships or social and economic structures. Would-be followers of Jesus need to reckon with the cost of discipleship. God's new order may be like the gift and celebration of a banquet, but there is a price to be paid: repentance is not cheap.

The harshness of Jesus' words in verse 26 is softened somewhat when we realize that this is the Hebrew way of saying that loyalty to Jesus must have no rival. Together with verse 33, these words may well have been uttered to those Galileans whom Jesus called to follow him around Palestine—people like Peter and the others, who did leave homes, families, employment, in order to 'fish' for people (5:10, and compare 9:57–62). Luke has included them in a Gospel addressed to a wider audience, probably living in an urban rather than a rural environment. Fifty years on from the time of Jesus' Palestinian ministry, Luke's first readers live out their discipleship in different circumstances from Jesus' first followers. So, for example, rich Christians are encouraged to be generous with what they have, rather than abandoning all their possessions (with v. 33, compare 6:30–38).

A literal following of Jesus may not be possible any longer, but Luke would be the last to say that the cutting edge of Jesus' call should be blunted. No one drawn by his life and vision can afford to treat his cause any less seriously than the first disciples did. So the sayings about building a tower, going to war, and salt lose nothing of their force by being heard in other settings. In George Caird's words, they remind us that discipleship demands as much consideration as business or politics. This is the only way to preserve the distinctive flavour of the kingdom of God, and thereby ensure that those who claim to espouse its cause in any age are going to be of any use. Jesus could never be accused of relegating his demands to the small print of the gospel. And what is more, he never asks others for anything which he himself is not prepared to give.

Can you share the joy of God? Luke 15:1–10

This chapter contains some of the best-known parables of Jesus. Luke has set them in the context of the controversy generated by Jesus' social behaviour: not for the first time the Pharisees and scribes arraign Jesus for welcoming and even hosting meals with tax-collectors and sinners (see also 5:30, 7:39). The latter group are not simply moral failures, but members of a disreputable class, whom even the Bible encourages the upright to shun (Psalm 1; Proverbs 2:11–15). Jesus' stories interpret and justify his offensive behaviour.

The parables of the lost sheep and the lost coin are virtually identical: something is lost, there is a persistent search and the joy of finding proves infectious. Indeed 'joy' is picked up in the statement which concludes both stories. The points Jesus makes are quite obvious: finding a lost sheep or coin restores wholeness to the flock or purse; and an outcast sinner's repentance reveals the joy of God in finding a lost person. To his critics Jesus confidently says: 'What you find offensive brings great joy to God. What I am doing is God's search for the lost, his way of restoring wholeness to the divided family of Israel' (compare 13:34). His stories raise an important question for all who wish to be faithful in the practice of their religion: 'Can you let God's joy be yours?'

One final point: throughout his Gospel, Luke is fond of drawing attention to women: gender is no bar to authentic faith and discipleship. In the second parable he goes one step further and allows a woman to symbolize the activity of God. The fact that Jesus could draw on female as well as male imagery to speak about God invites us to free ourselves from any exclusive reliance on male language. There may even be times when it is more appropriate to refer to God's nature and intentions in female rather than male terms, following the example of Jesus in 13:34, when he compares himself to a mother hen.

The party is for you too   *Luke 15:11—32*

To call this 'The Parable of the Prodigal Son' is probably a misnomer— if anything the father is the central character. In fact this is a story about two sons, each of whom falls short in his own way. If we title the preceding parables 'The Lost Sheep' and 'The Lost Coin', we ought to call this one ' The Lost Sons'.

How would the Pharisees have responded as they listened to the story? As they heard about the younger son, their horror and disgust could only have increased. In the demand he makes of his father, he as good as wishes him dead. Not only does he waste the money which presumably would have kept his father in his old age, he also associates with Gentiles: Jews would consider looking after pigs a sinful way of making a living. It would not be surprising if the Pharisees felt exactly the same way about the younger son as they did towards 'tax collectors and sinners'.

We might expect the righteous hearers to identify more closely with the older son. Yes, he has dutifully served his father, and distances himself as far as possible from the profligate younger son, even refusing to recognize him as his brother. But the Pharisees could hardly have been enamoured of the older son. For all his faithful obedience he is jealous of the brother he disowns, and incapable of entering into his father's sorrow and joy. Behind his protest of loyalty lies the bitterness of one whose devotion to his father has amounted to nothing more than unrewarding, unremitting servitude.

Each of the sons needs to repent; they are both lost—and both loved. The father goes out to younger and older alike, lavishing his generosity on the one who was as good as dead, and inviting the other to share his joy. The welcome return of the prodigal can make the family whole once more, if only the dutiful son will treat him as his brother and join the celebrations. The story's ending is as open as the door to the party. We do not know what happened to the older son, but there is no avoiding the questions put to him, and left with the Pharisees. Can we identify with the father's intention to restore his family? Can we share the joy of God at the return of the lost?

This last section of the Gospel has held before us two inextricable elements of the Christian life: joy and demand. One without the other produces a religion of froth or gloom. They belong together because Christian faith is an adventure of redeeming love, and love is as joyful as it is costly.

The costliness of faith is what W.H. Vanstone calls 'love's expense', in his Love's Endeavour, Love's Expense (DLT). Love is exhausting, it invites misunderstanding, even rejection. Loving God is costly because he is committed to a healing and reconciling work which reaches deep into the brokenness of human life and embraces every aspect of it. The joy of faith comes out of the return of love. As on earth, so in heaven, there is great joy when the beloved returns to love to the lover. Salvation is fired by the divine energy of love. To enter the kingdom is to lose all and gain all. It is at the same time total demand and fulness of joy.

When we can no longer face the demands of love, we can ask God to draw us back to himself, so that we might hear that joy which echoes throughout heaven.

Use money to benefit others   *Luke 16:1—12*

Teaching about discipleship continues to dominate Luke's narrative. Following on from the generosity of spirit advocated in the previous chapter, the stories and sayings in chapter 16 concentrate largely on wealth: how should the followers of Jesus handle their money? The central character in the parable is variously thought of as dishonest, crafty or wise. The problem is partly one of translation in verse 8. The best clue to his character is provided by the story itself. Here is a manager who deservedly faces the sack for inefficiency and incompetence. How then will he make his living? Certainly not as a labourer or a beggar! He decides to make sure his boss's customers will take pity on him when the inevitable happens. So in the last days of his stewardship he reduces their debts. There is some debate as to whether he was sacrificing his own commission on their accounts, or waiving the interest charged by his boss (charging interest to fellow Jews was forbidden by Scripture—see Exodus 22:25; Leviticus 25:36; Deuteronomy 23:19–20). Either way, his quick action is commendable—even if it meant a loss of interest, his boss would gain an entirely undeserved reputation for piety in the community.

If verse 8 is Jesus' comment on the story, it suggests that its original point was not about handling money. Jesus wanted to encourage the people of Israel to have a similarly quick-witted, astute response to the crisis provoked by his ministry—as we have seen in 12:54–13:9. Luke, however, has placed the parable in a section which deals with wealth, adding his own comment in verse 9. Money is 'tainted' or 'unrighteous' because it belongs to the sinful world, but disciples are still to be trustworthy in their financial dealings. Money is not for personal gain, but 'to win you friends'. Disciples will be 'received into eternal habitations'—that is, meet with God's approval—if they invest the money which is entrusted to them by God in people, not in their own profit.

Once again there is an important word here for the richer members of Luke's church: God approves when money is invested in the poor (6:20–38; 14:12–14). This message is hardly exhausted by the time it reaches us.

The 'either/or' of the kingdom of God   *Luke 16:13–18*

As Jesus continues his teaching about wealth, he reaches behind the way it is used in order to uncover its power. Money can easily be promoted from its place as a very useful servant to become master of personal and communal life. It can even attract the devotion and service which belong to God alone. If wealth is one of God's potential rivals, then it stands in an 'either/or' relationship with him. 'You cannot be the slave both of God and money.'

The Pharisees who overhear Jesus are not merely a religious élite. They probably own property and benefit from the power and privilege that their wealth confers. They have a ready religious interpretation of their good fortune in Deuteronomy 28:11–13, where material prosperity is a sign of divine blessing for those who obey him. 'How can this man tell us to choose between God and money, when God has blessed us with our wealth?' Just as Jesus disallowed the connection between tragedy and sin in 13:1–5, so here he severs the link between prosperity and uprightness. Wealth may be prestigious in the eyes of other people, but it cuts no ice with the one who 'knows your hearts'. So the power which orders life must be *either* God *or* money.

In the sayings in verses 16–18, which appear quite disconnected from their setting here, Luke has Jesus make the point that traditional teaching, including Scripture, is now being reassessed. The ministry of John the Baptist heralded a major shift: the authority which now orders life is the kingdom of God, not the Law and the Prophets. Just as in the parables of chapter 15 Jesus claimed to know the mind and heart of God, so here he makes the audacious claim to be able to interpret God's will for everyone in Israel. The shape of God's intention and purpose is now being revealed in the work and teaching of one whom the Law's devotees choose to jeer at. Jesus' remark in verse 17 is heavily ironical, and shows that he does not underestimate the strength of the opposition to him: the end of the world is more likely than a change in the Pharisees' interpretation of the Law! The saying about divorce illustrates the new state of affairs Jesus has introduced. What the Law of Moses allows, Jesus now forbids (see Deuteronomy 24:1–4). A man can no longer treat a woman as if she were his disposable property, which was the basis of the Mosaic law. Every attempt to regard people as commodities, by making their humanity subservient to wealth, is disallowed by the 'either/or' of the kingdom of God.

The peril of dissolving the 'either/or'   *Luke 16:19–31*

Jesus' well-known parable, an adaption of a popular folktale, builds on the preceding verses, and illustrates the consequences of failing to use money to win friends. What Jesus said earlier about there being no direct connection between wealth and righteousness is vividly exemplified by the fabulously rich man in the story. His attitude to Lazarus betokens the fact that he holds in utter contempt the teaching of the Scriptures (e.g. Deuteronomy 15:4; Proverbs 15:31) and the needs of the poor: he chooses to ignore them both. The ultimate fate of both men fulfils perfectly the hope of the Magnificat and the Beatitudes, and is another example of the difference between divine and human values.

The point of the story is not to provide details of the afterlife. Jesus depicts very clearly the character of one who abuses wealth, and thereby falls foul of God's judgment. Not only is the rich man self-indulgent, deaf to God and blind to the poor man, he is unable to see Lazarus as anything other than an object, one who makes no moral claim on him at all. Even in his torment, Lazarus is no more than a lackey, evidenced by the refrain 'Send Lazarus . . .' in verses 24 and 27. There is surely some connection between the rich man's inability to recognize the humanity of one whose daily presence he could hardly have missed, and his (and his family's) need for something more than the obvious message of the Bible to warn them about the judgment of God. Living under the authority of God and valuing the humanity of others do seem to be linked. Jesus is not saying that wealth in itself is evil. But he does warn of its power to possess those who think *they* are its owners, to deafen them to God and the needs of others—especially the poor. Hence the importance of the 'either/or'. No one can avoid the power of money, but we must all ask how we will channel it, so that it remains a servant and never becomes master.

Four hallmarks of the Christian community *Luke 17:1–10*

The rather sombre picture in the previous story, of a man dominated by the love of money, is followed by a collection of sayings which express in clear and positive terms the attitudes and behaviour that Jesus looks for in his disciples. Luke has brought together four hallmarks of Christian community life. First, there is a call for particular concern for the 'little ones' (vv. 1–2). Whom does Jesus have in mind? They may be those, like children, who in Jesus' day were given few rights in society (Mark 9:42). Or they may be disciples whose faith was weak (Matthew 18:6–7). Jesus' followers must be careful not to abuse those whose lowly social standing or tender conscience makes them easy victims of the strong and powerful.

Second, Jesus demands persistent forgiveness (vv. 3–4). No community is ever spared disagreements and conflicts. Among the disciples, offences must neither be swept under the carpet, nor give cause for resentment. Healthy community life depends on disputed issues being brought into the open and rebuked, after which unlimited (this is the meaning of 'seven times' in verse 4) forgiveness must follow. Of course, concern for the weak and the practice of forgiveness never come easy, because they often entail swimming against the tide of wider society's values. In the sayings which follow, Jesus shows how what he demands becomes possible, by drawing on the resources of God.

So his third hallmark of community life is for disciples to recognize the power even of what little faith they have (vv. 5–6). The mustard seed is tiny; the mulberry bush has deep, well-developed roots. The faith which opens up a community to God's concern for the weak and his unlimited forgiveness will have a great impact, something we have seen time and again in Jesus' teaching. The fourth hallmark qualifies the third—faith shows itself in the humility of obedience (vv. 7–10). The 'unworthy' (v. 10—not 'useless' as in some translations) servant who carries out his double task only does what is expected of him. Disciples likewise have no claim on the goodness of God. A humble and obedient faith is content to carry out God's work by showing particular concern for the weak and practising unlimited forgiveness.

> The language and imagery of divine judgment have appeared in several recent passages, notably in relation to the use of wealth. We have seen a fascinating mixture of the mundane and the eternal, combining down-to-earth warnings about the right use of money with other-wordly descriptions of torment, bliss and the sudden inevitability of the day when God will call the world to account.
>
> If we are to be encouraged to change our behaviour, we often need to have the consequences of 'business as usual' spelt out vividly and clearly. The picture language of divine judgment may carry less weight these days than the global threats of nuclear war or ecological catastrophe, but its purpose is much the same. It warns us to change our ways, or face the consequences.
>
> The fact that the language of divine judgment seems old-fashioned, even in many Christian circles, should not blind us to what it is trying to say. If human beings are entrusted with life, then we are accountable—not merely to the electorate, the hungry, the oppressed, the planet or future generations, but ultimately to the one who has placed all this in our hands. What we do with the mundane has eternal consequences.

Faith and wholeness

This healing story follows on naturally from the previous section by delineating the character of obedient faith: it is seen in what the lepers did as Jesus told them that they were cured. We have already read a similar story earlier in the Gospel (5:12–16). This one also reminds us of the healing of the Gentile Naaman of his leprosy in 2 Kings 5. There, as here, the request for healing is met by the call to obey the man of God; and Naaman, like the Samaritan, returns to give thanks for his cure.

It is obvious that the legal requirement for verifying the cure of a leper and enabling his reintegration into society (Leviticus 14:1–32) was no empty ritual for the Samaritan. It spoke to him of God's grace in his healing, and sent him back to Jesus full of praise and thanksgiving. For his part Jesus distinguishes between the *cure* of the other nine and the *salvation* which had come to the Samaritan: ten were *made clean* but only one was *made well* (RSV) or 'saved'. The Samaritan's response reveals that his cure has opened up a relationship with God. We might say that on account of this, he is more 'whole' than the other nine. All this suggests that it is unwise to identify physical cure and salvation. Even when it is given in response to asking, healing is incomplete. Salvation—wholeness—is more than the removal of illness: the body may well be healed, but wholeness touches body and *spirit*, the human being in relation to God.

It is not difficult to see why Luke includes this story, because it conveys one of his favourite themes. Gentiles—like the centurion in 7:9, and even the Samaritan in 10:25–37—are capable of faith. The healing of the Samaritan leper points ahead to a still broader dimension of wholeness in Luke's two-volume work: the salvation which the kingdom of God brings embraces not merely body and spirit but also Gentiles and Jews.

Faith, not speculation

According to Luke, Jesus uses the language of the 'kingdom of God', sometimes with his own ministry in mind, sometimes referring to the present and sometimes to the future (4:43; 9:27; 10:9; 11:2, 20; 13:29; 14:15). In Jewish sources 'the kingdom of God' carries a range of meanings: associated with it are the coming of the Messiah, the resurrection of the dead, the day of judgment, the great banquet, the gift of the Spirit, final victory over Israel's enemies, the renewal of creation, and so on. Holding these various expressions of hope together is the conviction that the kingdom is the work and gift of *God*. Coming from an occupied people awaiting the liberation of Jerusalem, the Pharisees' question to Jesus makes sense, not least because the possibility that he was the Messiah encouraged speculation that he would soon establish the kingdom (see 24:21; Acts 1:6). Jesus' reply discourages the guess-work for which the Pharisees were known. The kingdom will not come as they expect, not least because the clue to its nature is 'in the midst of you', found in the teaching and activity of one whom they find difficult to associate with God.

The Pharisees were not the only ones to speculate about the coming of the kingdom. The early Christians believed that he Messiah had come, and that a new age had dawned in the resurrection of Jesus and the gift of the Spirit. Jesus' reply to the Pharisees may unwittingly have encouraged some of his later followers to believe that there was nothing more to wait for (a view reflected in 2 Timothy 2:18). Others (perhaps in Luke's church) wondered when the world would end, and so allowed themselves to become distracted from the more important tasks of daily Christian living.

So Jesus' warning applies to Pharisees and disciples alike: 'Do not speculate!' There will be no mistaking the end when it comes (vv. 24, 37), although the run-up to it will be marked by business as usual, as if nothing is about to happen (vv. 26–30). Disaster will strike a world not ready for it (vv. 27, 29), even separating the closest of companions (vv. 34–36). Rather than waste their energy on idle speculation, Jesus' followers must rely on the resources of their faith in two ways. Firstly they must believe that the chain of events which will bring about the end has already been set in motion by Jesus' rejection and passion. The end *will* come, but first the Son of Man must suffer (v. 25). Secondly, they must remember that the agent of divine judgment (the Son of Man) is the rejected Jesus whom they follow as Lord. Disciples can only guess the time or place of the end. What is beyond speculation is that the benchmark of faithfulness to the will of God is the pattern of life laid down by Jesus. In the end, this is what counts more than anything else.

Prayer and the disadvantaged *Luke 18:1—14*

This passage contains two parables on one of Luke's favourite themes, prayer. Like the earlier story in 11:5—8, the first parable encourages Jesus' followers to persist in prayer. Maybe they are tempted to give up; perhaps some of the more hard-pressed of Luke's first readers found prayer a particular problem, because they wondered whether the Son of Man would ever come to vindicate them (17:22). Jesus' story makes the point that if a poor widow's perseverance finally wears down the indifference of a judge who prefers the quiet life, then how much more will the persistent prayer of God's chosen people elicit *his* help! The parable would bring particular encouragement to the poorer members of Luke's church, who would readily identify with the widow. But richer church members could hardly read the story without seeing themselves as being, in some way or other, the answer to the prayers of their disadvantaged sisters and brothers, especially so soon after reading 16:19—31! Luke suggests that the Son of Man will look for the kind of faith which is ready to go on praying, and (where appropriate) to see oneself as the answer to the prayers of the disadvantaged for justice.

If economically hard-pressed Christians can take comfort from the first parable, those who feel morally and spiritually inferior can be encouraged by the second. The Pharisee's prayer, with its repeated 'I . . . I . . . I . . .', is nothing other than an exercise in self-centred self-congratulation. It even maximizes the religious and moral distance between himself and others—especially reprobates like 'this tax collector here'. In complete contrast, the tax collector's prayer centres on the undeserved mercy of God; he is all too keenly aware of the distance between himself and the one to whom he prays. But the distance is overcome by the character of his petition, so that he—and not the outwardly pious Pharisee—meets with God's approval. There is another lesson here about humility (compare 14:11), but also about the kind of praying which creates solidarity among those who pray. Just as the prayers of the disadvantaged for justice can build relationships between rich and poor, so the prayers of sinners for mercy draw together all who know their need of God.

What does it mean to be (dis)advantaged? *Luke 18:15–34*

What does Jesus mean by welcoming the kingdom of God 'like a child'? He may be encouraging his disciples to allow their faith to be characterized by child-like attitudes of dependency and trust. Or he may be saying that his followers should go out of their way to welcome those who, like the children of their day, have little in the way of social prestige. Either way, Jesus issues a sharp challenge to some prevailing ideas about receiving God's blessing. Access to salvation is not for those who rely on what the world counts as strength, neither does it allow us to sweep the weak and insignificant to one side. What appears to the world as 'disadvantaged' is in fact 'advantaged' in the eyes of God, because his kingdom belongs to the likes of children—with all their vulnerability, and their capacity for wonder, trust and growth.

This re-ordering of advantage and disadvantage runs through the story of the rich man and the comment which follows. The advantage of wealth can be a disadvantage: the rich find it hard to enter the kingdom. The man had kept all the commandments referred to, but then Jesus omitted to mention the tenth: 'You shall not covet' (Exodus 20:17). Only by selling his possessions and becoming a disciple would he overcome the idolatry of his covetousness, and reinstate God in place of Mammon (16:13). Once again, to the amazement of his hearers, Jesus severs the link between riches and God's blessing (compare 16:14–15). In his response to Peter, Jesus goes on to say that disadvantage can be an advantage; those who renounce everything for the sake of the kingdom will receive more in return. In the first instance he is referring to those who have literally left homes and families, but his words apply to all who want to enter the kingdom. Its blessings invert the world's values and priorities: the poor are blessed (6:20), the humble raised, sinners justified (18:13–14), children welcomed, advantage becomes disadvantage and disadvantage becomes advantage.

Hard words for the disciples are once again not far from a reference to Jesus' own suffering, as was the case earlier, in 9:22–27. Sayings about the Passion punctuate these discourses on discipleship. The inversion of values brought about by the kingdom finds its clearest demonstration in Jesus' rejection, suffering and death. The very heart of the gospel lies in God's power to overturn even the disadvantage of crucifixion.

Opening the eyes of faith

In common with Matthew and Mark, Luke includes this important story as Jesus draws near to Jerusalem (Matthew 20:29–34, Mark 10:46–52). Luke omits the reference to the request from James and John for places of honour in the kingdom, found in the first two Gospels between the third prophecy of the Passion and the healing of the blind man (Matthew 20:20–28; Mark 10:35–45). But what is clear from all three accounts is that the disciples cannot yet grasp what is in progress (18:34). In their own way, they are as poor and blind as the beggar by the roadside. They cannot take what Jesus has said, because they are blind to the Scriptures. Just as they struggled with Jesus' attempts to invert their understanding of salvation, so they find it hard to alter their ideas about the work of the Messiah. But if they are to share the blessings of the kingdom which Jesus brings, they need the faith which allows them to 'see' that the bringer of salvation must embody the reversal of values he has so often spoken about. In all this, he fulfils the will of God, by going the way spoken of by the prophets.

Those in front of the beggar in the crowd obstruct rather than help him, so he shouts all the louder. Like the widow in the earlier story in 18:5, he persists in his struggle against all that would keep him in his place. When he eventually reaches Jesus, he makes the simple request to 'see again'. Jesus' words to him—'Your faith has saved you'—have been heard several times already in the Gospel (7:50; 8:48; 17:19). He has precisely the kind of faith which the disciples need for their own salvation. So if the disciples are to recover their 'sight', they must persevere in faith, even when they cannot see what Jesus means by his words about rejection, suffering, death and resurrection. The time will come when their eyes will be open (24:31–32, 44–47). For the moment they must hold on in faith.

Another lost son returns

This well-known story, which is similar to the call of Levi the tax collector in 5:27–32, is virtually a dramatization of the parables in chapter 15. The one whose ministry was to seek out the lost here finds one who had strayed from the family of Israel. Tax collectors were not much liked. The fact that they worked for the occupying foreign power, as agents for Rome's appropriation of Palestine's wealth, did not endear them to their fellow Jews. In addition they had a reputation for lining their own pockets by fraudulent means. Like the prodigal son, Zacchaeus was effectively squandering the inheritance of Israel, while at the same time working for foreigners.

He appeared in public and mingled with the crowd at some risk to himself. We might speculate as to what prompted him to go to the lengths he did. Did he perhaps want an end to the ostracism which his work forced upon him? Was he disturbed by his conscience? We shall never know. What is clear is that something in him drove him towards a man with a reputation of welcoming outcasts. Though Zacchaeus had climbed the tree to get a better view of Jesus, it is Jesus who notices and finds him. The tax collector's joy is a perfect foil for the crowd's disgruntlement, and he demonstrates what the coming of salvation means for a rich man. Unlike the respectable man in 18:18–23, this 'sinner' is prepared to share his wealth with the poor, and even go beyond the legal requirements for restitution after robbery (Leviticus 6:5; Numbers 5:7). No longer will money be allowed to separate Zacchaeus from the rest of the family of Abraham. He promises to use it to 'win friends' (to borrow the language of 16:9).

Once again the salvation which Jesus brings inverts human estimates of what is good and acceptable. But unlike the reaction of the blind beggar in 18:43, there is no mention here of rejoicing as this lost son of Abraham comes home and the family of Israel is restored. In view of the nearness to Jerusalem, the silence is ominous.

Investing in the mission of the kingdom   Luke 19:11–27

Jesus' remark at the end of the previous story that 'today salvation has come to this house' could raise similar expectations to his earlier statement in 17:21 that 'the Kingdom of God is in your midst'. As we noted then (17:20–37), Jesus managed to excite what he saw as false hopes of the imminent liberation of Israel. The parable in today's reading guards against the wrong sort of expectations. It looks very much like two stories rolled into one, a conviction which is strengthened by comparing it with the very similar story in Matthew 25:14–30. A tale about a nobleman who goes off to a far country to be made king, against the wishes of his compatriots, is combined with one about a man who goes away, leaving his servants to trade with his money. The nobleman-become-king story is based on actual events: the first-century Jewish historian Josephus records the journey of Archelaus, son of Herod the Great (the king of Judea), to Rome following his father's death in 4BC. The son wanted to succeed his father, but his fellow Jews objected and sent a fifty-strong delegation to Rome to oppose him.

Earlier in the Gospel we have come across stories about the behaviour of servants while their master is away (12:35–48). Now, as then, the main theme is what the servants do with that which belongs to their master. Two servants invest what is entrusted to them, a third does nothing other than keep it safe. In view of 19:7, we may well wonder whether Jesus is criticizing those religious leaders who are quite content to preserve the traditions and teaching which God had given to Israel, rather than investing them in a mission to all sections of society.

Christians reading this story will readily identify the man away in the far country with Jesus. Opposed as he is by his compatriots, he has not yet returned as king and judge. His followers can rest assured that he will come back to establish his rule, but not yet. In the meantime, they are to invest what he has given them in the work he approves of, which is nothing less than the all-embracing mission of the kingdom of God. All investment involves risk, but in the judgment of God, a 'saftey-first' approach to mission brings the greatest danger.

The Messiah's humility is his glory   *Luke 19:28–40*

The road to Jerusalem is almost at an end, as Jesus and his disciples join the pilgrims going up to the holy city for the Passover festival. The Jews were gathering to celebrate the exodus of their ancestors from slavery. It was a time when expectations of another exodus ran high; those who remembered Moses were hoping that the promised Messiah would appear at Passover-tide, and free Israel from her enemies. We have known from the very beginning of Jesus' journey that he has been heading for the place of his departure (the Greek word in 9.51 is 'exodus'). According to 4:18–19, Luke's whole Gospel has been one of liberation, as Jesus has released those oppressed by illness, prejudice, greed, poverty and death. Israel's most powerful enemies are not the occupying armies, which hardly feature in Luke's account, but the forces which order life within Israel. Like Moses before Pharaoh in Exodus 5:1–5, Jesus will confront those whom he believes are chiefly responsible for Israel's present oppression. As the agent of the kingdom of God, he will give them their last chance to repent.

Jesus makes a deliberate choice to enter the city on a donkey. 'The Master needs it' (repeated in vv. 31, 34) because he cannot afford to allow any further misunderstanding about his messianic role and intentions. His acted parable recalls Zechariah 9:9–10, with Jerusalem's king coming on a colt, banishing war and proclaiming peace to the nations. Throughout the Gospel we have seen the way Jesus inverts some of the leading ideas and values around which life is organized. In his entry into Jerusalem, he also inverts the popular image of the Messiah. He comes as king, but with no intention of leading an armed revolt against Rome. The words with which he is greeted recall the message of the angels at his birth (with v. 38 compare 2:14), which suggests that his whole life has been pointing towards this moment. The Pharisees are still worried that the presence of a crowd of his supporters may attract the unwelcome attention of the Romans, who would view Jesus' action as seditious, whatever he had in mind (with vv. 39–40 compare John 11:47–48). But the whole of Israel's history has been building up to the coming of her messianic king. If the disciples are silent, the stones by the side of the road will greet him instead!

The way Jesus enters the city reveals the magnitude of his authority. He is prepared to take his cause into the very nerve centre of Jewish life. There he will represent those who have benefited from his ministry. His concern for all who need the salvation he brings is measured by his willingness to stand on their behalf in the place where the risk to himself is greatest.

It is almost impossible not to be drawn to people who manage a degree of consistency in their lives. By contrast, those who regularly say one thing and do another, or expect from others what they would not entertain for themselves, only confuse and irritate.

As Jesus has approached Jerusalem, Luke has depicted him as a model of consistency. When he asked for persistent prayer and persevering faith, he did so because these were the fuel of his own vocation. When he called for the inversion of the values which ordered his own society, it was because he exuded humility, welcome and forgiveness, and felt at home with the lost.

In the end, the surest measure of consistency is whether a
person is prepared to put his or her own life on the line, if this is
what it costs to stay true. As he edged closer to Jerusalem, Jesus
revealed his consistency for what it was—the divine longing for
peace, the glory of heaven itself.

JERUSALEM AND ITS TEMPLE: THE ── END OF JESUS' PUBLIC MINISTRY ──

The journey which Jesus began in 9:51 reaches its destination at last: he
is back in Jerusalem for the first time in this Gospel since his Passover-
tide visit as a twelve-year-old (2:41ff). Then he sat among the teachers
of the Law and astounded them with his questions. Now he is the one
whose teaching draws the crowds and carries the weight of divine
authority.

Reclaiming the temple   *Luke 19:41—20:8*

Jesus' approach to the holy city is marked by sadness, rather than the joy
of the pilgrims in whose company he was doubtless travelling. In his
lament over the city, he reveals himself as a realist. Desirous as he is for
Jerusalem to live up to its name ('Jerusalem' means 'city of peace'), he
has already realized that his mission will provoke division (12:51), and
that Jerusalem's rejection of divine visitation will bring about her
destruction (13:34–35). The language of verses 43–44 is drawn from
scriptural descriptions of the fall of Jerusalem 600 years before (Isaiah
29:3; Ezekiel 4:2). Jesus is a shrewd enough observer of political reality
to know that the tragedy will be repeated if his vision of Israel's
salvation is brushed aside.

The major obstacle to Jesus' cause throughout the Gospel has been
official religion. In Galilee, the Pharisees were its embodiment; here in
Jerusalem, they fade out of the scene, to be replaced by the temple
authorities (chief priests, scribes and elders), in whom religious,
economic and political power is vested. Rome has struck a deal with
them: if they manage to keep unrest at bay and ensure that the imperial
taxes are paid, Rome will not interfere in the government of Judea. Such

compromise has its price, as we shall see increasingly. So when Jesus takes his case to the power centre in Jerusalem, he must be prepared for more than a theological debate.

Compared to the other evangelists, Luke plays down Jesus' action against the temple. He attacks the way in which the necessary purchase of coinage for the temple tax and unblemished animals for sacrifice has degenerated into a racket of religious tourism, exploiting the pilgrims to line the coffers of the authorities. Sharp financial dealing has forced out prayer—so Jesus acts to reinstate the primary purpose of the holy place. In the teaching which follows, he offers the authoritative interpretation of God's will which he believes is sorely lacking from the centre of Israel's life. Though the pilgrims were ready to hear him, the powers-that-be saw only one way to deal with an upstart who posed a threat on so many levels. There could be nothing corresponding to the compromise they had struck with their Gentile overlords in their relationship with this Galilean Jew.

Their early attempt to trap him proved futile. Were he to claim unambiguously that he derived the authority for his words and deeds (especially his most recent, the action against the temple) from God, he could be handed over to Pilate as a political threat. He would clearly then be presenting himself as an alternative to the Jewish leaders, and this could only have a negative impact on public order in the city, at a time when nationalistic feeling traditionally ran high. Were he to deny any divine authority, he would be exposed as a sham before his admirers. Not only does Jesus' reply allow him to side-step the trap, it also reveals something of the response he is still looking for. Although this is Jerusalem's last chance, he refuses to coerce his hearers into accepting his message. Even at this crucial moment, what he looks for is faith—the conviction that his message and ministry are indeed 'gospel' (20:1) for Israel.

The price of withholding
what belongs to God   *Luke 20:9–26*

Jesus now goes on the offensive, by accusing Israel's leadership of failing to give God his due. Those who heard the parable would recognize only too well the scenario it describes. Absentee foreign landlords who removed wealth from Palestine were much resented by the Jews. When money was tight or if nationalistic feelings were stirring, tenants might well refuse to pay the landlord his share. Murdering the heir would give the occupants first claim on the property, and prevent the drain of wealth—but then they had the owner to reckon with. Jesus' parable has another resonance, though: in Isaiah 5:1–7, the vineyard stands for Israel, and in contemporary interpretation of the image, for the temple. Jesus' words are right on target, as verse 19 indicates. The custodians of Israel's heritage have taken advantage of their position, and failed to give God his due.

The same message comes out of the exchange about paying Caesar's poll-tax. It was deeply resented by the Jews, not only because it allowed a foreign power to cream off some of Israel's wealth, but also because the coinage in which it was paid offended their scruples about graven images. Once again the trap is set for Jesus: if he agrees with payment, he will alienate his hearers; if he disagrees, he could be accused of treason. As in the earlier incident, he plays the ball back into the questioners' court. Those who have compromised themselves by accepting and benefiting from Roman rule must pay the price. But there is one who has the highest claim on their loyalty—and the clear implication is that they have not given him what is his due.

Christian readers could hardly fail to interpret the parable in the light of subsequent events. The murder of the son *outside* the vineyard here and in Matthew 21:39 (see also Hebrews 13:12) may be an indication of the way the story's details were influenced by what actually happened to Jesus—in Mark 12:8 (which is likely to be the earliest Gospel version of the parable) the son is killed *before* being thrown outside. The death of Jesus the Son is followed by the birth of a new community, the Israel of the Church, of which the rejected and vindicated one is the cornerstone (language from Psalm 118:22–23 is also used of Jesus' relationship with the Church; see Acts 4:11, Ephesians 2:20 and 1 Peter 2:6–7). In Luke's narrative, the Christian community is a sign of what is due to God. It exists as the fruit of Jesus' faithfulness and loyalty, now released and made available as the power which, according to Acts 17:6, turns the world upside down. By contrast the temple, and the whole system centred on it, came to an end at the hands of the Romans in AD70.

There are no grounds here for triumphalism or attitudes of superiority on the part of the Christian community. The Church is only saved from these if it does not make the mistake of thinking that Jesus' words about giving God his due are only aimed at their original target.

Running what is God's as if it belongs to the tenants still receives its due reward.

No higher authority   *Luke 20:27–44*

At first sight, this passage looks like a couple of straightforward theological exchanges, in which experts throw texts at one another in the hope of scoring the all-important winning points. But there are deeper issues at stake. The Sadducees were a priestly party whose interests centred on the temple, and who were more at home than most in the collaborationist atmosphere of Roman occupation. They believed nothing which could not be proved from the first five books of the Bible; so unlike the Pharisees they objected to the idea of the resurrection of the dead. They did not find it in Moses, and furthermore they believed it owed much to foreign (Persian) influence on Israel's belief.

The Sadducees' question draws Jesus into a more general debate about which group had the authority to interpret the will of God for Israel. The scenario they present to Jesus is an attempt to use the Law of Moses in Deuteronomy 25:5–6 to discredit belief in resurrection. 'It is absurd to think that at the resurrection a woman might have seven husbands, therefore resurrection itself is absurd'—so their argument goes. Jesus dismisses it on two grounds. First, he states that in the entirely different order of the resurrection life, marriage is no longer appropriate. And second, he maintains that the idea of resurrection *is* consistent with the teaching of Moses. It can be argued from Exodus 3:6, which Jesus interprets in a way which would be familiar to the rabbis, if not to us.

Then it is Jesus' turn to put a controversial question, which may be paraphrased as: 'Is David really to be the role-model for the Messiah?' Some Jewish groups were waiting for a 'son of David' (based on 2 Samuel 7:12–16), who would fight to restore Israel's boundaries to what they were in the days of the greatest king, and cleanse Jewish territory of the supposed ethnic impurity represented by the Roman occupying forces. But Jesus does not believe that the warrior David provides the messianic pattern: the Jews must look for someone greater. So he asks, 'How can the Messiah be "son of David" when in one of David's Psalms (Psalm 110:1), the Lord (i.e. God) calls the Messiah "Lord"?' Again, the interpretation of the Psalm is at home in Jesus' world, not ours—but his question suggests that Passover-tide Jerusalem is buzzing with different ideas about the Messiah. And behind

257

all the arguments lies the issue of who had the authority to say how Israel's liberation would come.

Christians read the records of these debates with the benefit of hindsight. Luke's story is leading inexorably towards the rejection and resurrection of one who was announced early in his Gospel as 'Christ the Lord' (1:32; 2:11). Luke has made it clear from the beginning that all that happens to Jesus the Messiah is rooted in the Scriptures, which means that he—not the Pharisees, Sadducees or anyone else—has the authority to interpret the will of God and define the way to liberation.

The most worthy offering
Luke 20:45—21:4

After the heated theological debates of the last two readings, Luke brings us down to earth with a vivid contrast between two kinds of religious practice. The scribes are teachers of the Jewish Law in the synagogues, and in view of their approval of Jesus' teaching about the resurrection of the dead (v. 39), probably Pharisees. There is no doubt that they are important people, with the responsibility of interpreting the word of God in the Jewish community. But Jesus' description of them suggests that it has all rather gone to their heads. He can agree with the words they use to express their belief, but not with the way that belief shows itself in action. These teachers of the faith live out of the importance of their position in the community and their economic power, rather than on the basis of heartfelt trust in God. What is worse, their opinion of themselves makes them insensitive to the weaker members of society—like widows who have fallen on hard times, and whose houses they are prepared to take in lieu of unpaid debts. They epitomize those who cover their service of Mammon with a religious veneer (compare 16:14–15).

By contrast, the poor widow makes the smallest offering allowed by the Law. By giving all she has, she shows that she lives out of real faith in God and not self-interest. She reminds us of other women in this Gospel: like the two Marys, she is ready to live by the word of God (1:38; 10:38–42); like Anna, she is prepared to trust him (2:36–38); like the women who accompanied Jesus and the Twelve, she too is generous (8:1–3); like the unnamed prostitute, she relies on God's mercy (7:36–50). The widow's example comes as a typical and welcome Lucan touch, as the struggle between Jesus and his opponents is about to intensify. She reminds us of what is more important than anything to Jesus—the character and behaviour of those who belong to the people of God. Those who take their stand on the niceties of religion—whether skill in theological debate or prominence in public office—could do much worse than learn from this widow. In her offering, Jesus sees something of immense worth.

No short cut to the end of the world *Luke 21:5–19*

Luke's account of Jesus' public ministry is drawing to a close. He has entered Jerusalem and reclaimed the temple as a house of prayer (19:46). He has stormed the citadel of the authorized teachers of Israel's faith, and established the temple as his own base, teaching there every day and drawing great crowds (21:37–38). He is under no illusions, though, about the institution he has usurped: the days of its splendour are numbered. His statement calls forth the obvious questions from those who heard this startling and unwelcome remark, and in the discourse which follows Jesus gives his answer.

We would be unwise to view the rest of the chapter as a verbatim report of Jesus' last words in the temple. Like Matthew, Luke has based his account on Mark (compare Matthew 24; Mark 13), but there are small though significant differences between them. Some of the language and ideas are very similar to material found in the so-called 'apocalyptic' literature of Jesus' day. Here we find sketches of the days leading up to the final revelation of God's puposes for Israel and the wider creation, often using cartoon-like imagery drawn from Scripture. Within the Bible, Daniel 7–12 and Revelation are the nearest to these writings, which are intended to support the faith of the people of God in the tribulation and distress leading up to the day of judgment.

Reading through Luke 21, we can see the same desire to encourage the followers of Jesus. Some of the material here is not new to us. We have read similar things before in the Gospel—repetition allows Luke to underline his message. So, no one should be taken in by those who say that the end of the world is imminent (vv. 8, 9; compare 17:22–37). The unrest which marks the last days should come as no surprise (vv. 10–11). It is a familiar theme in apocalyptic literature, where the final liberation of God's people is preceded by distress similar to the plagues of Egypt (Revelation 9 and 16). Disciples should be ready to face opposition—even persecution and martyrdom—trusting the Lord for words to say (vv. 12–19; compare 12:11–12). In all that befalls them, perseverance is to be the hallmark of their faith (see notes on chapter 18).

Luke gives us the strong impression that, like the first followers of Jesus, his own church was facing upheaval and stress. Christian groups since then have often wanted to short-cut the responsibility of bearing witness to the gospel in a stressful world, by wishing that the end would come soon. For both Jesus and Luke, this is not faith, but fantasy and delusion.

Between the end of Jerusalem and the end of the world
Luke 21:20–38

Jesus now addresses more directly the question prompted by his announcement of the destruction of the temple. Just as surely as buds herald the approach of summer, so the fall of Jerusalem will be signalled by Roman armies surrounding the city before sacking it. All this will happen within a generation. The words in verses 21–24 do not reflect the actual course of events in AD70—for these we must rely on the Jewish historian Josephus. Drawing on biblical references to the fall of Jerusalem in 587BC (Isaiah 3:35; 29:3; Jeremiah 20:4–5), Jesus can foresee the consequences of Israel's rejection of his vision of salvation. The city's fate will mark the recurrence of God's judgment on the unfaithfulness of his people. The 600-year-old lesson has still to be learned.

Luke is insistent on reiterating the point made earlier in 17:22: however much the disciples may want to see one of the days of the Son of Man, they will not see it; the master is taking his time coming (12:45); the end will not come at once (21:9). So he is at pains to separate the fall of Jerusalem and the glorious coming of the Son of Man; the 'time of the Gentiles' holds them apart (with v. 24 compare Daniel 8:13). Once again we hear the now familiar injunctions to occupy the time responsibly: what was earlier referred to in terms of faithfulness to the given task (12:42–44), or investing capital in the master's service (19:12–27), here takes the form of wakeful prayer. In the period of the Christian mission, this will be the Church's sure footing, and guard against worldly distraction (with vv. 34–36 compare 8:14; 17:26–30).

Luke 21 is one of the most difficult chapters in the Gospel. However much uncertainty surrounds its interpretation, it does make the important point that when the Church carries out its mission in a stressful world (as it certainly did in its earliest days), it has to live with two equally strong temptations. One is to wish that the world were other than it is, which lies behind the hope for a quick end to it all. The other is to look for some way of dulling the senses to the pain and agony of life in the wider world, rather than searching for ways of responding to its stress.

Both temptations are a form of escapism, which is an all-too-common way of shielding ourselves from the shock waves of change, in a world which is reaching for something new. Some kinds of escapism are more religious than others, but in all its manifestations there is a denial of what is so clearly exemplified in Jesus. Luke's account of Jesus' final days in Jerusalem points unmistakably to one who holds his Church to the task of mission in the face of the world's distress. In all this, we are reminded again of the priority of prayer (19:46; 21:36).

FROM THE UPPER ROOM TO — THE HIGH PRIEST'S HOUSE —

Though Luke has sown the seeds of Jesus' passion early in his account, it is Jesus' movement from the temple to the upper room—and thereafter from the fellowship of friends to the inquisition of adversaries—which marks the beginning of the actual Passion narrative.

Preparing for the Passover in secret   *Luke 22:1–13*

The opening scenes of the passion narrative depict two ways in which the disciples prepared for the events of Passover. Both are equally secretive: Judas conceals his intentions from Jesus and the others, while Peter and John activate a plan which ensures that the location of the last supper will not be widely known.

Why does Judas betray Jesus? We can be reasonably sure why the chief priests want to be rid of Jesus. They see him as a threat to their authority as custodians of Israel's faith, and a danger to the survival of their privileged position as beneficiaries of the prevailing political order. But we do not know what motivated Judas to act as he did. The evangelists shed little light on the matter: John puts it down to greed (John 12:6), while Matthew's story of his repentance after the event suggests he was misguided (Matthew 27:3–10). He may have reached the point where he found himself siding with Jesus' opponents. Perhaps he simply wanted to arrange a meeting between Jesus and the authorities away from the glare of publicity, to give his master a chance to explain his intentions more clearly. Or maybe he was frustrated or disappointed with the course of Jesus' ministry, and sought to force his hand by confronting him with his adversaries. Whatever Judas' intention, the chief priests were only too glad to reward him. Luke sees a sinister side to Judas' secret dealing. Dark forces are at work; Satan has found the opportune moment referred to in 4:13. As he approaches his death Jesus is pitted against the powers of evil.

The contrast between Judas and the other two disciples could not be greater. Peter and John follow Jesus' instructions to the letter. It may well be that he has secretly made plans for the Passover meal, just as he had earlier arranged to have the donkey available. The unmistakable man with the water pot on his head (traditionally, this was woman's work) leads the disciples to the upper room. The fact that they find everything in accordance with Jesus' instructions only enhances the authority of Jesus' word. Like the crowds in the temple, the disciples do well to listen to Jesus. Those, like Judas, who allow their secret dealings to separate them from God, risk becoming tools of the evil one.

Remember me this way   Luke 22:14–23

Luke's account of the last supper focuses on Jesus' final instructions to the twelve apostles, the nucleus of the restored Israel. In an atmosphere heavy with betrayal, misunderstanding and impending denial, Jesus reveals *his* abiding trust in *them*, by directing them to what will sustain their common life in the future. The first of his instructions alerts them to the way they should remember him: 'Do this in remembrance of me'—remember me *this way*.

The ritual of the Passover meal—the lamb, the herbs, the bread, the four cups, the recital of the ancient story—brought Israel's past vividly into the present (on the scriptural basis of the Passover, see Exodus 12 and Deuteronomy 16:1—8). None of the evangelists goes into detail about Jesus' last meal; the accounts fasten on to those parts of the ritual which became especially significant for the Christian Church, as it obeyed Jesus' command to 'do this'. Remembering what God had done for their predecessors fuelled Jewish hopes for freedom from those who were still their enemies: the Passover looks forward to Israel's total liberation. In this his final Passover, Jesus also looks forward to the day when all that the meal celebrates is fulfilled in the kingdom of God. The first cup of wine (mentioned only in Luke) will be Jesus' last before the day of the great banquet (13:29; 14:15).

Jesus reinterprets the significance of the bread and wine in terms of his own 'exodus' (9:51), rather than the deliverance from Egypt. Like wine poured into a cup, so his life will be poured out in death 'for you'. Just as God's covenant with Israel was ratified by sacrifice in Exodus 24, so a 'new covenant', promised in Jeremiah 31:31—34 and Ezekiel 36:24—27, will be sealed in blood. This time, the ultimate act of generosity and grace is the sacrifice of Jesus' life for the benefit of a new community. The Israel of the Church must remember its founder, and allow its life to be nourished by one who received freely from his Father and gave freely to everyone. Its common meal will celebrate all that he stood for throughout his ministry, all that his vision of the kingdom holds before world, all that he looked forward to in the goal of total liberation.

Eucharistic liturgies as far back as 1 Corinthians 11:23ff associate the Last Supper with 'the night that he was betrayed'. Remembering Judas at the same time as we remember Jesus provides the starkest possible contrast between concealed self-interest and open self-giving. One leads to death (Acts 1:18), the other to unlimited life.

The leader must be servant
Luke 22:24—34

After the solemn words over the bread and wine, it may seem an inopportune moment for the disciples to engage in a trivial squabble. But this scene, like the others which deal with the supper, makes its point through the most powerful irony. Jesus has just told the disciples that he is ready to relinquish his hold on life in accordance with God's purpose for salvation. His readiness to *give up* his life will nourish them in the future. And yet Judas, who has already done his bit to help those who will *take* Jesus' life from him, eats at the same table. Now

Jesus sets the disciples' jockeying for position, and the fundamental misunderstanding it represents, against the servant pattern of his whole ministry.

The disciples have heard Jesus speak of a kingdom many times (as they will again in a moment), but never of one ordered by worldly values. In his vision of God's kingdom, the first are last, the outcast are brought in, the lost are found, the irreligious are justified, the poor are wealthy, the sick are whole and the greatest are the least. So the master behaves like a servant—which means there is no place for a dispute about greatness in which one tries to elbow another out of the way. Throughout his ministry, Jesus has been challenging the way power is used to the disadvantage of the weak. The sharpest image of all that he has been trying to convey is that of the servant who is willing to lose his life in death: weakness is strength, humility is greatness, when they define self-giving love.

Jesus' words are particularly pertinent for those who have stood by him, and are about to be entrusted with his ministry of the kingdom, even having a share in his work of judgment (vv. 28–30). Because they have identified with his struggle against evil, they too are experiencing the unsettling, buffeting attention of Satan, who wants to test Simon Peter as he once did Job (see Job 1:6–12). Peter has apparently forgotten that when he first met Jesus, he was overcome by a sense of unworthiness which kept Jesus at arm's length (5:8). This is now replaced by a confidence in his own ability to stay close to Jesus. But he lacks the master's insight, and only Jesus' prayer for him will enable him to pick up the pieces, once his bravado is seen for what it is.

Again Jesus is presented as the one who knows and meets the needs of his followers. His own sacrifice is the food and drink which nourishes the community in its break with worldly ways of exercising power. The Church is ordered and strengthened by the authority of service and the victory over evil, both alike the fruit of Jesus' faithful prayer.

Pray in the face of testing   *Luke 22:35–46*

Jesus' disciples have been slow in the past to fasten on to his teaching, particularly as they approached Jerusalem with the warnings of what awaited him there (9:45; 18:34). Not surprisingly, in the charged atmosphere of the upper room where Jesus has fed the disciples with symbols of his suffering and referred them to the patterning power of his

264

service, their insight fails them again. What they need most of all at this moment is the faith which once propelled their teaching and healing mission in Galilee (with v. 35 compare 9:1–6). But for the moment, this is beyond them. Jesus wants them to realize that times have changed significantly since then. Once he was a popular figure whose missionary followers could take hospitality for granted. Now he is about to be seen in a very different light, and so are they—as associates of a common criminal, a man 'reckoned with the rebellious' (Isaiah 53:12). But in one sense, nothing has changed. In the old days, their needs were met— their faith saw them through. Jesus wants to impress upon them that they need that same ability to trust God now, especially in the testing time he and they are about to endure. But this is not the time for razor-sharp perception on the part of the apostles—they think he wants them to arm themselves!

Jesus is sufficiently gracious and realistic not to put them through further explanation. Teaching must give way to prayer, and so after the meal they return to the place where they have been camped (with v. 39 compare 21:37–38). Jesus looks to his disciples to support him in the ordeal he is about to face, asking them to focus their intercession on the last petition of the prayer he taught them in 11:2—4: 'lead us not into temptation'. But he must face his agony alone: as Jesus' anxiety drives him to prayer, their grief submerges them in sleep. Only Luke reveals the intensity of Jesus' anguish, and that in the words of verses 43–44, which are missing from some of the earliest versions of the Gospel.

The scenes in the upper room and at the Mount of Olives reflect words from the Lord's Prayer. Today Jesus has given his disciples the daily bread of his own body, and spoken of the coming of the kingdom. Now he asks the Father for strength to do the Father's will, as he and the others face the severest test of faith. Jesus puts his own teaching about prayer into practice, and invites all his followers to do the same. One of them is conspicuously absent from this place of prayer. Judas is the only one who remains awake—but then his faith faltered at the first stages of the test.

Character revealed in crisis   *Luke 22:47–62*

Though we may pray to be preserved from crises, it is often the case that they reveal our true character. This is certainly so in this passage. Judas, Peter, the other disciples, the chief priests and elders, and Jesus all reveal their true colours amidst the stress and anxiety of Jesus' arrest. Judas' kiss is the action of a man who does not really know where his loyalties lie. The hands which took the wages of a secret deal also received the bread and cup from the one he has so cheaply betrayed. Judas enters the camp at the head of an armed band. He brings what has remained a secret out into the open, and the intimacy of his kiss overcomes the distance of his deception in an instant—or does it?

The other disciples were too tired to arm themselves with the weapons of prayer, but are only too ready—for all Jesus' teaching—to wield the swords of misunderstanding (with vv. 49–50 compare v. 38). The Jewish authorities are unable to pursue their course in the light of publicity. They prefer the dark, undercover activity of dealing through a traitor and illegal arrest, arming themselves against one who entered their city on a donkey. For all their godly piety, they are agents of the evil one, the power of darkness. Of all the disciples, only Peter follows Jesus after his arrest. But now it is his turn to be tossed in Satan's sieve. His loyal protest at the meal is swept aside by the ever-advancing tide of recognition in the courtyard.

What is true of those around Jesus is even more so of him—crisis reveals character. Jesus' concern for those around him shines through the narrative. He reserves his rebuke, not for the confused Judas but for the dark hypocrisy of his real opponents. He heals their servant, a victim of his own followers' impetuous attempts at self-defence. He makes no attempt to push the cup to one side (v. 42) by resisting the temple police, because his agonized prayer has borne fruit in his ready acceptance of the Father's will. He casts a compassionate glance towards Peter, at the moment when his trusted friend denies him for the third time; it is enough to set the tears of repentance flowing.

Jesus is undiminished, but hardly unaffected, by this crisis. He is carried forward by the conviction that although the hour appears to belong to his enemies, in truth this particular time is belongs to his Father.

The heart of the matter   *Luke 22:63—23:1*

What is the point of asking a blindfolded prisoner to identify his assailants on the evidence of nothing more than their blows? The mockery of the guards (vv. 63–64) shows the contempt in which the ministry of the Galilean prophet is held by the powers-that-be at the centre. But the power-brokers gathering informally in the high priest's house know that they must move beyond mockery if they are to deal effectively with the threat posed by Jesus. This is hardly a trial; if John is to be believed, their minds were already made up before they arrested him (John 11:53). They are simply looking for a way to get rid of him (19:47; 22:2).

It is vital to be clear about the issues at stake. Claiming to be 'Christ' or 'Son of God' was not in itself a capital offence. The titles meant much the same in Jesus' own day—God's 'anointed', or God's agent of salvation. Their real force lay in their reference to divine authority. The heart of the argument between Jesus and his opponents does not lie in a messianic title, but in the disputed claim to God-given authority. Who speaks for God in Israel? Who says what God wills for his people? Whose vision of the kingdom of God is right? In all this Jesus did not merely stand *outside* the recognized channels of authority (he was not a priest or a scribe), he stood *against* them. In the name of *his* vision of the kingdom of God, he was accusing Jewish officialdom of failing to give God his due (20:9–16).

The council's questions try to push Jesus into coming clean about the source of his authority. This is a tactic with a proven record of failure (11:14–22; 20:1–18), and it runs true to form. What actually resolves the issue for the council is Jesus' enigmatic statement about the Son of Man. By alluding to Daniel 7 (see notes on 9:18–27), he is making the audacious claim that God will stand by him and his cause, not by them and theirs. Ultimately God will demonstrate that he, not they, is the judge of what is right. As so often in this Gospel, the tables will be turned—this time, in Jesus' favour. It is not hard to appreciate that Jesus is doubly dangerous to those arraigned against him. He challenges every dimension of a system which serves their interests. And if they do not act decisively against him, they know that the level of popular support he enjoys from the Passover pilgrims in Jerusalem could attract the unwelcome heavy hand of Rome. They have no alternative but to take their case to Pilate.

It is important to identify Jesus' adversaries carefully. They are certainly not the Jewish people as a whole, but members of the ruling classes of Jerusalem—chief priests, elders, scribes. They remind us not of the culpability of one particular race of people, but of the temptations we all face over the way we exercise power over others. We do well to pray for deliverance from the darkness of unrestrained self-interest by the power of Jesus' self-giving love.

FROM THE GOVERNOR TO GOLGOTHA TO THE GRAVE

In this final part of the passion narrative, the opposition to Jesus runs its full course. He appears before politicians and the public, receiving responses which range over curiosity, mockery, violence and grief. What is remarkable in Luke's depiction of Jesus is the fact that even as his life is being taken from him, his power to give himself to others is undiminished.

Enemies and friends
Luke 23:2–12

By framing their case against Jesus as they do (only Luke spells it out in such detail in verse 2), the Jewish leaders try to gain Pilate's interest. He is not convinced, though, that the tired, undemonstrative figure who stands before him represents any threat to Caesar's authority: Jesus has nothing of the defiant energy of the leader of an armed revolt. But the governor has as little success as the council in persuading the prisoner to provide a straight answer. A further attempt to jolt Pilate into punitive action allows him to squirm off the protagonist's hook: the mention of Jesus' ministry in Galilee opens the door for Pilate to send Jesus to Herod. It is not hard to sense Pilate's relief as Jesus is taken to the puppet king of Galilee. In view of Luke's earlier note of Herod's intentions against Jesus in 13:31, we might expect Herod to be more sympathetic to the Jewish leadership, but this is not the case. He sees this chance encounter with Jesus as an opportunity to satisfy his long-held curiosity, but Jesus' unwillingness to respond to interrogation proves yet again to be an obstacle. Herod is reduced to treating the whole affair as a joke, before returning Jesus to Pilate.

What are we to make of the charges against Jesus? Two representatives of Roman political authority find him innocent, but in the minds of his enemies Jesus is not without guilt. His whole ministry was indeed leading the nation astray. His words about the poll-tax in 20:25 may well have been sufficiently ambiguous to allow the Jews to represent any ambivalence towards Rome on Jesus' part as opposition. What is more, he has made no attempt to deny any messianic claim before the Jews, Pilate or Herod. Though Jesus and his interrogators see messiahship differently, there is enough common ground for him not to dissociate himself entirely from their accusations, and to persist in the diffidence of his replies. He may not be an insurrectionist, but he certainly is a liberator from the tyranny of a self-interested, unjust and ungodly order, presided over by the Jewish leaders.

The scene ends on a note of poignant irony. The Jew Herod and the Gentile Pilate—enemies who share a lack of real feeling for the accused—become friends by being drawn into the story of Jesus, now well and truly on the way to the cross. How much more, then, are the Jewish and Gentile members of Luke's church reconciled, through their common faith in the one who has given his life for them!

A dilemma and a way out   Luke 23:13–25

Neither Pilate nor Herod can find anything to make Jesus worthy of execution. Pilate's offer to have him flogged before releasing him is firmly rejected—not surprisingly, because it is nothing more than a sop to his accusers. At this point, the Jewish leaders play their ace card. They have been insisting throughout that Jesus is a threat to public order, but so far their claim has fallen on deaf ears. It needs amplifying, and who better to turn up the volume than the crowd which has up to now been waiting in the wings? They find their voice by taking up the cause of a genuine agitator. We know nothing of the custom of releasing a prisoner at the Passover feast, though as a symbol of Israel's release from the prison of slavery in Egypt it could not be more fitting. Barabbas is evidently a popular man—to suggest his release is a sure way of drawing attention to the power of the crowd. Now that he is having to deal with a mob rather than a council, Pilate can make no further headway.

At this moment perhaps it occurs to the governor that Jesus' accusers have a point after all. They insist that he poses a threat to the public order—here is that threat, yelling for his execution. In the volatile atmosphere of Passover, when Jerusalem is packed with excitable pilgrims, the last thing Pilate wants is a riot. He cannot afford to ignore what might turn out to be the first stirrings of trouble. It is easy to accuse Pilate of weakness, but his dilemma should not be underestimated. As far as public order is concerned, the buck stops with him. No one would thank him for releasing a man whose potential for disorder was even now ringing in his ears. In fact, if the unthinkable happened, everyone would rightly accuse him of failing in his responsibility to prevent a riot. He has little choice but to extinguish the sparks before they ignite the highly inflammable vapour in the Jerusalem atmosphere—and there is only one way open to him.

Once again the scene ends in poignant irony. Jesus is handed over—Barabbas is released. As an innocent man takes another step towards his execution, a notorious wrongdoer is set free. The release of Barabbas contains a message for Luke's readers in their mission to society's moral failures. If the death of Jesus meant freedom for a wrongdoer who had no interest in him, how much more does the cross offer the hope of liberation to sinners who are penitent!

Shouldering the burden   *Luke 23:26—34*

A condemned criminal was expected to shoulder the extra burden of carrying his own cross-beam to the place of execution. Though Luke does not dwell on the suffering of Jesus, it is clear that his strength has been considerably reduced by the emotional and physical pressures he has endured. Simon of Cyrene may well be a Passover pilgrim; by shouldering Jesus' burden, he becomes a model disciple, perfectly fulfilling the master's earlier words in 9:23. Weak or not, Jesus' interest in those around him is far from exhausted. Perhaps the mourning women of Jerusalem offer him a sedative to relieve his impending agony. But he is more concerned about what will befall them when his words to the city come true.

Jesus uses language of divine judgment from the prophets to warn Jerusalem one last time about her fate. He has already identified his own suffering with that of the prophets who were martyred before him (13:33—34). In the imagery of green and dry wood, drawn from Ezekiel

20:47–48, he associates himself with what will happen to Jerusalem. In some mysterious way, Jesus' lot is also part of God's judgment on his people. True, he is on the way to execution because he has kept faith with his vision of God against those who have opposed him. But he shoulders the burden of a collective sin which has rejected his vision, his God and his salvation. It is as if Jesus' crucifixion marks the beginning of the process of a divine judgment which has to sweep away the sins of the old order, before the new one finally appears. This is devastating enough for Jesus, but nothing compared to what will finally descend upon Jerusalem. What Jesus endures is like green wood, not yet ready for the fire but burning nevertheless. But Jerusalem's devastation will be like a raging fire made out of dry wood, when the rejection of his way to peace eventually leads Rome to take action against the city (19:42, 21:20–24). On that day, the presumed disgrace of barrenness will be a blessing—a childless woman will at least be spared the suffering of her own children—and people will pray for the end of their lives (with vv. 29–30 compare Hosea 9:14; 10:8).

It could hardly have been easy for Jesus to shoulder the burden of God's judgment on Jerusalem in his own suffering. Yet as he does, he manages to extend his compassion to those who carry out what is for them a routine execution. His prayer—'Father, forgive them'—shows him continuing to live by what he taught as he nears his end (6:28; 11:4). There is no clearer example of the power of God made perfect in human weakness (2 Corinthians 12:9).

Weaving the patterns   *Luke 23:32–38*

Jesus' disciples may have dropped out of the story by now, but he is not alone in his death. The presence of criminals on either side recalls the words he quoted from Scripture at the supper (see 22:37, which quotes Isaiah 53:12). In the same way, the soldiers' mercenary practice of dividing up clothing reflects words from Psalm 22:18. The stories of Jesus' Passion are shot through with biblical allusions and quotations, especially from passages which refer to the lot of the suffering righteous person. The way the Bible is used here does not suggest that Jesus' career has to confirm to a highly predetermined programme. It is more the case that his death weaves a pattern which is part of the fabric of God's dealings with Israel. Those who proved to be faithful to God in the past faced hardship, abuse and rejection. If this is the pattern woven

271

into the stories of faithful response to God, how can it be otherwise for his most faithful son?

All four evangelists agree that Jesus was executed as a messianic pretender, 'the King of the Jews' . In the eyes of those who taunt him, the very shame of crucifixion ridicules any claim to be God's Messiah, because he is under God's curse (see Deuteronomy 21:23; Galatians 4:13). How can God anoint with shame and blessing at the same time? Nothing could be more appropriate than for earth to echo the mockery of heaven. But for the Christian reader the mockery is heavily ironic: the fact that Jesus *cannot* save himself from the cross is the clearest evidence that he *is* God's Messiah. What his adversaries cannot realize is that he has reached this point precisely because of the exercise of his Spirit-given liberating power (4:18–19). In his loving solidarity with all Israel he did indeed 'save others', but at the same time he exposed himself to the risk of rejection and suffering. Establishing Israel's salvation has brought about his execution, because he has faithfully refused to abandon the Spirit-inspired vision of liberation which provoked such determined opposition from the authorities.

In all this Jesus weaves another pattern—not only of faithful love for God, but also of the faithful love of God for his people. Even all-embracing divine love cannot insist on a welcome. It has to be prepared to meet with abuse, suffering and rejection, as is all too clear in the fabric of the Old Testament. Execution is the supreme price Jesus had to pay for his anointing with the Spirit of God, which inspired and enlivened the way he set about serving and saving others. Jesus can only endure the taunts of those who condemn him. Far from turning him into an object of scorn, the inscription above his head invites us to see his powerlessness as the supreme manifestation of his power to save.

A turning point in human history and human hearts
Luke 23:39–49

At the end of his ministry, Jesus is tempted to renounce his way of being Messiah, just as he was at the beginning. The three-fold refrain of Satan in the wilderness—'If you are the Son of God . . .'—is echoed in public by the mockery of the leaders, the soldiers and one of the criminals: 'If you are the Christ, save yourself . . . save us' (vv. 35, 37, 39). But Jesus remains true to his cause, and this is surely the secret of the effectiveness of his death. Luke depicts this in two ways. First, the

272

imagery in his account demonstrates the cosmic consequences of Jesus' Passion. The three hours of darkness symbolize God's judgment on the world's injustice and the end of the present age (see Amos 8:1–10, Joel 3:15). The tearing of the temple curtain picks up Jesus' earlier words about the destruction of the temple in 21:6. The cross marks the turning point in human history: as one era ends, so another begins.

Second, Jesus' death as the faithful martyr makes a profound impression on those around the cross—the criminal crucified next to him, the centurion, the crowds. His undeserved suffering enables the other criminal to reflect on his own fate, and he utters a prayer of faith, which picks up some of Jesus' own words at the last supper (with v. 42 compare 22:16, 18). Jesus responds by promising him an immediate share in the salvation he brings. 'Paradise' means garden, and is part of the rich Jewish language about life beyond death. Luke probably understands it as equivalent to 'Abraham's bosom' where the beggar Lazarus waited for the day of resurrection (16:22). The Gentile centurion has seen that Jesus did not revile those who executed him or added insult to his injuries. Instead he prayed for those who drove in the nails, and showed compassion towards the dying criminal. Jesus' final utterance—a prayer of trust drawing on Psalm 31:5—moves the soldier to confess his faith in words which highlight the pattern woven throughout Jesus' Passion: 'Truly this man was righteous' (a better translation than 'innocent' in v.47). The dying Jesus also makes an impression on the crowds drawn to the spectacle of crucifixion. In Luke's account, they do not mock Jesus: they stand and watch, returning home moved to sorrow. It may be that some of them were among the three thousand Jews in Jerusalem who repented and were baptized on the day of Pentecost (Acts 2:22–41).

Jew and Gentile, a criminal and a Roman official—all drawn towards salvation by the dying Jesus. If Jesus makes such a profound impression on human beings when he is at his weakest, what do we make of the impact of one whose risen life has been released into the whole world?

Devotion and preparation   *Luke 23:50–56*

After all the abuse Jesus' body has suffered since his arrest, it comes as something of a relief to find people who are prepared to take care of him, even after he has breathed his last. It is also good to be reminded that not all members of the Jewish council have been corrupted by

273

power. Between them, Matthew and John tell us that the wealthy Joseph of Arimathea was a secret disciple of Jesus. Mark and Luke mention nothing of this, only that he was expecting the kingdom of God to come. A sympathizer who may not have been able to stem the tide of opposition to Jesus within the ruling council, he can at least now make a final act of public devotion. It is safe to assume that Joseph, like those in the previous reading, has also been deeply moved by the events of the last day. His devotion prepares us for those Jewish officials who will join the Jerusalem church after Pentecost (Acts 6:7). Like Joseph, the Galilean women must also have been overwhelmed by what was happening to Jesus. They had kept their distance from the place of execution, but now they too are drawn closer. They begin their own preparation for the first day of the week as they observe the details of Jesus' burial.

Everything is done in accordance with the requirements of Jewish Law and custom. Joseph wants to make sure that one executed as a criminal is buried before nightfall (Deuteronomy 21:22–23), and the women resolve to wait for the Sabbath to pass before they perform the customary anointing. In many ways, we are reminded of the earliest scenes in this Gospel. There, in and around Jerusalem, we met Elizabeth and Zechariah, Mary and Joseph, Simeon and Anna, living according to traditional piety and hope. By recalling the beginning of the story on this day of preparation, Luke is inviting his readers to prepare for the new beginning at the dawn on the other side of the sabbath.

In his version of the Passion of Jesus, Luke achieves something which none of the other evangelists manages. By depicting Jesus as the faithful martyr who remains true to his cause, he brings out the fact that Jesus' death is of a piece with his life. On the cross, he reveals the very commitment to the will of God and the good of others which led him to make that final journey to Jerusalem. His love is undiminished, even in death. His cross seals his willingness to suffer, in loving solidarity with all.

> *Jesus' costly solidarity with God and human beings is a theme of some recent Latin American theology. In his Passion of Christ, Passion of the World (Orbis), Leonardo Boff writes of the way the cross of Jesus shows us what love can do when it is prepared to enter into the sorrow and suffering of the world. On this understanding, the crucified Jesus not only invites our contemplation and wonder, he also asks us to allow ourselves to be moved by his living and dying, to take up our cross in the same committed love which we see in him, and to discover him to be at the very heart of God. Only in this way can we and the whole world be saved.*

— JERUSALEM: A NEW DAY BEGINS —

We now reach the climax of Luke's Gospel, as the power of life overcomes death—for Jesus, his followers and his cause. The one crucified as 'King of the Jews' is vindicated, because God has raised him from the dead. Those who have been thrown by his earlier words about rejection, death and resurrection finally come to believe them. And the cause which had all but died with Jesus is taken up and extended by the apostles, as they become the agents of the world-wide liberating work which the Messiah still has to do.

A new day   *Luke 24:1–12*

The details of the evangelists' accounts of the early morning visit to the tomb differ slightly, but they all agree that a group of women unexpectedly find Jesus' tomb empty. Their shock soon gives way to the beginnings of faith in the resurrection. These Galilean women (compare v. 10 with 8:2–3) have already begun to overcome the distance which separated them from their crucified friend (23:49, 55–56). For them, it is enough to interpret the evidence of their eyes by the memory of Jesus' words. Characteristically in Luke, women have a capacity for faith that men find harder to come by. Whereas the women remember and believe, the men go on stumbling over the words about death and resurrection. Peter's visit to the tomb (recorded in verse 12, which is not found in all manuscripts of the Gospel), allows him to

275

confirm an incredible story, but as yet he can only wonder what it is really about.

Despite Luke's stress on the empty tomb, he is careful to show that on its own, it provides an inadequate basis for resurrection faith. Other explanations for a missing body are possible. It may have been stolen (John 20:13), though Luke guards against this with his observation about the grave-clothes in verse 12. Something more than an empty tomb is needed if we are to believe in the resurrection of Jesus from the dead. By drawing attention to the truth of Jesus' prophetic words, Luke makes a start on the 'something more'. As the story of this unexpected new day unfolds, so the foundations of the Easter faith will be uncovered.

From the afternoon of incomprehension to the evening of recognition *Luke 24:13–35*

From the startling events of the early morning, Luke takes us on to the late afternoon, when two of Jesus' disciples are presumably returning home after what for them has been a disastrous Passover. The word is about that their friend who was crucified and buried two days earlier is in fact alive, though they cannot believe it. As they walk, they are quite naturally reminding one another of the events which have so shocked and bewildered them. The appearance of another traveller, surprisingly ignorant of all that has gone on in Jerusaelm over these past few days, gives them yet another chance to go over the story.

Why can they not recognize him? For one thing, they certainly do not expect Jesus to be alive. Though he had excited their hopes for the liberation of Israel, he had not managed to free their imagination. Whenever he spoke of what lay ahead of him in Jerusalem, his disciples were unable to share his convictions about the outcome of his ministry—vindication by God, resurrection. And now the fact that he has been rejected by the guardians of his own faith and culture, and made to look as if God himself were condemning him, means that they cannot possibly share the women's sense of wonder at the angelic message and the empty tomb. Their general state of mind only makes matters worse. Grief and disappointment combine with the confusion generated by the women's story to cloud their vision to anything but their own sorry predicament. It is also possible that their ability to recognize Jesus is hampered by some alteration in his appearance, though here we are in the realms of speculation.

We should not underestimate the difficulties these two disappointed people had in recognizing the one who walked with them. If anything, their blindness only alerts us to the 'something more' which resurrection faith thrives on. Reports of an empty tomb and angelic messages, no matter how well meaning, are simply not enough to break through difficulties of belief, sadness, confusion, disappointment and whatever else the two friends were taking home with them to Emmaus. The penny finally drops for them, as 'something more' transforms the women's story from rumour to reality. According to Luke, resurrection faith is born as the dawn message is interpreted by the Jewish Scripture and the breaking of bread.

The stranger points to a theme which runs through the whole of Scripture, with its story of the relationship between God and his people. Israel is forever facing suffering and humiliation as she struggles to live out her vocation in a world which tends to resist God's purposes. But her story never ends in defeat: God faithfully delivers his people from suffering to glory. What is true for the nation as a whole is particularly so in the case of her representative leader, the Messiah. 'It is necessary that Christ should suffer' (v. 26) precisely because he is the true Israelite, and the recurring theme in Israel's life is represented supremely in his experience.

The stranger insists that the humiliation and suffering of the one they hoped was the Messiah should not have surprised them—but neither should they be content with a story that ends at the cross! The fire which the fellow-traveller's exposition of Scripture kindles in their hearts really begins to blaze once they sit down to a meal with him. He is their guest, yet he takes the initiative of saying grace. A familiar ritual performed in a way which they immediately recognize convinces them that they have sat at this man's table before. The dawn message, the stranger's explanation of Scripture, and now the memories evoked by the way he breaks bread can only mean one thing.

We now know what the 'something more' necessary for Easter faith consists of. We need the Bible and the Eucharist if we are to make sense of the early morning message of the women. The empty tomb is part of Scripture's story of God's commitment to his people. If he does not abandon the often unfaithful Israel, how much more will he vindicate his utterly faithful Son! The aliveness of Jesus beyond Good Friday is the victory of all that he lived and died for over all that opposes the liberating purpose of God. And he still makes himself known to those who live by his cause today as they meet to remember him. We too have sat with him at his table. We have read in the Gospel about his meals with all sorts of people—Simon the Pharisee (7:36–50), the great crowd (9:12–17), Martha and Mary (10:38–42), the Pharisaic ruler of the synagogue (14:1–24), sinners like Zacchaeus (15:2, 19:1–10), and finally with the disciples in the upper room (22:19–20). We have also shared in the eucharistic meal by which the Church has remembered Jesus from the beginning. With the two on the road to Emmaus, we have recognized the risen Jesus, to whom Scripture bears witness, in the breaking of the bread. Like them we are nourished in the Easter faith by the risen Lord himself, through holy word and sacred food.

The day of transformation   Luke 24:36–43

Having laid the foundations of Easter faith, Luke devotes the rest of the chapter to drawing out some of the implications of Jesus' resurrection. Up to now, the risen Jesus has appeared to one (Simon—v. 34; 1 Corinthians 15:5) and then to two disciples. His third appearance involves the larger body of his followers. This is appropriate, because the resurrection of Jesus has a considerable bearing on their future life together. But before we hear about this, Luke is concerned to say something more about the resurrection of Jesus, by underlining its *physical* reality. The risen Jesus is no ghost: he can be seen and touched; he is able to interact with matter. Yet Jesus is also different as a result of the resurrection—he has in some way been transformed. He can appear and disappear at will; he is clearly no longer limited by the dimensions of time and space. But he is recognizably the same Jesus who taught and healed, who was rejected, crucified and laid in the tomb.

One of the reasons for Luke's emphasis on the physical reality of Jesus' resurrection may well be to draw attention to the nature of the salvation which Jesus brings. Liberation is not about escaping from a world which often acts in defiance of God, but about redeeming and transforming it into the sphere of his kingdom. At the same time, the experience of God which the risen Christ opens up is not other-worldly or ethereal. It has 'shape' and content; it is defined by the life and cause of the one whose body is marked by the wounds of compassion. This is why the risen Lord greets his followers with words he has used before in his ministry (with v. 36 compare 7:50; 8:48; 10:5; 19:42). His work of bringing peace to broken people and a fractured world goes on, and it will occupy the lives of his followers in ways they can hardly imagine. In this scene, they begin to be touched and transformed by the celebration which characterizes God's new order. For the first time since Jesus entered Jerusalem in 19:37, joy returns to the narrative, only to become an infectious hallmark of the life and work of the Church as it carries forward the transforming work which Jesus has begun.

The promise of tomorrow   Luke 24:44–49

Jesus goes on to share the interpretation of the Bible he has earlier offered to the two journeying to Emmaus with the wider body of disciples. But he adds a reference to the future world-wide work spreading out from Jerusalem. This too comes under the category of what 'is written' (v. 46). Luke has often reminded us that Jesus' ministry in Galilee and Judea fulfils the Jewish Scriptures (see the notes on chapters 1–2; 3:4–6; 4:18–19; 7:22). By rooting the next stage of the Messiah's ministry in the same Scriptures, Luke shows that the work which culminated in Jerusalem is of a piece with what will happen from Jerusalem. This will assure his first readers that the Church's life and concerns are no mere novelty. In a world in which the pedigree of a new religious movement was highly prized, Luke is saying that the impact of the resurrection of the crucified Jesus (seen in the growth of the Christian Church), far from being a corruption, is in fact the legitimate development of the ancient faith of the Jews.

'Repentance for the forgiveness of sins' in verse 47 is useful shorthand for the gospel. It achieves the very opposite of any attempt to narrow down the apostolic message to the concern for an individual relationship with God. Jesus prayed from the cross for the forgiveness of his persecutors (23:34), as if to remind us that the sin from which the world must repent is that which nailed him to the cross. In concrete terms, this showed itself as the rejection of God's liberating purposes announced and embodied by Jesus. We have seen in Luke's story how those who opposed Jesus preferred to hold on to their power and privilege, whether religious, racial, political or economic. In so doing they went against the grain of God's salvation. According to Jesus the indiscriminate mercy of God for the undeserving has no truck with prejudice, greed, injustice and whatever else ruptures communion between humankind and God, and between one person and another. The gospel which the risen Lord entrusts to his followers is to be as multi-dimensional for them as it has been for him, if it is to transform the whole of life.

If they are to be faithful to their calling, the disciples will need an energy which is beyond their own resources. And so Jesus assures them that they will be able to rely on nothing less than the Spirit which has energized his own ministry in Israel. Once again we are being drawn towards Luke's second volume, which might best be called the 'Acts of the Holy Spirit'.

The day of worship, praise and prayer   *Luke 24:50–53*

In the final chapter of his Gospel, Luke has compressed the end of Jesus' earthly life into a single day—the first Easter Sunday. However, at the beginning of Acts, he goes over the same ground from Easter to the Ascension, but spreads the story over forty days (Acts 1:3). St Paul also suggests that Jesus' appearances to his followers extended over a longer period of time (1 Corinthians 15:1–8). It can hardly be a matter of which version is right and which is wrong, as if Luke is at variance with himself! The way he ends Volume One and begins Volume Two allows him to make different, though connected points. The conclusion to the Gospel suggests that Luke wants us to see that the resurrection of the crucified Jesus, the promise of the Holy Spirit and the mission of the Church belong inseparably together. The beginning of Acts picks up the words in 24:49, and emphasizes the need to wait prayerfully for God's next step (Acts 1:14). So the Church in any age can recognize the risen Lord as it commits itself to continuing his work, living in the day of God's mission, in the power of the Holy Spirit and the dependency of prayer.

The end of the Gospel also reminds us of its beginning, because we are once again in the temple, in an atmosphere of worship and prayer (see chapters 1–2). By ending where he began, Luke cleverly ties the whole story of Jesus together. Just as he has insisted on the identity of the risen Christ and the crucified Jesus (v. 39), so he now reminds us that the story which ends on the high notes of resurrection, universal mission and the promise of the Spirit is the one which began with a humble, childless priestly family. Without the ending, the story of Jesus would have had no beginning, because it would never have been told. But without the beginning—among the concerns of ordinary people like Zechariah and

Elizabeth, Mary and Joseph, the shepherds, the Roman authorities, Simeon and Anna—the ending might tempt us to distance the ascended Lord Jesus from the rough and tumble of everyday reality. It is all too easy to associate the day of worship in which the Church is called to live with a rarefied spiritual experience. But if Luke directs our attention towards the glory of the Lord Jesus on the day of resurrection and Ascension, he will not allow us to lose sight of the world which God is still in the process of redeeming.

> The end of the Luke's Gospel prepares us to read all that led up to its beginning with fresh eyes. From the vantage point of Easter, we can see the significance of the coming of Jesus for all people in every age. The one whose place in Israel was prepared by God's love and patience can no longer be constrained by race, gender, class, creed, nation, history or space. His life, his cause, his love, his benefits are offered freely to everyone, everywhere.

JOHN

From the earliest days, the Fourth Gospel has attracted some Christians and repelled others. It was said of Bishop Westcott, a famous commentator on St John: 'He speaks of St John's Gospel with a kind of hushed awe; it is like Fra Angelico, he cannot venture to criticise a verse without prayer.' Others have felt that the Jesus of John strides over the earth like a god—he is not the compassionate friend of sinners of the synoptics, or the anguished saviour of Gethsemane and the cry of dereliction, but has a trace of Stoic apathy. This Gospel has also been branded anti-Semitic. This last is a facile charge, anachronistic and historically unaware of the hostile and persecuting opposition of orthodox Jews at the time when the Gospel was being written, and unappreciative of John's symbolic—if in retrospect unfortunate—use of the term 'the Jews' to describe not only Christ's original enemies but an attitude to him which persisted.

It is impossible to find any scholarly consensus as to the Gospel's origins, authorship or purpose, though there are some penetrating insights in the immense labours of academics. What follows is based on certain presuppositions about the Gospel, not without scholarly support, though not all undisputed:

◇ That it emanates from a small, exclusive, Christian community, rather like the disciples at supper with Jesus in chapters 13–16. The believing community was hard-pressed by Jewish opposition, and also by heretical denials of the humanity of Jesus and the importance of his history, in the interests of an esoteric or 'spiritual' religion.

◇ The Gospel makes clear that the Word was made *flesh*. Jesus has a body, grows tired, hungers, thirsts, weeps, dies. It may, however, mark the unmade beginnings of the road to the Council

of Chalcedon and the dogma, for better or worse, of the divine
and human natures in one person.

◇ Though history is all-important and the Gospel is addressed to the
issues of its own day, it is not misguided to believe that it deals
with timeless questions. Its happenings are not simply of the past.
In the words of Robert Browning, ' . . . that Life and Death / Of
which I wrote "it was"'—to me it is' (*A Death in the Desert*). For
the writer of this Gospel, judgment and eternal life are here and
now.

◇ The evangelist has his own methods and literary techniques,
especially his use of irony, misunderstanding and symbolism; and
a distinctive, haunting, though not scintillating, style. Those who
claim to have heard Jesus speaking to them in our time nearly
always hear him in the accents of St John's Gospel.

◇ Authorship is an insoluble problem. There is a genius here at
work, perhaps the greatest theologian the Christian Church has
ever known, though there may well have been an editor involved
too (chapter 21 certainly appears to be an appendix, added to an
original which finishes with 20:30–31). Was the genius the
beloved disciple, an actual follower of Jesus many years before,
and now an aged presence in the community? Or is that disciple
simply an ideal, one who—amid the impenetrable blindness of
'the world', and even of some near-believers—understood the
mind of the Lord, the enigma of his revelation and his mission to
bring his disciples into union with himself and the Father? These
are not mutually exclusive options. But the Gospel 'is unthinkable apart from a particular kind of religious community' (Wayne
A. Meeks).

◇ The best clues to the date of the Gospel occur in 9:22, 12:42 and
16:2. These references to expulsion from the synagogue for
confessing the messiahship of Jesus reflect a situation towards the
end of the first century—perhaps AD85–90—when relationships
between Church and synagogue were increasingly strained.
Scholars disagree as to whether there was official Jewish
opposition to Christianity for leading people astray from the

Torah at this period, but it is beyond doubt that relations were far from good between the synagogue and the particular Christian community addressed by the Fourth Gospel.

The translation used is the Revised English Bible.

Further reading

R. Bultmann, *The Gospel of John*, Westminster, 1971

K. Grayston, *The Gospel of John*, Epworth Press, 1990

Barnabas Lindars, *John*, JSOT New Testament Guide, JSOT Press, 1992

G. Wakefield, *The Liturgy of St John*, Epworth Press, 1985

Outline of John's Gospel

The Prologue: The Word made flesh is the true light	1:1–18
Witness to the Word made flesh	1:19—4:54
Authorities in conflict: Whose work is Jesus doing?	5:1–47
The Word made flesh: The bread of life	6:1–71
Authorities in conflict: Jesus' origins and destiny	7:1—8:59
The Word made flesh: The light of life	9:1–43
Authorities in conflict: The true leader of God's people	10:1–42
The Word made flesh: The resurrection and the life	10:40—11:53
'The light is with you for a little longer'	11:54—12:50
The hour of glory for the Son of Man	13:1—17:26
The Lamb of God finishes his work	18:1—19:42

The risen Jesus opens the eyes of faith   20:1–31

A later editor brings the Gospel up to date   21:1–25

THE PROLOGUE: THE WORD MADE — FLESH IS THE TRUE LIGHT —

There is a parallel between the opening of this Gospel and that of Genesis. The story of Jesus Christ begins not at the River Jordan with his baptism (Mark), nor in a miraculous virgin birth (Matthew and Luke), but before the first creation. He is the revelation and the deed of the divine Word, through whom the creation was spoken into being (compare Psalm 33:6), the reason or wisdom (compare Proverbs 8–9) which brings order and light out of chaos. This light has never been overcome by the world's darkness. It shines in nature and in human life.

Jesus is the Word made flesh, taking our nature upon him, dwelling among us in a human life. This is a new role for the Word, the supreme revelation. In the Word made flesh we—the community of believers—see the glory of God's unique Son. This implies four things:

◇ The Word of God is a person, the Son of God, 'of the Father's heart begotten', and in the closest intimacy.

◇ He does not come to bring a new law, but a new relationship. As the New Testament elsewhere insists, the Law of Moses is superseded. 'Grace and truth came by Jesus Christ.' These words might have come from Paul. Grace is the infinite courtesy and condescension of God. Jesus is the revelation of the divine love in action and of ultimate reality, which has ethical as well as metaphysical consequences.

◇ 'No one has ever seen God' (compare Exodus 33:20). Jesus, the incarnate, has revealed his glory. The glory of God is not something which the incarnate Word attains; it is his from the beginning. Seen in a humble human life, it will be completely shown in his return to the Father through death.

◇Notice the dual attitude to the world. It is the creation of God by the Word; as such it must in origin and divine intention be good (3:16). Yet for the most part, in this Gospel 'the world' means that organization of human affairs resulting in cosmic disorder, which is almost irretrievably against God and outside Christ's prayer (17:9). This should make us think what part in 'the world' Christians may have.

WITNESS TO THE
WORD MADE FLESH

The witness of John
John 1:19–34

John the Baptist's preaching of repentance is not mentioned in John. He is simply the forerunner who is to prepare the way of God's true revealer, simply a voice. John's voice, though immensely significant, is of course nothing to the voice of the Son of God, which wakes the dead (5:25; 11:43). In this Gospel, John's baptism in water is not the response to his preaching, but a sign and the shadow of the one whom he foretells.

When the Baptist sees Jesus approaching he recognizes him at once: 'There is the Lamb of God who takes away the sin of the world', a declaration repeated the next day. Here Jesus is seen as the lamb of a new Passover analogous to the old, in which the lamb's blood, sprinkled on their doorposts, protected the children of Israel from the destroying angel and made possible their journey to liberty and the Promised Land. Through his sacrifice, Jesus' followers are delivered from the guilt and power of sin and set free for a life in which they share his glory and oneness with the Father. 'Followers' is a significant term, for after John's second declaration two of his disciples throw in their lot with Jesus.

The baptism of Jesus is not described as in the other Gospels, but the Baptist tells of the descent of the Spirit on Jesus, like a dove. The image is not necessarily one of gentleness. In his 'Little Gidding', T.S. Eliot, fire-watching in the London blitz, saw incendiary bombers as a dove, 'with flames of incandescent terror'. The Holy Spirit does not always come 'with peaceful wings outspread'.

The first disciples

The Baptist must surrender his disciples to Jesus. The call of the Twelve begins not with the summons to fishermen by the lake of Galilee, but with the beginning of the end of John's mission. As the two of them follow Jesus, he turns and utters his first words in this Gospel: 'What are you looking for?' They want to know where he lives, a question which will be taken up again in 14:2–6. The consummation of discipleship is 'that where I am you may be also'. For the moment we may assume that in spending the day with him, they learn what they need to know if they are to become disciples, though not what they will discover in the future after many a hard lesson. As yet, they simply believe that Jesus is the promised Messiah.

Is the unnamed disciple the evangelist himself, the beloved disciple? This is a fascinating question with no certain answer. One of the two is Andrew the brother of Simon, doubtless familiar to the Gospel's readers and prominent in the sequel (chapter 21), as in the early Church. Andrew finds Simon and brings him to Jesus the Christ. Jesus, who presumably has not met Simon before, immediately knows him. This is characteristic of Jesus in this Gospel. He knows and sees in advance, and not only observes Nathanael under the fig-tree, but penetrates the deepest recesses of the human heart (2:25). This is not because he is an omniscient god of mythology, nor a celestial psychologist, but because of his union with the Father in the Holy Spirit. He prophesies Simon's new name—Cephas, Peter, the Rock—and foretells what in spite of weaknesses he will become.

Jesus now decides to move to Galilee. It is not clear whether he has arrived there when he meets Philip to whom he says, 'Follow me.' Philip goes and tells Nathanael about Jesus. Nathanael makes his one appearance here apart from his mention in 21:2. Nathanael is superior and scornful when he learns that Jesus has come from Nazareth. This is not mere snobbery. Messianic impostors from Galilee had already caused trouble (Acts 5:36–37). Nevertheless he does respond to Philip's invitation. Jesus greets him as a true Israelite and Nathanael is impressed. Jesus has seen him under the fig-tree, a place recommended for studying the Scriptures. This 'seeing' cannot be physical; it is due to the spiritual discernment we have noted. Nathanael hails it as a miracle and is immediately converted to Jesus whom he confesses to be Son of God and king of Israel. But this is nothing to what he will see.

Verse 51 is one of the most important in the Gospel. It is the first of those solemn sayings which begin with a double 'Amen', obscured in most English versions. It is based on a mystical Rabbinic interpretation of Jacob's dream in Genesis 28:10–17 in which the ladder is Jacob himself. The verse introduces one more title of Jesus, 'Son of Man', familiar from the other Gospels. Here it means that the historical Jesus, as representative of true humanity, is our direct link with God (see also 3:13).

The sign at Cana   *John 2:1–11*

In D.H. Lawrence's novel *The Rainbow*, Brangwen and Anna in a tempestuous marriage quarrel about this story. She is contemptuous of some of the beliefs of Christianity, but he clings to them out of sheer love. 'The water had not turned into wine. But for all that he would live in his soul as if the water *had* turned into wine. For in truth of fact it had not. But for his soul it had.' That is the case with many who cannot let go of this sign. The fact that it is chemically impossible for water to be turned into wine will not deter those who would assert Christ's authority over all so-called laws of nature. But that is not the world in which the Fourth Gospel dwells. For the evangelist this impossible change is as nothing compared to the supreme miracle of Christ's 'hour', the bringing of life from the dead. Christian tradition and liturgy have seen this story as Christ's hallowing of marriage, but that is very much a side-issue—though a not invalid point for meditation.

The first sign is a manifestation of Christ's glory. He does not show much filial affection towards his mother: 'woman' is formal, rather than discourteous; but afterwards to say in effect, 'Leave me alone' is rather rough. This Gospel never calls the mother of Jesus by the name Mary and she does not appear again until she stands beneath the cross (19:25–27). Does Jesus repudiate the natural relationship and, by giving her then to the beloved disciple, make her the mother of those who most reciprocate his love?

When the wine runs out at the wedding feast, Jesus' mother would have him engage in precipitate action to reveal himself and disclose his whole and finished work. But that means his death and glorification, and he has much to do first. His 'hour' has not yet come. His mother is not altogether deterred. She knows that Jesus will not be inactive—he will give some token of his mission, some manifestation of his glory, and she instructs the servants to do whatever he tells them. He changes a huge amount of water—120 gallons—into wine. The change is a sign that all religions and ways of salvation are inferior to Jesus and what he brings. We are still drinking this abundant wine.

The cleansing of the temple   *John 2:12–25*

In the other Gospels this story comes at the end of Jesus' ministry; John places it near the beginning. Jesus is affronted by the trade in the temple, which has become a market more than a place for the worship of God. But the violent action is not only a sign that the end of animal sacrifice—together with its associated corruption and commercialism—is at hand, but that the *sanctuary* itself (the word used for 'temple' in verse 19), the Holy of Holies, will be destroyed. Jesus' reply to the Jews' questions about his authority is misunderstood. His body is the true temple—his life, his presence. Any building reared by human hands, however resplendent and monumental in labour and offerings, will always be partial and provisional, with the danger that it may be profaned by worldliness, human conflicts and pride. But Christ's body will be destroyed in death, and then raised up to a life which is indestructible. It will become the place where those the Father seeks will worship him in spirit and in truth (4:23). And this is not to be postponed to the end-time. It is taking place now in the life and destiny of Jesus.

After the resurrection the disciples understand. They realize that Psalm 69 is a biography of Jesus, that zeal for God's house has indeed consumed him, but that the true temple rises in his resurrection from the dead. They also become aware that this is prophesied in Hosea 6:2. 'The third day' has a meaning something like 'the eleventh hour' for us—a guest was not supposed to remain in a home beyond the third day; the spirit lingered about the body till then.

The Passover visit to Jerusalem seems to have been a success. 'Many put their trust in him when they saw the signs that he performed.' But Jesus is not impressed. He will not throw in his lot with them. They might have constituted a 'Jesus movement', but faith aroused by miracles is only a beginning. And with his power to see through these believers—as he saw the depths of goodness in Nathanael—he knows that they would not prove trustworthy in the decisive hour.

Jesus and Nicodemus John 3:1–15

Nicodemus is a Pharisee, one of the party which was seeking to bear witness to the true faith of Israel, and as a ruler of the synagogue was not identified with the temple. He comes to Jesus by night, secretly— because in spite of recognizing something of his God-given power, he is in the dark about him. In one of the rare references to the kingdom of God in this Gospel, Jesus tells him that real understanding demands nothing less than rebirth. This defeats Nicodemus, who is remarkably obtuse for a learned and intelligent man. He takes talk of being born again literally and deems it impossible.

The insistence on rebirth has been of immense influence in thought about what it means to be a Christian. 'The born-again' experience is still common and not only in Christianity. It is paralleled in Judaism, and it should not have been a new idea to Nicodemus. John Wesley said that the new birth 'is that great change which God works in the soul when he brings it into life . . . when the love of the world is changed into the love of God; pride into humility; passion into meekness; hatred, envy, malice into a sincere, disinterested love for all mankind'. Wesley dwells on the moral consequences. The new birth is not simply an 'experience'. The marginal alternative in English translations from 1884 must be noted: 'born *from above*'. It is birth of the Spirit, birth from God, birth from where the Son of Man has descended. It is the life of God in the human soul.

Jesus goes on to say that the new birth is 'of water and the Spirit'. This could be a reference to baptism. Baptism without the Spirit is an empty sign; the Spirit without baptism, the sacrament of Christ's finished work, may lead to an esoteric mysticism which ends in weird and superstitious fancy, a constant looking for signs, a dabbling in the occult.

But the Spirit cannot be imprisoned in institutions; it is like the wind, ultimately beyond human control. There is a great liberty of the Spirit (2 Corinthians 3:17). The conversation then takes up the notion of that which is 'above'. Human beings are incapable of contact with heaven. 'The new birth is not achieved by a process of religious ascent; hope lies only in the Son of Man who descended from heaven' (Barrett, *The Gospel According the St John*). But he who descended will also ascend, not by some miracle for all the world to see but by being strung up on a cross. Moses displayed a serpent on a flag pole for the people to receive life and healing (Numbers 21:9). Just as those who were bitten by scorpions in the wilderness looked and lived, so those who *with the eye of faith* see Jesus crucified will receive, not simply an extension of their mortality, but eternal life, 'the possession of unlimited life all at once' (Boethius).

> *William James made a famous distinction between the 'once-born' and the 'twice-born' as two different types of religious experience. Certainly some of us do not undergo any radical change in our personalities and are very much the same people at seventy as at seven. Others have an experience of conversion, which changes their spiritual allegiance and whole way of life, though change of personality is less certain. But the birth from above is not about datable religious experience. It may be taking place silently, imperceptibly, throughout the years, as the Spirit takes possession. Though old age may be a long and sometimes painful process of dying, there is a real life, 'hidden with Christ in God' (Colossians 3:3).*

Love and judgment   *John 3:16–21*

Nicodemus is now abandoned, though he appears again briefly and to his credit at 7:50–52 and 19:39. The discussion ends with some theological pronouncements, including verse 16, which has so often stood out of this context in Protestant liturgy and in the testimony and comforting of Christians. This is the evangelical faith in a nutshell and in some ways seems almost to be out of place in this Gospel, which usually denigrates 'the world' and would seem to limit believers to a small number. But this is a Gospel of God's abundance, as we have seen in the sign at Cana and will see again in the feeding of the five thousand. There is no limit to his love except by the self-exclusion of those who will not believe that its whole truth is there in Jesus, God's supreme revelation and gift (compare Romans 8:32).

God's purpose in sending his Son was not judgment, in the sense of condemnation, and those who trust in Christ need have no fear; but unbelievers condemn themselves, for they prefer darkness to light. Sin may be both profitable and enjoyable; it is alluring and exciting, sometimes even romantic, like the dark. But it has to be covert, because it is fundamentally dishonest, a denial of the truth, a breaking of trust; it dreads exposure and so fears and hates the light. Believers are people of the light; they have found the truth in Jesus and live by it; the light shines through them so that the whole of their life is a revelation of God (compare Matthew 5:14–16).

There is no sense here of a *last* judgment, a great assize. The saving event is also judgment. The light of Christ divides the whole of history of the past, present and future into those who follow it and those who continue to live in darkness.

The final witness of the Baptist   *John 3:22–36*

Jesus, who moves to and fro between north and south more in this Gospel than in the others, is now back in Judea. There was undoubted controversy between the Baptist's followers and those of Jesus which seems to have persisted after the resurrection and beyond Palestine (Acts 19:1–6). The Baptist's movement did not end with his execution. Here Jesus is seen as baptizing though there is no record in the synoptics. There is a hint of jealousy and rivalry on the part of John's followers, and it could be that the evangelist is addressing a situation which had continued into his own time.

According to the evangelist, the Baptist will have none of this. He knows his own limited and in some sense temporary role. As he has insisted before, he is not the Messiah but the forerunner or, in another analogy, the best man at the wedding, not the bridegroom. In Middle Eastern marriages this is no subordinate figure. He woos the bride, arranges the feast and stands guard at the door of the bridal chamber until he hears the bridegroom's voice announcing his arrival. The Baptist's joy is complete because the bridegroom has arrived even though this means that his responsibility is over. He takes satisfaction in a mission accomplished, and is ready for the festal celebrations (even though in this case they will be delayed). He is thus an example to all believers, whose vocation is not to their own fame or honour, but simply to be friends of their Lord.

Verses 31–36 seem to follow better from verse 21. We are back to the one who comes from above and the contrast between the heavenly and the earthly. The conclusion in verse 36 is severe and awesome. While belief in the Son guarantees eternal life, to disobey the Son unleashes the divine wrath, which for John is a reality. Could God be kind if he could not be angry? Luther, among others, did not think so.

The woman at the well

The Pharisees' hostility to Jesus (mentioned here for the first time) makes him withdraw to Galilee—his hour had not yet come. He has to pass through Samaria, though he could have avoided it. The Samaritans believed that they were the descendants of the lost ten tribes of Israel and accepted only the first five books of Moses. They and the Jews quarrelled over land; relations at best were frigid, and the Jews and Samaritans did not like to use common cups and dishes. Jesus, tired in the heat of the day, rests by Jacob's well and a woman comes along to draw water. Thirsty, he asks her for a drink. She, the woman, is astonished that a Jew should show no hesitation about sharing her vessel. For a moment she may wonder whether he is about to make advances like most men. Instead, he is going to engage her in a profound theological discussion, itself remarkable. He shows more respect to her than to Nicodemus. But at first he is concerned, not with relationships between Jews and Samaritans or women and men, but again with the temporal and the eternal, the earthly and the heavenly.

Water was scarce in the Middle East. It was not something which human ingenuity could create; it seemed to come direct from God. There is a paradox that the Jesus who asks her for water is the one who gives it—though not water from a well, however hallowed by its association with Jacob, but 'living water'. This means running as opposed to stagnant water. Jesus is speaking literally when he tells her that the water he gives will quench thirst forever and be an inward supply, 'welling up and bringing eternal life'. She is impressed and eagerly asks for it, but only because she thinks it will deliver her from the wearisome need to toil to the well. Jesus, in fact, spares us nothing of 'the trivial round, the common task'.

The true worship of God

The living water of eternal life is the knowledge of God (compare 17:3). It satisfies that longing of the Psalmist for the most intimate communion (Psalm 42:1). It may be typified by the water which with blood flowed from Christ's pierced side (19:34)—the water which in the end could be given only because of his dying thirst (19:28).

O Water, life bestowing,
Forth from the Saviour's heart,
A fountain purely flowing,
A fount of love thou art:

O let us freely tasting,
Our burning thirst assuage;
Thy sweetness never wasting,
Avails from age to age.

Thomas Aquinas

But there are conditions for receiving this water. Asking is not enough. 'Go and call your husband' says Jesus to the woman 'and come back here'. Once more, he who knows what is in human beings has discerned her manner of life, the long list of emotional disturbances and failures to find true satisfaction, and entered into her psyche. She is embarrassed but honest, and hails Jesus as a prophet. Her question about the place for God's true worship is far from a *non sequitur*. She needs to know where she may find the place of repentance. This, says Jesus, is no longer the sacred mount of the Samaritans, Gerizim, where they believed Abraham had prepared to offer Isaac (Genesis 22), Melchizedek had met Abraham (Genesis 14:18), and the priests had first made sacrifices after the crossing of Jordan (Deuteronomy 27:4). Nor is it in Jerusalem, even though 'salvation is of the Jews' and Jesus stands in their (and not the Samaritan) succession. Sites and cults are but provisional. They will not survive the end of the age. The 'hour' of Jesus reveals the truth that God is Spirit. This does not mean that he has no concern with forms and liturgies, or that true religion is inward and 'spiritual'. Rather God is that transforming energy beyond the human sphere by which Christians, through the revelation of Jesus, already live in the age to come. He is to be worshipped in the faith which recognizes Jesus (that is, 'in spirit'), and in union with Jesus (who is 'the truth'). Verse 24 is not, as some have thought, the text to be inscribed over the portico of a future temple to a single world religion. It is Christocentric, though Christ is the Logos, the light which enlightens everyone (1:9). When the disciples return they are 'astonished to find him talking with a woman'. But they do not question him. The woman departs for the town—leaving her jug behind in her eager excitement—to tell of the man who seemed to know all her past and might be the Messiah.

The harvest

The disciples, with typical anxiety and concern for his welfare, press food on Jesus. We are not told explicitly that he refused it, nor that his conversation with the woman had left him satiated so that his hunger and thirst are forgotten. We may infer from verse 33 that he did not eat on this occasion, but here he uses food (as he had earlier used water) as an analogy of his true sustenance to do God's will. It would seem from various hints in all the Gospels that Jesus had not much thought of food or drink for himself until his work on earth was done and he could be present at the feast of the consummation. In any case, there is a harvest to be reaped. Does he refer to the approaching Samaritans, visible on the horizon? This harvest has defied the course of nature in which there are still four months to wait. 'Harvest' in the synoptics normally refers to the end-time. But here there is no interval between sowing and reaping, no patient waiting. 'The decisive moment is the present moment. It does not belong to some future time but always to the present, and this because it is an event of the last things' (Bultmann, *The Gospel of John*).

There is reference here to the ministry of the disciples as well as that of Jesus. The passage is certainly written with an eye to their missionary experience and their discouragements in hard times of opposition and indifference. Sometimes there seems a long, unrewarding interval between sowing and reaping, seed-time and harvest. In the view of God's eternity they are simultaneous. This removes any jealousy between sower and reaper, and sadness because the harvest may be reaped by one who has not laboured and waited for it. Those who sow may not survive to gather the fruits of their toil; they must live by faith that their work will not have been in vain. Sower and reaper may be two different persons in time; in eternity, they are united in the harvest home of heaven. Jesus is the sower; the disciples are the reapers. He has done the hardest work, sown himself like the grain of wheat which falls into the ground and dies (12:24). The disciples may not therefore look back to their own good sowing and care of the crops. The glory is Christ's. Yet the sowing has been in history and no Christian preacher or missionary dare be oblivious of the past and those who have come before— supremely Jesus. For he is the author and finisher, the pioneer and perfecter; the mission finds its meaning only in him. All his disciples and their successors have to do is to reap the harvest of his life and Passion.

The woman has succeeded in converting many Samaritans, who are willing to receive Jesus. His two-day stay leads many more to faith. The lesson is the old evangelical one that it is the task of missionaries and messengers to bring people to Jesus and this is all that matters. Faith must rest not on other people's testimony, nor on dogmatic formulations, but on direct encounter with Jesus, though mediated by preachers, spiritual guides, or creeds. 'We have heard for ourselves': that is the criterion. The Samaritans confess Jesus as saviour of the world. 'Saviour' is not a common New Testament title and is mostly confined to the later writings. Here it asserts, as does John 3:15, that the mission of Jesus is universal, 'immense, unfathomed, unconfined' (Charles Wesley).

The second sign   *John 4:43–54*

Jesus now continues his journey into Galilee; there is a hint that the Galileans' acclaim, like that of the people of Jerusalem (2:23), is not true faith because it rests on signs and wonders (v. 48), and will later (6:14) turn to rejection.

The second sign takes place like the first at Cana in Galilee. A similar story is found in Matthew 8:5–13 and Luke 7:1–10. In both, a distressed officer seeks Jesus out and asks him to heal his son (or servant, in Luke), pleading with intense faith and humility, and the patient is cured from a distance. But there are differences. This miracle takes place at Cana not Capernaum, the suppliant is not a heathen officer but a Jewish official at the court of King Herod, and Jesus at first rebuffs him. John's story is briefer and less powerful and moving. He shows no appreciation of the officer's faith. He seems detached and admonitory, less human, less concerned with the boy's healing than with the attitude of the father. Is he not approaching Jesus merely as a wonder-worker? Is not his faith in miraculous powers, which will fulfil his own heartfelt desires, rather than in Jesus?

It is at first sight an unattractive picture of Jesus, remote and unlovable. He is different from the one who had declared 'God so loved the world . . .' But it points to the austere truth that faith must be in Jesus as the revealer of God, not in his ability to grant our wishes or perform miracles which meet our needs, however much they are those of sincerest human love. This is a hard lesson to learn. St John of the Cross learnt it, though it meant a journey through the dark night of sense and soul. And Charles Wesley could say 'Nothing beside my God I want/nothing in earth or heaven'. But then if God is the one desire of our hearts, all things are ours, even though he may not always seem to answer our prayers in the way we would wish. In this passage the wish was granted, the pleading heard, because it was an admission of total dependence on God, a need of a power not ourselves. This is the first stage of faith; and the father and all his household became believers.

> These early chapters tell of much misunderstanding of Jesus—by Nicodemus for instance, but even by those who claimed to believe. His mother did not see that his hour had not yet come, his disciples would not understand the true meaning of his words and actions till he was raised from the dead, Herod's officer may not at his first approach have known the meaning of faith. But John the Baptist knew who Jesus was, and the Samaritan woman—the least respectable—learned quickly and became his messenger. What then is necessary for faith?

AUTHORITIES IN CONFLICT: — WHOSE WORK IS JESUS DOING? —

Lame at the pool   John 5:1–15

Jesus is again in Jerusalem for an unidentified festival. The disciples do not seem to be present; at any rate they are not mentioned throughout this chapter of controversy with 'the Jews'—those of that religion who were already beginning to think that Jesus was dangerous and should be removed. They were mostly the religious authorities, certainly not the whole race, for many Jews believed in him (8:30; 1:12), and some were divided about him (10:19–21; 11:36–37). His mother and his disciples were Jews.

There was another miracle. Jesus, having ascertained that the man has the will to be healed, tells him to rise, take up his bed and walk. Immediately he does so. He has no need to wait any longer to go into the pool. The word of Jesus is effective for his cure. That, however, is not the end of the matter. The man was healed on the sabbath when the Jews deemed it unlawful for a person to carry a load, in this case a bed. When charged, the man replied that he was merely doing what the healer had told him to do; but he had no idea of who he was. Jesus had withdrawn to avoid notice and excitement. Jesus finds the man in the temple, where presumably he has gone to give thanks. Jesus is stern with him and implies that the man's illness was due to sin. If so, his misdemeanours must have been very much in the distant past since he had waited at the pool for almost forty years. Jesus does not automatically assume that illness, infirmity and handicap are due to sin (9:3). Yet his comment is puzzling, though as we are well aware these days, abuse of the body may cause the most terrible illness. Now the man knows the identity of his healer, reports to the authorities and disappears forever from the Gospel.

The sabbath, the Father and the authority of Jesus   *John 5:16–23*

The opponents of Jesus now charge him with sabbath-breaking—and worse, because in order to justify himself, he invokes God as his Father. Already they had thought that he should be disposed of; now they are more vehement in their determination to make away with him. He has seemingly revoked the belief that the origin of the sabbath lay in God's rest from the work of creation (Genesis 2:2–3; Exodus 20:8–11). The Jewish philosopher Philo (c. 20BC–AD45) and later rabbis qualified the tradition because God could never be totally inactive or cease from doing good. The rabbis came to argue that on the sabbath God rested from his work of creation but not from his work of judgment. Jesus dares to claim that the continuing work of God is seen in *his* signs. This is blasphemy in the ears of his critics.

In the Hebrew tradition a son reproduces the thought and actions of his father, and the father's love for the son is expressed in enabling him to do this. Jesus, the Son, is totally dependent on God the Father and the Father's love (vv. 19–20). Jesus says that the Jews have not seen in the signs so far anything compared to what will follow, for the Son will have the Father's power to raise the dead. The Father has delegated his own works to the Son and this means not only the giving of life but also judgment. In the historic Jesus the final confrontation between good and evil, life and death takes place. This is not only seen in the particular events which are unfolding, culminating in his death and resurrection. His freedom to give life to whom he will extends beyond the immediate provenance of his ministry to all ages and all peoples. Therefore all must honour the Son as they honour the Father.

This implies that the relation of Jesus to God is not that of a prophet called to proclaim God's message in a particular crisis. It is not a matter of calling but of being. Jesus may at this period have been thought of as subordinate to the Father, but as Son he is of the same nature. According to Austin Farrer, 'The Son has nothing that he does not derive from the Father, but he derives from the Father all the Father has to give.' This would be impossible were he not equal. 'He depends on the Father not less than we do, but for infinitely more. Like us, he depends on the Father for all things. We receive from the Father all we are, he alone receives from the Father all the Father is.'

The voice that wakes the dead   John 5:24−29

Jesus speaks words of great solemnity. Between verses 19 and 29, there are three sayings prefaced by the repeated ' Amen', translated as 'in truth, in very truth I say'. Notice the mention of 'the voice' of the Son in verses 25 and 28. Here again is the uttered Word of God, which was in the beginning (1:1). His word has the power of God to wake the dead and pronounce judgment. It does not initiate us into mysteries as contemporary myths and cults claimed to do. There is nothing to satisfy our speculative curiosity. Jesus speaks the words of eternal life.

The passage is cryptic. It is through the gift of his own life received from the Father that the dead are raised by the Son. The Father and the Son have life in themselves, the life of God as creator and judge. Believers have life in the Son: that is what his voice imparts. It may not always be by some mighty cry as at the grave of Lazarus, but by the word that he speaks as he talks in public or in private. This brings the resurrection and the last judgment into the here and now. The dead are not only those already departed this life and in the tomb. They are the men and women of the world, 'who live a life which lacks authenticity, for they do not know the true light (1:9) and the life which it gives' (Bultmann). 'Hearing' is more than the most attentive mental perception. It is listening and responding with faith and obedience (compare 12:47).

Verses 28 and 29 seem to revert to the old belief about a general resurrection and judgment, which the previous statements re-interpret.

Jesus also gives himself the additional title 'Son of Man' (compare Daniel 7:13, 22), the representative of our humanity before God. Because this goes back to conventional beliefs about the 'last things', some have thought that the verses are a later insertion to try to allay the alarm of those disturbed by the new teaching of eternal life in the very presence and word of Jesus. If authentic, they may simply be saying that the old view is a picture or parable of what is eternally true and manifest in the work and word of Jesus of Nazareth.

The witnesses and the glory   *John 5:30–47*

Underlying all these assertions of Jesus is the question of the authority for his signs and statements. He says again that he can do nothing of himself and accepts the axiom of ancient jurisprudence that his own testimony must be supported by witnesses. His all-sufficient witness is the Father, but his world-minded questioners will regard his claim to know that God endorses him as self-deceiving blasphemy. So he invokes three more witnesses. First, there is John the Baptist, a 'burning and shining light', but not *the* light. The greater witness is the works which God has given him to accomplish; these are not the signs themselves but what they signify—the power to raise the dead and judge the world. There are also the Scriptures, which the devout Jews pore over so avidly.

Christian conviction is that the whole of the Bible is about Jesus Christ. All the long centuries of Israel's vicissitudes, the proclamations of the Prophets, the laments and praises of the psalmists, their awareness of God and their desolation, find their fulfilment only in Jesus Christ. There are Christians who are embarrassed by this, who do not like to speak of the *Old* Testament, who feel that it is Christian imperialism to take over the Jewish Scriptures and regard them primarily as witnesses to Christ. There must certainly be an understanding, more reverential than it has often been, of their place within Judaism. Sometimes Christians have caricatured Jewish interpretation, whereas it is essential to a knowledge of Christianity. There must be as much agreement and sharing of insights as possible. But Christians cannot deny their beliefs, not so much that the Jewish Scriptures are inadequate and inferior as that Christ does fulfil those ancient expectations. It is his sufferings which are foreshadowed and shared by the anguish of prophets and psalmists, and the love revealed in him which is seen in the compassion of former saints and their defiant refusal to abandon belief in the divine mercy. There are many crosses before the one set up on Calvary to be the consummation in time of the sacrificial self-giving of God himself, which is his nature from all eternity.

Rejection of Jesus means that his opponents have not understood the Scriptures they revere: Moses' writings speak of a prophet to come (Deuteronomy 18:18). It is human pride and the desire for honour from one another which blinds them. The glory that comes from God, seen in Jesus, will utterly devalue their accepted standards and honours-system.

THE WORD MADE FLESH: THE BREAD OF LIFE

The feeding of the five thousand   John 6:1—15

The controversy with 'the Jews' is interrupted by the miracle of the loaves and the subsequent lengthy discourse. This is the one miracle reported in all four Gospels and the comparisons and contrasts are interesting. The crowds follow Jesus, and the fact that he sat down on the hillside suggests that he taught them before realizing their hunger. St John says that 'it was near the time of the Passover, the great Jewish festival'. The detail has possibly great significance. Does it foreshadow that last Passover of Jesus' death to which events are fast moving, and his vocation as Lamb of God? Must it not also heighten the atmosphere as the people begin to think of the feast of liberation from bondage? Philip and Andrew are both rather naïve, and our imagination must not play too freely on the boy and Andrew's bringing him to Jesus with his supplies. The emphasis is on the paucity of the disciples' resources: only Jesus can feed the multitude.

The old liberal expositors explained the miracle by suggesting that Jesus prevailed on the crowd to share the food they had brought with them. And it would be strange if the boy were the only one in a crowd of five thousand to have come with some refreshment. But that does not appreciate the thought-world of St John. It was a prophetic sign, not necessarily demanding Christ's divinity as explanation. Elisha seems to have performed a smaller miracle, feeding a hundred people from twenty loaves and some ripe ears of corn. And there was some left over then, though not twelve basketfuls (2 Kings 4:42–44).

The disciples are told to gather up the fragments that remain. The Church Fathers read into this the proper disposal of the eucharistic elements, but John does not regard the meal as eucharistic. There is bread and fish (compare 21:9) but no wine. The giving of thanks is Jewish—grace before meat; this would 'consecrate' it, not in the sense of separating it for holy use, but rather releasing it from God's domain for human consumption. The bread is his before it is the crowd's. They become excited, stirred up by the miracle and the Passover season. Jesus is undoubtedly the expected prophet. They want to seize him to make him king, a sort of Herod who would lead them to freedom from the new Egypt of Roman suzerainty. He withdraws alone to the hills. They do not understand the meaning of the sign which he will have to explain later. There are problems: Jesus repudiates a political role through which alone it would seem a more just society is possible; and in a world of starvation his primary mission is not what we know as Christian aid. But he *does* feed the multitude and relieve their hunger. He will simply tell them later that there are deeper needs than physical, and richer food than earthly bread.

The walking on the water   *John 6:16–21*

This story has become colloquial, in that banners are displayed on cricket grounds and at other sporting events proclaiming that a particular athletic hero 'walks on water'. Again, there have been those who have denied that it tells of a miracle, here and in Matthew 14:22–27 and Mark 6:47–52. Some think of John's as an earlier and more natural version—that the absence of wonder and amazement on the part of the disciples is due to the fact that the boat was already near the shore and that Jesus was walking on the sand. But a rational explanation is not true to the mind of the evangelist: for him the real point of the story is the miracle of Jesus walking on the lake (Bultmann). This may be spiritualized as in Paul Gerhardt's hymn, translated by John Wesley and including the lines,

Give to the winds thy fears...
Through waves and clouds and storms
He gently clears thy way.

These words greatly helped Bonhoeffer in the Nazi prison. Amid the storms and tempests of life Jesus comes. The sight of him in the darkness and the gale may add to the disciples' fears at first, but he is the I AM (translated in verse 20 as 'it is I'). He has the divine mastery over the forces of nature—material or spiritual—and in a moment brings them to the haven where they would be (compare Psalm 107:28–30). A mystical interpretation may not be out of place, as in Francis Thompson's well-known poem 'The Kingdom of God—In no strange land':

Yea, in the night, my Soul, my daughter,
Cry—clinging Heaven by the hems;
And lo, Christ walking on the water
Not of Gennesareth, but Thames!

> The Gospel is about God the Father. He is the one who does the works; but he has sent his unique Son, who though entirely dependent on him is his agent. His sole mission is to bring men and women to the Father. To deny him is to deny the Father. What understanding of God do we derive from these chapters of St John's Gospel? And what do the miracles mean for our lives today?

The pursuing crowd   *John 6:22–29*

This is a difficult passage, not made easier by the number of textual variations in ancient manuscripts. Though Jesus has withdrawn to escape the people's wish to make him king, they are still after him and crowd the boats to reach the opposite shore to find him in Capernaum, where he is presumably preaching in the synagogue. The matter of the kingship seems to have been forgotten. They ask him what he is doing in Capernaum, but Jesus does not answer their questions. He casts aspersions on their motives: signs have not kindled faith but merely their desire for material benefits (though these are not luxuries but basic necessities). Are people blameworthy for wanting their daily bread to assuage hunger and keep them and their families and neighbours alive? In the prayer he taught his disciples in Luke and Matthew, Jesus tells them to ask for bread (Matthew 6:11; Luke 11:3).

Here he tells the people not to work for perishable food but for the food of eternal life, which the Son of Man (speaking of himself in the third person) is able to provide. This is because he is 'sealed' by the Father (v. 27), that is owned and authenticated by God. It may also imply that he is consecrated, set apart for sacrifice, which may be why he uses the future tense: 'the food . . . which the Son of Man *will* give you . . .'

The people are Galilean peasants, who indeed earn their living by the sweat of their brows. They want to know how these assertions affect their daily work, which must be for their own and others' subsistence. Jesus says that the one work God requires is to believe in him as the one sent by God. The 'sending' is a very important idea throughout the Gospel. According to the late Hans Urs von Balthasar, a Roman Catholic theologian, 'Perhaps the going forth from God is still more divine than the return home, since the greatest thing is not for us to know God and reflect this knowledge back to him as if we were gleaming mirrors, but for us to proclaim God as burning torches proclaim the light.' This proclamation of faith affects the whole of life, for it is of that ultimate reality which includes God's total creation: time and eternity, body and soul. And it places our toil for daily bread and the relief of physical hunger in the context of lives which are destined for more than this passing earth.

The bread of life   *John 6:30–40*

There is demand for a sign. They have not seen the miracle of the loaves as such, but simply regard it as a marvellous humanitarian act. They have thus missed its significance. For them it has meant the satisfaction of physical hunger and nothing more. They hark back to the story of the manna in the wilderness, quoting Psalm 78:24–25 with a hint— important for further development of the theme—of Psalm 105:40. 'Bread' means food in general, including flesh.

Jesus rejoins that it was not Moses who gave the manna, but God, who is his Father. He gives not simply manna, which was rancid after a day and was not to be stored (Exodus 16:19–20), but the true bread of eternal life. Like the manna this descends from heaven, for it is he, Jesus, who dares to use the mysterious divine name, 'I AM the bread of life'. Once more there is the emphasis on the descent, the downward movement (compare 3:13), preparing the way for the understanding of the Incarnation as *kenosis*, self-emptying. This development from

Philippians 2:5–11 has been revived in recent theology; the eternal nature of the blessed Trinity is always pouring itself out in love, of which the historic Incarnation, the Word made flesh, is the revelation in time. This bread removes spiritual hunger, the awesome emptiness and desolation of life without God for all eternity. But the people will not believe that the bread of eternal life is Jesus. This leads to a statement of an almost Calvinist belief in election. There are those whom the Father gives to Jesus and those, it seems, whom he does not—a theme central to the rest of the chapter and the Gospel. Those the Father gives to the Son are safe for ever in his keeping.

Jesus says that it is the Father's will that 'I should not lose even one of those he has given me, but should raise them all up on the last day'. This introduces the idea of resurrection, which is important for the discussion of what is almost certainly the Eucharist a few verses down. For John, the Eucharist is not—as it was for Ignatius of Antioch early in the next century—the 'medicine of immortality'. It does give life and close communion with God, but the believer still has to be raised up at the last day. The Gospel takes bodily death, the irreversible coma which marks our departure from this life, seriously.

The bread is the flesh of God's Son   *John 6:41–51*

'The Jews', those hearers who are hostile, 'murmur' in dissent. We can almost hear them, those rumblings which, though not quite parliamentary roars, inarticulately form the background to public sentiments of which some members of an audience disapprove. If Jesus is now engaged in a typical synagogue sermon, it is interrupted at this point. The hearers cannot believe that this man, whose father and mother they know, can have descended from God. His birth was all too natural. There may be Johannine irony here, though he is not necessarily saying that the Jews are not aware that this apparently normal birth was the result of virginal conception; if they could accept its apparent scandal, it would establish that this is no mere man who speaks. Any hints that the evangelist may know of the birth stories are tantalizingly elusive. Belief in an unusual or miraculous birth of Jesus may destroy his main contention, for he is insisting that the revelation confronts humanity in history. This destroys the preconceived notions of Jesus' adversaries. It is a man—standing before them and speaking with a local accent—who has come down from heaven, dares to call himself the I AM and is the bread of life. Their real problem is that they think they know how God would reveal himself and this blinds them to the truth as it is in Jesus. He must be received with the openness of faith. This means 'coming' to Jesus, but this is only possible for a person who is 'drawn' by the Father. Jesus is recognized only by response to God's own teaching (v. 45, quoting Isaiah 54:13). This 'drawing' is not irresistible, nor does it override free will, a qualification of any hint of Calvinism here. It is certainly not magical. It is the response to listening, being taught by God. In verse 37 the visual metaphor is used: it is 'seeing', with the implication that it is not something hammered into a person by a barrage of words or intellectual concepts, but insight. Faith is sight and this is eternal life.

We are then back to the I AM saying and the bread of life. This means that Jesus is in some sense to be eaten. The nineteenth century German philosopher Feuerbach's cynical and degrading comment may be elevated to Christian truth: 'Man is what he eats'; by feeding on Christ one receives his life and will never die. What is to be fed on is Christ's flesh, his full humanity, given for the life of the world (compare 3:16).

The Lord's Supper   *John 6:52–58*

This scandalized the Jews as—taken literally—it has many Christians. Those who object to Cranmer's *Prayer of Humble Access* on grounds that it expresses a Christian cannibalism ('Grant us therefore gracious Lord, so to eat the flesh of thy dear Son, Jesus Christ and to drink his blood . . .') are not always aware that the real ground of offence is this passage of John's Gospel and not the free composition of a Protestant liturgist. There may be a reference to the Eucharist, whose institution at the last supper John does not record. His attitude towards it has been said to be one of 'critical acceptance' (Barrett). He does not repudiate it, though he may be aware of the danger of its becoming a 'stinted form' (Pascal) which exempts people from the duty of loving God. By his carnal language, John brings out its awesome and shocking nature. In 4:34 Jesus had said that his food is to do the will of the Father who sent him. In this sense he feeds on the Father. So the believer eats and drinks Jesus, in obedience and faith. By its very nature this means mutual indwelling, what Calvin and his English Puritan followers called 'the mystical union', a union as close as bread and eater, vine and branches. This is what the Eucharist signifies.

Jesus specifically calls himself the Son of Man in verse 53. The title 'Son of Man' implies, first, Jesus' descent from God as the bread of heaven, and also his ascent by way of the cross (3:13); and, second, it refers to the end-time, for which the early Christians prayed in their worship (1 Corinthians 16:22: 'Marana tha'—Our Lord come). All this is implicit in the Eucharist. A hymn of Charles Wesley is the best comment:

We need not now go up to heaven
To bring the long sought Saviour down,
Thou art to all, already given,
Thou doest e'en now thy banquet crown
To every faithful soul appear
And show they real presence here.

The scandal and the defection   *John 6:59—65*

It is not simply the unbelieving Jews who are now scandalized. Jesus' words sift out his few disciples from the majority who have followed hitherto. And the whole discourse in the intention of the evangelist is doubtless directed at some in his own day who are unable to grasp spiritual truths or 'heavenly things'. Jesus warns them of far greater shocks in store: they are to see the Son of Man 'ascending where he was before'. This refers to the lifting up on the cross, which for John is the beginning of Jesus' ascent to his glory. There will be no spectacular demonstration of divine splendour before the world, but what will seem to his disciples like utter shame and defeat. Already talk of eating his flesh and drinking his blood must have sounded like a premonition of death, the giving up and pouring out of life. Now it is made clear in Johannine terms. The words of Jesus are 'spirit and life'. He makes the astonishing and contradictory statement after all that has been said that 'the flesh can achieve nothing'. 'Flesh' does not here refer to the full humanity of Jesus and all that was accomplished through it in his human life and death, but to a carnal interpretation of the Lord's Supper. Like George Fox seventeen hundred years later, John is concerned about the reality of sacramental communion (our terms not his). True eating and drinking means an immediacy of fellowship with Christ and its ethical consequences, 'which makes perfect and redeems from all that is vain, fleshly and earthly, up to God, who is holy, pure, spiritual and eternal' (George Fox).

C.K. Barrett's summary is worth noting: 'The offer of flesh and blood calls for proclamation to make it intelligible and supply the necessary understanding of God's action; for faith on the part of the recipient; and (since with this there will be no hearing of the word and not faith) the predestinating prevenient action of God.'

The Twelve   *John 6:66—71*

Many now 'walk no more with him'. Jesus turns to the Twelve, not mentioned elsewhere in this Gospel apart from 20:24. We assume they are the especially chosen ones and include those who became disciples at the beginning of the Gospel. Peter, as at Caesarea Philippi in the other Gospels (Mark 8:29 and parallels), is their spokesman. It is significant that he does not use any of the titles found in the sayings of Jesus himself or applied to him in the tradition. He does not call Jesus the Son of Man, Son of God or Messiah, the one sent by God, come from the Father, the Saviour or even the Bread of Life. Peter's ascription declares that Jesus 'stands over against the world simply as the one who comes from another world and belongs to God and indeed that he is the sole one to do so' (Bultmann). This is echoed in much early liturgy, as in the *Gloria in Excelsis Deo*: 'You alone are the Holy One'. It also foreshadows the Passion, for the Holy One is the one set apart, consecrated as a sacrifice.

The Twelve have decided for Christ, yet they are not simply the instruments of their own calling. He has, ultimately, chosen them. But they will find the following of Jesus a hard path and there is no certainty that all of them will endure to the end. 'A gracious soul may fall from grace' (Wesley): one of them is a devil. The disciples did not know the identity of the traitor at this stage. The evangelist knows, of course, and names him Judas, son of Simon Iscariot. If John knew the words after Peter's confession in Mark 8:27—33, in which Peter, trying to dissuade Jesus from the cross, is called by Jesus 'Satan', then he is deliberately changing Jesus' words in order to condemn Judas. John's readers would find this all the more fearsome and disturbing, because there were Judases in the early Church who would denounce Christians to the imperial power.

> What light does this chapter shed on the meaning of the Eucharist and our own approach to it? Is faith necessary to right receiving? Does the chapter underline the necessity for word and sacrament to be the central rite of Christian worship? Does it teach that remembrance of passion and resurrection should be conjoined in the Eucharist and that it should also anticipate 'the last day'?
>
> And what do we learn of the dangers and cost of discipleship? Peter's confession was bold and brave; following Christ must combine total dependence on him with willingness to risk all, in the belief that we are able to endure to the end.

AUTHORITIES IN CONFLICT: — JESUS' ORIGINS AND DESTINY —

As the Gospel narrative has unfolded over the first six chapters, the revelation of Jesus has grown steadily richer—he is the one whom the Jewish Scriptures point to, the Messiah, the Son of God, the king of Israel, the Son of Man, the new temple, the one sent by God, the bringer of eternal life, the embodiment of divine love for the world, the source of the water of life, the true bread of life which has come down from heaven. His works are a sign of divine glory, his words come with the sole authority of God. We have seen the way people have been affected by him—some have become disciples and evangelists, some have been healed, some have remained uncertain, some have opposed him.

The progress of divine revelation has been accompanied by signals of Jesus' destiny. He can only bring life to the world by losing his own—his power to save lies in his 'lifting up', his ability to be heavenly food and drink rests in his willingness to give up his own life. Though Jesus has not set out to judge the world, St John has shown that this has been an inevitable part of the impact of his revelation of God's grace and truth. Many of those who encounter him are unwilling to accept what he reveals. The guardians of the religious heritage of his own people reject his central claim to be acting and speaking for God and God alone. And at the end of chapter 6, we saw that even some of his followers start to draw back.

As the narrative continues through the first half of the Gospel, up to the end of chapter 12, the revelation of Jesus becomes clearer and brighter as the shadows lengthen over his relationship with the Jewish leaders. The stage is being set for the supreme manifestation of his glory in the Passion.

The unbelieving brothers
John 7:1–13

Jesus is in Galilee because to be in Jerusalem would probably lead to his arrest and precipitate the hour which has not yet come. It is, however, the time of the Feast of Tabernacles, the autumn harvest festival, which according to the first century Jewish historian Josephus was 'the most sacred and most important feast of the Jews'. Jesus would be expected to go. His brothers urge him to do so, for they see it as an opportunity to display his powers to a wider audience: 'show yourself to the world' (v. 3). Like his mother at Cana in chapter 2, they are eager for him to fulfil what they think is his mission. They are neither hostile nor jealous. Rather they are proud of him and do not want him with his supernatural gifts to remain in obscurity. Yet the evangelist charges them with unbelief. They will not wait for God's moment. They are in fact opportunists. 'The right time for me has not yet come, but any time is right for you' (v. 6).

John does not show Jesus' natural family in an altogether good light. The Gospels, apart from the birth stories in Matthew and Luke, do not give any grounds for idealizing 'the Holy Family', nor regarding his mother as especially close to Jesus in understanding, though in John she is at least beneath the cross (19:25). This may be disconcerting at a time when there is a sense of the need to restore faith in the nuclear family, but however much it is the cornerstone of a stable and healthy society, it is not inevitably a nursery of heaven. Some, like Jesus and his disciples, may have to abandon it for the sake of the higher demands of the divine will.

Jesus, who will not go to the feast at the instigation of his brothers, goes nonetheless after some delay. This disturbed ancient editors and copyists and they altered verse 8 to read 'I am not *yet* going'. Many reliable manuscripts contain this: but the balance seems in favour of the hard reading. Cana may perhaps again be a parallel. Jesus rebuked his mother when she wanted him to act: yet he turned water into wine all the same. So he now goes to Jerusalem though not, as later, for his ascent to heaven by the cross. He went *in secret*, not on public pilgrimage; but this also may have the rabbinic and Aramaic implication that he was walking humbly before God (Micah 6:8; Matthew 6:4, 6). He is talked about in Jerusalem and is the subject of controversy. Opinions are divided as to whether he is a good man or a charlatan.

Controversy with 'the Jews'   *John 7:14–24*

This is a difficult passage, of which verses 19b–24 seem not only to hark back to 5:16ff, but possibly to belong there. In some sense the controversies in chapters 5–10 constitute a trial of Jesus, parallel to that which occurs later before the Sanhedrin and Pilate. There is first the contention that Jesus, not being a member of the Jewish schools of biblical interpretation, has no authority of sound learning. Jesus answers that he has his teaching direct from God and his knowledge is not scholastic so much as ethical. It comes from his doing of God's will in the obedience of faith, and the seeking of his glory who is the truth. 'The Jews', the religious leaders, lay claim to learning, but by desiring Jesus' death they transgress the law Moses gave them from God, in which they claim to be experts.

The people now become enraged and charge Jesus with being demon-possessed because of what they regard as his unworthy and paranoid suspicion. He then returns to the sabbath controversy, in a few very difficult verses. He has only broken the sabbath once and this for a work of healing of the lame man at the pool, a work which restored the man's whole being. The practice of circumcision on the sabbath is not thought to break this commandment because it was instituted by Moses, or rather by the tradition Moses inherited. Should not Jesus' one act of total healing be similarly condoned? His opponents do not understand Moses' real intention. They are legalists who judge by externals, not by the right judgment of those who obey the God to whom one responds in faith and love.

The advent and departure of the Messiah   *John 7:25–36*

The 'Jerusalemites', a term used only here in verse 25 and in Mark 1:5 to describe the permanent residents of the Holy City, speculate as to whether Jesus may not be the promised Messiah. Is the apparent reluctance of the Jewish authorities to arrest and be rid of him due to a fear that he may be the Messiah after all? After all, his signs are truly messianic. The problem is that every one knows where he comes from, whereas it is universally accepted that the Messiah will be a figure who suddenly appears, from where no one knows. There was a rabbinic saying, 'Three things come wholly unexpected: Messiah, a godsend and a scorpion.' Everyone knows that this man emanates from Nazareth. Here is irony: they think they know all about his human origins; in fact he has come from God and this not of his own accord. He has not chosen his own destiny. It is because they do not know God—although they think they do—that they do not know or understand Jesus' origins. He knows God because he has been sent by him. Jesus' words are few and cryptic. They are the raw material of the most profound insights of Christian theology, of its understanding of the whole nature of God. Jesus' being sent by the Father reveals the truth of the eternal being of God, and demonstrates the self-giving which is his very nature.

Many now believe in Jesus and this strengthens the resolve of the Pharisees and chief priests to remove him. They misunderstand his departure as much as his advent. When he says he will go away after a little while, they take this literally and think that he will go to the Greek Dispersion. He will in fact return to God where they cannot follow him, and this not because of their plots and manoeuvrings but at his appointed time, in fulfilment of his mission.

The promise of the Spirit   *John 7:37–44*

This dramatic scene is the climax of the chapter. On the last and great day of the feast when the worshippers are at their most numerous, Jesus stands and proclaims, 'If anyone is thirsty let him come to me and drink.' It is the message to the Samaritan woman over again: he is the living water. There is a problem of punctuation in the Greek. Verses 37 and 38 could be translated, 'If anyone is thirsty let him come to me and let him who believes in me drink. As the Scripture has said, ''Out of his belly shall flow rivers of living water'' '—that is, out of Christ not the believer. This is almost demanded by the picture of the living water flowing from the side of the crucified (19:34; 1 John 5:6–8). Yet the preferred meaning of the modern translators is also in the Fourth Gospel, when Jesus tells the woman at the well, 'The water that I shall give will be a spring of water within him, welling up and bringing eternal life' (4:14). Both meanings are therefore true. Jesus is the source of living water. It is out of him in the totality of his being and life, his words and actions, that the water flows; but those who drink it themselves become tributaries of the one great river of Christ, or channels from his reservoir.

The living water is the Spirit. But, to translate verse 39b literally, 'as yet there was no Spirit, because Jesus was not yet glorified'. St John insists—possibly against extreme charismatics in his own community who would dispense with Jesus because their religion was all 'Spirit'— that the gift of the Spirit is entirely a consequence of the 'glorification' of Jesus, that is, his ascent to the Father through the cross, which finishes his work. The saying should be linked with those about the Paraclete in the farewell discourses (14:16ff; 15:26ff; 16:7ff). At present believers have only Jesus, the Word made flesh. After Jesus has physically departed, 'the presence of the Spirit is required if the message of the Gospel is not to be confined to those who first heard it; for the Spirit has the great asset of being unfettered by limitations of time and space' (John Ashton, *Understanding the Fourth Gospel*).

This again divides the crowd. Some are convinced that Jesus is the prophet who would herald the Messiah: others that he is the Messiah himself. The unconvinced point out that the Messiah should come from Bethlehem (Micah 5:2)—a contradiction of the previous statement that his origins are unknown—whereas this man is from Galilee. Unlike Matthew and Luke in their birth stories, John does not attempt an answer to this difficulty; it is not his concern. The virgin birth is irrelevant to him, and in any case could be an embarrassment rather than a reassurance (8:41).

Nicodemus—another Gamaliel   *John 7:45–52*

According to 7:32, officers of the temple police had been sent out to arrest Jesus four days earlier, but they themselves were too impressed by his numinous power to bring him in. The Pharisees were furious in their frustration and at Jesus' hold on the crowd. Nicodemus, who has appeared not entirely to his own advantage in chapter 3, counsels against summary judgment. The Law does not countenance kangaroo courts. The man is at least entitled to a fair hearing. This is rather of the temper of another Pharisee, Gamaliel, who opposed those in the Jewish assembly who wanted to condemn the apostles to death (Acts 5:33–39).

313

He would leave the issue to the judgment of God. Here Nicodemus saves the leaders from precipitate and unjust action, though he only secures a postponement because Jesus' departure from this world is his divine destiny.

Nicodemus is disowned by his colleagues: 'Are you a Galilean too?' Galilee is more than a geographical region; it describes a different ethos from Judea, a different attitude to life. There is a striking physical contrast between the two regions. George Adam Smith wrote poetically of the difference between Galilee and Judea being like the difference between their two names, 'the one liquid and musical like her running waters, the other dry and dead like the fall of your horse's hoof on her blistered and muffled rock'. In the synoptic Gospels, the journey of Jesus from Galilee to Jerusalem is the journey from life to death. In becoming a 'Galilean', in the opprobrious words of those who disagree with him, Nicodemus is choosing life, while the fact that Jesus does come humanly from Galilee first provokes that hostility which will destroy him—and yet will be his way to God and eternal life for all who believe.

The witness of Jesus and of the Father   *John 8:12–20*

The passage begins with an I AM saying, one of the most familiar and important to the evangelist. The contrast between light and dark 'is an archetypal symbol, rooted in the deepest instinct of the human race' (John Ashton). It is in no sense original to Jesus or to John and yet it is vital to Christian understanding. The I AM is important, not only because it relates Jesus to God, but also because it states that he is the light which eternally shines and which the darkness cannot overcome (1:5). He is not the dawn, the light succeeding the darkness; he is the light which shines perpetually, though at its brightest in the incarnate Jesus. The world is in cosmic and moral darkness. But there is the light, the revelation of God's glory and truth; and all that is evil, clandestine and dishonest, and all that makes us doubt God and deceive one another is alike banished. The followers of Jesus walk in the light and are themselves light, as in the synoptic saying, 'You are the light of the world' (Matthew 5:14). They see straight, they have vision, they see God, which means they have communion with him and know something of his mind. The subject is not pursued in this section; its fuller treatment awaits chapter 9.

There follows a legal dispute. By the standards of the Jewish Law, Jesus' unilateral claims were invalid. He has not the necessary two witnesses to support what he asserts (Numbers 35:30; Deuteronomy 19:15; 1 Timothy 5:19). Jesus rejoins that the witnesses are himself and his Father, the one who sent him. This is absurd in terms of human law; but God's revelation does not have to answer before mortals. He says this near the treasury, the headquarters of the Jewish leaders. He defies them at the physical centre of their power, but they do not arrest him. His hour has not yet come.

> Jesus represents himself as one who is above the Jewish Law because he has come from God, and all his words and actions must be judged in terms of his descent and ascent. The Anglican theologian O.C. Quick once said that he regarded as the very touchstone of Christian orthodoxy the clause of the Creed, 'He came down from heaven'. What does this mean in our Copernican universe? And what was the mission Jesus was sent to accomplish? Is it not above all to reveal the true God? This means among other things that he releases the living water of the Spirit, and is eternal light in an otherwise dark world. Both of these have implications for the mission of his followers, who are to continue his work as streams of his grace and 'lights in a benighted land' (Charles Wesley).

Threats and warnings   John 8:21–30

Jesus warns his Jewish opponents that their time is short. Unless they decide for him quickly he will have gone away and they will die in their sin. Whereas earlier (7:35) they had thought that he was planning to go to the Greek diaspora, now they wonder if he is not contemplating suicide. This indeed would remove him from them completely for he would migrate into the gloom of Hades. They are naive, but there is irony in the saying for he voluntarily lays down his life. 'No one takes [my life] away from me; I am laying it down of my own free will' (see 10:18). Jesus more than once in the Gospel states the contrast between himself and his opponents in Hebraic parallel couplets (compare v. 23 with v. 15). They will die in their sins unless they believe 'that I am what I am'. Is there here a blatant claim to be Yahweh as in Exodus 3:14?

315

It does not provoke fury towards a blasphemer but a puzzled question, 'And who are you?'

C.K. Barrett writes, 'If a translation of the ''I am'' in these verses is sought I should be inclined to offer the colloquial English, ''I'm the one'', that is, ''It is at me, to me, you must look, it is I whom you must hear''.' The fuller answer is in verse 28. The supreme revelation is in the cross, which is also Christ's return to the Father from whom he came. They do not recognize him as such but he is the Son of Man, the apocalyptic figure, herald of the end of the age (Daniel 7:13), who is here and now active in the world as God's presence and obedient Son on earth. It is a paradox of the Gospels that the title 'Son of God' originally referred to a human being, and 'Son of Man' to a figure from heaven. A study of the Son of Man sayings in John (1:51; 3:13, 14; 5:27; 6:27, 53, 62; 8:28; 12:23, 34; 13:31) shows that many of them refer to ascent or lifting up on the cross. We may say simply that Jesus is the means of communication between heaven and earth, God and humanity; this is revealed supremely in the cross. He is the Son of the Father but also the Son of Man, the one with authority to bring the judgment of God to the world, to communicate God's justice and condemnation of evil (5:27). Whatever we think about verse 24, the divine claim with its echo of Exodus seems unequivocal in verse 28: 'I am what I am' brings many to faith (v. 30).

Jesus the liberator   *John 8:31—40*

'Truth' and 'freedom', especially the latter, are words much bandied about today. The ethical meaning of the former is paramount and it is generally recognized that society as a whole, especially political society, tends to be 'economical' with it. It does, however, have a metaphysical meaning; in C.H. Dodd's words, it means in this Gospel, 'the Eternal Reality as revealed to men—either the reality itself or the revelation of it'. It is an especial judgment on our age, at once of mistrust and credulity.

'Freedom' is one of the great demands of our time. There has been clamour for 'the free market', and armed struggle for deliverance from tyrannical oppression, such as apartheid in South Africa or the dictatorships of Latin America. There is also the strong desire to be free of all constraints on individual behaviour, to rebel against the family or the social *mores* . The tragedy is often that the bid for freedom may result in even greater slavery, and in individual cases to chaotic unhappiness if not terrible disease. The freedom Jesus offers is through the truth. He does not say 'through freedom you will find the truth', but 'the truth will make you free'. This was expounded with great profundity by the Cambridge scholar of late last century, F.J.A. Hort: 'The pursuit of truth begins in a sense of freedom . . . We are slow to learn that truth is never that which we choose to believe, but always that which we are under necessity to believe . . . A life devoted to truth is a life of vanities abased and ambitions forsworn. We have to advance far in the willing servitude before we recognise that it is creating for us a new and another freedom. The early dream was not false: only freedom comes last not first.' And that freedom is not political, nor that of a libertine. It is freedom as opposed to slavery in the household of God. It is gained through the truth as it is in Jesus.

Since the Son hath made me free,
Let me taste my liberty,
Thee behold with open face,
Triumph in thy saving grace,
Thy great will delight to prove,
Glory in thy perfect love.

Charles Wesley

The opponents of Jesus think they are free because they are descendants of Abraham. Yet they are not in the succession of his truth. They break the commandment by wanting to kill Jesus.

The condemnation of the unbelieving Jews *John 8:41–59*

This is a severe and disquieting passage. We have to remember that the Jews called God their Father and themselves his children, by virtue of their race and his choice. The rabbis discussed the question as to whether this was in fact their right, whether it was perpetual or depended on the acceptance of God's word and the doing of his will. So Jesus was casting doubts more fiercely—and it may be thought insultingly—of which the rabbis were aware. The Jews' representatives here protest their legitimacy, perhaps with a glance at rumours about the birth of Jesus. He retorts that because of their murderous

317

intent, they clearly have the devil for their father. They cannot recognize the truth in him because their father is the father of all lies. The Jews' evil is not in particular falsehoods they tell, but that they have 'the lie in the soul'.

Jesus insists that God is the source of his being; he has not come of his own accord, but has been sent by God. 'How' is of no interest to the evangelist; it is irrelevant. When Jesus asks, 'Which of you can convict me of sin?', he is not claiming moral unimpeachability by human standards, and this is not a basis for a dogma of his sinlessness in terms of this-worldly morality. He is saying that he is from God and therefore beyond human judgment altogether. His opponents dismiss him offhand as a charlatan. They do not listen to him and therefore fail to hear the Word of God, the Word of Truth. His opponents now charge him with being a Samaritan and demon-possessed. He does not refute the former, which is a charge of heresy in their terms and also of illegitimacy in the sense that they do not regard him as an authentic Jew, a member of their party. Judaism in Jesus' day was not a single tree with many branches, but a jungle of sects. The evangelist is not interested in which party Jesus came from any more than in his human origins; but he must affirm his place in the Jewish tradition and counter any suggestion that he is of the devil and not the true God. 'The party opposite' are so confused theologically that for them the work of God is the work of the evil one. Jesus asserts that God is his only judge and that those who obey his teaching will never see death—a claim surely to make us pause, as it did the Jews.

Jewish legitimacy is descent from Abraham, but Jesus' promise of eternal life is way beyond anything Abraham is able to do, for he is dead. The Jews see this as further proof that Jesus is possessed. He repeats that he does not glorify himself. 'It is the Father who glorifies me', the God whom they claim to know yet do not. But Jesus would betray the truth if he did not claim an especial knowledge of God and obedience to his word. He is the one whose day Abraham foresaw and in which he rejoiced. The Jews transpose this reference to a passage which is not easy to identify in Jewish writings, and turn it into what seems an impossible and ridiculous statement that Jesus saw Abraham. This in fact is the truth: 'Before Abraham was born, I am.' This is a claim to divinity and blasphemous to the Jews. They take up stones to throw at him but he somehow evades them and passes out of the temple. His hour has not yet come; but perhaps they are too blind to be able to observe his departure.

THE WORD MADE FLESH:
THE LIGHT OF LIFE

The man born blind

John 9:1–12

As in several instances in the synoptic Gospels, Jesus encounters a man physically blind from birth, on whom he may perform the messianic work of giving sight. The disciples interestingly address Jesus as 'Rabbi', and ask whether his condition is due to the man's sin or his parents'. Suffering, illness, disability were believed to be due to sin and, according to the view very prevalent in the ancient world, the sins of the fathers could be visited on children (Exodus 20:5; 34:7; Jeremiah 31:29, 30 and other passages). Jesus had given some credence to this belief in the case of the cripple at the pool of Bethesda, whom he tells to reform his sinful ways (5:14). But in this case, the blindness is not the result of sin. This does not permit any modern 'liberal' interpretation, fought for so vehemently earlier this century, that calamity is outside the direct will of God. The man's blindness is in order that God's power may be displayed in curing him, through the revelation in Jesus who is the light of the world. In some sense, the man is not to be seen as an individual but as a representative of benighted humanity. The miracle is a sign of what God's power may do to deliver the world from darkness, if only men and women will believe in his emissary, Jesus the Son of Man.

Once again the urgency of Jesus' mission is stressed. Night is drawing nigh. He will not be in the world to be its light much longer. Therefore he will not delay even for the sabbath (v. 14). As in Mark 8:23, Jesus heals the blind man through the use of spittle, this time mixed with clay from the ground. Like Caroline Abbot making two grief-stricken and bereaved contestants share the dead baby's milk-bottle in E.M. Forster's *Where Angels Fear to Tread*, he 'is determined to use such remnants as lie about in the world'. Even low, unhygienic matter may become a sacrament of God's healing power, though this method of curing the blind was by no means unique to Jesus in the ancient world. Sight is not given until the eyes are bathed in the pool of Siloam. The meaning of the name 'Siloam'—'sent'—is an allegory of Christ, the one sent from God, the living water. There may be a reference to baptism: Justin Martyr in the second century said of the baptized that they had been 'enlightened'.

The man, now able to see, is not recognized by all of his excited neighbours. He describes his cure and identifies his healer, but when they enquire as to Jesus' whereabouts, he does not know. There is mystery both in the revelation and the revealer.

The first examination of the healed man   *John 9:13–23*

The story now has a dual pattern. The formerly blind man comes increasingly to spiritual sight—from acknowledging Jesus as a prophet to faith in the Son of Man, who is more than a human emissary. The Pharisees on the other hand reveal more and more that they are the spiritually blind. They have the right to question the man, though they do so in terms of the old dispensation whose guardians they are. We are now told that the healing took place on the sabbath, like the earlier one at Bethesda (5:9). This poses a dilemma. The miracle is such as could have been wrought only by an agent of God. And yet how could a sabbath-breaker be such? The Pharisees are divided. They question the man further about Jesus. He is convinced Jesus is a prophet. Thus, like the Samaritan woman in chapter 4, he takes the first step of faith.

The Jewish authorities, presumably still the Pharisees, now send for the man's parents. The 'miracle' may have been a trick. They want to make sure that the man really had been born blind. The parents cannot deny this, but are agnostic about the miracle because they are afraid to acknowledge Jesus as the Messiah, since this would mean excommunication from the synagogue. This detail would seem to belong to the situation in the evangelist's own time, rather than to the historic ministry of Jesus. Like so much in this Gospel, there is constant interplay between the story of Jesus around AD30, the Johannine community decades later and the whole future of Christianity in the world. The onus now rests with the man who has been given his sight, the convert.

The second examination and
the blindness of Jesus' opponents   *John 9:24–41*

The man born blind is now summoned again before the court of enquiry. It is axiomatic for its members that Jesus is a sinner. Once more they demand that the man describes what happened. They are probably hoping for inconsistencies in his account. He grows impatient and ironic: 'Do you also want to become his disciples?' They abusively charge him with being a disciple of Jesus and assert their fidelity to Moses, to whom indubitably God spoke. Yet again they declare their uncertainty of Jesus' origins.

The man is now angered and astonished and speaks with the freedom of an articulate disciple rather than a beggar. Such a miracle, 'unheard of since the world began', could be performed only by one who had come from God! The interview ends in abuse. They have no doubt that the man's original blindness was due to sin. They imply that he was born out of fornication and brought up in a sinful home. They turn him out, which for the evangelist probably anticipates the excommunication from the synagogue of those in his day who confessed Jesus as Messiah. Jesus now reappears—the examinations have taken place in his absence. He wants to lead the man on to a deeper faith than that in Jesus as Messiah, to faith in the Son of Man, a divine figure, the bringer of the salvation promised at the end time yet revealed *here and now* (see also the note on 8:28). It is not sufficient simply to honour Jesus as prophet or teacher. The only true response is to fall down on one's knees. But the man does not recognize Jesus' true identity until Jesus has told him.

The narrative ends with a general declaration by Jesus. He has come into the world for judgment, for a drastic reversal. His word and actions will give sight to the blind, but afflict with blindness those who claim to see and yet cannot recognize God's salvation when it comes. We find the way to God when we know that in our natural state we are blind, yet ask for sight.

These chapters of the Gospel show how early Christians were plunged into controversy about Jesus. Here the controversy is not political, nor social, but theological. Who is Jesus? Is he an impostor, a charlatan, a deluded prophet-poet or the one sent from God the Father, whom future orthodoxy, by developing these texts, would affirm as the very Being of God in the life of a human being, the revelation in time and history of the eternal Trinity? The proof is in his Word and in the testimony of those to whom he has brought liberty, life and light. The challenge is in the words of Robert Browning: 'Call Christ the illimitable God—or lost'. We are left wondering how far such controversy should be the continual state of the Church in the world.

AUTHORITIES IN CONFLICT:
―THE TRUE LEADER OF GOD'S PEOPLE―

The good shepherd *John 10:1–6, 11–18*

This is the one section of the Fourth Gospel nearest to a parable, the word actually used in verse 6 of the REB. Like the parables in Mark 4, it confuses and darkens the understanding of Jesus' opponents. The parables are often adduced as examples of the simple, homely clarity of Jesus' teaching and contrasted with the theological obscurity of some of the Church's academics today. In fact, many of the parables have been riddles from the start and only the initiated have been able to comprehend them.

The analogy starts easily enough. Jesus contrasts the thief who clandestinely climbs into the fold with the shepherd who enters by the door. The sheep know the shepherd's voice—a universal fact about sheep farming—and they will follow him. It is otherwise with a stranger. The image of the shepherd is found far and wide throughout history. It is one of the dominant figures of the Old Testament (see especially Psalm 23; Jeremiah 23:1–4; Ezekiel 34), where Israel's leaders are likened to the shepherd. But as well as correspondences, there are differences between the Old Testament and Jesus' words here. The shepherd is no king; the flock is neither the people of Israel, nor the crowds on whom Jesus has compassion (as in Mark 6:34), but rather his own, with whom he has a deep, intimate relationship. Jesus is the *good* shepherd (v. 11). The adjective could have been 'true', the usual word for 'good'; instead it refers not only to the revealer's 'absoluteness and decisiveness, but also to his "being for . . ."' (Bultmann). He lays down his life for the sheep, whereas the one who is out only for himself runs away when the wolf approaches the sheep grazing in the open. The sheep thus have life because the shepherd sacrifices his own for their sakes.

The parable now returns to the mutual knowledge of shepherd and sheep. This is not rational or theoretical knowledge, but total relationship, a binding together, the realization of one's being in the other. It is the relationship of Jesus to the Father, which the disciples may share through Jesus' laying down of his life. Disciples are not

322

restricted to the immediate circle of Jesus' ministry and the community from which this Gospel came. Jesus looks beyond all these to a universal mission and to those brought to faith over all the Christian years, from many lands: they too are his sheep. His longing prayer—here (v. 16) as in chapter 17—is that they all may be one.

Jesus the door $\qquad$ *John 10:7–10*

This figure of speech is offered by Jesus to elucidate what has so far been incomprehensible. In some ways it interrupts the discourse about the shepherd, and it raises important questions for our time, which is why we are treating it separately.

Jesus is the way into the fold of God's people, the only way. A door not only opens but excludes. It keeps out those who have no right to enter and protects those within. It also gives them freedom of movement to go in and out and find pasture. Through Jesus the sheep may safely graze and return to the fold. Verse 8 is difficult. Does Jesus denounce *all* who came before him—his great predecessors, the patriarchs and prophets? This cannot be so, for it would contradict the whole tenor of the Fourth Gospel and the New Testament. But must we exclude other faiths and those whom our supposedly Christlike tolerance would admit as 'anonymous Christians'? The statement seems more of the temper of Jesus' opponents in this Gospel than of what we have learned of him. Claims for Christian exclusiveness and for the authority to guard it have led to persecutions, inquisitions and a denial of the freedom and life Christ came to bring.

We need to remember the dangers to the Johannine community both from the religions with which the ancient world teemed and the many false interpretations of the Christian faith. Even more is our own world, full of fundamentalist, fanatical sects—plunging into weird prophecies, nature worship and the occult—which are capable of capturing the most intelligent people. Religion as such is not all good. There is much in it that steals human hearts, despoils and destroys lives and communities, and as a result leads to death. Jesus, on the contrary, offers life—life to the full.

There is intolerance in the Gospel. It claims to contain the whole truth about the universe and human life. This does not mean that Christians themselves should be intolerant or fail to learn from other religions and their adherents, and often be shamed by them; but they must test them by Jesus Christ. And Christianity is not merely the choosing of an intellectual path. It is union with Christ in his utter self-giving. To go in and out through this door is about commitment as well as refuge. It is to graze in the green pastures and beside the still waters of eternal life.

Further controversy   John 10:19–39

There is continuing difference of opinion among 'the Jews'. Some regard Jesus as insane, possessed. Others cannot believe that his works—above all the cure of the man born blind—are of the devil. Once again there is the demand that he disclose his identity, as though he had not done so enough already, metaphorically in the sayings about the good shepherd and the door, but supremely in the I AM which prefaces them. He does, however, present his deeds done in his Father's name as his chief credentials. That 'the Jews' cannot recognize who he is because of them shows that they are not sheep of his flock.

The Fourth Gospel is not universalist, even though God loves the world (3:16). There seems no hope of all being saved. Some are wilfully blind or deaf, others are invincibly ignorant. Listening is vital here. Jesus' own sheep are those who listen to his voice. He speaks in recognition of them, and out of deep knowledge. Thus they have eternal life (17:3) and they are safe for ever. Security is what Jesus promises: 'No one will snatch them from my care.' They are the Father's gift to Jesus and he is greater than all, so that this is their ultimate security. Although he asserts the Father's supreme greatness, Jesus makes his most outstanding and audacious claim yet: 'The Father and I are one.' This is not a claim to co-equality as in later Trinitarian doctrine. It does not conflict either with the distinction of persons in the Godhead or with the later statement 'The Father is greater than I' (14:28). The union is not of 'substance' or 'being' as in the Nicene Creed, but of will. The Father and Jesus are one in their guardianship and care for the sheep. This is enough to provoke one more attempt to stone Jesus. Good deeds or no, he utters blasphemy. His bewildered opponents believe that he has claimed divinity.

Jesus refutes them out of their own law. Psalm 82:6, 'You are gods, sons of the Most High, all of you', is addressed not to human beings but to a pantheon of the gods of the nations, who are guilty of injustice and ignorance and therefore will be condemned by Israel's God to die like mortals. Jesus follows rabbinic custom, by disregarding the context and applying the saying to those human beings to whom God's word came, the sheep who have heard his voice. If *they* are sons of God—in some sense partakers of the divine nature—how much more is he, the one especially consecrated? This may give some scriptural warrant to the Eastern Orthodox doctrine of deification, which many in the West regard as highly dangerous—though it can be stated in terms which make it simply an affirmation of human destiny in Christ, the attainment of perfect love, as in the Wesleys.

THE WORD MADE FLESH:
⸺ THE RESURRECTION AND THE LIFE ⸺

Jesus' delay
John 10:40—11:16

The story of the raising of Lazarus begins and ends with two withdrawals by Jesus from Judea and Jerusalem (10:40 and 11:54). The first returns him to where the Baptist testified, and the crowds once more come. The second has him in retreat with his disciples. We are for the first time introduced to intimate friends of Jesus, three whom he especially loved—Mary, Martha and Lazarus. In his human life, there were those with whom he was more intimate than with others, whom he found more *sympathique*. At this stage there is the temptation for the expositor to become a novelist, to fill out with the imagination the scanty yet alluring details supplied by the evangelist. In fact we know very little of the household at Bethany, though it is almost certain that the Mary and Martha of Bethany are the same two sisters in the unnamed village of Luke 10:38ff.

News reaches Jesus that Lazarus is ill. Jesus knows that the illness is, humanly speaking, mortal, but he waits two days until he knows that Lazarus is dead and beyond human help. There may be significance in the fact that it is not until the third day that he makes the journey. Delay, an interval long or short, is a characteristic some have found in the miracle stories of the Gospels (Mark 2:1–12; 5:25–53). Here it is one more instance of Jesus choosing his own hour; and also of the fact that this journey is the way of the cross. The disciples are well aware of this and when he does decide to go they try to dissuade him for they remember the stone-throwing of his enemies. The supreme irony of history is about to be played out. He will manifest his glory in awakening Lazarus from what he says is the sleep of death, but more in the fact that he who is the resurrection and the life is going to die as a direct consequence of this miracle. Thomas, whose Greek name was used as the equivalent for the Semitic word for twin, is bold at the prospect: 'Let us also go and die with him.'

The resurrection and the life   *John 11:17–27*

When they reach Bethany, Lazarus has been four days in the tomb. In Jewish belief it was already too late for any revivification, for the soul left the body after the third day. The mourning is at its height and many, presumably of the Jewish authorities and officials, have come to condole with the sisters. In this story they do not threaten Jesus. As soon as she hears that he is on the outskirts of the village, Martha hurries to meet Jesus, though Mary remains at home; this difference between the sisters is important to the narrative. There is regret rather than reproach in Martha's declaration that Jesus could have saved her brother from death, though she is quick to affirm that even now God will grant whatever Jesus asks. Martha has faith in the power of Jesus' prayer. He is no magician: what he does is through his complete union with the Father.

Martha thinks Jesus' reply is simply a conventional restatement of belief in a general resurrection at the end of the age; and she is not satisfied. Jesus replies with the tremendous assertion, 'I AM the resurrection and the life.' In him the future hope is brought into the present. Two different concepts are joined together: *eternal life* , 'the possession of unlimited life all at once' (Boethius)—in some ways a Greek idea, though we have to be careful about finding Greek influences in this Gospel; and *resurrection* , a Jewish apocalyptic notion of a cataclysmic act of God on the last day, bringing the dead of all ages out of their graves. What John is saying, however, is that whether you believe in eternal life as a present and continuing possession or as a recovery of life after the death of the body and the end of the world does not matter: eternal life is the gift of God in Christ (C.H. Dodd, *The Interpretation of the Fourth Gospel*). We may also agree with Bultmann: 'Life and death in the human sense—the highest good and the deepest terror—have become unreal for [the believer]'. They are mere formalities for those who have Jesus Christ. He is the life both before and beyond the grave. Martha confesses her faith in what was probably the basis of an early creed of the Church. Note the additional 'one who was to come into the world' in verse 27 and think what it means about Christ's destiny and mission.

The summons from the tomb   *John 11:28—44*

All this time, Mary has remained at home. Martha goes to bring her to Jesus since he has asked for her. It is hard not to think of Mary in the light of Luke 10:38ff, silent and adoring, waiting on Christ's word in faith, though this may go beyond John's story. Mary indeed falls at Jesus' feet and greets him with the same words as her sister; but Martha has greater certainty than faith. Mary and the mourners are wailing and Jesus, too, is overcome with distress. He is moved to tears—of grief, of sympathy, or anger? Perhaps all three; but since he knows that Lazarus is to be raised to life again, and the tears soon turned from sorrow to joy, it is possible that he is indignant because of lack of faith. They will not suspend their wailing in hope of a miracle. Set this against the history of the Church from John's day to our own and there is cause for tears because of lack of trust and of love: Christ's gospel has been ignored. Yet it may be that Jesus is aware that death is still a tragedy, in spite of its being natural and necessary to the continuance of life and the hope that he brings. In the world as it is and remains, 'there are situations where love and sorrow combine with protest and indignation' (Kenneth Grayston, *The Gospel of John*). Nor is the situation at the grave of Lazarus a simple confrontation of divine omnipotence and death. The harsh realities of human life and history, bitterness, pain and destruction, the grief inseparable from love are there too.

Jesus goes to the tomb and tells them to move the entrance stone away. Martha protests: it is nauseating and ghoulish. She has to be reminded of her professed faith. The glory of God is to be revealed. Jesus adopts the posture of prayer (Psalm 123:1), but he does not make a request. He thanks the Father for hearing him always and in advance. The miracle is the consequence of his union with the Father. It is God's gift to him—no crude manifestation of sovereignty. It is an effect of that union which is leading him to the cross. Jesus' loud cry reminds us of that which Mark records at the moment of his death (Mark 15:37).

Lazarus stumbles out still fast bound in the grave clothes. He has returned to ordinary life. One day he will die again and no voice will call him out of the tomb. 'It is almost as though the writer (who is a supreme ironist) is reminding his readers that very soon they will realise, if they follow the story to the end, that this is not "the real thing". Rather it is an episode that must take place in order that the substance, as distinct from the shadow of divine omnipotence, may be shown' (Donald MacKinnon). Contrast Lazarus' grave clothes with Christ's on Easter Day (20:6): *there* is the final act of God.

Expediency and politics *John 11:45–53*

The division between the Jews continues. Some believe in Jesus because such mighty works as his cannot but come from God; others may not, as formerly, ascribe his miracles to the power of evil, but they are fearful that he will attract such popular support as to become a political force which will lead to Roman suppression of their temple and nation. There is throughout subsequent history an ambiguity about Jesus' relationship to politics. Some have used him as the justification of political action, sometimes violent, both of right and left. Extreme examples this century are General Franco and the liberation theologians. These latter are not easily dismissed. They have biblical support, though not so obviously from St John's Gospel. More often, Jesus has been ignored for reasons of expediency, or in some sense crucified again because his message from outside this world makes too great demands on human faith. There seems little doubt that, historically, he was removed by leaders of 'church' and state because they feared he might promote a bloody revolution. They interpreted his message solely in worldly terms and were blind and deaf to God in spite of their religious conformity.

Caiaphas has been seen as the embodiment of evil—crafty, cruel, duplicitous. So he has been portrayed in Passion plays throughout the centuries, to the undoubted fostering of anti-semitism. But was he not in the case of Jesus placed in a dilemma often faced by statesmen, most acutely but not invariably in war? Is it not the statesperson's responsibility to try to preserve those institutions which, however imperfectly and at times unjustly, maintain some order? Must not the course of expediency be followed, and the ethics of 'the greatest happiness of the greatest number'? Better one die than a whole nation be destroyed. In

Caiaphas we are faced with the problems of statesmanship. Here is a signal instance of Johannine irony. Caiaphas, the astute politician, speaks of what is beyond his utilitarian comprehension. Jesus will die, but his death is not absolutely the result of political plotting for the sake of expediency. It is the will of God, for he will die both for the Jewish people and for the children of God scattered throughout the world. John leaves us with a number of questions. Is this universalism after all, or does Jesus die only for those who have responded and become the children of God, the sheep of his flock? And in what sense is his death for them? Does it save them only as they accept it and are united with it as the Son ascends to the Father in divine self-giving love?

'THE LIGHT IS WITH YOU FOR A LITTLE LONGER'

Doubtless aware that official opposition to him is about to take a new course, Jesus withdraws again, this time into private retreat with his disciples, before his entry upon the final conflict.

The anointing—extravagance and abundance
John 11:55—12:11

It is Passover time and the crowds flock to Jerusalem. They are there early to undertake the necessary purifications (Exodus 19:10ff.; Numbers 9:10; 2 Chronicles 30:17–18). Jesus is back in Bethany at the house of Lazarus for a supper given in his honour. Again it is impossible not to read this without recalling the synoptic stories, both of Martha and Mary (Luke 10:38–42) and of anointings—by the prostitute in Simon the Pharisee's house (Luke 7:36–50) and the unnamed woman at Bethany in the house of Simon the Leper (Mark 14:3–9; Matthew 26:6–13). Martha and Mary here have something of their roles in Luke (note that Lazarus never utters a word in the incidents which concern him). Martha serves; Mary performs the act of devotion. Its tenderness and love cannot be exaggerated. Some preachers have thought that she is the woman of Luke 7:36ff, reclaimed by Christ, who repeats the anointing in grateful reminder and yet deeper love. We do not know enough to be certain. In the

Marcan story, which is after the entry into Jerusalem and presumably on the Wednesday of what we call Holy Week, the woman anoints Jesus' head, maybe symbolizing his kingship. Here the act is of greater humility—perhaps with the wiping of the feet with her hair—and intimacy. The fragrance fills the house as the odour of the gospel fills the world. But it is an act of extravagance and abundance. The disciples are embarrassed by it in Matthew and Mark. Here Judas is singled out as protester, and not for the philanthropic reasons he states. He has no concern for the poor, but as treasurer of the Jesus community he wants to pilfer the common purse. This blackguarding of Judas in addition to his betrayal rather takes attention from the real point of John's story.

The question of extravagance in devotion is always timely. Should the Church spend resources in art and music and things of beauty in a starving world? In a submission on Worship to the General Assembly of the World Council of Churches at Uppsala in 1968, the American novelist John Updike wrote that the Church must always be what the world is not and where life is poverty-stricken and depressing, there needs to be some colour and splendour in Church; austerity belongs with affluence. We may think that it is in times of affluence that the arts may flourish most. But beauty is an eternal and Christian value, and in its truth flows from the Christian gospel. There should also be an extravagance in discipleship. In the words of the German Pietist Paul Gerhardt's hymn: 'Too much to thee I cannot give/Too much I cannot do for thee'. The difficult words of verse 7 probably mean that Mary's act is prophetic, as in Mark and Matthew. She has anointed Jesus' body in anticipation of his burial. Because of the popularity of Jesus and of the spectacle of Lazarus called out of the tomb, the chief priests are resolved to do away with Lazarus too. The friend's lot, like that of his Lord, may be to suffer in extravagant devotion to him.

The triumphal entry   *John 12:12–19*

This is a somewhat different story from that in Matthew 21:1–10 and Mark 11:1–10. There is no preparation beforehand. The people (there are no children) are not in a procession accompanying Jesus but come out of the city to greet him. He then finds a donkey, mounts it and fulfils the prophecy of Zechariah 9:9. Whether this is intentional is not clear, but the disciples only made the connection after Jesus had been glorified.

So much in Christian faith is the product of reflection on events and actions which must have seemed enigmatic and mysterious at the time. Jesus says this will be true of his washing of the disciples' feet (13:7). It is all bound up with the assertion that Christianity is a historical religion. History is not only the narration of what we believe actually happened in the world of time and space; it is also interpretation in the light of later experience. Two thousand years later, we are still discovering more of the truth as it is in Jesus, not simply through new and challenging discoveries such as the Dead Sea Scrolls, but as we apply the Christ-event to our world and our lives. It is strangely provocative, in view of Jesus' earlier refusal to be taken and made king (6:15), that he should allow the acclamations of what has become known as Palm Sunday (only John's Gospel mentions palm branches, waved to celebrate victory). Was the ride thrust upon him? Did he, on the spur of the moment, see the opportunity for a prophetic act which would declare that he comes as king, mounted on the donkey of peace, not the war horse, his victory already won? He still has to endure the conflicts, the trials, the tortures of the next few days, and death itself. He awaits the supreme hour of his glorification on earth and yet all is already accomplished. This motif runs through the next chapters of the Gospel.

The excitement of the crowd, inspired by the raising of Lazarus, justifies the alarm of the Pharisees: 'All the world has gone after him!' Again there is irony; for they, too, like hostile Caiaphas and loving Mary, are unconscious prophets.

Glory in the cross   *John 12:20—36*

The prophecy of 12:19 immediately begins to be fulfilled. Some 'Greeks', Gentiles attracted to the worship of Israel, ask to make the acquaintance of Jesus in words which used to be displayed in the inside of some pulpits to remind preachers of their task. This is reported to Jesus by Andrew who has been told of it by Philip, forecasting that the world outside Judaism will be brought to Jesus by his disciples. The Greeks then disappear from the story; no more is heard of them. But for Jesus the hour of his glorification has come: 'Jesus is making the first identification of the Passion and the glory' (Michael Ramsey). The verses which follow (vv. 24ff) interrupt the sequence of thought and may be a later insertion (with v. 24 compare 1 Corinthians 15:36—38; v. 25a is a traditional saying). The sacrifice of Jesus is movingly described by an analogy from nature which humbly compares him to a mere grain of wheat.

The next verses are John's counterpart to Gethsemane. Michael Ramsey quotes the comment of the eighteenth-century Lutheran scholar J.A. Bengel about the concurrence of the horror of death and the ardour of obedience. It is almost a union of Gethsemane and the transfiguration, the prayer for deliverance transcended by the prayer for the glory of the Father's name, and then the heavenly voice. This last declares that the Father's name has already been glorified in Christ's ministry hitherto and will be again in his Passion and resurrection. The hour of glory is also the hour of judgment for this world, not in the future but now in what is going to happen to Jesus Christ. The evil ruler who holds this world in thrall will be cast out. And Jesus by being lifted up from the earth will draw all to himself. The 'lifting up' of course has a double meaning. It means Jesus' exaltation in glory, but also recalls 3:14 and the suffering servant in Isaiah 52:13. The comments of Bultmann are the profoundest: 'The promise of verse 32 therefore is spoken under the sign of the cross: like verses 25 following, it is bound to the law of discipleship unto the cross'. The drawing to himself is a drawing to Christ's humiliation as well as exaltation.

The people cannot accept that a heavenly emissary—a Messiah or Son of Man—will be impaled on a cross. This is not what they have been taught to expect. Jesus rejoins in words which seem to belong to the sayings about light and to follow from his claim to be the light of the world (8:12). But the light will not shine forever; they must trust it while they have it. And so he goes into hiding once more, which does not fit in with the synoptic accounts of the last week of his life.

Blind eyes, dull minds, over-cautious faith, true faith and the judgment   *John 12:37–50*

This is an interruption of the narrative, but it summarizes the ministry of Jesus and its effect. There will be no more public appearances except as a prisoner and on the scaffold. What has he achieved? What has been his mission?

There is some qualification of the previous reports that many of 'the Jews' had come to faith in Jesus. There would not be enough to save him from the cross. The evangelist is here more concerned with the comparative ineffectiveness of the signs. It is what one would expect from the experience of the prophets. It is simply not true that 'we needs must love the highest when we see it'. Unknown to the evangelist, though wrongly believed by some later Christians to have been influenced by Old Testament teachers, Plato had said that should the perfectly righteous man appear, he would be impaled, crucified. Why should this be? Isaiah attributes it to the deliberate act of God. Here we glimpse the fact that Christianity is near tragedy and its God not simply 'the Great Companion, the fellow-sufferer who understands' (A.N. Whitehead), but a strange, inscrutable being who sometimes seems to be as much against us as for us. God appears to forsake us as much as to be with us, mysteriously to tolerate human obstinacy and opaqueness to good, and place us in situations in which evil is able to have its fling.

There are those amongst the Jewish authorities who believe, but they will not acknowledge Jesus openly. They are afraid of excommunication. This must have been the case when the Gospel was written. It is a perennial problem, even among those in our time who profess and call themselves Christians. We value our own reputation in the world more than the glory of God and are afraid to witness for Christ because our careers may suffer or we may lose the good opinion of our friends. As with statesmanship this may not always be a simple issue if, say, our families may suffer through our witness, and not simply ourselves.

The last proclamation of Jesus' public ministry—shouted out but carefully constructed—reaffirms that faith in him is faith in God. He speaks the Father's word; he has the Father's authority. This suggests that discipleship 'is not a cult of Jesus but a faith in God' (Hoskyns). He is the light of the world; 'No one who has faith in me should remain in darkness.' He is not the world's judge but its Saviour (3:17), though those who disregard his words judge themselves, as will be apparent on the last day.

As we reach the end of the first part of the Gospel, it is worth asking yourself where you stand in the story it tells. Have you Martha's practical and serving faith, or Mary's adoring and extravagant devotion? Are you a Lazarus, brought by Christ from death to life, a convert? Are you compromised by the work you have to do, the decisions you have to take in the world? Are you afraid to be too convinced a Christian according to St John, either because of intellectual reservations or because of what it may cost you?

THE HOUR OF GLORY
FOR THE SON OF MAN

From the thirteenth chapter onwards, the pace of the Gospel slows down considerably. Whereas the evangelist has spent twelve chapters outlining the course of Jesus' public ministry in Jerusalem, Samaria and Galilee, he now devotes the rest of his account to the few days surrounding Jesus' Passion. In addition to telling the traditional story of Jesus' arrest, trial, execution and resurrection (though he does this in his own way), St John uses this part of his Gospel to address the needs of his readers, the Church whose roots lie in the little band of men and women who followed Jesus from Galilee to Jerusalem. One of their leaders, Peter, had earlier pledged his allegience to Jesus as the one who has the 'words of eternal life' (6:68). Now, as Jesus prepares to leave Peter and the others, the evangelist underlines and draws out the significance of the whole message of the Word made flesh for those who must live with the physical absence of their Lord. Like the first disciples after Easter, the Church rests in the assurance of the unseen—though not unreal—presence and support of the divine world. It shares in something of Jesus' own relationship with the Father. It embodies his love, and can confidently expect to live in his joy and peace. But it must also live with the hatred which sought to snuff out the light of that love. So as the narrative reaches its climax, the Gospel encourages the followers of Jesus to continue in their faith come what may. Their allegience to the way of truth and life may threaten to destroy them as it did him, but they must never lose sight of the Lord who has been 'lifted up' through his crucifixion, to open up the very life of heaven to them.

The foot-washing—portent and example   *John 13:1–17*

The solemnity of the first verse cannot be exaggerated. There is a change of tone in the Gospel at this point. The public ministry of Jesus is over. There is an end of signs in mixed company or before crowds, and of the sometimes bitter controversies reflecting not only the historic situation of Jesus but that of the evangelist's own community *vis-à-vis* the local synagogue. All this is superseded by the intimate disclosure to 'his own' of the Lord's departure and return, the knowledge of God which he reveals and the glory which is his with the Father 'before all worlds'. Here Jesus speaks in love, even when in rebuke or exposing their ignorance to those in whom—in spite of their weakness and desertion—he is joined forever by the Father's gift. There is one, Judas Iscariot, who is lost eternally; he soon leaves on his nefarious enterprise, though not before Jesus performs an unexpected and dramatic act. In its primary meaning, the foot-washing anticipates what is going to happen to him and its effect on them. The act is homely and domestic, no more in our civilization than a host cleaning his guest's shoes. This does not amount to much in our age, when servants are few and we all share in the washing up. It is a menial task for one whom they call Teacher and Lord, something which they will understand only in the light of events which are to follow. There cannot be full comprehension of Jesus' meaning and message while he is still in the world. The foot-washing portends the seemingly utter humiliation of the cross which is his way to resume the glory he has always had.

Peter resists. This is too great a reversal of roles. He is affronted by a servant-Christ. Jesus tells him that the washing is essential if he is to 'have a part' with or in him, to share in his fellowship and his life. There may be a reference here to baptism, that washing which imparts the cleansing of Christ's death to his disciples; that is the complete bath. Golgotha is, in fact, the world's baptism. Our individual experience of conversion flows from that, and once we have entered into it by baptism, all we need is to have the dust and mud of life's journey daily washed from our feet. Peter misunderstands completely. When he is told that he cannot belong to Jesus without having his feet washed, he wants as much washing as possible—'my hands and head as well'. He has been too proud to accept the humble service of Christ's love which is in fact the sacrifice of his dying. Now he interprets the benefits of this materially, either like those who might think that Christianity is nothing but an earning of merit by regular attendance upon sacraments, or those who believe that perfection is obtainable 'at a clap'. To have a part with Jesus is a journeying on through life with a constant return to the cleansing of his life and death. It is also, as the next part of the story enjoins, a following of the Lord's example of service.

The washing of the disciples' feet is both a foreshadowing of the cleansing through the cross, and the setting of an example of humility. There may be a parallel in Mark 10:43–45 on which this passage from John 13 is a commentary (whether either evangelist knew it or not). The nations of the world, says Jesus, have rulers who lord it over their subjects. 'It shall not be so with you; among you, whoever wants to be great must be your servant, and whoever wants to be first must be the slave of all. For the Son of Man did not come to be served but to serve, and to give his life as a ransom for many.' There, as in the foot-washing, is the link between the utter self-giving of Jesus and the humble service of his followers. Notice that Jesus does *not* say 'Just as I your Teacher and Lord have washed your feet, so must the one who takes my place as leader', but rather, 'you also ought to wash one another's feet'. This is not a task to be performed by prelates or sovereigns. It is to be mutual. We are to impart to one another the cleansing of Christ and to serve one another in the most menial ways, not only as bestowing our distinctive, individual gifts for the benefit of all Christ's disciples but by doing the humblest services for one another. The hallmark of the community of Jesus' followers, which John never calls the Church, is ministry, understood not as authority but service. That is the one qualification and should be the one desire:

> *O that I may be counted meet*
> *To wash thy dear disciples' feet.*

Charles Wesley

To make a liturgy of this—whether in the (probably) fifth-century Greek 'Liturgy of Towel and Basin', or at a service on Maundy Thursday—may be a moving and valuable reminder, but it must not be a substitute for the constant helping of one another in the ordinary tasks and troubles of life. A more relevant application of it in our time may be in spiritual direction, whether one-to-one or in a group like the traditional Methodist class-meeting. But neither director nor leader must be a 'lord of faith', rather a 'helper of joy' (2 Corinthians 1:24, AV), one who is alongside as a fellow-disciple who also needs cleansing.

The foot-washing incident haunts many today, guilty because the Christian Church within a few centuries and thereafter became a worldly corporation influenced by many different cultures, with hierarchies in disregard of the exemplary actions and the admonitions of Jesus. Yet would it have survived throughout the ages and in all the world had it remained a Johannine community without organization and influence in human affairs? The dilemma is agonizing. It cannot now be as though Constantine had never lived, or there had not been sacerdotal presbyters or prelatical bishops, or constitutions which were both reflections of human government and in some cases models for it. The foot-washing, like the existence in history of fellowships of the humble poor, remains a perpetual question-mark and warning over the Christian acquisition of worldly power and secular authority. The temptations of political influence may be unavoidable, yet they may deny and even betray Christ.

The departure of Judas   John 13:18—30

Jesus is not at ease with his disciples because the traitor is there, though as in the synoptic Gospels the others do not know who he is. But entwined with the distressing disclosure is a solemn statement, prefaced in the original by the repeated 'Amen' (vv. 20, 21), which complements though does not belie the foot-washing. For these disciples, who must not shun the humblest role of mutual service, are to be those whom the Lord sends. In them he is received, and through him the Father who sent him. They are destined for an apostolic ministry, though John does not write literally of apostles and has no notion of a special order within the community. They are all, in a Hebrew term, the *shaliachim*, representatives of Jesus: and it was said that a man's *shaliach* is as himself. This is an almost unbearable dignity, and yet the one whom they represent is the lowly Jesus who washes his disciples' feet and reigns from the tree of the cross. This is common to all the Gospels even though the foot-washing is unique to John (compare John 13:16; 15:20 with Matthew 10:24; Luke 6:40).

The traitor among them is typical of the most dastardly—one who has eaten bread with the person whom he betrays, infringing all Middle Eastern laws of hospitality and breaking the most solemn bonds of table fellowship. The disciples do not recognize him and even the one most beloved has, at Peter's instigation, to enquire. This mysterious disciple, who appears for the first time at this point, is impossible to identify. He represents the ideal of discipleship in spiritual discernment and closest communion with the Lord, though as a historical figure he seems to be the one whose teaching about Jesus is contained in this Gospel. As the Hebrew metaphor has it, he is in the bosom of Jesus as Jesus is in the bosom of the Father (v. 23; compare 1:18). As for Judas, Jesus does not so much dismiss or excommunicate him, as expose him to himself and let events take their course. His words are echoed centuries later when Lady Macbeth says of the murder she plans, 'If it were done when 'tis done, then 'twere well / It were done quickly.' Jesus does not expostulate or plead with Judas or try to dissuade him. He expects his treachery as inevitable, the action of the father of lies, the enemy of all good. He is relieved when Judas receives the bread dipped in the dish and goes out into the full light of the Paschal moon, yet into the darkness of the kingdom of evil: 'it was night'.

The departure of Judas highlights one of our spiritual deficiencies: the other side of our failure to know God is that we may not recognize evil. We lack moral insight. We may not know our own real sin, nor where treachery lies in the Christian community.

The glory of the Son of Man and the new commandment
John 13:31–38

As in his response to the request of the Greeks in 12:20–23, Jesus declares that the departure of Judas is the time of his own glorification and of God's in him. The 'now' is all-important. Jesus will be glorified not only at some far-off return in the clouds of heaven with hosts of angels but now in the seemingly dire events of the next days, in his departure from the world and the visible fellowship of the disciples. His going is sorrowful; it will leave the disciples bereft and with no security, for they cannot accompany him. The farewell discourses to which this announcement is the introduction offer many consolations. The first is here in the new commandment (Latin *mandatum*, corrupted into *maundy* and giving its name much later to the Thursday of Holy Week): 'love one another; as I have loved you, so you are to love one another'. Jesus will be with them in their mutual love and by this 'everyone will know that you are my disciples'.

This replaces in John the second commandment taken from the Jewish Law, 'Love your neighbour as yourself.' The disciples are to love one another. There is no mention of anyone outside the circle, which seems at first to be exclusive. But the real test of Christ's love—and Church history bears tragic witness to its failure—is that of his followers' love for one another. Love is no universal happy benevolence towards those whom we hardly know and might soon dislike if they were brought close to us. Love of all humankind is possible only to God. In the love of those with whom we are involved in the Christian mission we may love as Christ loves: here our love is tried and tested in partnership. It may be costly as we recognize differences and overcome

338

jealousies and wash the feet of those with whom we disagree, or who seem to be meeting with recognition denied us. In a sense they are our neighbours because they have been brought close to us in Christ. We did not necessarily choose them. Love in John's Gospel is closely connected with the Word—with speech, communication, self-giving—which is Christ. To love as he loves is to be the interpreter of the love of God, to communicate the divine love beside which our own is so fallible.

Peter is a sign of this fallibility. He continues puzzled as to Jesus's destination, but seems to be aware that it involves a path of danger. He excitedly promises to lay down his life for Jesus, should this be necessary, but is told that his loyalty will not survive till cockcrow.

Departure and return: the promise of Jesus' presence
John 14:1–3

Jesus comforts his disciples and reassures them on the eve of his going away. It may be that the words are especially precious to the evangelist because the witness, possibly the Beloved Disciple on whom this Gospel depends, is aged and on the point of death; it is as though in him Jesus is departing once more. The Cambridge scholar, F.J.A. Hort, in his profound study *The Way, the Truth, The Life* (1893), says that the night before his Passion is not the only time when Christ has seemed to his disciples to be departing from the earth and leaving them to themselves. Our age is one such time, not only because of the state of the world after 2,000 years, but also because of the decline of Christianity, at any rate in the West and North. It is disappearing from our culture and remains only in fragments. These verses may be read as in part a comment on Psalms 42 and 43 in which the Psalmist is oppressed by the seeming absence of God. This is almost a commonplace of Jewish and Christian experience: 'Where is your God?'.

Jesus assures the disciples over and over that he goes away for their good and that he will come back. Here he says that he is returning to the Father's house, from whence he came. The assumption seems to be of a universe of two or more storeys, though we must not anachronistically envisage it in terms of Dante's *The Divine Comedy*. There is no trace in this Gospel of any 'descent into hell', unless Jesus' occasional moments of distress (12:27–28; 13:21) are interpreted as such—as Calvin did the cry of dereliction (Mark 15:34)—but this is unlikely. There is some difficulty between verse 3 and the later verse 23. In the former, Jesus says that he will go to prepare dwelling places in the Father's house for the disciples, and then return and take them to himself, presumably to dwell with him in that house. In verse 23 he says that he and the Father, in love of the one responsive to his Word, will come and make their dwelling with him, presumably where he is on earth. Both together may mean the fulfilment of an Old Testament promise: 'Let them make me a sanctuary that I may dwell among them' (Exodus 25:8, AV). The house or home of God, incompletely revealed in the temple at Jerusalem, will descend upon each believer, who will be a room of it. John Ashton says that the coming mentioned here is not the resurrection, nor the coming of Jesus at the end, nor the mission of the Holy Spirit: 'It presages a mystical union of awesome intimacy, one that indicates the profoundly contemplative character of the Johannine community.' Hort discerns the consequences when he writes: ' . . .the earth itself is no distant or foreign shore, but lies within the heavenly precincts . . . and even when Jesus refers to their journey to come, he at last resolves the place to be prepared for them into a simple sharing of his presence'.

Departure and return: the way, the truth and the life   *John 14:4–6*

In answer to Thomas's question Jesus says that he himself is the way to his destination, so that with him we are already there: 'my Lord, my Life, my Way, my End'. His claim is absolute: 'I am the way, the truth and the life; no one comes to the Father except by me'. This is alien to many in our multi-faith society. It asserts the necessity of the historical Jesus against those in the early Church whose religion was entirely of the Spirit and who felt they could dispense with Jesus and God's deed in him. They have had their successors in history, such as Joachim of Fiore (c. 1132–1202) with his belief in the age of the Holy Spirit to succeed that of the Father and the Son, and those in the nineteenth and early twentieth centuries who, largely in literature, have used his teaching as the inspiration of a new 'religion of humanity'. Ironically, they have often found the writings attributed to St John the most congenial of the New Testament. Jesus' claim affirms the distinctiveness of the Christian faith, what Bultmann calls 'the intolerance of the revelation'. This does not imply a refusal to listen to those who are not Christians or to enter into dialogue with them. It does not mean their persecution, or discrimination against them, or a failure to recognize that they possess truths from which we may learn in the understanding of our own faith: their lives often shame Christians. It means that Jesus leads a radical assault on all religions, including Christianity itself, all systems of human thought, all our misunderstandings of liberty and love. The way is not *our* quest for God or reality; it is *his* for us.

Jesus says also, 'I am the truth and I am the life.' Both, as has already been evident, are key concepts of this Gospel. Truth is eternal reality, not the vain, artificial shadow in which we spend so much of our lives. Jesus makes it possible for his followers to live in the real world, the world in which, in spite of the appearances of their earthly existence, God has a purpose for them. This is true life in contrast to the meaninglessness which ends in frustration, boredom and death. And truth and life are not mere philosophic abstractions, nor doctrinal formulae. They are found in Jesus and in our relation to him. This is personal and particular; and so truth and life are not open to all, only to those of the Way. This implies not only commitment to Christ but also its moral outworkings.

A question and a thought:

- Do you find the real presence of Jesus in the mutual love of Christians?

- '. . . the whole seeming maze of history in nature and man, the tumultuous movement of the world in progress, has running through it one supreme dominating Way, and . . . he who on earth was called Jesus the Nazarene **is** that Way' (Hort).

Eternal God,
Whose Son Jesus Christ is for all humankind
the way, the truth and the life:
grant us to walk in his way,
to rejoice in his truth,
and to share his risen life;
who is alive and reigns with you and the Holy Spirit,
one God, now and forever.

Alternative Service Book

Jesus and the Father, faith and prayer *John 14:7–14*

Jesus declares that through knowing him, the disciples have known and seen the Father. Philip, who has had a good record as a go-between hitherto (1:43–46; 6:5–7; 12:21–22), is all uncomprehending. A theophany—a sudden appearance of the Father, God himself—will overcome all his doubt and fear. But he has evidently spent a long time with Jesus and has not really known him, not come to realize that he is the Father's representative on earth. It has not dawned on him that the revelation is not in some earth-shattering, numinous manifestation of overwhelming deity but in the human life of the one with whom they have journeyed and are now at table.

The Lord's question pierces our hearts. In all our devotion, in all our worship and service, have we known Jesus? Has the Church? Has it developed according to his mind and recognized in him the true God, the Father? Or have we not made him in our own image, the clone of our own ideals and predilections? Yet we must not forever regard the Church as a mass of failure and apostasy. It is not a succession of *faux pas*. Jesus, the true and living way, is revealed in its long history. Hort says that in the rebuke to Philip 'we may still hear our Lord recalling to us an undervalued and imperfectly used experience'. We must not neglect the Christian centuries or the witness of the saints. 'They wrestled hard as we do now with sins and doubts and fears' (Isaac Watts), but they knew Christ and their knowledge was no pre-scientific antiquarianism. He was with them and may be with us through them.

Jesus speaks of the mutual indwelling of himself and the Father. If this is too hard and mystical an idea then the works he has done are revelation enough. And he promises that the believer will do even greater works because he is no longer confined to one small corner of the earth and brief period of history. He is going to the Father and his continuing action through his followers is universal in its scope. And more: the believer's works will be the result of his or her union with the Father and the Son through Christ's death. The means of this union is faith, which comes through the story of a person and his deeds, not through concepts or authoritarian dogma. And Jesus will act in answer to requests made in his name. This exercises a kind of censorship; nothing can be granted which is incompatible with him. Prayer is the activity of the union. Its end is not our glorification or success in human, earthly terms, but 'that the Father may be glorified in the Son'.

The triple promise John 14:15–24

The proof of love for Jesus is the keeping of his commands. Love is not simply passionate feeling or ardour of desire. It is listening to Jesus' words with loving attention, like Mary in Luke 10:39. So often erotic love cannot wait on words or keep commandments. It burns with impatient longing for physical possession. The love of which Jesus speaks is akin to faith, which must always be patient. It is ethical, its passion is for the truth. We shall not misrepresent it if we borrow a phrase from the seventeenth-century (by no means orthodox) Jewish philosopher Spinoza: 'the intellectual love of God'. Thought and reason are not the antitheses of the emotions. Law is not inevitably the opposite of love as the writer of Psalm 119 knew. The application of God's commandments to our conduct in the often agonizing situations of human life is a labour of love. There is an affinity here with the Sermon on the Mount in Matthew 5–7.

As he leaves them, Jesus makes three promises to the faithful and loving disciples. First, at his request the Father will send the Paraclete, the Spirit of Truth. 'Paraclete' is a very strange term, for which there is no one satisfactory English translation. Is it 'Advocate' in the legal sense, or 'Comforter' (in the sense of 'Strengthener'), or 'Counsellor' or 'Friend in need'? 'Sponsor' sheds some light. The Spirit will vouch for believers, commend them to God as well as support them in their confrontation with the world. As the Spirit of truth he is the Spirit of Jesus who is the truth, and he will be with them forever to represent Jesus and testify to his authenticity when his bodily presence is removed. 'The world'—human society organized according to its own values and temporal interests—cannot receive him any more than it did Jesus. Jesus' second promise is that he will come again. Jesus and the Spirit are inseparable—the historic figure, God-incarnate, and the one released by his departure through death, who continues his work and revelation. The evangelist unites the hope of the Lord's return with the tradition of Pentecost. But the world is unaware of this, thinking that Jesus is safely dead and buried. Yet not only is he alive, but for that reason, those who believe in him will live also. Death will no more destroy them than it did him. That this will be known only within the Christian community puzzles 'the other Judas' (v. 22, see Luke 6:16; Acts 1:13), for it was believed that Jesus' coming again would be a public spectacle in view of the world (Revelation 1:7). The third promise refers to the mystical union mentioned in 14:1–3. The Father and the Son will take up their abode with the lovers of Jesus. This is different from the promise of the continuing revelation and work of Jesus in the community of disciples with the sponsorship of the Spirit. It places this Gospel at the fount of later Christian contemplative experience, with its immediacy of union with God.

The legacy of Jesus   *John 14:25–31*

This passage seems to sum up and conclude the farewell discourse. It ends with the summons, 'Come, let us go'. Older commentators thought that the next three chapters record conversation away from the supper table *en route* for the Garden, and that the teaching about the vine (15:1–8) was actually spoken either as the group passed through vineyards, or in the temple court where a golden vine upon the gate represented Israel. Many modern scholars now believe that there were two or more editions of the Gospel and that our chapters 15–17 were rather clumsily inserted in the second. In them we find teaching about the departure of Jesus which reflected slightly different situations in the evangelist's community from chapter 14.

Verse 26 introduces the second promise of the Paraclete, called here the *Holy* Spirit for the only time in this Gospel. The revelation in Jesus does not end with his departure but will be renewed by the Spirit, who will not simply remind believers of what Jesus has told them but reconstitute it so that it is a present reality. 'Peace', Christ's parting gift, is more than that for which humanitarians long and statesmen negotiate, and which seems forever to elude them or be attained imperfectly through temporizing and often unjust settlements. It is 'the realised confidence of faith and fellowship with God' (Westcott) and with one another, with Christ in God. It is the salvation promised for the end-time, but bestowed by Jesus here and now, though at the cost of his death. It is found at the other side of suffering. It is there even as human conflict rages. So the disciples should not grieve at Jesus's departure. He is going to be with the Father completely, which is both joy for him and the accomplishment of his mission in the unity of the Godhead. What he does for them is possible because he will no longer be contained in the sphere of human relationships, for these limit him as the Father is not limited. 'The Father is greater than I'—greater, that is, than the incarnate Jesus on earth. He leaves this world to be with God the Father, Lord of all the worlds.

Jesus tells them this because dire events are to befall, which they may regard as unrelieved suffering and defeat. A chill falls over the table as the prince of this world approaches, but he has no claim against Jesus. His sinister advent will not destroy Jesus, much less expose him as a charlatan. It will be the supreme opportunity for him to show the extent of his love for the Father and his obedience to the Father's will.

The true vine   *John 15:1–8*

In the Old Testament, the vine is the symbol of Israel (Psalm 80:8–13; Isaiah 5:1–7; Jeremiah 2:21; Ezekiel 19:10–14). It was apparently often neglected by God who planted it, and so ravaged by beasts and passers-by; or it became wild through disobedience. Jesus says that he is the *true* (the real, the genuine) vine. Life and growth are possible only through remaining in him, that is, in closest union with him, as branches in the vine. This union is not the end or goal of discipleship, or prayer, as in traditional mysticism. It is that belonging to Christ which is the very beginning of discipleship, that being in him as the vine which is the only possibility of life and growth and fruitfulness. This teaching was very important to the Protestant Reformers, especially John Calvin.

Pruning is necessary, undertaken by the Father who is the vinedresser. The barren and withered branches are cut off and cast away, or burned on the garden bonfire; the fruitful are made more so by the pruning, which the evangelist calls cleansing. This figure of speech is used only here and in 13:10. It does not refer to ritual purification—there is no mention of water in this passage—but to the effect of the Word. This is no single utterance but the total words and work of Jesus. There may be a reference to Church discipline in all this—the excommunication of some, asceticism for all who remain—but the essential meaning is of spiritual death, which is not brought about by ecclesiastical condemnation but is already a reality for the one who is not truly in Christ. Everything is under the Word and loyalty is the prerequisite: 'Dwell in me as I in you.' The image of the vine makes plain that 'the loyalty that is demanded is not primarily a continued being *for* but a being *from*; it is not the holding of a position, but an allowing oneself to be held' (Bultmann).

Fruitfulness is the test of being truly in the vine. Its life is not flowing through the branch that is withered and barren. Discipleship is total dependence on Christ, unbroken communion with him: 'Apart from me you can do nothing.' This means that every request made in prayer is answered, for it is the expression of perfect union and therefore cannot be contrary to the mind of Christ or the will of God. It is also the way in which the Father is glorified, just as he is glorified in the Son Jesus. Thus the glory does not separate the disciples from Jesus and the Father: it unites them. Here also is the definition of discipleship. It is to abide in the true vine and bear much fruit. And for this evangelist, there is no higher state or office for believers. Whatever functions they exercise or titles they bear, there is no promotion out of discipleship.

Love and the friendship of Jesus   *John 15:9–17*

The themes of the previous section are continued and amplified. The love of Jesus for his disciples is as the love of the Father for him. It is to be the environment in which we dwell. 'To abide in love, which is what is demanded of the disciple, means continuing in the love he has received, in the state of being loved' (Bultmann). It means keeping Christ's commands. This love is corporate, not simply *Jesus loves me* but *Jesus loves me in the fellowship of his disciples.* 'As always, this love is not personal affection, but the being of the disciple for his neighbour that completely determines his own existence' (Bultmann). This is what is meant by 'love one another, as I have loved you'. It is the eve of Christ's death, yet he speaks of joy, for the result of love—whatever the heartbreak and sacrifice—is joy. This is the test of its validity (compare 16:20–24; Hebrews 12:2). He goes on to tell them that they are his friends. This is not exactly the offer of a reciprocal relationship as in human friendship. It is almost the language of an oriental king at whose court the friends were distinguished from the servants because they were in the king's counsels. They knew what he was about, were in his confidence, shared his secrets and his plans. It was similar with Abraham, the friend of God (Isaiah 41:8; 2 Chronicles 20:7; James 2:23; from the apocrypha, compare Wisdom of Solomon 7:27), from whom God did not hide what he was going to do (Genesis 18:17). There is an analogy with human friendship, whose supreme manifestation is in the laying down of life on behalf of one's friends. This is what Jesus is about to do. His death is a sacrifice for his disciples, but not to divert God's wrath or to cheat the devil, or to bear God's punishment for sin in their place. His self-giving leads them into his glory and makes his

346

presence permanent in their lives, with his love as their abode. The initiative in this friendship is Christ's. 'You did not choose me: I chose you'—words found in Greek over the entrance to the Chapel of the Queen's College for ministerial training at Birmingham. And the purpose of the choice is that they may bear fruit, 'fruit that will last' in the love that will mark their lives and those of their converts, and in the complete unity of their prayers with the Father's will.

The world's hatred   *John 15:18–27*

Love provokes hatred. This is a sad mystery of human life and history. 'We needs must love the highest when we see it' is alas a falsehood. As has been mentioned earlier (see notes on 12:37–50, pp. 332-33), the Greek philosopher Plato said that if the perfectly righteous man appeared, he would be impaled, crucified. So it was for Jesus and will be for his disciples. This is not what we are inclined to expect. We still think in terms of myriads of converts, and of our so commending Christ by a Church free from faults and skilled in communication that 'the world' will be bound to respond. But in John's understanding 'the world' is incorrigible, a society implacably estranged from God, the coalition of all false values—all the greed, lust, cruelty of human nature, all the rebelliousness against what is good. Once again Jesus warns the disciples: 'A servant is not greater than his master' (13:16; Matthew 10:24; Luke 6:40). At this point those forms of Christianity (such as Methodism) which preach 'universalism'—the belief that God wills that all shall be saved (though this is 'an optimism of grace' which must never be lost)—may lack the resilience of Calvinism for hard times, when Christ's cause does not prosper and only a few live by his love. There is a doctrine of election in these sayings, the concept of the faithful few chosen by Christ and called out of the world. They will be despised and hated as Christ was, their gospel not conquering the earth, though eternal in the heavens. There are dangers of sectarianism in this, of 'holier than thou' attitudes and, taken to extremes, the horrible belief that God has chosen the majority of humankind for damnation. Yet it may save Christians from a failure of nerve and from a sense of guilt if they accept that they will attract the hatred and not the mass response of the world. The tragedy is that it is the very coming of Jesus and his gospel of love which has inflamed the world's hatred and added to its sin. His devout and orthodox opponents might have continued undisturbed in their personally honourable and law-abiding ways had it not been for his confrontation and exposure. This turned them into conspirators of his death, into murderers. This is often the consequence of good. Evil cannot remain submerged by easy tolerance and quiet consciences.

The passage ends with a third promise of the Paraclete. The legal connotations are more evident here. He is the witness to Jesus before the world's tribunal. And the disciples who have been with Jesus from the beginning will also testify to him.

> Think of the parting gifts of Jesus to his own—the Paraclete: his peace; his joy; answer to prayer. Notice that they are all dependent on the commandment, 'Love one another as I have loved you.' How does this qualify our understanding of them? What is the nature of his love and of ours in consequence?

Faith strengthened by persecution and the Paraclete
John 16:1–15

Jesus reiterates his warnings of persecution and martyrdom. 'It is the way the Master went/Should not the servant tread it still?' (Horatius Bonar). In view of the previous questions of Peter (13:36) and Thomas (14:5), it is strange that Jesus should say that, plunged into grief by his foretold departure, none of the disciples has asked him where he is going. The verses seem to be from an alternative account of Jesus's farewell. The failure to question Jesus about his destination is a failure both human and spiritual. Wrapped up in their own sorrow, the disciples at table show no interest in what is going to happen to him. Jesus assures his first disciples that he goes away for their good. Otherwise the Paraclete will not come. This is to be more to their advantage than the continuing physical presence of Jesus, which being in a human life would be transient however long he might be with them.

Verses 8–11 are among the most difficult in the Gospel. Does the word which REB translates 'prove the world wrong' mean 'expose', 'convict' (in the sense of 'convince'), ' reprove' or even 'punish'? At the same time, 'sin, justice, and judgement' are terms which could call for abstract ethical discussion. This Gospel teaches us to think of them in a new way and not as the world does—even the respectable world living by the codes of law-abiding citizens—or those who long to see right prevail in human affairs and oppose 'the system'. Sin here is not moral failure but unbelief, the refusal to accept the revelation in Jesus and its questioning of all worldly standards and values. Justice is the vindication of Jesus, who goes not into oblivion at death but to the Father, so that he is the truth and meaning of the whole cosmos. Judgment is not some great assize in the future, but the present overthrow of the devil in what Jesus is about to accomplish.

Jesus has said (15:15) that he has disclosed everything to his friends, yet here he seems to imply that he is withholding some things as too great for them to bear at this stage. What he means is that while the whole revelation is contained in him in his words and deeds, its full elucidation must wait on the future guidance of the Spirit. 'You do not understand now what I am doing, but one day you will' (13:7). Only when he is gone will it all become clear. The future is all-important. For the disciples with the gift of the Spirit, it is full of hope, in spite of foretold persecutions, because the Spirit will guide them into all truth. They will see the whole design of God's mercy and its application to countless lives and to the whole universe. But the future does not displace the past; it fulfils it. The Spirit does not guide into new truth, rather the truth as it is in Jesus. There was the danger in the charismatic movement of New Testament times that in Calvin's phrase, the Spirit might be 'plucked away' from the word of Christ and the gate left open 'unto all manner of dotings and seducings'. That may be a danger today, not so much with the Christian charismatic movement, as with the various 'spiritual' religions which combine certain Christian insights with nature cults and theosophies.

Nor does Jesus promise private inspiration or 'inner light'. The Spirit elucidates the word of Jesus spoken to the community. He will also make known the future. This is not prophecy as in the foretelling of the things which are coming upon the earth. It is the glorifying of Jesus in human history and experience in the light of his death, resurrection and ascension.

The 'little while' John 16:16–24

These verses refer to two short intervals—the few hours until Jesus' disappearance from the disciples' view and the time after that until they see him again. They are mystified but Jesus understands. They will know grief and sorrow, mourning and tears, 'cosmic loneliness', because all worldly support will be gone. They will be alone in a world they never made and by rational calculation all seems lost. Meanwhile the world rejoices because Jesus has apparently gone and it could not accommodate so disturbing a person, who seemed to fault it on every count, to turn its values upside down. He was at once its fierce opponent and yet, though suspected as such, not a political rebel or freedom fighter. Jesus compares the disciples' situation to that of a woman in childbirth. The travail is indescribable, yet forgotten in the joy that a child has been born. And would there be such joy apart from the preceding anguish? Sadness will be theirs for a time, but Jesus will see them again. This, surely, is the promise of Easter, which for the evangelist is at once the second coming of Jesus and Pentecost. Though the world will go on and the suffering and grief be in some sense perennial, they will be overcome by a joy which no one can take away.

Like Christ's peace, this is not joy as the world gives it. The world's joy may be a very real human happiness, not simply the temporary pleasures of hedonistic indulgence. But it is never free from anxiety, always accompanied by fear that circumstances may change and it may be turned into sorrow overnight. The Greeks were afraid that too great a happiness might call down the envy of the gods, and similar feelings persist. The stars may be against us, or false friends, or the national economy, or human inability to solve the world's problems or conquer disease, or even divine wrath because of our sins. Ignatius Loyola advised the retreatant experiencing 'consolations' to think how it will be in the desolations which follow, but according to this Gospel such realism is not to deprive the disciples of their joy in the returning Christ and the Paraclete. They will live in the eternity beyond this world. Their joy will be completed in answered prayer, the fulfilment of the injunction of Matthew 7:7 and Luke 11:9: 'Ask and you will receive.' There is freedom with God, confidence, perfect ease in which to make any request, qualified only by the fact that it must be in the name of Jesus. However, verse 23 solemnly introduces a new thought. The asking of 23a refers to questioning Jesus, as the disciples have understandably been doing, if sometimes in rather crass ignorance. In the remainder of the verse, 'ask' refers to a request made in prayer. Perhaps, then, our questions and doubts should be turned into prayer.

Riddles and plain speech

It is popularly said that Jesus was the most lucid of teachers whose homely clarity has been obscured by a power-hungry Church, beginning with St Paul. In fact, according to Mark 4:11–12 his parables were deliberately intended to bewilder and confuse those outside and would be intelligible only to those who understood the mystery of the kingdom of God. John does not write here of parables, but of riddles ('figures of speech'). Not only does Jesus in these discourses use a private language which only the community will understand (such as his talk of 'going away'), but, as we have seen, he declares that much of what he says and does will be apparent later in the light of what is going to happen to him and of the gift of the Paraclete. Here he confesses that he has hitherto spoken in riddles but promises a future of plain words. Then there will be prayer in his name, but no need for him to intercede to appease an angry Father because the Father himself loves them and the Father and he together listen and respond to those who ask. The disciples claim now to understand what he means when he says that he came from God and returns to God. They affirm their faith and certainty and conviction. Jesus is not convinced by their assurance. 'I warn you, the hour is coming, indeed has already come when you will be scattered, each to his own home, leaving me alone.' Those are terrible words. There is an awesome solitariness in Jesus's vocation. He treads the winepress alone, to use words from Isaiah 63:3, which so moved preachers of a former day. Yet he is not alone for the Father is with him.

John does not regard Jesus' words at the end of verse 32 as a denial of the cry of dereliction in Mark 15:34, which for some in our time seems to be the heart of the Gospel. It is possible that those words were intended as a reference to Psalm 22 as a whole. This influences the Passion story in all four Gospels and proclaims that in spite of calumny and suffering the righteous person is not deserted by God. In any case, as an old writer said of that bitter cry, 'The Father withdrew his presence, but did not break the union.' The aim of all Jesus' words is that his followers may find peace in him in contrast to their experience in the world. And he has conquered the world.

Courage! your captain cries.
Who all your toil foreknew.
Toil ye shall have: yet all despise.
I have o'ercome for you!

Charles Wesley

Jesus prays for his glorification   *John 17:1—5*

This long prayer of Jesus, more like the often-ridiculed extempore prayers of Christian history than a liturgical form, is in part his report to the Father of what he has done on earth, his 'de-briefing'; for the third time in this Gospel he 'lifted his eyes', according to the Greek, (6:5; 11:41). Unfortunately the REB blurs this in the interests of idiomatic English. Verse 1 should read ' lifting up his eyes to heaven', possibly 'into the heaven' (Psalm 123:1—2). His prayer is not with eyes cast down like those of the publican (Luke 18:13) but in filial confidence with a vision of the dwelling-place of the Father to whom he speaks. Some have found it difficult to conceive of God praying to God, but the Son's conversation with the Father is the sign of their perfect union of love.

'The hour has come,' says Jesus, but there is no specific mention of the terrible ordeal of crucifixion. The dark night that he is to pass through will be in the reader's mind, and the prayer is the prelude to the account of his trial and death. He is not agitated or afraid: with perfect calm he contemplates what is no malignant fate but the completion of his work of revelation, the consummation of the divine act of love. His concern is that the Son may be glorified in what is about to happen, and so glorify the Father who has made him sovereign over all flesh, the humanity he has taken on himself, in order that those the Father has given him may have eternal life. He looks beyond the cross to the glorification which is its meaning, his ascent to heaven and the total life of God, which makes possible the gift of eternal life to his own. This does not mean that the glory of God was not revealed in the incarnate life (1:14); rather that that life was the disclosure or projection of a glory in a human being, which has its fullness with the Father. It is to this mutuality of heavenly existence that he prays to return. Verse 3 defines eternal life as the knowledge of God and of Jesus Christ his emissary (the latter name is used only here and in 1:17). There can be no knowledge of the one without the other. This knowing is both knowledge about— distinguishing the true God from false deities—and knowledge in the intimacy of personal union. It is parallel to believing: both have intellectual as well as emotional elements. It is one of the key concepts of the Fourth Gospel: words for it occur in every chapter. Jesus says that he has glorified the Father because his work on earth is complete. He has made known the Father's name, whose nature and whose name is love. Now he prays that he may be raised out of his earthly existence to the glory which he had with the Father before the world began.

The prayer of intercession
and consecration
John 17:6–19

Having prayed for himself, Jesus now intercedes for those whom he is leaving behind. They are not called 'disciples' nor 'apostles' nor 'the Church'. They are not a human organization founded by Jesus in his earthly ministry. They are a heavenly entity, the possession of the Father and his gift to his Son (vv. 6, 9, 24). Notice how John 17 is dominated by the verb 'to give'.

First Jesus reports to the Father on what he has done for them. He speaks as though their misunderstandings, sorry behaviour and defection were already overpast. He has confidence that they have come to know the name that is not some magic *abracadabra* but the true nature of God and of himself as sent by God. The 'now' in verse 7 is all important. It is this present moment of the Lord's departure which brings them to the truth. They find their true relationship to him for the first time in the face of death, which is normally the final end of human association, and find faith through his apparent failure. Jesus prays for them, not for the world. The world, which God loves to the extent of giving his Son (3:16) is not altogether excluded from the prayer, for the unity for which Jesus pleads is that the world may believe (v. 21, 23). But the community of disciples are now to reveal his glory. In the world they need the protection of the name, again no magic incantation but the truth of God and the holiness of the one who is invoked as 'Holy Father'. They must be holy, that is, separated from the world, not out of indifference to its coming to faith, but in lives consecrated to God and uncontaminated by the profanity of ambition, lust and greed. This means their unity, but the word for 'one' is not masculine as in Galatians 3:28, where Paul declares

353

that different races, sexes and social stations are transcended and become one humanity in Christ. Here the word is neuter and the unity is with the Father and the Son. It is not a prayer to be answered in a World Council of Churches or a unity scheme, but in the sharing of the very life of God, in the divine love. Jesus is able to say that on earth he has kept the disciples safe in the Father's name. Only one perished. He was a satellite of the power of evil, and the first letter of John makes plain that in the last years of the first century there were many antichrists who, like Judas, 'went out' (1 John 2:18–19; compare John 13:30). It has been so ever since. They may have been comparatively few, or only one from any group of disciples, but who may be sure that he or she is not perhaps that one?

Jesus' prayer is that the disciples may share his joy even while in the world. They are not to be taken out of the world, in order to escape from its harsh realities, but to be kept from evil, which is an ever present danger. They are sent into the world just as Jesus has been. They succeed him in his mission. Jesus prays for their consecration, not by some occult ceremony but by the active word of truth, the revelation of God in Jesus. This is not esoteric or a private experience. It is objective, in history, and it has a cleansing and sanctifiying power more than a mere symbol or rite, important as they are in proclaiming the word and confronting us with the divine being and action in Christ. There may be an echo of a rite in the next verses. The consecration of the disciples follows from the consecration of Jesus. The words of verse 19, 'For their sakes I consecrate myself', could be the equivalent in this Gospel of the words of the institution of the Eucharist in Mark 14:22–25 (compare 1 Corinthians 11:23–25). Over the bread and wine Jesus said, 'This is my body'—that is, 'I, myself'—and 'This is my blood'—that is, 'my life'. There he made himself over to God, laid 'his consecrating hand upon the life now drawing to its close, at once bestowing its fulness upon his disciples and setting it upon the altar of his Father's will' (Donald MacKinnon).

The prayer for future believers and their perfecting in the divine unity   *John 17:20–26*

Centuries on, Christians have believed that here Jesus prayed for them—and indeed still prays, for the Puritan Thomas Goodwin described John 17 as 'a platform of Christ's heavenly intercession'.

The prayer is for their participation in the divine unity, which will show to the world that Jesus is the authentic messenger of God and so bring it to the true knowledge of faith. The prayer is for perfect unity (v. 23), the unity of the end, of the finished work of God in Christ. The unity of Christians on earth is the anticipation of this. Perfectionists in the history of the Church have sometimes been morally dangerous, judgmental and divisive, but at their best—like John Wesley in his wiser statements—they have emphasized that Christian faith should make a difference to human beings and their behaviour, and that there should be no limit to the efficacy of divine grace. And perfection is the victory of the Father's love in those who are Christ's own.

In verse 24, Jesus says no longer 'I pray' but 'I will', misguidedly weakened in REB to 'my desire is'. Jesus abandons the language of supplication for that of sovereign purpose (Michael Ramsey), though there is tenderness in the prayer, both towards God and his own. He wills that they should see his glory in the fullness of his being in the Father's love before the world began. This points to their future life beyond this world, and is paralleled in 1 John 3:2: 'What we shall be has not yet been disclosed, but we know that when Christ appears we shall be like him, because we shall see him as he is.' The visual metaphors are important: 'Man is a unified being who sees' (Iris Murdoch). Sight may transform, especially when it is insight, the word apprehended by the response of our own faculties, not simply spoken from outside. The ignorant and unbelieving world remains (v. 25), but there is the little group of those who know that Jesus knows, and that he has been sent by the righteous Father. The accomplished mission of Jesus has been to make the Father's name known to them and this he will continue to do. Out of all its rich complexity, 'the prayer finally comes to rest with the word love . . . in this prayer the last word and not the first. And in the light of its use in Christian history, and of our present use of it, in which it can mean anything or nothing, it had better not be spoken until a great deal else has been said first' (Christopher Evans).

THE LAMB OF GOD
FINISHES HIS WORK

The garden

John 18:1—11

Jesus has said in his prayer that he has already finished the work the Father gave him to do (17:4), but he still needs to speak the word from the cross, 'It is finished.' He does not simply pass from the prayer to a peaceful yielding of his spirit into the Father's hands. As all the world knows, he had to die violently by a cruel Roman form of torture which in its bitter pain and public calumny could destroy soul as well as body. Yet in this Gospel he approaches his death in perfect command, with no terror or dismay. It is his destiny, his royal way, the ironic symbol of his exaltation to the Father, though the cross is but a few feet from the ground, within earshot of sometimes taunting sightseers. In this Gospel Jesus is no passive victim. He takes the initiative from first to last. In the garden, he does not pray in agony that the cup of suffering may pass from him, nor do the disciples sleep. Although not named Gethsemane, the garden is a familiar rendezvous and Jesus cannot have gone there to escape from those who seek his life, rather to await them. Judas and the soldiers, a mixed force of Romans and temple police, come to arrest him. His encounter with the Roman state, which is so significant for John, begins here. They represent the 'Prince or ruler of this world' (14:30). Jesus advances to meet them and identifies himself in words reminiscent of the I AM sayings in the Gospel: 'I AM he'. The soldiers draw back and fall to the ground before his numinous majesty. He gives himself up but is concerned for his disciples and asks that they may be let go, softening the terrible assertion in Mark that they all forsook him and fled. They will be scattered, but as a result of the care of Jesus as well as their own fear. The high priest's servant is attacked and his right ear cut off. John says that this is by Peter, not an unnamed bystander as in Mark. From chapter 13 onwards Peter is represented in an unfavourable light, oscillating between self-assertive boldness and cowardice and totally lacking in judgment. Jesus restrains him. He must drink the cup to be placed at his lips, for, though bitter, it is in fact yet one more gift of the Father.

Peter's denial

Jesus is first tried, presumably before the Sanhedrin, though the proceedings are brief. No witnesses are called and there is no mention as in Mark and Matthew of Jesus' sayings about the temple and its destruction. Above all, the question by the high priest about his messianic claims, which in Mark led to Jesus' condemnation to death by the Sanhedrin, does not occur. The only abuse of Jesus is the policeman's slap in the face. There is a problem about the status of Annas, as elsewhere in the New Testament (for example Acts 4:5). Annas was the deposed high priest but he still exercised great influence. His son-in-law, Caiaphas, was the actual holder of the office. No further discussion with the leader of Judaism was necessary after the controversies of the ministry. Furthermore the Jesus of John would hardly have answered the high priest's question of Mark 14:61 in the apocalyptic terms of that Gospel. This evangelist is most concerned with the trial before Pilate, but also at this stage with Peter's denial, recorded in all four Gospels. It is remarkable that the story should have been preserved and given such prominence. At a time when apostasy was causing the early churches so many problems and sin after baptism might be an unforgiveable offence (Hebrews 3:12–14; 10:26–27), here is the story of the chief of the apostles denying at the hour of trial that he had anything to do with Jesus. Yet he was forgiven and restored, though it could have been argued that he sinned before conversion (Luke 22:31–32) and the gift of the Spirit. John does not tell the story as movingly as Luke. There is no mention of the Lord's look, nor Peter's tears. It is left as a record of fact and a count against Peter who had earlier boasted his fidelity (13:37).

The scene when Peter is brought in by an unnamed disciple—not the beloved as has sometimes been imagined—is vivid, with the fire and Peter standing round with the police, warming himself. The narrative is brief, but many of us may have stood there at some time, and our hearts have failed us for fear as we have sought to keep warm in the world's cold, with Christ on trial before unbelievers.

Jesus is handed over to Pilate

The opponents of Jesus are determined that he shall perish by the most terrible and shameful of public deaths which only the Roman authorities can impose. Therefore they take him to Pilate, the procurator, but since it is the day of the Passover (which John makes a day later than the synoptics) they will not defile themselves by entering the quarters of a Gentile. There is irony here. They are delivering up the true Paschal victim, yet meticulously regarding their ceremonial rules. They remain outside the praetorium. Jesus is inside and Pilate hovers between the two. Pilate was a vicious and corrupt governor, given to outbursts of uncontrollable temper. Here he is rather different: far from exemplary—weak, vacillating and superstitious—yet patient, discerning that this prisoner is no ordinary criminal or imposter, wanting to release him and anxious to score over the Jews if he can.

The evangelist is a profound student of 'the world' he so much opposes to Jesus. He understands the importance of government and the state. He is not simply concerned to ingratiate Christians with the Romans or to exonerate the latter from the crucifixion of Christ. He is aware of the age-long debate between the rule of the state and the rule of Christ, of the compromises and accommodations forced upon government. Although he did not foresee either the holocaust or apartheid—or for that matter the British Empire or the rule of W.E. Gladstone or Margaret Thatcher—he knows that there will be dialogue (at times of the deaf) while he believes that Christ and his followers are no menace to lawful authority. Sometimes, though, they will be its victims and martyrs, their power only spiritual. This is one of the motifs of the trial before Pilate. There is another. His enemies want Jesus crucified to humiliate and destroy him utterly, but this is the manner of death purposed by God. It is a lifting up, the symbol of his ascent from shame to glory, the public declaration to the world of the healing, saving love of God. The cross symbolizes the divine movement in loving activity which unites earth and heaven, and a compassion that would be all-embracing, even though but few accept it. In words found in the *Alternative Service Book*, 'He opened wide his arms for us on the cross'.

The King of truth or the bandit?   John 18:33–40

Pilate first interrogates Jesus on the charge of sedition: that he has claimed to be King of the Jews, leader of rebellion against the authorities in order to restore the kingdom to Israel. This charge could have substance in view of the teaching of Jesus in the synoptic Gospels about the kingdom of God, almost without echo in John. Pilate, totally mystified by Jesus' replies, which bewilder his cynical mind with metaphysics, concludes that he is a harmless crank and no danger to the state: only the malice of his opponents has tried to make him one. He ought to release him but has not the strength to withstand the clamour of those who want Jesus killed.

There are deeper questions here of great importance in our time. Jesus admits that he is a king, but not of a kingdom that has its origin in this world. This does not mean that his kingdom is unconcerned with this world or irrelevant to it, totally of a 'spiritual' order. But it is not a kingdom supported by earthly forces to fight on his behalf. 'King' is not in fact a term which Jesus himself would use, either of himself or God (compare the synoptic Gospels). It is Pilate's word, disliked by some today, who feel it not only outdated in human government but incompatible with the spirit of Jesus. Earthly government, so Christians have always believed, is necessary to human life, devised to 'order the unruly wills and affections of sinful men' and to secure justice. It is an ordinance of God, what the Protestant Reformers called 'Christ's strange work' in contrast to his 'proper work' of salvation. But his kingdom is no worldly institution. It is of the truth, that is, of the ultimate meaning of the universe, where 'faith prevails and love adores'. Truth cannot be defined in a few sentences in answer to Pilate's question. That would lead to the bigotry of ecclesiastics or the closed minds of fundamentalists, and drive others to scepticism. It is an ethical as well as metaphysical issue. It is seen in the life of Jesus who is the truth.

Pilate—who cannot make head or tail of Jesus and cynically shrugs his corrupt shoulders at the mention of truth, but feels that the prisoner is a harmless eccentric as far as the government goes—makes a futile gesture, common to all the Gospels. He invokes a custom that one prisoner should be released at Passover. (The custom is not attested elsewhere and its orgins are quite unknown. Perhaps Pilate invented it!) The angry crowd shout instead for a certain Barabbas, who was a bandit. There is irony here. They have wanted Jesus condemned to death as a political insurgent and now they ask for the release of one presumably found guilty, if not of political violence, of mugging innocent victims to rob them of their possessions. Underlying the crowd's demand is both a psychological and theological fact. Public opinion, especially when inflamed by vindictiveness and hatred, may find it easier to show mercy towards a sworn enemy, even one who has engaged in terrorism, than towards one whose fundamental message is of peace and love, and whose teaching and presence seem to go against the assumptions of society. At present, there are many signs of furious hatred of criminals and desire for revenge and most brutal punishment. The tabloid press would hardly want to set Barabbas free. Yet the fiercest opposition is often against those who would not meet violence with violence. There is, however, a deeper theological meaning. Was it in the evangelist's mind that in this incident there is a profound truth of the gospel? The just is condemned and the sinner is free. Jesus died instead of one whose deeds, by the laws of the state, deserved death. 'In *my* place condemned he stood.'

'Behold the man!' *John 19:1—7*

It was the custom to flog a condemned man immediately before he was led out to be crucified. Pilate, in order to delay his decision and try to satisfy the Jews by making Jesus look ridiculous, has him flogged at this point. More than that, he is delivered to the soldiers for their brutal teasing. They plait a crown of thorns and put it on his head, a caricature of the halo of Hellenistic rulers (Mark 15:17; Matthew 27:28—29). They clothe him in the red or purple mantle of a victorious king. They taunt him and smite his face. In this sorry state, Pilate presents him to his adversaries. 'Here is your man!' he says. 'This pathetic creature, so clearly a human being, powerless and derided, cannot possibly be a king!' Here is one more instance of John's irony, for this humiliated figure is indeed *the* man—in Luther's phrase 'the proper man'— representative of humanity and, more, the Word made flesh. He is, in language Pilate would not use, the Son of Man come down from heaven (3:13). Here 'is the lowest depth of his condescension . . . immediately before his exaltation on the cross' (R.H. Lightfoot).

Pilate's ploy is ineffective. The sight of Jesus, so humiliated, evokes no pity. The chief priests and the temple police cry out in fury. 'Crucify! Crucify!' is not the clamour of a crowd incited by the chief priests, as in Mark, but the audible rage of the priests themselves and the guardians of the shrine. Pilate, exasperated and bitterly ironic, tells them to crucify him themselves, knowing that they cannot do so. They then bring up another charge. This man has sinned against the Jewish law of blasphemy (Leviticus 24:14—16) because he has claimed to be the Son of God. This demands the death penalty, and Pilate, as Governor required to indulge the religious scruples of the populace, should not ignore it. Underlying the scene is the whole question of God and the state. The latter, ordained by God, is not 'of the world'. It is the arbiter between God and the world and should not yield to the world's clamour, whether riotous shouts or tabloid headlines.

> From the trial hour of Christ—from the Cross of the Son of God—there arises the principle to which all his life bore witness, that the first lesson of the Christian life is this: Be true. And the second this: Be true. And the third this: Be true.
>
> Robertson of Brighton

A second examination and the condemnation of Jesus
John 19:8–16

Pilate hesitates. A superstitious man, he is seized by the fear that the one whom he had regarded as a harmless and rather pitiful victim may after all have divine powers, so that to crucify him would result in awesome vengeance. So he asks about Jesus' origins. Jesus is silent, as he had been in the synoptic accounts, and as were many just men on trial in classical antiquity. His divine origin and glory are manifest only to believers. It may be that like Socrates he refuses to argue against the authority of the state even if its decision is unjust. For Jesus, the fact that the state is going to act wrongfully does not constitute a sin equal to those whose hatred and envy have arraigned Jesus before it. It is they who have prostituted the state, which in itself is a neutral and impartial ordinance of God. There is no anti-semitism here, nor any attempt to ingratiate Christians with the Roman authorities at a time when, through the denunciations of their enemies, they may be in danger of condemnation. There is an implication of respect for the state, even though it may be perverted by those possessed by evil, in their demonic cry, 'Crucify'. Its authority is from above and in this case its yielding to injustice serves a divine purpose.

Pilate almost pleads with the Jews to let him discharge Jesus. But they have a final trump card. They threaten to denounce Pilate before Caesar. Pilate once more brings the two parties together. The scene portrayed from verse 13 is of the utmost gravity. It is pictured in detail of time and place. Pilate takes his place on the seat from which sentence had to be pronounced. The language could mean that he sat Jesus there and that John intends an ironic ambiguity, for this bedraggled Jesus, not Pilate, is the real judge. It is about noon when the Passover is being prepared. At that very hour, the religious representatives are repudiating their history and heritage, while the true Paschal victim is about to be slain. Pilate still pleads: 'Here is your king! Am I to crucify him?' But the Jewish authorities are implacable in their vehement hatred. They deny their whole patriotism and national identity by the cry, ' We have no king but Caesar!' Pilate finds this irresistible, and gives in.

The crucifixion   *John 19:16b–25a*

The popular Roman Catholic devotion of the stations of the cross—the imagined stopping-places on Our Lord's agonizing progress from the judgment hall to Calvary depicted around the walls of churches and kept by pilgrims along the Via Dolorosa in Jerusalem—is totally alien to St John's Gospel. However bedraggled the flogged Jesus, bruised, bleeding and crowned with thorns, may have been, for John the procession is a royal progress. Jesus is on his way not simply to the gallows but to God. He will be lifted up not very high above the bystanders, but this is the beginning of his ascent to the Father. So, Simon of Cyrene is neither mentioned nor required: cross-bearing in John is not part of the summons to discipleship. Jesus carries the cross himself. 'Whatever may have been the facts about the bearing of the cross of wood, no man can lighten the Lord's burden for him, or share his achievement with him' (R.H. Lightfoot). Nor is it said by John that anyone mocked him, nor, once he was crucified, told him to come down from the cross. Neither is there darkness at noon, which for John is apparently (v. 14) the time of the crucifixion and not its awesome climax. Jesus is crucified between two others but there is no mention of who they were or why they were there. The title Pilate orders to be written and fastened to the cross is no taunting of a false and rebellious claim. It is a final assertion of himself against the Jewish authorities to whom he has reluctantly succumbed. It is prophetic of one of the offices of Jesus and of a universal lordship, written in the languages of the three cultures of the ancient world. These have influenced the presentation and understanding of the faith as much as they have been baptized into it. Our Christianity comes via all of them.

Psalm 22 influences the story as in the synoptics: 'They shared my garments among them and cast lots for my clothing.' This is done in an orderly fashion and with some respect. The undergarment, woven from one piece and without a seam—doubtless a precious gift—is not torn. We may think that that has been left to Christians, tearing Christ's unity asunder with quarrels and divisions of a tragically seeming inevitability. There is no evidence that the evangelist has such allegorizing in mind, but it is not altogether inappropriate to his method. What is a fact is that the Son of Man, crucified, hung between earth and heaven naked.

The mother and the Beloved Disciple   *John 19:25b–27*

In this Gospel, the dying Jesus is not alone; he is not entirely deserted by his followers. The women (possibly four of them) are not watching from a distance as in Mark and Luke, and one of the men is with them at the foot of the cross. He is the Beloved Disciple, whose faith and love do not fail Jesus at the last extremity and through whom (and not Peter) is founded a new family of love. The Lord's mother has been mentioned only once before, at Cana in Galilee (2:1–12). She then, but dimly understanding, wanted to precipitate an hour which had not yet come and would be different from her hopes, though she showed faith that her son's likely action may be something of an epiphany. Now his hour has come (again the REB is unsatisfactory in translating verse 27 as 'from that moment', for 'the hour', as elsewhere in John, means the hour of Jesus' death), and it marks the beginning of something new.

Though appearing so briefly the mother of Jesus seems to be closer to the company of disciples than Mark 3:31–35 would suggest. Here, as at Cana, Jesus addresses her as 'woman'. It is a title of grave courtesy and it is incomprehensible that the REB should translate the Greek as 'mother', for John is concerned more with spiritual than with natural relationships. Ties of flesh and blood are now dissolved in the Lord's imminent death, but he creates a new family as he gives his mother and the Beloved Disciple each to the other. Some scholars have seen the two as types, the mother representing Jewish and the disciple Gentile Christianity. The two traditions are reconciled at the cross in Jesus's dying gift. A community is born which transcends natural associations, while sharing their inheritance. It is not misguided to infer from this that the mother of Jesus is given to be mother of believers too. Marian devotion has sometimes been excessive. There is no hint here that she is

363

co-redemptrix, any more than the Beloved Disciple is co-redemptor. Both stand at the foot of the cross and their new relationship is the gift of the dying Jesus and from a work not of their own, except that they have followed there and are with Jesus to the last, sharing in his sufferings and his victory. This is the place where the new family is born, and we enter it as we are there too, witnesses of Jesus' dying as 'more than standers-by' (Charles Wesley).

The thirst and the finishing of Jesus' work *John 19:28–30*

We may infer that the group remained beneath the cross until the end, the consummation. This is at hand, all is fulfilled; but first Jesus gives the only hint of his physical sufferings when he says, 'I am thirsty.' He who is the bread of life began his ministry in the other Gospels hungry; here he who is the source of living water dies thirsty. Yet it is at this moment, 'when he suffers the most absolute thirst, that he pours himself forth as the everlasting spring' (von Balthasar). It could also be, as Kenneth Grayston has suggested, that by accepting the wine his executioners offer, Jesus enables them to earn merit, as in Proverbs 25:21–22: 'If your enemy . . . is thirsty give him drink . . . and the Lord will reward you.' They soaked a sponge with the wine and fixed it on hyssop, a herb which 'grows out of the wall' (1 Kings 4:33), to prevent the wine running down their arms. They could easily lift it to his lips, for he hung only a few feet above the ground. Hyssop is symbolic both of the cleansing of the sinner (Psalm 51:7) and of outcasts (Leviticus 14:4–6), and of the protective sprinkling of the blood of the Paschal lamb on the Israelite doorposts (Exodus 12:22). It both offers his enemies the possibility of cleansing through his death and fulfils the prophecy of the Baptist, hitherto not recalled: ' Behold the Lamb of God, who takes away the sin of the world'.

Jesus' mission is now accomplished, wrought out in events terrible though salvific. There is his last cry, 'It is finished', and the bowing of his head in death. Older evangelicals dwelt much on these last words in John. What was done on the cross was final, done once for all, unrepeatable (compare Hebrews 9:25–28). They would endorse the reading of verse 30 with exclamations of deep fervour. Cranmer's prayer over the words of institution in the Prayer Book rite declares in a militantly Protestant phrase that by his suffering of 'death upon the Cross for our redemption', God's Son 'made there (by his one oblation of himself once offered) a full, perfect and sufficient sacrifice, oblation and satisfaction for the sins of the whole world'. This, like the letter to Hebrews, may be an extension of John's understanding of the meaning of Christ's death, though it is not unwarranted. For John the cry may be the equivalent of the cry of dereliction in Mark 15:34, not its substitute. We have already noted that the whole of Psalm 22 is a cry of hope and assurance: though God seems to have forsaken his servant and handed him over to tormentors and despisers, there is divine vindication. In the eyes of the world, the crucifixion may seem the total defeat of Christ's cause and evidence that he does not have divine approval. For the believer this is the victory that overcomes the world. Christ's work on earth is now done. 'The Incarnation is ended. There remains but that formality—death' (Charles Péguy).

There is also the implication that the ultimate end of time and of the universe has been reached. This is the judgment, the verdict, the revelation of the whole counsel of God. There is nothing more for him to do. Yet Jesus' work is not over. It is bequeathed to his followers. He dies of his own free will when the time is right and all is accomplished. In full possession of his faculties, perhaps revived by the sips of wine, he literally 'handed over the spirit'. Assuming that the little group of verse 25 is still beneath the cross, it could be that in the very moment of death, Jesus bestows on them the promised Spirit, for he is now glorified (7:39). 'In the unitary event of *krisis* (judgment) and glorification which is the Cross, the Spirit becomes "free" in the moment Jesus breathes his last, and thus can be breathed into the Church, undelayed, by the Risen One (20:22)' (von Balthasar).

The piercing   *John 19:31–37*

According to the Jewish Law (Deuteronomy 21:22–23), bodies of executed criminals must be removed before sunset, otherwise the land will be defiled. On this account, the Jewish authorities are anxious that the three crucified men, who had been hung as late as noon, and who by this form of death might linger on well into the night, should have their end hastened. In addition it was a Friday, the eve of the sabbath and that sabbath seems to have coincided with the Passover, so that speedy despatch was more necessary than ever. The soldiers brutally smash the legs of the other two, but to their surprise Jesus is dead already. His ordeal, of which he has been in charge throughout, has not been unduly long. John does not think of the work of Christ in terms of the amount of agony, the terrible toll of human suffering, which he endured on behalf of us all. It is doubtful whether he would be altogether in sympathy with Bonhoeffer's words, so vital to modern theology: 'Only a suffering God can help.'

The piercing is of profound significance and of almost innumerable meanings. It obliquely declares that Jesus is the true unblemished Paschal lamb (Exodus 12:46); also that he is the righteous sufferer, no bone of whose body will be broken (Psalm 34:20). There is also the fulfilment of Zechariah 12:10, in which a disobedient people grieves for the one they have wronged, a grief which the author of Revelation postpones until the apocalyptic coming of Christ (Revelation 1:7). There could be more than grief in John's use of the text: there may be a reference back to 3:14 and the lifting up of the serpent in the wilderness. The Salvation Army song, 'There's life for a look on the crucified one' may convey part of the meaning. The piercing, however, opens the heart of the saving victim. There may here be another reference to the paschal lamb in the reference to the blood and water in verse 34, for rabbinic legislation laid down that 'the heart of the slain lamb be opened, and its blood flow forth'. Devotion to the Sacred Heart of Jesus has its origin here, though it has often been too carnal and too sentimental, and far from the ethos of this Gospel. The Puritan, Thomas Goodwin, thought that the prayer of John 17 rather than this passage revealed the 'heart of Christ in heaven towards sinners on earth'. It is what comes from the heart—Christ's very self, not just the ruptured organ of his physical body—that is of greatest significance. The 'flow of blood and water' is a reference to baptism, birth from above of water and the Spirit (3:5), but not baptism of the Spirit alone apart from the cleansing of Christ's blood. There is evidence from the first letter of John that the community to which that and the Gospel were addressed included dissidents who accepted entry to the Church by water-baptism, but then demanded a second stage of membership when the divine gift of the Spirit was received in its fullness. After this Christians could not sin, so the cleansing blood of Jesus was not needed. Against this the letter declares, 'This is he whose coming was with water and blood: Jesus Christ. He came, not by the water alone, but both by the water and the blood: and to this the Spirit bears witness, because the Spirit is truth' (1 John 5:6).

Is this for John the institution of both the Gospel sacraments? It certainly implies that both Baptism and the Eucharist are necessary. The one signifies the new life in the Spirit, the other is the perpetual remembrance of Christ's death, through which alone the Spirit is given and through which alone we are made one with God in Christ. Augustus Toplady's hymn *Rock of Ages*, still sung in the inner cities and not least among black Christians, has another interpretation of the piercing:

Let the water and the blood,
From thy riven side which flowed,
Be of sin the double cure,
Cleanse me from its guilt and power.

The burial
John 19:38—42

Joseph of Arimathea appears in the Gospel for the first time, though he is also known in the synoptic tradition (Mark 15:42—43 and parallels) as a wealthy disciple. According to John he has kept his allegiance secret so far, but now he boldly goes to Pilate to ask for Jesus' body. He wants to give it a worthy burial, not to see it as vultures' prey or cast into a common criminal's grave. In this he is assisted by Nicodemus, making his third and final appearance, who brings an immense quantity of spices. This is typical of the abundance of this Gospel—the water turned into wine at Cana, the quantity of food left over at the feeding of the five thousand. This is to be a burial fit for a king! The body is reverently wrapped with the spices in grave-clothes, which are going to be significant in the first resurrection story. There is a garden in the place where Jesus was crucifed. Does John intend his readers to think of the paradise garden of Genesis in which man and woman fell from their original state of innocence, which is now restored in the garden of the cross? This is uncertain and must not be pressed too far. John may simply intend to emphasize that the burial of Jesus was seemly and in a place of beauty, where there was a new tomb, not yet used for burial, so that he was not laid with sinners or paupers. But it may all be due to the need for haste, to bury Jesus in the nearest available space since time was short, the Sabbath was at hand and its sacred hours must not be defiled.

What must not be overlooked is that Jesus, as much as Lazarus in chapter 11, is altogether dead and buried. There is no question that he has survived crucifixion, or merely fainted on the cross so that his friends could revive him. He is dead. And all the devotion of converted sinners and sanctified saints, of apostles and martyrs, of scholars and preachers, of architects, musicians, poets, embroiderers and silver-smiths can do no more than bury him—albeit with reverence and love—so that his life is not forgotten and his memory does not lose its power.

> The Gospel story has insisted throughout that Jesus lives because he has gone to the Father. His death, though no counterfeit, is the finishing of his work on earth and his ascent to the Divine glory. By the time we reach the end of chapter 19, we may share these sentiments: 'If the Gospels omitted all mention of Christ's Resurrection, faith would be easier for me. The Cross by itself suffices me' (Simone Weil, 1909–43). Why then does John need stories about the resurrection?

THE RISEN JESUS OPENS THE EYES OF FAITH

John must make vivid through stories the teaching of the farewell discourses—that in the future the conditions of the relationship between Jesus and his own will be different from those of his incarnate life, though he is the same Jesus. And so chapter 20 contains four stories, the first three unconnected. The Gospel could have ended with any one of them.

The race to the tomb   John 20:1–10

Mary of Magdala goes along to the tomb. She is not in a group of women as in the other Gospels and she goes earlier, in the darkness before the dawn and presumably to mourn rather than embalm, which has already been done at the burial. She was one of the women beneath the cross (19:25), and is mentioned in the Gospels only as present at Calvary and the tomb (apart from the statement in Luke 8:2 that seven demons had come out of her, implying what we would call psychological illness). She is clearly important in the tradition of the cross and resurrection. Here she finds that the stone has been rolled away from the entrance to the tomb, presumably suspects grave robbers (common in those days) and in alarm runs to Simon Peter and the Beloved Disciple to report that the Lord's body is missing. They immediately hasten to see what has happened. The other disciple outruns Peter. He is, metaphorically as well as literally, the one who gets there first, the one with deepest understanding and most immediate insight. Hans Urs von Balthasar has said that Peter represents the Church of office, while the Beloved Disciple stands for the Church of love. When the latter arrives he looks into the tomb, sees something strange about the burial clothes, but pauses outside. Peter, on arrival, rushes in, but apparently can make nothing of it. The other disciple then enters, sees and believes. There is no angelic presence, no appearance of a risen Jesus, no recall of Scripture. The disciple has but the empty tomb and the grave-clothes. These and these alone convince him.

Only a mystic would have been brought to faith by emptiness, by the absence of the body. Yet it is when God seems to have withdrawn any signs of his presence that the mystic believes more than ever in his reality. There is no asking for signs of evidence, for visible and tangible reassurance. The state of the grave-clothes may have borne the silent witness which endorsed the Beloved Disciple's faith. There is probably a deliberate contrast with the raising of Lazarus, who stumbles out of the charnel-house, bandaged and bound to resume his mortal life. Jesus is alive forevermore, in the eternal order. This the disciple sees with his inward as well as outward eye and believes. He is the one person that first Easter who was convinced by the empty tomb.

The disciples went home again. They made no announcement. They were presumably left for the time being to carry on with their daily lives. But for the Beloved, emptiness and apparent loss were filled with all the fullness of God, with the victorious life of him who has gone away not to leave us desolate but that he may fill all things. In his resurrection Jesus has made this earth no derelict outpost of creation but the centre of the Father's love, because of one forsaken grave.

Mary in the garden   *John 20:11–18*

Mary has somehow returned to the tomb and stands there in tears. The word 'maudlin'—the old pronunciation of Magdalen(e), as in the Oxford and Cambridge colleges—is derived from her name. She looks into the tomb and sees two angels who had not been there for the

Beloved Disciple, but they are no help to her (perhaps John borrowed the account from the synoptics). They portend an awesome glory, but she needs a body even if dead, and a grave to act as a shrine where she may show her love and await the resurrection on the last day. She then turns and sees Jesus but, as is common in the Easter stories, does not recognize him. She thinks he is the gardener, who may have removed the body, until he speaks to her, as to his own sheep, by name (10:3). She then hails him by his name of Teacher—not a title redolent of deity—and would embrace him, but he forbids her. He is alive and ever her friend, but he cannot be retained on earth, nor can the old relationship be restored. The transition foretold in the discourses is coming into sight, as Hort said, 'the transition from a presence taking its character from their circumstances to a presence taking its character from his'. He is the ascending Lord, and Mary of Magdala is made the first emissary of this truth to his male disciples, his brothers, to tell them that they too are to share his relationship with the Father.

But why does Jesus say 'I am ascending' when all was complete by his lifting up on the cross? Did not his ascension take place *then*? John has no description of it as Luke has at the end of his Gospel and in the first chapter of Acts. For him it is an event unseen by mortal eyes, except for those who could discern the real meaning of the cross. But in Mary's experience it has not yet taken place. To bring her to new understanding and the new relationship with Jesus—with whom she can enjoy 'the fellowship of sight and hand' no longer, but who is more than ever her teacher and Lord—what is simultaneous in reality is made successive: death, resurrection, ascension. Once she knows this, she is to proclaim it, the consequence always of resurrection appearances of Jesus. Unlike the women in Mark, Mary is not fearful, and obeys. Notice what is so often brought to our attention these days, that in the Easter stories the infant Church is both feminine and masculine.

Behind closed doors   *John 20:19–23*

This story seems independent of the previous two. Mary's message cannot have been received, or if it had, it had not brought reassurance, for the disciples—how many we do not know—are gathered fearfully in a closed room. It may have been like this when the Gospel was written and the Christians assembled in secret because opponents were lurking to denounce them to the Roman authorities. Suddenly Jesus comes: no doors or locks can keep him out. He greets them with peace, words both to dispel fear and create unity, and the origin of the 'kiss of peace' in ancient Eucharists, now revived in modern liturgies. His wounded hands and side are his marks of identification. It is not his face or, as with Mary of Magdala, his voice that they recognize, but his wounds, proof that he, the crucified, is risen from the dead and that 'the whole of his past rises with him' (Henry Scott Holland). Resurrection does not obliterate his life and death. It is the vindication, not the reversal, of what went before. His departure in sacrificial love is still a reality of his life with the Father in his glory.

The promises of the farewell discourses are fulfilled (14:27, 16:33). The legacy of peace is twice bestowed and the timid, frightened and bewildered disciples are filled with joy. They are sent out on the mission Jesus himself received from the Father. And just as in the Genesis story, God breathed into Adam's nostrils the breath of life and he became a living being (Genesis 2:7), here the disciples receive the Holy Spirit from the breath of Jesus. It is important for this Gospel, as we have already seen, that the gift of the Spirit is totally dependent on Jesus and his glorification. The Spirit is his breath, his 'self', his risen life. Easter and Pentecost are one, and the end-time too, since the Spirit was to be given in the last days (Joel 2:28–32; compare Acts 2:17–21). The consequence of this gift is the power to remit and retain sins, which introduces notions not hitherto found in the Gospel, where nothing so far has been said about the forgiveness of sins. The promise is not given to a priestly caste but to the disciples at large. There is no hint in this Gospel that there is an especial order of apostles. The precise title is not used, but all Christians are sent as Jesus was. In a Church which spans the earth and has millions of members, it has been deemed necessary to set apart a special order with particular responsibilities 'to declare and pronounce to his people being penitent the absolution and remission of their sins' (*Book of Common Prayer*): but the humblest disciple has this authority and must not be afraid to use it. It is however a charge given to the disciples as a group not simply as individuals. There is a link here with the foot-washing and its mutuality (13:14). There may be those who refuse to accept forgiveness because they do not see the need of it, or resist the offer of divine grace. Their sins are retained and—to interpret this in the light of later penitenial customs of the Church— they cannot be restored to the Christian community.

Thomas' confession and the
conclusion of the Gospel
John 20:24–31

The synoptic Gospels honestly assert that some of those who heard of the supposed resurrection or even saw Jesus doubted (Matthew 28:17; Luke 24:11). Thomas has been portrayed as a type of scientific sceptic demanding visible, tangible proof, but it was the wounds he needed to see. Could he be instead a type of those whose devotion has been centred on the Passion? This has sometimes been unhealthy, not only morbid but compatible with cruelty. It is not the ethos of the New Testament and cannot be derived from this Gospel above all. But the company of disciples needs those who, as Daniel Jenkins once wrote, 'know something of the depth and agony and the infinite burden of the cosmic wounds of Christ by which we are healed'. This may not be the understanding of the fourth evangelist, but suppose Thomas was a man of intense and somewhat withdrawn devotion, deliberately absent on Easter evening because the last thing he wanted at a time of such bewilderment mixed with grief was company, above all in a house-group. He was in deep distress, ashamed of himself, in despair about his own salvation, not unlike Martin Luther and John Bunyan wondering if they could be saved, fearful lest they might be predestined for damnation. In Luther's intellectual and spiritual dark night, his confessor, von Staupitz, warned him, 'Leave such thoughts and begin with the wounds of Jesus.' Rumours that Jesus has come back from the dead do not suffice for Thomas. Has he not returned for judgment? 'If only I could see the wounds.'

Next week, significantly on the eighth day (that is, out of time and in the kingdom), Thomas is there. Jesus shows him what he so desperately needs to see. At once he is brought to adoring faith. He goes far beyond Mary in the garden, who rapturously greeted her beloved teacher. He acknowledges Christ's deity: 'My Lord and my God'. This is not a rehearsal of the Nicene Creed of centuries later. It is believing, personal trust, total adoring worship. Yet it has been inspired by what is denied to those for whom John wrote and to future generations. They will not see Jesus any more, yet to them is given what is only the second beatitude in this Gospel (the first is in 13:17). The contemporaries of Jesus, those who saw with their own eyes and felt with their own hands the Word of Life (1 John 1:1–3), are not so privileged as those who live in union with the exalted Lord by the faith which transcends time and

372

distance and the circumstances of our mortality. They have an immediacy greater than that of those who first believed, and to them is given also the long experience of the saints of all ages: 'the historic Christ in his fulfilment'.

Thomas' confession of faith brings the original version of the Gospel to its conclusion. The evangelist has written all that is necessary. He has made a selection from the many signs which Jesus did. His sole purpose is that his readers may come to faith in Jesus as the Christ the Son of God and that believing they may have the life which Jesus offered, in his name.

A LATER EDITOR BRINGS — THE GOSPEL UP TO DATE —

The Gospel has been brought to an end most fittingly, but someone other than the original author felt it necessary to add an appendix with many motifs. There is need to give some account of the restoration of Peter after his denial of Jesus; to clarify the relations of Peter and the Beloved Disciple and their vocations in the early Church; to give reassurance of the presence of the risen Jesus at a time when there were many discouragements and the Church's mission might seem to be without success. The writer of the appendix also feels that he must vouch for the Gospel and its author, with his unique account of Jesus Christ.

The appearance by the lakeside   John 21:1–14

This story from the Easter tradition is not easy to reconcile with what has gone before. These disciples are not as those who have been solemnly commissioned and received the Holy Spirit. They have gone back to Galilee, where indeed they were told to go in Mark and Matthew, though Luke says they must remain in Jerusalem. There is, however, no rendezvous with the majestic Christ back on the mountain which in Matthew he seems to have made his own. The seven mentioned have gone back, disconsolate, to their fishing, though nowhere else in St John's Gospel are we told that many of them were fishermen. Nor have the sons of Zebedee been mentioned before. Like those in a similar story in Luke 5:5, they toil all night and take nothing. There is, though, a stranger on the shore. He tells them where to throw out the net and this time there is a tremendous haul. The Beloved Disciple, hitherto not said to be in the company, recognizes Jesus, and Peter, so desperate to encounter the one whom he had failed, plunges into the sea and makes for the shore, though covers his nakedness in the process. The others drag in the net. We are not expected to think that they counted the 153 big fish. We pass now into allegory. The disciples, as in the synoptics, are fishers of people and under the risen Lord's direction. They have made the perfect catch and the net is unbroken. Evangelism has not, as so often, destroyed the Church's unity. They do not eat of the fish that they have caught, though some evangelists have devoured their converts. There is a meal awaiting them which Jesus himself has prepared, a sort of Eucharist, a meal of reconciliation. The Lord has provided it—there is no offertory procession. They are his guests and they receive what he offers.

The charge to Peter   *John 21:15–25*

After the meal is over comes the test for Peter. The other disciples fade into the background: he and the Beloved Disciple alone figure in what follows. This is one of the most moving scenes in all the Gospels, one with which some of us will always associate William Cowper's hymn, 'Hark my soul it is the Lord'. Peter had denied Jesus three times. He is now given a threefold opportunity to declare his love. The fact that two different words for love are used is not significant. There is only one in Aramaic, of which presumably this is the Greek translation. More important, it is a feature of the style of this Gospel to alternate between synonyms, to interchange words of the same meaning. In this account two words for 'sheep' as well as for 'love' are used. The questions and commands are of the utmost significance. Jesus addresses Peter formally, using not his nickname but his proper name, Simon 'son of John'. Love for Jesus is not exclusively the gift of the Beloved Disciple. Peter, too, is called to an intensity of love, though in his modesty and in the presence of the risen Christ he dare not claim that he loves Jesus more than do the others and leaves it to the divine omniscience to assess the degree of his love. What is made plain is that Peter's love for Jesus must be shown in pastoral care. It is not a one-to-one relationship apart from the sheep of Christ's flock. And the sheep are not Peter's but

Christ's as in the words of the Prayer Book ordinal: 'Have always therefore printed in your remembrance, how great a treasure is committed to your charge. For they are the sheep of Christ which he bought with his death, and for whom he shed his blood.'

Peter is here made the chief pastor and there is a different ethos from that of the foot-washing or the commissioning on Easter evening. There pastoral care was mutual. Here there is an emerging hierarchy. But love is the *key* (if we may go back to the charge to Peter in Matthew 16:19). In von Balthasar's distinction between Peter and the Beloved Disciple, the Church of office must also be the Church of love, though the latter represents a more mystical communion than the former. Peter's vocation is to follow Christ almost literally to crucifixion. The self-determination of his youth will be replaced by binding and martyrdom. His arms too will be stretched out on a cross. This will be the cost of leadership. Just for a moment there is a glint of jealousy. Is the Beloved Disciple's lot going to be easier than Peter's? The question may have arisen because there was a belief that the disciple on whose testimony the Gospel rests had, unlike Peter and others, lived to an old age, so much so that those who shared the more conventional hope of the Lord's return (that is, that he would soon return on the clouds of heaven—a view corrected in this Gospel) had thought that he might survive until the Lord's coming. Now he has either died or is on the point of death. But what matters is not the differences in length of service or manner of death but the following of Christ, whatever our fate in this world.

The postscript ends with a guarantee of the Gospel's impeccable credentials, not everywhere accepted in the early Church, and with an assertion that the full record of Jesus' life would be beyond the compass of the world. It is inexhaustible, for it is the eternal grace and truth of the divine Father incarnate in Jesus.

There are many forms of death which assail us in our world, not least by lingering and decayed old age. Are we able to take comfort from the fact that God's judgment of a life cannot be determined by the manner of our leaving it and to pray that God will 'direct the end of our lives to be Christian and well-pleasing in his sight, taking us to himself when he will and as he will, only without shame and sin'?

375

The Collect for St John the Evangelist

Merciful Father
Whose Son is the light of the world:
so guide your Church by the reading of your apostle and
evangelist St John,
that we may walk by the light that has come among us
and finally know him as the light of everlasting life:
who is alive and reigns with you and the Holy Spirit, one
God, now and forever. Amen.

Alternative Service Book

Editor's note

No comment has been made on John 7:53—8:11, the story of the woman taken in adultery. This passage is found in a number of places, and with variations in its text, in the earliest manuscripts of the Gospels. The most ancient authorities omit it altogether, and so it is generally not regarded as an authentic part of John's Gospel.

ACTS

The story of the road to Emmaus in Luke 24:13–35 could be described as the introduction to the Book of Acts. As the two travellers journey with the mysterious stranger along the road from Jerusalem, they also journey back through the Old Testament which their fellow traveller explains to them. 'And beginning with Moses and all the prophets, Jesus interpreted to them in all the scriptures the things concerning himself' (24:27). It is only when the past is at last properly understood that the light of the resurrection can be revealed and the future begin to beckon. Acts too is the story of a journey from Jerusalem. And it also travels frequently into the Old Testament, as well as into the past of Jesus' own life and ministry. Luke seems to be saying that only if we are prepared to take Israel's history seriously can we fully understand the significance of those early years of the Church's existence, and begin to move into the future. Memories, the psychologists tell us, do need to be explored, and sometimes healed, if tomorrow is to be lived to the full. So these notes on Acts draw frequently on the Old Testament. This is necessary if Luke's vision in Acts is properly to be comprehended. For Luke and the early Christians, the Old Testament was the only Bible, a resource that they knew so well that it had entered the very fibre of their beings. It was the tool they used to try to discover what their experience of Jesus, his death and his resurrection could mean, and what it meant to be part of the earliest Christian community.

Who or what is the hero of the Book of Acts? In spite of the title 'Acts of the Apostles' it is clear that we do not hear about the mission and ministry of all the 'Twelve'. So is it Peter, or Paul, or perhaps even Stephen who receives star billing in this book? Certainly Peter looms as large in chapters 1–12 as Paul does in chapters 13–28. But for all their importance the figure that unifies the book and is its chief actor is no human agent, but the 'Spirit' of God himself. Throughout the writings of Luke, both his Gospel and Acts, the Holy Spirit plays a crucial role in prompting new developments, whether it be the beginning of Jesus' life and ministry, the inclusion of the Gentiles in the Church, the commissioning of Paul for his missionary work, or even directing him to Jerusalem and the fate that awaited him there. The 'word of God' is another thread that runs through these writings. At times it seems like something concrete, almost personified, and certainly active in what it seeks to do. Luke retells the parable of the sower and its interpretation (Luke 8:5–15) with small but subtle differences from Mark (Mark 4:3–20). These differences serve to emphasize the importance of the seed, 'the word of God'. Perhaps Luke had that parable particularly in mind as he wrote his second volume. So often, the story as it unfolds seems to illustrate the working out of the parable in the life and history of that early Church. Luke's focus on the 'word of God' also serves another purpose. 'The word of God' is not restricted to the period of the Church, nor even the period of Christ's own life. For Luke, as for all early Christians, God's word was also to be found in the pages of the Old Testament. So to emphasize, as he did, the power of the 'word' in the growth of the Church binds together Old and New Testaments, suggesting that the activity of God from creation to consummation should be seen as one unified whole.

One feature of Luke's narrative can be quite troubling for today's readers. Because Luke regards the early Christians as the inheritors of the Old Testament promises to Israel, he often presents a very negative picture of the Jewish people, particularly the Jewish leadership responsible for the temple. Whatever the historical rights and wrongs of such a presentation, it is certainly true that Christians have been guilty of appalling anti-semitism in the past, and they have justified such attitudes by reference to parts of the New Testament, including the writings of Luke. In response to this, it is not helpful to play down the hostility Acts shows towards official Judaism, but it is important to remember that the ultimate target of such attacks is a false religiosity which believes that power, security and control are more important than travelling where the Spirit might lead. Christianity, like Judaism or any other religion for that matter, can easily harbour such false religiosity.

For ease of communication, the followers of Jesus are referred to as 'Christians' throughout the notes, even though it was only when the faith reached Antioch that they took this name (Acts 11:26).

The translation used is the Revised Standard Version (RSV).

Further reading

F.F. Bruce, *The Book of the Acts*, Eerdmans, 1988

I.H. Marshall, *The Acts of the Apostles*, Tyndale New Testament Commentaries, IVP, 1980

Donald Juel, *Luke–Acts*, SCM Press, 1984

P.S. Esler, *Community and Gospel in Luke–Acts*, Cambridge, 1987

Outline of the Acts of the Apostles

Between the Passion and Pentecost	1:1–26
Pentecost—the promise and power of the Spirit	2:1–47
Cameos of the Jerusalem Church	3:1—8:1
From Jerusalem to Samaria	8:1—9:43
The Gospel, the Gentiles and the Jerusalem Church	10:1—12:25
A door of faith to the Gentiles	13:1—14:28
An uneasy compromise with the Jerusalem Church	15:1–35
Opening the door of faith still wider	15:36—21:14
Paul and the authorities in Jerusalem	21:15—24:27
From Caesarea to Rome	25:1—28:31

BETWEEN THE PASSION
— AND PENTECOST —

Introducing Luke's second book *Acts 1:1—5*

In his second book Luke begins a new literary and theological adventure. Before he wrote Acts nobody had considered it necessary or important to tell the story of the early Church. It was different with the Gospels: whatever might have been the original motivation for Mark to set down his account of the life of Jesus, his teaching, his miracles, above all his death and resurrection, by the time Luke wrote *his* Gospel he could feel that he was following in a valued and esteemed tradition. But what was the value of the history of Luke's own near contemporaries—the adventures and failures of the first Christians?

Mark's Gospel may give the impression that after the resurrection there was really little else for the disciples to do except wait fervently and expectantly to see 'the Son of Man seated at the right hand of Power, and coming with the clouds of heaven' (Mark 14:62). Nor was Mark alone in focusing on the future. Paul's letters, particularly those to the Thessalonians, often paint vivid pictures of Christian communities so concerned for the future that their present experience seemed meaningless and unimportant. But the Second Coming, that moment when all their hopes would be obviously consummated in power and glory, had not arrived by the time of Luke's writings. So he sought to provide a new framework of history, one which did not restrict its interest to the past life of Christ and the future of his coming again.

This concern of Luke comes across in the dedication of his work to Theophilus. These few lines of introduction carefully focus our attention on Luke's purposes in writing. Most importantly he draws out the connections between this writing and his first book: the history of the Church is the true continuation and completion of the life of Christ. Both works are dedicated to the same person. 'Theophilus' may have been an important Roman official, or—in view of the fact that the name means 'lover of God'—a 'code name' for all Christians. In other ways too Luke reminds us of his earlier work: there is the theme of the 'kingdom of God', so central to the Gospel, and the mention of 'forty days' which would have led Luke's readers to recall those significant forty days in the wilderness that preceded Jesus' own mission. Above all there is a reference to a promise of baptism with the Holy Spirit, such as Jesus himself experienced. John baptized with water, but the disciples will be enabled to continue Jesus' mission in the power of the Spirit, the same Spirit that had rested on him at his baptism (Luke 3:22) and remained with him throughout his ministry. At his death he committed it to his father and by its power he was raised.

Power to be witnesses to the end   Acts 1:6–11

'Why do you stand looking into heaven?' The angels' question seems paradoxical, for if Jesus is to 'come in the same way' as the disciples saw him go, then they—and we—have good reason to continue looking skywards in anticipation of an equally dramatic return. Yet it is a characteristic insight of the biblical tradition that mountain-top experiences, such as the transfiguration or the ascension as here, should never be viewed as ends in themselves, but rather as a necessary preliminary to commissioning for service before returning to the plain below. Perhaps this is the clue to the meaning of these verses: for the very last words of Jesus to his disciples are words of mission. The disciples are to be witnesses to Jesus and his resurrection throughout the known world. So, in one sense at least, if the disciples are to look for a return of Jesus that fits the manner of his departure, they should be prepared to follow his command to mission and service, rather than over-emphasize speculation about 'the end'. There is certainly a strong strand within the New Testament writings which holds that Christ will not and cannot return to complete all things until all human beings have had the gospel preached to them (Mark 13:10).

If Luke is indeed recounting the story of the ascension in such a way as to remind his readers that events on earth matter as much as events in heaven, then he has chosen his words well. The phrase 'times and seasons' is used elsewhere in the New Testament (e.g. 1 Thessalonians 5:1) as part of the vocabulary of those who fervently waited and did little else; here, of course, the disciples are discouraged from such preoccupations. One reason for this may be that the promise of the Holy Spirit is associated with 'power' (v.8). Power was a word which was traditionally associated with the return of Jesus in a spectacular and triumphalist fashion (see for example Mark 13:26). It may not be the whole or the end of the story, but for Luke and his readers the coming of the Spirit at Pentecost, when the disciples were empowered and the mission of the Church really began, did mean that in one important sense the old promise of the return of Jesus had been fulfilled. The Holy Spirit who came to the disciples at that time was none other than the Spirit of Jesus himself.

Foundations for a new beginning   *Acts 1:12–26*

On their return to Jerusalem the little company of Jesus' followers devoted themselves to prayerful waiting for Jesus' final promise to be fulfilled. One of their first actions was to restore the number of male witnesses to the Easter message to twelve after the defection of Judas. We may wonder why it was necessary to replace Judas, curiously choosing one 'by lot' from the 120 believers that made up that pre-Pentecost Christian community. It is interesting that when comparing the lists of the apostles given in the various Gospels and here in Acts, the number twelve seems to be more constant that the names of the individuals who make up the list. The reason must surely lie in the desire of the New Testament writers, and especially Luke, to present the early Church as the continuation of Israel, and the recipient of the promises that had been made to the chosen people of the Old Testament. So the twelve apostles are the founding fathers of the twelve Christian 'tribes'.

In fact Luke has already shared his view of the Church with us earlier in the chapter, for he means the 'forty days' of verse 3 to recall the wilderness experiences of Israel as well as Jesus. Indeed the whole of Luke's second book is an attempt to work out how the restoration of the kingdom to Israel (v. 6) is accomplished in the life and mission of the Church. Luke is not the only New Testament writer with this vision of the relationship between Israel and the Church, but he works it out perhaps more consistently than anyone else. Luke's vision is not without its problems—it certainly creates tensions in relationships between modern-day Jews and Christians—but it is an important contribution to Christian theology. For it insists that the God who is active in the history of early Christianity is not a fickle deity whose ways are incomprehensible, but one who is the same 'yesterday, today, and forever', and whose steadfast love and mercy have been known since the beginning of human history. The strange method by which Matthias, rather than Justus Barsabbas, is finally chosen seems to fit into this picture, for the 'Urim and Thummin' (a system of lots) was the method by which the priestly community of Old Israel made many of its important decisions.

PENTECOST—THE PROMISE
— AND POWER OF THE SPIRIT —

Harvest of the Spirit   *Acts 2:1—13*

Having restored the original number of the apostles, the followers of Jesus were ready for the next stage of God's work of renewing Israel. Christians have taken over Pentecost so thoroughly that we tend to forget that the 'day of Pentecost' was really a Jewish festival— Pentecost is the Greek name for the Feast of Weeks or *Shavuot* referred to on several occasions in the Old Testament. This was originally a harvest festival, marking the season of the wheat harvest, but later Jewish tradition had also given it a historical reference. It was taken to commemorate the time when Israel received the law and covenant at Sinai, and thus in an important sense the moment when God made Israel his special people. So it is no accident that in Luke's view, the Spirit was given to the Christian community on this particular day. The Spirit, which brooded over the waters and was active in the creation of the world, once again takes the form of a rushing mighty wind to create a new people of God whose mission it will prompt and guide. As we read on through the Book of Acts we shall notice this feature on several occasions: any new or creative development in the life of the Church always takes place under the auspices of the Holy Spirit. If we compare the Gospel of Luke with the other Gospels we notice the same stress on the work of the Holy Spirit. Jesus is often described by Luke as being 'full of the Holy Spirit'. He began his ministry in Nazareth with the proclamation, 'The Spirit of the Lord is upon me' (Luke 4:18). Now, as his followers begin to follow in his steps, they are energized by the power of the same Spirit.

In the pages of the Gospel the Spirit has rested pre-eminently on one person, Jesus; now it is stressed that the Spirit descends upon *all* the disciples. But the images used to convey the presence and work of the

Spirit emphasize a unifying power: the Spirit has the ability to connect the many members of the Church with the one Jesus. The fire that is distributed upon the heads of the disciples recalls the pillar of fire that had symbolized God's presence at Sinai; yet fire is also a visual way of portraying interconnection. The energy of fire is indivisible even though there may be many flames.

The theme of unity continues in the dramatic account of the gift of tongues which accompanied the Pentecost events: the one Spirit has the power even to overturn the division of humanity that was provoked by the Tower of Babel (Genesis 11). At Babel God had scattered humanity over the face of the earth and 'confused' their tongues. At Pentecost comprehension replaces confusion, and as the mission of the Church 'to the end of the earth' begins, the hope is that the divisions between human beings can be overcome by the integrating power of the gospel.

Prophecy and Jesus   *Acts 2:14–36*

The Spirit has come: it is now the time for Peter and the apostles to begin their mission. They do so in dramatic form, with a powerful sermon by Peter which leads to 3,000 people being added to the Christian community. Jesus himself had also begun his mission with a sermon, at Nazareth (Luke 4: 16–30), and Luke probably wants to remind us of the parallel. Peter is apparently more successful than Jesus had been on that occasion, for the Nazareth sermon had led to Jesus being rejected and almost put to death by his own people! But, like Jesus, Peter makes a great deal of use of the Old Testament to try to explain the events that are now taking place. It helps to remind us that Peter's audience is likely to have been composed either of Jews, both from Jerusalem and from the Jewish Dispersion, or of people such as proselytes who were very closely connected to the Jewish people. This is the moment for 'the house of Israel' (v. 36) rather than the Gentiles to hear the gospel, a second chance for those of Jesus' own people to hear the message they rejected from his own lips and in his lifetime.

Of course, in this post-Easter period the message has explicitly become one *about* Jesus, rather than one proclaimed by him. So in Peter's words we may see the first attempts by the early Christians to wrestle with the significance of Jesus. Some of the terms used to describe him may sound a little strange to those of us who have been nurtured in the full trinitarian faith of the Church. Peter describes him as 'a man . . . attested to you by God' (v. 22) and having been made, seemingly at his resurrection, 'both Lord and Christ' (v. 36). We see that 'Christology' (a technical term which refers to our attempts to understand who Jesus was and what he did) did not spring fully developed from the lips of Peter and the other apostles in the earliest days of the Church. Rather it was something gropingly, and sometimes painfully, worked out as the disciples held together their faith in Jesus' resurrection and continued presence and power among them with their knowledge of the Old Testament Scriptures and prophecies. And as the early Church encountered new situations, it discovered that new ways of describing Jesus became necessary. So the Book of Acts begins a theological journey in which the 'man Jesus' is ultimately discovered, by those who have faith, to be Lord of all.

Yet it is characteristic of God, according to the New Testament, not to compel faith, and this is true even on the day of Pentecost. There are those who interpret the disciples as being drunk with 'new wine', perhaps a deliberate irony by Luke, since the self-same phrase is used elsewhere in the New Testament (Luke 5.37–38) to describe the effervescent joy that Christianity can bring. Moreover, though Peter proclaims that the prophecy of Joel has now been fulfilled, it is only so for those who have eyes to see. There is indeed fire on the earth on this day (v. 19), but it does not visibly consume the world. Instead it cleanses and empowers a small group of disciples inside a house on the back streets of Jerusalem.

Believers together   Acts 2:37–47

Luke's vision of the early Church is of a tree—perhaps a mighty oak, rooted in Christ and through him in the Old Testament—whose trunk comprises the twelve apostles and especially Peter. Any branches which grow must be integrally joined to and dependent upon the trunk. As we shall see in moving through the Book of Acts, the true picture may have been more complicated than Luke suggests, but in these verses his ideal of the unity of the Church is expressed with particular strength. The entire group of Christians listens faithfully to the teaching of the apostles. They share in fellowship'—the Greek word *koinonia* could also be translated 'community'. As an expression of this community, there is a voluntary sharing of goods. We also hear of worship which includes the breaking of bread. By this means the disciples celebrated the presence of the risen Lord among them, for Jesus had made himself known at Emmaus in the breaking of bread (Luke 24:35). But, according to the ancient prayer in the *Didache* (an early Christian writing, dated somewhere between AD70–130), the breaking of bread also celebrated and fostered unity—of the Church certainly, and potentially at least, of all humanity. 'As bread that was scattered on the hillside is made one in this loaf . . . so may your church be gathered from the four winds into your kingdom.'

CAMEOS OF THE JERUSALEM CHURCH

A healing in the temple
Acts 3:1–10

To any Jewish person of the New Testament period, Jerusalem and its temple were inseparable. From all corners of the Mediterranean world the temple had drawn the throngs to whom Peter had preached at Pentecost. And though the early Christians broke bread and prayed together in their own community, they still faithfully attended the regular hours of prayer in the temple, morning and afternoon, on a daily basis (Acts 2:46). It was an important way of continuing to affirm their identity as Jews. In the early part of his Gospel Luke focuses attention particularly strongly on the temple: there the events of salvation are set in train with the promise of the birth of John the Baptist, and there too the exquisite story of the encounter between the infant Jesus and the aged Simeon and Anna is placed. Later in the Gospel, it is true, hesitations about the role of the temple seem to arise; it needs to be cleansed by an angry Jesus, and it is surely the central focus of Jesus' tears as he weeps over a city that has rejected him.

The temple is too crucial to Israel's faith not to be given a second chance, and so it features once more in these early chapters of Acts. Among those who joined the Christian community at this time there must have been many Simeons and Annas, and even priests like Zechariah too. They were people who were deeply imbued with the spirit of the Old Testament piety which believed that Israel's longed-for salvation and redemption would embrace the temple. So it is appropriate that the first miracle explicitly recounted in Acts should take place within the temple boundaries. Luke underlines the continuity between the new life and health which faith in Jesus brings and the salvation promised and given by the living God of the Old Testament. Yet even as the man who had sat by the Beautiful Gate is given something more precious than silver or gold, questions start to arise in the mind of the thoughtful reader. Why had he been sitting at the gate? This was because the lame were considered too 'unclean' to enter further into the temple; they were not eligible to be full members of the community of Israel. Can a temple, then, whose gates are exclusive barriers remain a central focus for a group who believe that God has entrusted them with a promise for 'all that are far off, everyone whom the Lord our God calls to him' (Acts 2:39)? Luke will have us wait until Stephen's speech in chapter 7 for his answer.

Peter's appeal to the Jewish people   Acts 3:11−26

A miracle of healing has just taken place in the temple: it is right, therefore that it is also in the temple that Peter makes what Luke regards as his definitive appeal to the Jewish people. The great figures of Jewish history—Abraham and the other patriarchs, Moses, the prophets—are summoned to bear witness that Jesus was indeed *the* prophet expected by the Old Testament writers, and explicitly referred to by Moses in Deuteronomy 18:15−16.

Yet alongside this history of promised fulfilment, Luke acknowledges that there has also been a pattern of rejection of Jesus by his own people. This is a consistent theme of these early speeches in Acts (e.g. 2:23; 4:10−11; 7:51−53), and reminds us of the response Jesus himself encountered when he spoke to his fellow townspeople in Nazareth (Luke 4:28−30). Why does Luke so stress this? Part of the answer must lie in the perplexity that the early Church felt over the issue. Given that, by Luke's own time, the majority of the Jewish people and their religious leaders had *not* accepted Jesus as their Messiah, how could Jesus really be the one who fulfilled the expectations of the Old Testament? One way of responding to this puzzlement was to focus on the almost deliberate perversity of those who had not responded. Note how Luke contrasts the determination of the Jewish people to execute Jesus with the desire of Pilate to release him (v. 13). Luke then goes on to suggest that it was precisely part of God's plan that 'the Christ should suffer' (v. 18), so that even his rejection was in a sense foreordained. These speeches in Acts are some of the few occasions in the New Testament when Jesus is explicitly called God's 'servant' (3:13, 26; 4:27, 30), a title which reminds us that the persecution predicted in Isaiah 53 was part of the allotted role of God's chosen instrument of salvation.

Will the people listen to this passionate appeal? There is an edge to the conclusion of Peter's speech. Those who do not listen to Jesus, the promised prophet, will be destroyed from the people (v. 23)—an implicit threat that Jews who do not accept Peter's message can no longer be considered part of the Israel of God. Now the potential recipients of God's promise extend beyond those who are Israelites by birth, for it is with the universalist promise to Abraham (v. 25) that Peter, foreshadowing later developments (Galatians 3–4), draws his speech to an end.

Jesus—the rejected cornerstone
Acts 4:1–12

Many—5,000 men—believed: but their religious leaders, particularly the Saducees who made up the high-priestly party and controlled the temple, did not. Luke here points up the divisions that existed within the Jewish establishment of the time. The Sadducees were a theologically and politically conservative group, noted for their refusal to accept the innovations that had crept into the Jewish faith in the previous couple of centuries. They were especially opposed to the novel doctrine of the resurrection of the dead, whether it was being applied to one man—Jesus—or to all the faithful. This is not the only reference to the theological position of the Sadducees in Acts: Paul later escapes from a potential lynching by sowing dissension between the Sadducees and the Pharisees, who did believe in resurrection (23:6ff). The early Church was not hostile to the Sadducees on theological grounds alone: the Church also took exception to their concern to maintain the political status quo. They were prepared to collaborate with the Roman occupying powers, as much to preserve their own vested interests centring on the temple as to secure the safety of the ordinary citizens who bitterly resented the Roman occupation.

Peter's quotation from Psalm 118 about the stone (v. 11) in his confrontation with the leadership is appropriate. For that Psalm is clearly set in the temple, and the 'stone that the builders rejected' was one which was not considered good enough to be a part of the very building that these high priests controlled. By applying this text to Jesus, Peter argues that the crucified and risen Messiah has now become 'the head of the corner', the stone on which the whole structure depends. These were challenging words for those who regarded the temple as their personal prerogative and power-base.

Brave words before the Jewish leaders   *Acts 4:13–31*

'Boldness' is the key word in this passage, framing it in verses 13 and 31, and appearing again in verse 29. It is a deliberately chosen word: it is not intended to mean that the disciples were being cheeky! Its significance is revealed by the fact that Luke has used it in the very last verse of his book to describe Paul's preaching in Rome. (In Acts 28:31 it is translated 'quite openly', but is the same word in Greek.) Indeed 'speak the world boldly' or 'openly' was what Jesus himself did (Mark 8:32), so Peter and John and the others stand firmly in the Gospel tradition with their bold speech.

There is possibly a tantalizing connection with the Gospel at this point. The preaching of the apostles has just led to the conversion of 5,000 men, who are clearly intended to represent the people of Israel. It is fascinating to note that the Gospel story of the miraculous feeding of the 5,000 is followed first by a prediction of Jesus' rejection by the 'elders and chief priests and scribes'—*exactly* the same group of people who reject Peter's and John's preaching of Jesus here in Acts—and then by a prediction of his resurrection, which is precisely the point of debate here (Luke 9:18ff). Then, significantly, the Gospel states that Jesus' own followers must not be ashamed of him and his words, and predicts that the disciples must also expect to share a similar fate to that of Jesus himself (Luke 9:23–27). It seems that Peter's readiness to speak with 'boldness' in the face of danger fulfils the words of Jesus in the Gospel.

There is a sense, then, in which Israel has been fed in the conversion of the 5,000 men—but what of Israel's rulers? The Psalm that Peter and John sing with their friends after their release has an ominous ring. Psalm 2 speaks of the rejection of the Lord's Anointed by the Gentile rulers. But it is now used to refer not only to Pontius Pilate, but also Herod, the Jewish leader. Is the Jewish leadership beginning to be equated with the

Gentile 'kings of the earth', in the eyes of the Christian Church? And what about the 'shaking' of the room where the disciples are gathered? In the Old Testament it was the temple that shook (Isaiah 6:4) when the prophet had a vision of God there. Is God beginning to move from the temple to be with the disciples, as they are removed from the temple by its guardians? Once again we are directed forwards to Stephen's speech (Acts 7:48ff).

Community life   *Acts 4:32—5:11*

Luke did not regard the sharing of goods between rich and poor, to which he also refers in Acts 2:44, merely as a gesture of humanitarian goodwill; they did it for important religious reasons. The early Christians were not the only group within Judaism to follow such a practice: those who were responsible for the Dead Sea Scrolls (probably the Essenes) clearly had a similar custom. (There were other beliefs and practices that the Essenes shared with the early Christians, as we shall see later.)

The Essenes believed that their community was engaged in a 'holy war', fighting a final cosmic battle against the forces of darkness. They believed that this holy war took precedence over the habitual features of human existence, such as owning land or marriage. It is possible that a similar instinct lay behind the practice of the Jerusalem Christian community. They saw themselves living in a 'new age', the time of the resurrection; as they awaited the final triumph of the kingdom, they still needed to engage in 'holy war' with the forces of evil. The era of resurrection stands outside the normal canons of human existence: according to Jesus, those who attain the resurrection from the dead 'neither marry nor are given in marriage' (Luke 20:35)—and perhaps do not own property either. Notice that Luke carefully inserts a comment on the apostles' witness to the resurrection (4:33) between two remarks about holding goods in common: he wants us to link together resurrection and revolutionary custom.

Perhaps this helps to explain Luke's description of the awful and (to the contemporary Western reader) quite shocking fate of Ananias and Sapphira. Interestingly enough, the language used in the story is reminiscent of the tale of Achan who, in the Old Testament, broke the laws of the 'holy war' and kept back part of the spoil seized at Jericho (Joshua 7). As Achan had broken the rules of his 'holy war', Ananias and

390

Sapphira had broken the laws of theirs, and paid a similar penalty. Death is a harsh punishment, but perhaps Luke sees its appropriateness for those who, like Ananias and Sapphira choose not to live the resurrection life.

No easy answers Acts 5:12–42

The healing ministry of the leaders of the Jerusalem church, and the popular responses it evoked, remind us of the Galilean ministry of Jesus. Like their Lord, the apostles drew great crowds, and occasionally those who came for healing approached more in superstition than faith (compare verse 15 with Luke 8:44). The apostles' healing also provoked the anger of the Jewish authorities, on this occasion the Sadducees (see also Luke 11:14ff). In view of the fact that the Sadducees did not believe in either angels or the resurrection, it is gloriously appropriate (and somewhat ironic) that the apostles should be released from prison by 'an angel of the Lord', who then commands them to continue speaking about the resurrection life!

In this account of official reactions to the apostolic ministry, some of the tensions between Sadducees and Pharisees on the Jewish ruling council (the Sanhedrin) emerge. The words of the Pharisee Gamaliel, propounding a principle that remains associated with his name to this day, provide the focus of this passage. They come in response to the last major speech that the apostles address to the Jews of Jerusalem and their leaders. They are an important reminder that the Pharisaic movement, for all the bad press it receives in the Gospels, contained many people who were honourable, reflective and genuinely anxious to further the will of God. Gamaliel came from a great rabbinic family, 'the House of Hillel', who provided leadership for the Jewish community stretching from the pre-Christian era to the second and third centuries AD. Perhaps the thoughts of Gamaliel provide a necessary corrective to some of the sentiments that the apostles have been expressing up to this point. Though Peter and the others have maintained, in the fervour of their testimony, that it was clear beyond any shadow of doubt that Jesus was the Christ, Gamaliel counsels caution. Other charismatic figures had appeared on the scene, and like Jesus they too had attracted a following. But their impact had been short-lived, and had failed to survive their deaths. Better patience, then, than premature judgment of the Jesus movement. Gamaliel's wisdom reminds us of the ambiguities that often form part of true religion: we cannot judge authenticity simply by the ability of an individual or a movement to satisfy even the most basic human needs. That certainly was the tenor of Jesus' own message, for it was characteristic of him to ask questions of his hearers rather than provide easy answers.

Jerusalem is for Luke the place of the resurrection. Alone of the Gospel writers, Luke does not tell us of any resurrection appearances by Jesus in Galilee: the disciples encounter the risen Lord in Jerusalem and the nearby village of Emmaus, where he is known in the breaking of bread.

Resurrection and life dominate Luke's account of the Jerusalem church, like a melodic fugue. We are told of Jesus 'the Author of Life' (3:15), of the Sadducees' anger because they hear preaching about the 'resurrection from the dead' (4:2), and of the apostles' testimony to the resurrection of the Lord Jesus (4:33) as they speak to the people the words of 'this Life' (5:20).

We were reminded near the beginning of Acts that the primary function of an apostle was to be a witness to the resurrection (see 1:22): they are certainly living up to this task! But we have also heard of the unity of a community which holds all in common and breaks bread together (2:46, 4:32). This link between resurrection and koinonia is not accidental: they belong inseparably together, for it is as bread is broken in a community 'of one heart and soul' that the presence of the risen Jesus can most powerfully be experienced. Those who fracture the unity, like Ananias and Sapphira, are aliens to the resurrection.

The theme of the temple provides a vital counter-point. For the psalmist the temple in Jerusalem was the place to which the faithful journeyed to seek the 'living God' (Psalm 84). The early disciples continued to worship there, praising God for all he had done in Jesus and the Spirit. Yet the temple hierarchy had engineered Jesus' death, and continued to oppose the community which grew out of his resurrection. So there is certainly life in Jerusalem: but Luke makes us ask whether it is within a temple building or among a community of disciples?

At the end of this series of cameos of the Jerusalem church, we find the apostles in the temple, which is where they were at the beginning of chapter 3. But we discover that they are steadily being driven away from the focal point of the life of Judaism, whether they like it or not. Luke is preparing us for the developments that will come in the next chapters, with the preaching of Stephen.

The seven—doing more than serving tables *Acts 6:1–7*

The account of the appointment of Stephen and the other 'men of good repute' is one of those moments in Acts when there appears to be more to the story than at first meets the eye. The ostensible reason for the selection of the seven men is to 'serve tables', that is to administer equably the common resources of the community. However, what we then hear of the seven suggests that their real role was the 'apostolic' one of preaching and teaching, rather than concern with financial and welfare matters. And this is true not only of Stephen—to whose preaching Acts devotes almost as much space as to the sermons of Peter himself—but also of Philip, who in Acts 8 is responsible for some important moves in the Church's mission.

Luke acknowledges that a fair amount of tension had sprung up in the nascent Church, as the number of disciples had begun to grow. The 'Hellenists' to whom he refers were perhaps Greek-speaking Jews resident in Jerusalem on a semi-permanent basis (Stephen and his colleagues all have Greek-sounding names), the 'Hebraists' being members of the Palestinian Jewish Christian community whose mother tongue was Aramaic or Hebrew. One may suspect, however, that the tension between the two groups extended beyond the distribution of food, and that some quite significant theological differences between the various elements of the Jerusalem Christian community were beginning to emerge.

Luke's picture of the selection and service of the seven represents his concern, or even over-concern, to stress the unity of the first Christians. He also wants to highlight the authority of the twelve apostles, to suggest that they, and they alone, led the community during this period. All the same Luke is aware that something significant and new was beginning to happen in the life of the Church; the creativity of the Holy Spirit is once more to the fore. Notice how three times in this chapter the Spirit is linked with Stephen and his preaching (vv. 3, 5,

10). As so often in Acts, developments have been foreshadowed in the Old Testament and the Gospel. In Numbers 11 Moses had been confronted by the people of Israel grumbling over food, and had appointed seventy men to 'share the spirit' and assist him in his work (vv. 24f). Luke may also have seen Jesus' own choosing of seventy disciples (Luke 10) as a precursor of what is now happening.

Whether preached by the apostles or the seven, the 'word of God' increased (v. 7), so this initiative in ministry was clearly justified. Yet this verse contains a curious irony of which Luke was surely aware. Why should he tell us of the conversion of large numbers of the Jerusalem priesthood at precisely the point in his narrative which precedes the temple (their *raison d'être*) coming under sharp attack from Stephen?

The Passion of Stephen Acts 6:8–15

The suffering of Stephen, the first martyr, is told in such a way as to draw a close parallel with the Passion of Jesus himself. It is recounted with consummate artistry: almost every detail is significant as Luke shows us that the injunction to disciples to be imitators of Christ is not just a pious metaphor but a matter of life—and death. Along with Christ the other figure that Luke has in mind as a prototype for Stephen is Moses; this makes particular sense for Luke since he believed that Christ was the fulfilment of the Old Testament prediction that a prophet like Moses would be raised up by God (Acts 3:22).

As a Hellenist Stephen has been speaking in the synagogues of Greek-speaking Jews, who had come to live in Jerusalem from parts of Asia and Africa. If he had expressed any hesitations at all about their place in Jewish life, they might be expected to have taken strong exception to his words, since it was the temple that had largely been responsible for drawing them to the Holy City. Charges are thus brought against Stephen: that he had spoken blasphemous words against Moses and God, and also spoken against 'this holy place and the Law'. According to Luke these charges are made by 'false witnesses'. Immediately we are reminded of the trial of Jesus, which also took place before the council, and the claim then made by 'false witnesses' that Jesus had spoken against 'this temple' and threatened to destroy it . Intriguingly while we find this recorded in the Passion narrative of Matthew and Mark (Matthew 26:60–61, Mark 14:56–58), Luke himself does not refer to this in his account of Jesus' trial. He seems to have deliberately held back these words about the temple until this moment. It is as though he is wanting to say: 'Let us give the temple and the city of Jerusalem every possible chance. It may be that when people hear about the resurrection of Jesus and experience the coming of the Holy Spirit they will realize that faith in Jesus and a love for the temple are not necessarily mutually exclusive.' But, as we have already seen in Acts, the disciples have gradually been driven away from the temple by the authorities— and the conversion of the priests (v. 7) is perhaps intended as a symbol of the temple's increasing redundancy. The scene has thus been set for Stephen's dramatic speech in chapter 7.

But the comparison between Stephen and Jesus does not stop at the charge with which they were accused. Once again the address which Jesus gave in the synagogue at Nazareth springs to mind (Luke 4:16–30), a speech which almost ended in *his* death there and then. The description of Stephen as 'full of grace' echoes the 'gracious words' with which Jesus had spoken. Luke also uses the same Greek word when stating that all in the council 'gazed' at Stephen as when previously mentioning that all eyes in the synagogue were 'fixed' upon Jesus. In fact a study of the word 'gaze' reveals some interesting details. The word is used twice in an important chapter of Paul's Second Epistle to the Corinthians, to which we will return. Other than that, the only New Testament writer who uses the word is Luke, and when he does it is generally in situations where the divine presence is breaking into the world of human beings. So the disciples 'gaze' on Jesus as he ascends into heaven (Acts 1:10); similarly Peter uses the word in recounting a vision from heaven (Acts 11:6). All this suggests that when the council 'gaze' at Stephen and see that 'his face was like the face of an angel' something very significant is meant. Is it possible that Stephen has so imitated Christ in his life that he is transfigured, so that his face resembles the divine?

There is, of course, an Old Testament parallel, for the face of Moses shone after he had talked with God (Exodus 34:29ff). Moses is so much part of the background to the story of Stephen that Luke is almost certainly alluding to him here. Indeed on those two occasions that the word 'gaze' appears in 2 Corinthians, it describes the way the Israelites 'gazed' on Moses while his face was shining and reflecting the glory of God (2 Corinthians 3:7, 13). One of the charges against Stephen is that he had 'spoken against Moses'. Here then is Luke's defence of him: how could such an accusation possibly be true if Stephen had so visibly taken upon himself the radiant likeness of Moses?

Israel's men of faith
Acts 7:1–16

Stephen provides no mere craven defence: indeed it would be fairer to call his speech an attack, not on the Old Testament itself but on the way it had been misunderstood throughout the history of Israel, and particularly by those who had brought him to trial. He begins by attributing the call of Abraham far away in Mesopotamia to the 'God of glory' (7:2). Glory is a biblical metaphor for the visible presence of God, so Stephen seems to be saying, quite deliberately, that God is even more present outside the Promised Land than within it (compare Ezekiel 1). He goes on to focus on three quite deliberately chosen Old Testament figures: Abraham, Joseph and Moses. All are used in different ways to suggest that God is not bound by holy places or a holy land but can, and characteristically does, act to save his people in places far away from Jerusalem.

It was in Mesopotamia that God had first appeared to Abraham to begin Scripture's story of salvation. Even when God had brought him to Canaan Abraham only remained there as a 'sojourner', owning not a scrap of its land. Similarly the great events in the life of Joseph, which enabled the people of Israel to survive a disastrous famine, took place in the hated land of Egypt. Undoubtedly these links with land form the main reason why Stephen refers to these two patriarchs. It is possible though that they are also regarded as foreshadowing Christ. Certainly the New Testament elsewhere (Romans 4, Galatians 3) draws a direct line from Abraham to Christ. The pattern of Joseph's life—he so nearly died in the pit and in prison before being exalted to bring life to others— meant that he could be viewed as Jesus' forerunner in a special way (as he was by many in the early Church).

The holy land of Midian
Acts 7:17–41

The pivot of Stephen's speech is provided by the person of Moses—not surprisingly, in view of the charge against him. With Abraham and Joseph, the example of Moses is used to suggest that God's greatest actions have not taken place in Canaan at all. The 'holy ground' where Moses encountered God was at Sinai in the land of Midian, and it was this encounter that led to the deliverance from Egypt. But Stephen then takes his attack further: the story of Moses also proves that throughout history the people of Israel have tried their utmost to reject God's graciousness towards them. Notice the way in which Stephen relates the account of Moses' intervention between the quarrelling Israelite and Egyptian: the people failed to understand that God was giving them deliverance by Moses' hand (v. 25); they rejected Moses (v. 35). These are aspects of the tale which were not given prominence when it was first told in the Book of Exodus. And of course in the saga of the golden calf Stephen has plenty of fuel for his fire. Like fathers, like sons—the implication is first made in verses 39–41, and then categorically stated in verses 51–52, that those who accuse Stephen are behaving just like the rebellious Israelites of old.

There is one more way in which the figure of Moses is used. The words of Moses predicting that a prophet like him would arise (v. 37) were regarded by Luke and the early Church as an important scriptural testimony to the coming of Christ (Acts 3:22 and the notes on page 388). Stephen hints that if the prophet yet to arise is like Moses, then the destinies of Moses and the Messiah are intermingled. Moses brought 'salvation' to the people (v. 25); as Israel's 'redeemer' (v. 35) he was nevertheless 'rejected' by them. The RSV translation conceals the way in which Luke uses these same words of Christ. How then, implies Luke, can preaching Christ as saviour and redeemer—though rejected—mean speaking against Moses?

Opposition parties

Acts 7:42–53

Stephen's argument moves towards its culmination with his claim that the God of glory who travelled with his people from the holy land was far better worshipped in a moveable tent than in a static temple. From within the Old Testament itself he calls into question the role and very existence of the temple. Here Stephen stands within a venerable and respected tradition which hesitated about the rightness of a temple building for the people of God. At the time of David there were many who saw a temple as a pagan building, and Nathan the prophet expressed his qualms (2 Samuel 7:5). Again after the return from exile there was bitter dissension in the community about whether it was necessary to rebuild the sanctuary, and the words of Isaiah 66:1–2 quoted in verses 49–50 reflect this controversy. By the time of Jesus, however, the temple was cherished by mainstream Judaism, and a generation later it was to be defended bitterly in the Jewish-Roman war (AD66–70). But there still remained some groups within, or on the fringes of, Judaism who were marked out by their opposition to the Jerusalem temple. Among these were the Samaritans, who preferred to focus their attention on Mount Gerizim, near Shechem. The writers of the Dead Sea Scrolls, referred to earlier (see the notes on Acts 4:32, page 392), also expressed strong opposition to the current worship at the Jerusalem temple. They regarded it as corrupt, and in their 'Temple Scroll', an exciting discovery made only 20 years ago, they offered a blueprint for a purified temple of the future. It is possible, though impossible to prove, that Stephen and the Hellenists had links with one or other of these groups. Certainly the title 'Righteous One' used by Stephen (v. 52) cannot help but remind us of the 'Teacher of Righteousness' venerated by the Essenes.

Sharing the Passion   *Acts 7:54–60*

Whatever the relations between Stephen and these anti-temple groups, his words were bound to provoke those, such as the high-priestly party, for whom the temple was meat and drink. They would defend their precious place at all costs, even (as Luke saw it) at the ultimate price of denying their own continuity with the Old Testament. Stephen must die for his blasphemy against their holy place, and in his death, as in his trial, he reminds us of Jesus—and perhaps of Moses too. For at the end he sees the 'glory of God', which according to Numbers 12:8 was the special privilege of Moses. Glory has disappeared from the temple, and the visible presence of God is instead with this first martyr of the Christian Church as he 'gazes' into heaven. The barriers between the human and divine worlds are breached.

Luke deliberately has Stephen echo the words which, according to his Gospel, Jesus himself had used on the cross. Both Jesus and Stephen pray for the forgiveness of their persecutors (Luke 23:34), and both commend their spirit (Luke 23:46). Significantly though, as Jesus had committed his spirit to his Father, Stephen commits his to Jesus himself, whom he describes as 'Lord'. Luke's account has moved quite a long way from the first speeches of Acts, when Jesus was viewed as 'a man . . . appointed by God'. We can see how Jesus is beginning to take over the roles and titles which once belonged to God alone. In the furnace of the disciple's martyrdom a new understanding of Jesus is born.

Stephen also uses the title 'Son of Man' for Jesus. This is the only time it is used in Acts, although it appears frequently, and sometimes cryptically, in all the Gospels. There the Son of Man is a figure who *must* suffer, but is then promised vindication and glorification. Some think that the phrase 'Son of Man' suggests that the task of suffering does not just belong to Jesus alone, but is an invitation to Peter and his other companions to join Jesus in his Passion and to share in his resurrection. This explains why the 'Son of Man' appears at this point in Acts. Though Peter and the others had turned aside in Gethsemane and been unwilling to play the role, in Stephen the early Church meets the first of many whose suffering is joined to that of Jesus himself. Stephen has shared in the Passion, and even as he dies he is beginning to experience the glory.

In the story of Stephen, we have journeyed far into the past, and far away from Jerusalem. Before we can move forward to a new phase of the Church's life, we need to go further back than Jerusalem, the place of the resurrection, and Galilee, the place of Jesus' humanity. Stephen takes us back to the wilderness (7:30–44), where Israel was stripped of the subterfuges that it employed throughout its history, and forced to face God, for good or ill. The wilderness was also important in Jesus' own life, as the place for that necessary preparation which preceded his ministry in Galilee. Jeremiah reminds us that the human heart is deceitful above all things, and desperately corrupt (Jeremiah 17:9). But in the physical and spiritual wilderness we are forced into a new self-knowledge and awareness of our dependence. It is only as we realize our humanity that we can see the face of God, and be enabled to fulfil the mission which has been given to us. So it was for Moses at the burning bush.

The vision of God is more powerfully expressed in chapters 6–7 than anywhere else in Acts, a vision not merely reserved for Moses and the Old Testament. It is a major motif in the story of Stephen: he himself sees God face to face, and he becomes the means by which others like Saul can ultimately share in the vision. God must be experienced in the consuming fire of a burning bush and a martyr's death if we are to travel beyond a Galilean springtime and a Jerusalem temple.

— FROM JERUSALEM TO SAMARIA —

Impulse to mission

So far Luke has concentrated on events in Jerusalem; from this point he narrates the spread of the gospel beyond the holy city. We see how the death of Stephen exemplifies the principle enunciated by Tertullian, a second-century theologian: 'The blood of the martyrs is the seed of the church'. The stones thrown at Stephen were some of the blows that were later to goad Saul into submission to Christ. The first Christian martyrdom leads inexorably to the conversion of Saul into Paul, the apostle to the Gentiles.

Nor can the Holy Spirit be defeated. The persecution that followed on the death of Stephen may have led to the scattering of the Jerusalem church, but this dispersion became the means by which the gospel was carried further afield. Luke now turns his attention away from Jerusalem, though groups of believers remained in that city at least until the Jewish-Roman war of AD66. Luke believed that with the death of Stephen Jerusalem had killed the prophets and stoned those who had been sent to her. Jerusalem had not recognized and thus had now forfeited her visitation.

The apostles do not remain in Jerusalem. Symbolically this is Luke's way of saying that the new branches about to sprout have grown authentically from the original trunk that sprang to life on the day of Pentecost. It seems, however, a little strange that the leaders of the church should be able to remain safely in the city while lesser beings are subjected to imprisonment. Luke is probably aware, though he does not say so explicitly, that the persecution was directed primarily at the Hellenist wing of the church, those like Stephen who were particularly critical of the Jewish hierarchy and temple. The more traditional 'Hebraists', among whom were the apostles themselves, were at this stage still being tolerated.

Philip, appointed as one of the 'seven' at the same time as Stephen, preaches the gospel among the Samaritans. The Samaritans were considered 'half-breeds' by the Jews of Jerusalem, the product of intermarriage that had occurred back in 722BC between the northern Israelites and their Assyrian conquerors (2 Kings 17:24). So the spread of the gospel among the Samaritans was a definite development in the life of the Church. The temple in Jerusalem has rejected Christ: with a certain amount of irony the Holy Spirit now leads the way to the Samaritans who had themselves rejected the Jerusalem temple.

Authentic growth   *Acts 8:9–25*

The Holy Spirit dominates this account of the conversion of the Samaritans. In part this is because Luke is anxious to show that what is happening is a new initiative being directed by God himself. Pentecost must visibly spread to unite these 'outsiders' in Samaria with the original nucleus of the church of Jerusalem. The Spirit fosters the unity of the Church not only by drawing individuals together, but also by working in different groups, communities and ultimately races. The visit of the Jerusalem apostles, and their prayer that the Samaritans too might receive the Spirit, is a sign that the new developments in Samaria need to be recognized by the centre of the Church. This passage has occasionally been used to suggest that it is only at confirmation that believers receive the Spirit: Christian baptism is in the name of Jesus alone. This is something that I vividly remember being told in my childhood! Such an idea is rather economical with the truth—again and again in the New Testament there is a close connection between *baptism* and the giving of the Holy Spirit. The exceptional nature of the conversion of the Samaritans is responsible for their receiving the Holy Spirit in these two stages.

The power of the Holy Spirit is also prominent in this story. There is a contrast between the authentic 'power' that the Spirit has given to the apostles, and the false 'power' of Simon. In spite of the title which had been given to Simon (v. 10), it is clearly a situation of no contest! Simon's attempted 'simony'—trying to purchase this new and better power for himself—illustrates something very important about the Spirit: it blows where it wills, and it is not under human control. That God cannot be manipulated by human beings is an insight which stretches back at least to the Book of Exodus and the disclosure of the divine name 'I am who I am'. Later Church tradition saw Simon the magician (the Magus) as the founder of Gnosticism, an influential heresy which began in the second century and wove together elements of Judaism, Christianity, Greek philosophy and Persian religion. Gnosticism stressed the importance of possessing esoteric knowledge (*gnosis*) in order to be saved. Whatever the direct historical connections may be, it is certainly true that Gnosticism sought to constrain God and, like Simon here, hold him captive to human desires.

All the ends of the earth   *Acts 8:26-40*

The words of Jesus spoken at his ascension (Acts 1:8) are steadily being fulfilled. The gospel has already been carried to 'Judea and Samaria' (Acts 8:1, 4). Now, with the conversion of the Ethiopian under the guiding of the Spirit, it begins its journey 'to the end of the earth'. This is symbolized powerfully by the Ethiopian's travelling back to his own land after a visit to Jerusalem, for Ethiopia marked the farthest limit of the known world at that time.

Perhaps it is not surprising that the Ethiopian eunuch was reading the Book of Isaiah, which more than any other book of the Old Testament seeks to bring 'good news' to the Gentiles, and lead them to the light of Jerusalem. 'My house', proclaims God, 'shall be called a house of prayer for all peoples' (Isaiah 56:7). Yet the Ethiopian, both as a Gentile and as a eunuch, would not have been allowed to share fully in the worship of the temple. And even if he had rectified the first condition by becoming a proselyte, there was nothing he could have done about the second. He would have found some consolation in a promise addressed specifically to eunuchs in Isaiah 56:3–5, noble words but with little practical significance.

Still it was the Jewish Bible that had brought him to Jerusalem, a Bible whose injunctions he had tried to honour by bringing the 'merchandise of Ethiopia' (Isaiah 45:14) and worshipping God alone. Without his struggle for faith, he would not have been wrestling with the mysterious reading from Isaiah 53 when Philip encountered him. The prophet predicted that God's servant would be humiliated and suffer uncomplainingly, perhaps even be put to death, but then be restored and exalted. Isaiah 53 does not identify the servant clearly, but Christianity has always treasured this passage as a prediction of Jesus. Luke has prepared us for this interpretation by naming Jesus as the 'servant' on several previous occasions (for example, Acts 3:13).

As the story of Acts has developed, the speeches of Peter and Stephen have suggested that the life of Christ is truly in accordance with Scripture. Now a further step is being taken as this Ethiopian is baptized: Luke is telling us that without Jesus the Jewish Scriptures simply cannot be properly understood.

The light of Christ

Acts 9:1–9

If repetition is a mark of importance then Saul's conversion must be of the most significant event in Acts. Through Saul/Paul's own mouth the story is repeated on two further occasions (Acts 22:3–16; 26:12–23). A consistent theme that runs through all three accounts is the blazing light that results in temporary darkness for Saul but then is followed by illumination. Christ is a light to enlighten Paul and through him the Gentiles: the words to Simeon in the temple at the beginning of the Gospel are being fulfilled (Luke 2:32).

Paul is journeying to Damascus in order to persecute 'those belonging to the Way'—the disciples are not yet known as Christians, a name they will only acquire later, in Antioch (Acts 11:26). Yet strangely the voice from heaven accuses Paul of persecuting Jesus himself, an accusation which is reinforced through repetition. The Lord Jesus is one with the community of persecuted disciples, something that is also strongly suggested by the story of Stephen. In later years the apostle Paul proclaimed that Christians were 'the body of Christ', a powerful image of the way in which members of the Church were 'members' of Christ and also of one another. Is it possible that this vision of 'Jesus, whom you are persecuting' was the initial impetus which led Paul to realize that Christ and Christians were part of each other? After all the vision was powerful enough to turn Paul's whole life upside down!

Disciple and apostle

Acts 9:9–31

After such a vision it would have been particularly inappropriate if Paul himself had tried to be a Christian in isolation; so he must be united to the body of Christ. That is why Luke tells us so much about Ananias, this otherwise insignificant disciple who has such a crucial part to play in the conversion of Paul. The ministry of Ananias—carried out with some reluctance—enables Paul to join with the community of believers in Damascus. Luke has written nothing about the beginnings of the church in this city. Though Damascus was further from Jerusalem than Samaria, its church had a Jewish background. So its founding was not as significant as the breakthrough that had happened in Samaria. We are reminded here that Luke is quite selective in what he shares with us.

Paul's conversion is also a call: in verse 15 we are told of Paul's future mission. Note the order—the Gentiles are now placed before 'kings and the sons of Israel'. For the New Testament Paul is *par excellence* the one sent to the Gentile world. It may be that Luke has deliberately set the baptism of the Ethiopian eunuch immediately before the story of Paul's conversion as a 'taster' for what follows in his account: the Ethiopian is a symbol of all those at 'the end of the earth' who will ultimately be converted by the preaching of Paul. Paul preaches Jesus as 'Son of God'. This is the first time in Acts Jesus has been called by this title, but it is one that Paul uses many times in his preaching and letters. Though referring to Jesus as 'Son of God' was particularly scandalous for many Jews (see for example John 5:18), the title would not have seemed strange to many Gentiles: noble and illustrious men were often addressed in this way. Paul seems already therefore to be paving the way to the Gentile mission.

The account of Paul's initiation into the Church ends with him suffering persecution both in Damascus and in Jerusalem: the words of verse 16 are already being fulfilled. The former persecutor has been overturned so completely that in his flesh he 'completes what is lacking in Christ's afflictions for the sake of his body, that is, the church' (Colossians 1:24).

Like the prophet   *Acts 9:32–43*

Though the narrative of Acts will soon focus almost exclusively on Paul, Luke does not at this stage allow Peter to fade completely from view. He is the human focus of the Church's unity, and will himself have an important role to play as the community moves towards the Gentiles.

Luke reminds us of Peter's importance in the miracles at Lydda and Joppa. Both episodes recall similar events in the life of Jesus. Jesus healed a paralysed man and told him to carry his bed (Luke 5:18–26). He also brought back to life a little girl, Jairus' daughter, and in so doing used an expression that was virtually identical to Peter's words in verse 40 (Luke 8:40–42, 49–56). Peter, then, is walking in the steps of Jesus—and perhaps also of the Old Testament prophets, for Elijah also brought a dead person back to life (1 Kings 17:17–24). In his Nazareth sermon, Jesus pointed out that the woman whose son was revived by Elijah was from Zarephath, in the land of Sidon (Luke 4:26), and not therefore an Israelite. Is Luke preparing the way for the changes that will shortly occur as Peter meets Cornelius?

It was while they were 'on the way' that first the Ethiopian and then Paul met Jesus. Discovering while journeying is the keynote of the section of Acts that we have just read. It is probably no coincidence that we are introduced to the disciples as those who belong to 'the Way' for the first time in Acts 9:2. This was one of the oldest titles used for the Christian community, perhaps alluding to the command in Isaiah 40:3 to 'prepare the way of the Lord'.

The term may originally have referred to 'the way' taught by Jesus. But the metaphor gained increasing power as it was used of the path to suffering that Jesus had himself travelled, and which he invited his disciples to journey with him. The 'way' joined disciples and Lord in the closest bonds of fellowship. We glimpse something of this in the account of Paul's conversion: 'on the way' he had seen the Lord (9:27). We may wonder whether it is merely on a physical road that the revelation occurs, or does Luke also hint that the suffering of those 'belonging to the Way' whom Paul had so ardently persecuted was a decisive factor in changing his life?

Paul is about to become the most important figure in the Book of Acts. His life is not overturned in Galilee, Jerusalem, Caesarea or Antioch, but on a dusty road. As Luke's account unfolds, we see Paul continuing to journey, ever farther afield, as God's apostle to the Gentiles. The 'way' is an important picture of our faith too, reminding us that it must never be static. And as we travel on the way, Jesus meets us anew.

THE GOSPEL, THE GENTILES
— AND THE JERUSALEM CHURCH —

Under his roof?   *Acts 10:1−23*

Developments are not haphazard in Acts: the Lord, through his angel or his Spirit always prepares the way. So also does Luke himself: he is a master of polished literary techniques. He leads us towards the story of

Cornelius at Caesarea by several paths. Firstly, after he had met the Ethiopian, Philip journeyed to Caesarea, the Roman capital of Palestine whose ethos and inhabitants were predominantly Gentile. Secondly, the resurrection of Tabitha has reminded us that even in the Old Testament God was at work outside Israel. Thirdly, in Joppa Peter has been staying with a tanner, a member of a despised and unclean trade, and not the normal choice of lodgings for a pious Jew. Then fourthly, the God-fearing centurion Cornelius, notable for his love of the Jewish nation, has his forerunner in the Gospel—the centurion of Luke 7:1–10, whose servant Jesus had healed, sounds very like Cornelius. But that earlier solder had believed that, as a Gentile, he was unworthy to offer Jesus hospitality. By contrast Peter and his friends will stay with Cornelius for several days.

Hospitality and food are central motifs in Cornelius' conversion and its aftermath. It is no accident that in Peter's vision he is commanded to eat, and demurs because he saw animals that were 'unclean' according to the Jewish food laws. It is clear, not just from this account in Acts, but also from Paul's letters (especially Galatians 2, Romans 14, 1 Corinthians 8 and 10) that the single greatest obstacle to Jewish and Gentile Christians forming 'one body' was their different attitudes to food: how might those of Jewish origin continue to observe the biblical food laws and remain in fellowship with their Gentile brethren? Among the Jews, the sharing of food was (and still is) sacramental, making visible some fundamental beliefs and prejudices concerning Jewish identity. The Jewish food laws established and maintained boundaries between Israel and the wider world, and also between Jewish groups of varying degrees of devotion to the Law. For observant (practising) Jews it would have been impossible *both* to keep the food laws *and* to eat with Gentiles, or even with non-observant Jewish 'sinners'. In the Gospels Jesus had eaten with such people, and this was a major cause of his incurring the anger of the religious leadership.

So the vision of Peter is especially appropriate as the gospel begins to make an impression on the wider world. Its symbolism of food, the very nub of the problem for the growing Church, picks up the Jewish attitude to Gentiles, people whom God had created but whom Judaism regarded as 'unclean'. Peter may not have grasped the whole message immediately, but he certainly moves in the right direction, for he invites Cornelius' messengers to be his house-guests. The puppy dogs *are* beginning to eat the crumbs from the children's table (Mark 7:28;

interestingly the story of Jesus' encounter with the Syrophoenician woman is not included in Luke's Gospel).

The Spirit's breakthrough *Acts 10:23—48*

Peter catches on quickly. Moving from his non-committal greeting of Cornelius' messengers in verse 21, through his observation to Cornelius that he would not have associated with Gentiles had it not been for what God had revealed (v. 28), he boldly proclaims in verse 34 that God shows absolutely no partiality: Jew and Gentile are the same in his eyes. The speech that Peter makes on this occasion has interesting features. It gives more detail than we find in Peter's earlier speeches about the life and ministry of Jesus, presumably because he supposed that Cornelius, as a Gentile, would not necessarily know such facts. Peter also mentions that he and the other witnesses of Jesus' resurrection 'ate and drank with him after he rose from the dead'. Since eating and hospitality are so central to what is happening in this story, it is right that Luke refers to sharing food and drink with one another and with the risen Lord as a hallmark of the new age that has dawned. Peter does not mention the gift of the Holy Spirit in this speech, because the Holy Spirit takes over before he has the chance!

What now happens is often referred to as 'the Gentile Pentecost'. The Holy Spirit is poured out as powerfully as it had been on the original disciples in Jerusalem, 'even on the Gentiles' (v 45). This is a sign that something both new and formative is happening in the life of the Church. No less significant, though less obviously dramatic, is the note at the end of the chapter that Peter accepted the invitation of Cornelius to remain 'for some days'. Accepting Gentiles into the Church means more than sharing religious rituals and allowing them to be baptized. The one Spirit that has fallen on Jew and Gentile alike demands that barriers must come down and hostility be replaced by mutual hospitality, at the human as well as the religious level.

Peter's day of reckoning *Acts 11:1—18*

Since chapter 8, we have read of three conversions: first the Ethiopian eunuch, then Paul, and finally Cornelius and his friends. All are crucial to the movement towards the Gentiles which is proceeding apace.

Not surprisingly, the church in Jerusalem needs to catch up with the way in which the Spirit has been leading! The story of Cornelius in particular has been concerned as much with the conversion of Peter to a vision of a wider mission as with the conversion of a Gentile to Christ. The conservative elements in the church at Jerusalem are less than entirely happy with developments, so they ask Peter to account for himself. There may be a hint here that although Luke regarded Peter as the true leader of the Church (after all, before visiting Cornelius he, like Jesus, raised someone from the dead!), Peter himself did not automatically command the loyalties of certain of the Jerusalem Christians. They need to be convinced, and so the account of Peter's dealings with Cornelius is related in some detail. It is ultimately Peter's description of the Spirit's initiative that wins the day: to oppose what is now happening would be 'hindering' God— just as Gamaliel had previously suggested to the Jewish leadership that to persecute the original Jerusalem church also risked 'fighting God' (5:39). Luke is aware that an inbuilt conservatism is not the prerogative of Judaism.

Names are important in the Bible, and there is an interesting detail about Peter's name which surfaces in these chapters. Cornelius is told to enquire for one 'Simon who is called Peter' (10:5). This form of the name is carefully repeated several times (10:18, 32; 11:13). These are the only times in Acts that Peter is called Simon (though he is referred to as Simeon in Acts 15:14). Perhaps we are meant to remember that Simon was only called Peter when he became a disciple of Jesus. The new understanding that dawns upon Peter as the Spirit leads him towards the Gentiles is as significant as his own original conversion. He can still be referred to as Simon until he realizes that God has no partiality: only then does he become well and truly 'Peter'.

Intellectually the Jerusalem church seems convinced by Peter's appeal. But we sense that they have not really absorbed the practical consequences: could Jews be expected to share food and drink with Gentiles? The problem was to create tensions later in Acts 15 and even more among the Christians of Antioch (see Galatians 2).

Capital development   Acts 11:19–30

Antioch, on the river Orontes, was one of the three great cities of the Roman world, along with Alexandria and Rome itself. It was large (perhaps a million inhabitants) and important, the capital of Roman

Syria. It was also a cosmopolitan city where the people and culture of the exotic east met and mingled with the more austere spirit and traditions of Greece and Rome. In Antioch Jews and Gentiles would necessarily encounter each other. The city also knew a great variety of religious groups and sects, so it is not surprising that it was there that the name 'Christians', originally perhaps a distinguishing nickname, was first applied to the believers. But even if it was outsiders who first, probably sarcastically, called them 'Christ's men and women', this naming reflected a true development in the Church's life. With the regular admission of Gentiles, both in Caesarea and at Antioch itself, the disciples were no longer merely a 'Way' within Judaism but were fast becoming a new and separate faith.

Christians can now be distinguished from Jews, but their unity with each other is still crucial. Clearly the leaders in Jerusalem are concerned about what is happening in Antioch, and this explains why Barnabas is despatched on a journey of inspection. Barnabas appears as one of the most human and loving characters of Acts, willing to give others a second chance—whether Paul who had previously persecuted the Church (9:27), or John Mark who had failed to live up to the arduous challenges of missionary work (15:37). Notice too the gladness Barnabas feels about the new happenings in Antioch: normally Luke tells us of people being glad for themselves; Barnabas is marked out by being glad for others.

It is appropriate that Barnabas should later carry the relief sent by Antioch to the church in Jerusalem (compare Acts 4:36–37). This marks a genuine concern on the part of the Christians of Antioch for the welfare of their fellow disciples in Jerusalem, reminding us again that real Christian fellowship has its practical dimensions. Beyond that, the famine relief is an acknowledgment by Antioch of the debt it owed to the church of Jerusalem, and a gesture which must have helped to alleviate some of the unease felt in Jerusalem about their wholesale admission of Gentiles. Later on, during the ministry of Paul, another collection for Jerusalem was to figure prominently (Romans 15:26; 2 Corinthians 8–9), and it too seems to have signified more than simple charity. Unity was stretched as Gentile Christians became the dominant force in the Church: sending money to Jerusalem was a way of looking back to the roots and the trunk from which the faith had first sprung.

Passion parallels

Life was clearly difficult for the Christians of Jerusalem, and probably became increasingly so as more Gentiles were admitted by the wider Church. The events in Antioch would not have escaped the eyes of the Jewish hierarchy. 'Herod the king' here is Herod Agrippa. Between AD41–44 he ruled most of the territory that had forty years earlier been controlled by his relative, Herod the Great. For a brief period the system of Roman prefects (like Pontius Pilate) was abolished, and the Jews enjoyed a political renaissance and the feeling of semi-independence from Rome. The associated mood of self-confidence exacerbated hostility towards the Church, and persecution and martyrdom ensued.

The imprisonment of Peter sounds ominously and deliberately like a re-run of what had happened to Jesus himself. It too takes place at Passover, and there is a Herod involved. In the New Testament, members of the Herod family consistently play a sinister role: Herod the Great ordered the massacre of the innocents (Matthew 2:16–19; Herod Antipas (whom Jesus referred to as 'that fox' in Luke 13:32) shared with Pilate in the responsibility for Jesus' condemnation; and now death is also associated with Herod Agrippa. But death is not yet Peter's fate: he is still needed to guide the Church safely through the problems caused by the admission of Gentiles before he disappears completely from the pages of Acts (chapter 15). Peter's moment for the imitation of Christ in death as well as life will come in the Emperor Nero's persecution of the church in Rome, a story which Luke does not tell us.

The disciples of Jerusalem have been praying so hard for Peter's release that they do not believe it when it happens! The description of poor Peter being left outside John Mark's house by the enthusiastic maid is particularly vivid and memorable. However, after briefly recounting what happened, Peter has to leave Jerusalem. The apostles had weathered the storm after the death of Stephen, but they cannot expect to do so any longer. Jerusalem is left to James, brother of Jesus, and to the other brothers of the Lord. They made a brief appearance in 1:14, but then disappeared completely from view till now. We shall meet James again in chapter 15, as leader of the Jerusalem Christians. His name is associated with a very conservative form of Christianity which was determined to stay close to its Jewish roots.

A Jewish king's end
Acts 12:20—25

The Lord has preserved Peter, like Daniel in the lions' den. In turn Peter's persecutor meets the same fate as Belshazzar (Daniel 5:22ff). The dramatic tale of the end of Herod Agrippa was famous in the New Testament world. Josephus, the contemporary Jewish historian, tells a slightly different version of it: Herod died of stomach pains after being acclaimed as a god. Acts sets the scene in such a way as to suggest that though Agrippa died first of all for his blasphemy, his death could equally be viewed as a punishment for his oppression of the Christians. He is eaten by worms, as was the Gentile king Antiochus Epiphanes, who had persecuted the Jews two centuries previously (2 Maccabees 9:5ff). Antiochus, like Agrippa, had also claimed divine status. But in the way Luke tells the story of Agrippa, he invites us to see a deeper issue. Antiochus was a *Gentile* king who oppressed the *Jews*: Agrippa is a *Jewish* king who is oppressing the *Christians*. Who then now constitutes the Israel of God?

With this question, Luke sets the scene for what follows: Barnabas, Saul and John Mark return from Jerusalem to Antioch, which becomes the centre for Christian mission to the Mediterranean world. In the next chapters they will range far afield, both geographically and theologically, but Luke reassures us that they have their roots in Jerusalem, where the Church began. Once again the Spirit is preparing to lead the way: where will the road travel from Antioch?

> The last three chapters have taken us from Caesarea, symbol of the Roman political presence in Palestine, to Antioch, a centre of Greek language and culture on the edges of the Middle East where the successors of Alexander the Great had built a metropolis. Thus the movement that will occur later in Acts is foreshadowed: the gospel will travel west to Greece, and in Athens meet the heart of Hellenism; then further west to Rome and be forced to face the power of the Caesars. That is the direction in which Luke saw the Spirit leading the Church.

411

But the road also led east from Antioch: to Syria, Mesopotamia and Persia. In the early centuries of the Church's existence, vibrant and creative Christian communities existed in these regions: they produced theology of great beauty as well as great power. Luke has chosen not to relate their beginnings. Today the churches east of Antioch have been weakened by centuries of persecution and internal strife, but there still remains a faithful remnant, who perhaps know more of the difficulties of the earliest Christians than we who are cushioned in the West.

Astride the pages of Acts the Holy Spirit has so far blazed a path with dynamism and clarity. Yet the Spirit often speaks in tones that are more muted and ambiguous, and of this the struggling Christians east of Antioch provide a helpful reminder. God is not only the energetic Spirit making direct links between Jesus and the Church. He is also the mysterious stranger with the hidden face, who—like the Lord at a meal in Emmaus—vanishes from our sight as soon as we recognize him. The invitation 'Stay with us' must now become a prayer.

A DOOR OF FAITH
— TO THE GENTILES —

The call of the Spirit
Acts 13:1–3

Up to now Luke's account of the acts of the Spirit in the spread of the gospel has largely concentrated on events in Judea and Samaria. There have, however, been hints of a wider work of the Spirit. At the end of chapter 11, we were told that Antioch was an important centre of Christian mission among the Gentiles. Luke now takes us back to the church there, and shows how it became the base for Paul's missionary activity in the cities and towns around the eastern end of the Mediterranean.

Antioch is clearly a place of new beginnings. Luke signals this by his references to the role of the Holy Spirit in these verses. The Spirit plays such an important part in Luke's writings, and is responsible again and

412

again for new beginnings—the birth of Jesus, the start of his Galilean ministry and the birth of the Church in Jerusalem on the day of Pentecost. Now, another new development—the mission and ministry of Paul—is indicated by a sudden direct intervention of the Spirit. Paul, or rather Saul, is listed with the other prophets and teachers of the church in Antioch. They are a motley crew, showing the potential universality of the Church. One, possibly two, of them come from Africa, Barnabas is a native of Cyprus, while Manaen presumably originated in Galilee. Saul himself was brought up in Tarsus, on the southern coast of modern Turkey. Note the order of the names—Saul almost seems like an afterthought in the list. Even when he and Barnabas are the ones specially selected by the Spirit, it is Barnabas who is mentioned first. Saul's past history as a persecutor and his comparatively young faith must have meant that he was regarded with caution by many of the more long-standing Christians at Antioch. But he will very shortly and dramatically assume the leader's role—his works and words on the journey will lead to this.

Saul's inclusion in the names of the leaders of the church at Antioch is the first (and only) time in Acts when he is called a prophet. We know from Paul's letters that he respected the gift of prophecy (for example, see 1 Corinthians 14), but he did not normally describe himself as a 'prophet'. However Luke often refers to prophets and prophecy at significant milestones in the story. The infant John the Baptist is heralded as 'prophet' by his father (Luke 1:76), Jesus in the synagogue at Nazareth claims to fulfil the prophetic role predicted in Isaiah 61 (Luke 4:17–24), Peter at Pentecost recalls the book of Joel and proclaims that all humanity will prophesy (Acts 2:17–18). So Saul/Paul stands in a long line which includes Jesus himself and reaches back into the Old Testament. As the Spirit leads the Church to make new strides of faith, it is important that it still holds fast to its roots. The wine which prophecy served was therefore appropriate, for it was both vintage and yet new.

Paul leaves Saul behind   *Acts 13:4–12*

Barnabas and Saul started their missionary work by travelling to Cyprus, where Barnabas had once lived. They began by preaching in the Jewish synagogues; this became their regular practice, and it was one of the ways in which early Christianity held fast to its Jewish roots. However they soon moved beyond these Jewish religious centres, into the court of the Roman governor Sergius Paulus. Barnabas probably assumed the leading role as they addressed the pro-consul and met with a sympathetic reception. But then they were confronted by a powerful antagonist, the Jewish magician Bar-Jesus (Elymas in Greek). He was like John the Baptist in reverse—trying to make crooked the paths that John had so carefully prepared, and seeking to snatch away the word of God that had just been sown. It is no accident therefore that Luke calls him a 'false prophet'—it helps to heighten the contrast with John the Baptist and with Paul, both of whom Luke saw as prophets. Yet for all Luke's antipathy towards Bar-Jesus, he underlines his importance, mentioning him before Sergius Paulus, who seems to be under his influence.

This early missionary encounter with magic and false prophecy is Paul's moment of trial, almost the equivalent of Jesus' own temptation and struggle with the devil. Bar-Jesus represented what Paul might have been, if he too had remained hostile to the new faith. Saul's own religious and political career had been going well, until he happened to be on the road to Damascus one day and found his world turned upside down. But he had made his decision for faith in Jesus as Messiah, and in the Governor's court he stuck to it. With the power of the Spirit, and in the strength of his new name (this is actually the first time he is called Paul) he denounced Bar-Jesus and pronounced the punishment of temporary blindness on him. Paul had of course suffered the same fate on the road to Damascus; in his case, though, the darkness was not punitive but the result of seeing the great light to which he was subsequently led.

With the defeat of the enemy Bar-Jesus came the victory, as so often in Acts, of the word of God. The pro-consul Sergius Paulus, far more important than the centurion Cornelius converted by Peter (Acts 10), came to faith. If Paul is eventually to be the apostle to the Gentiles, he has made a powerful start with his first convert.

Leading towards the Gentiles   *Acts 13:13–41*

The next stage of the journey took 'Paul and his company' (v. 13; note how from this point in the narrative, Paul becomes the leader of and spokesman for the missionary group) away from Cyprus to what is now southern Turkey. However John Mark, who had travelled with them to

Cyprus, returned to Jerusalem. Luke is laconic about this, but it may be that John Mark was not happy about Paul's new position, or the move towards the Gentiles that the conversion of Sergius Paulus foreshadowed. Travelling north to Antioch in Pisidia, the company assumed their regular practice of visiting the synagogue. The sabbath-day worship of the Jewish community is the setting for Paul's first recorded missionary sermon.

In the Gospel, Luke has Jesus following his temptation in the wilderness with a keynote sermon in the synagogue at Nazareth which declared his intentions for his ministry (see Luke 4:16–30). The pattern is repeated in Paul: after his trial with the 'son of the devil' Bar-Jesus, he set out his vision and the themes which would be central to his preaching in the future. Even though it is difficult to be sure that Luke has given us the exact words Paul used on this occasion, it is reasonable to suppose that we have the kind of sermon Paul would have preached. Its language and ideas are characteristic of Paul, and different from what Peter or Stephen might have said.

It is a sermon addressed not only to the Jews in the synagogue but also, Paul stressed, to the 'others who fear God' (v. 16). These were pious Gentiles who were attracted to the Jewish vision of God and the ethical conduct of the synagogue community, without wishing to be circumcised and practise the full Jewish ritual law. It was among such God-fearers that the Christian faith was to leap the boundaries drawn between Jew and Gentile: as a group they would prove crucial wherever Paul's travels took him. The sermon seems on the surface to be a simple retelling of the Old Testament, but a second look makes clear just how sharply Paul focused his thoughts to meet the needs of the moment. A key theme is the element of *newness* in God's dealings with Israel. The God who is at work in Israel's history does not stand still. Rather he strides ahead, always prepared to use new situations and new people to fulfil his purpose. For a while he was with his people in the wilderness, for a while he gave them the land of Canaan. For a while he called judges, and then Saul, but both were eventually replaced by David. David, in turn, was used by God to speak of one who would come after him. Even John the Baptist, the herald of the kingdom, was aware that he was only the forerunner. His task was to prepare the way for the Messiah, who has now inaugurated a new freedom, the newness of resurrection and the forgiveness of sins. Undergirding the message is a hint that God's creativity may lead him to embrace a new people!

415

A second theme in the sermon is the hostility and incomprehension of those in Jerusalem. Ironically, even their inability to realize that Jesus is the Messiah who fulfils Scripture was in itself a fulfilment of Scripture, as the quotation from Habakkuk 1:5 at the end of the sermon indicates. But it is the leadership in Jerusalem, not Judaism as a whole, that is pilloried. Though Acts is rapidly moving away from Jerusalem and Palestine it has not yet left Judaism itself behind. Indeed Paul identified himself with his brothers and sisters in Judaism when in verse 26 he proclaimed that this salvation is given *to us*.

Glory beyond Israel   *Acts 13:42–52*

Paul's testimony to Jesus was evidently used to great effect, as he and Barnabas continued their preaching over the following Sabbaths. But not all their hearers were pleased with the message. The delight of many Gentiles among the congregation is matched by the antipathy of some Jews. This leads Paul to the first of three solemn pronouncements in Acts of his decision to turn towards the Gentiles: here in verse 46, again in 18:6, and finally in the concluding words of the book at 28:26–28. This repetition is matched by the three accounts of Paul's conversion and his commission as the apostle to the Gentiles (9:1–18; 22:4–16; 26:9–18). In both cases the repetition is a mark of importance. And perhaps the fact that this threefold repetition occurs twice suggests that the two things are interwoven: the light that Paul saw on the Damascus road was a light that would ultimately and inevitably shed its glow over the whole world. So it is appropriate that the words Paul and Barnabas quote from the Book of Isaiah to justify their decision speak of darkness dispelled by light (v. 47). Luke has used words like this before: Simeon in the temple had spoken of 'a light for revelation to the Gentiles' (Luke 2:32)—but Simeon had continued by suggesting that it was also to be 'the glory of your people Israel'. Pointedly, words such as these are now absent. Instead it is the Gentiles who glorify God.

The writings of Luke feel at times like a spiral: again and again we return to the centre, but each time the journey then leads further afield. At the beginning of chapter 13 we read of Paul and others 'worshipping' the Lord in Antioch. 'Worshipping' is an unusual word in Luke's writings, recalling as it does the kind of service that took place in the Jerusalem temple. So we have been reminded of the temple where Luke's story began and where Simeon sang his song. But as the chapter progressed we saw that though the Jewish Bar-Jesus was blinded by the light, it was a beacon the Gentiles were glad to receive through the ministry of Paul. The circle has expanded, and in the course of such growth Paul himself is to grow. The words from the Servant Song of Isaiah 49 quoted in verse 47 are often used to describe Christ himself. But here they refer to Paul and Barnabas. Previously Stephen had mirrored Christ so closely that he resembled him in life and death (Acts 67:55–60). Now it is Paul's turn to be caught up into Christ's own mission and ministry. Surely we have here the seeds of Paul's vision of Christians as members of the Body of Christ.

Apostles, but mere men   *Acts 14:1–18*

From Pisidian Antioch Paul and Barnabas moved in a south easterly direction through Iconium to the region of Derbe and Lystra. Wherever they preached the now familiar pattern of belief and rejection was repeated, but Luke is at pains to show that opposition only served to spread the gospel into new areas. It is interesting to note that they are called 'apostles' in verse 4; we know that there were those in the early Church who wanted to restrict that term to the Twelve. Paul's apostleship was clearly a contentious issue, and something that he himself had to fight for.

But however willing Paul may have been to be included among the apostles, he drew the line at divinity! The healing of a cripple in Lystra provoked the pagan population there to worship the apostles as gods. Superficially it seems a not entirely unhappy conclusion: the problems of success are ones that many Christian ministers today might wish to have. But the response of Paul and Barnabas reminds us that spectacular signs and wonders are not an end in themselves; they are always intended as pointers to the good news that can transform human beings inwardly as

417

well as outwardly. Paul and Barnabas made it clear that they were *not* gods—neither the pagan deities Zeus or Hermes, nor the living Lord who is at the heart of both Old and New Testaments. Though Luke does draw out links between Paul and Christ (in Luke 5:17–26 Jesus also healed a crippled man, and used a similar form of address to that of Paul here), he also makes it clear that there are essential differences, not least that Jesus Christ is the unique Son of God. When an audience cannot comprehend this, the gospel inevitably makes little or no headway. This failure may have been compounded by another factor at Lystra. Paul's hearers seem to have extended well beyond the 'God-fearers' we met earlier. He tried to speak theological language that they would be familiar with—his description of God as creator and provider has many links with Stoic philosophy. But whenever he addressed those with little or no knowledge of the biblical traditions (Acts 17:16–34), the gap of belief was too great to be bridged easily. Christianity needed the foundations that Judaism provided, even if it was to move beyond them.

Suffering for the peaceable kingdom   *Acts 14:19–28*

The crowds' dramatic change of opinion about the apostles, aided and abetted by earlier opponents, had violent consequences. Paul's stoning fleshes out some words he wrote to the Corinthians: 'Be imitators of me as I am of Christ' (1 Corinthians 11:1). For Luke the death of Christ had many meanings, one of the most important being a model and pattern for Christians themselves to follow. Paul himself recognized as much in his comments on the persecutions he received as a servant of Christ (see 2 Corinthians 11:24–27). Left here for dead, he is certainly now treading the road his Lord had trodden before. And the converts are warned that the same journey may well lie ahead of them. Entry into the 'kingdom of God' meant turning upside down the normal worldly standards of power and success.

And yet the kingdom of God *was* a matter of power—but it was power perfected through weakness. The language of the 'kingdom of God' does not appear very often in the Acts of the Apostles. As the early Church moved out into the Roman Empire the term could easily be misunderstood, suggesting that the Church was an overtly political challenge to the imperial status quo. For Luke this was a miscomprehension of the nature of the kingdom of God. And yet at the deepest level Luke was well aware that the kingdom of God presented a frontal challenge to the

Realpolitik of the era. The Caesars may have been able to grapple with rebellions and political pretenders; but they were utterly discomfited to be faced with those who believed that leadership and service belonged together. The words of Jesus in Luke 22:25–27 must have sounded like a total subversion of all that Roman emperors held dear. If we really listened to them they would be just as dangerous today.

The violence directed at Paul is a sign of the rejection of the gospel, and once again Luke shows how such opposition served to scatter the word of God still further to Derbe. From there the apostles began to retrace their steps and head back to their commissioning base in Syrian Antioch, taking the opportunity of the homeward journey to encourage the churches they had founded. When they arrived home, they told of the 'door of faith' which had been opened to the Gentiles. The door is ajar, a chink of light is shining through. However, doors can be slammed shut again . . . and this one almost is, as we shall see in the next chapter.

Notice how both 'Spirit' and 'word' have important roles to play in the first missionary journey. The Holy Spirit, as so often in the writings of Luke, is the creative force which initiates and empowers new developments in the life of the Church (Acts 13:1–3, 4, 9). The word of God has a chequered career: preached before Sergius Paulus (13:7), meeting joy and opposition in Pisidian Antioch and Iconium (13:44–49, 14:3), and spreading throughout the region. Indeed it seems that it is precisely when the word encounters opposition that it is most able to show its power, and ultimately triumph. As the parable of the sower in Luke 8:4–15 suggests, it shows its worth by its joy and endurance in adversity. Isaiah 55:10–11, which Luke surely knew, likens the action of the 'word of God' to the fructifying power of the rain and the snow: it will be effective, whatever adverse circumstances confront it.

In the Church today we need both the Spirit and the word. The word links us with our Christian and Jewish past, with the treasure-store of tradition, so that we can stand firm on the shifting sands at the end of the millennium. The Spirit promises to guide us into that new and uncertain future with truths that perhaps we cannot yet fully grasp. Together, as for those early disciples, the Spirit and the word can surprise us with joy (13:52).

AN UNEASY COMPROMISE
— WITH THE JERUSALEM CHURCH —

Not an easy yoke
Acts 15:1–11

As so often happens when major changes occur in relations between separate groups, the opening of a door of faith to the Gentiles was not readily welcomed by the whole Christian community. And so we find, not for the first time in Acts, the Church as a whole having some catching up to do as it comes to terms with new developments. As in chapter 11, there is a temporary pause in the gospel's breathless expansion while the centre ratifies the actions of those who have been leaping ahead.

It is appropriate that the discussion takes place in Jerusalem. Although Luke's story has by now shifted away from the city, it is still the root from which all new branches of the tree have sprung. If the Church as a whole is to remain united—and such unity was a particular concern of Luke—it must be from the roots upwards that any momentous shift occurs. Jerusalem was the centre of Luke's theological world as it had been of the world of the Old Testament, and of course it is still an important religious centre for Jews, Christians and Muslims. If things can be got right in Jerusalem, then they will be right everywhere. There are, however, some question marks about this 'Council of Jerusalem'. It doesn't quite fit with the picture presented in Paul's letters, particularly in Galatians. Was there ever such a formal council as is suggested here, in which amicable agreement was reached, or was the real story much more messy and contentious? We may feel that the pleas of Peter expressed so strongly in verses 7–11 sit uneasily with the description of his backsliding in Galatians 2:11–14.

As Luke tells the story there is a deep and immediate threat to the successful missionary endeavours of Paul and Barnabas. It is posed by a conservative group within the church of Jerusalem who still hold their Pharisaic origins very dear. We are becoming increasingly aware of the diversity of Judaism at the time of Christ. Most of his original disciples came from Galilee, and probably from groups that sat lightly to the more rigourous demands of the Law. Converts from Pharisaism, however, brought their old respect for the Law and Jewish traditions into their

420

new faith. They felt that the action of Paul in baptizing Gentiles without requiring circumcision undermined the very foundations of their ancestral faith. The scene was set for conflict. Perhaps deliberately, Peter in his speech sought to defend his own and Paul's actions, and suggested that to impose the Law on Gentile converts would place an intolerable 'yoke' upon them. The Pharisaic Christians would have been familiar with this term. They often called the Law their 'yoke', but they genuinely regarded it as one which was easy to bear! These deep divisions clearly needed some reconciliation.

A delicate decision   *Acts 15:12–35*

The reconciling voice is that of James the brother of Christ, who seems by now to have assumed the leadership of the Jerusalem church. James was a fascinating character, of whom we hear in the histories of Josephus and Eusebius. He was revered for his piety, which some would describe as religious conservatism. Any connection he may have had with the New Testament letter that bears his name would suggest that he did not find some of Paul's ideas, such as his stress on faith rather than works, altogether congenial. There were Christians in the second century who adhered fiercely to Jewish practices and venerated Jesus as a prophet and no more. They regarded James as their spiritual father. But here, at least, James quotes the Old Testament in support of a wider vision. There are not many extended Old Testament quotations in the writings of Luke. When they do occur, it is at critical points of the story, to give sanction to new developments taking place.

Somewhat strangely, James quotes from Amos in its Greek translation which is at variance with the original Hebrew. In the Old Testament, where it is translated from the Hebrew, Amos 9:11–12 reads:

'"In that day I will raise up the booth of David that is fallen
and repair its breaches,
and raise up its ruins,
and rebuild it as in the days of old;
that they may possess the remnant of Edom
and all the nations who are called by my name,"
says the Lord who does this'.

421

This has quite a different flavour from the Greek version, and would not have served James' argument at all! The Greek version enables James to claim that to extend God's providence towards the Gentiles was not an innovation, but rooted in the pages of Scripture.

The council's concluding compromise, which Paul and the others took back to Antioch by letter (thereby underscoring its importance), required the Gentile converts to adhere to some basic requirements. Unfortunately what these were is not completely clear to us. Our problem is that we cannot be sure whether the phrase 'and from what is strangled' in verse 20 was part of the original text of Acts. If it was, then it seems that besides sexual misconduct and idolatry the Gentile converts were also being asked to keep some of the more basic Jewish food laws. If it was a later addition, then it is likely that the code was primarily concerned with moral rather than ritual behaviour. Whatever the textual evidence, the compromise ultimately has a slightly uneasy feel to it, leaving both Jewish and Gentile Christians with problems still to be sorted out in the future. Even James' visionary quote from the Old Testament posed as many problems as it solved. For though it made it clear that the Gentiles were encompassed by God's love, it still left unaddressed the question of whether Gentiles 'seeking the Lord' would need to become Jews as part of that process.

OPENING THE DOOR OF
FAITH STILL WIDER

Problems and possibilities   *Acts 15:36–41*

Preparations for a second missionary journey are drawn into the wake of the council of Jerusalem. We do not need to probe very far below the surface of Luke's account to sense the unease in the events which follow the council: there is more going on than we are told. Paul's quarrel with Barnabas was certainly a clash of personalities, and Barnabas' characteristic generosity of spirit towards John Mark's earlier failure (13:13) may have had something to do with it. But Galatians 2:13 also suggests that Barnabas was finding it increasingly difficult to follow Paul down a road which alienated him from his fellow Jews and some Jewish Christians.

Then there is the account of the circumcision of Timothy. It is true that as the son of a Jewish mother Timothy was technically Jewish by birth, and that by circumcising him Paul was acknowledging that Jewish Christians were entitled to hold on to their Jewish traditions. But Paul's action here sits uneasily alongside his proud refusal in Galatians 2:3 to allow Titus to be circumcised, and with his categorical dismissal of the value of the practice in his letters. Was Paul being put under pressures about which Luke does not tell us?

Next we read of the Spirit behaving rather strangely, by obstructing the apostles' attempts to preach in Bithynia. Normally the Spirit encourages rather than prevents movement—so why does the Spirit stop Paul entering into a new area of ministry? The first letter of Peter implies that this was a region where Peter himself was active (1 Peter 1:1). Perhaps to avoid possible conflict between different viewpoints, it had been agreed that the apostles should divide the work between themselves on a geographical basis.

Finally we meet Lydia, the first named woman convert in Acts. Paul has evidently not abandoned his practice of taking the gospel first to the Jewish community: there was no synagogue in Philippi, and the Jews met for prayer by the river. Luke's description of Lydia as 'a seller of purple goods who was a worshipper of God' indicates that she was both a Gentile and a God-fearer, and probably an influential business woman in the city of Philippi. She followed up her baptism with an unusually pressing invitation to Paul to come and stay with her. The council of Jerusalem had debated the admission of the Gentiles in terms of theology. Here we see its practical outworkings. For the Jewish Paul to accept hospitality from a Gentile was a sharp break with Jewish custom, and perhaps even Paul hesitated at taking that step (this may be implied by the ending of verse 15). Yet it was a leap that had to be made, for such table-fellowship was, as the the ministry and parables of Jesus make clear, at the very heart of the gospel.

Citizens in captivity   *Acts 16:16–40*

As we read of Paul's work in Macedonia, we notice that we have almost imperceptibly slipped into the first of the 'we' sections in Acts, beginning with the vision at Troas in 16:10 and continuing until the incident at Philippi reported in 16:17. Does this indicate that the author of Acts had joined Paul on his journey at this point? This may be the case, although we have evidence that ancient authors did sometimes write in the first person to give their travel narratives extra vividness. But we have also slipped into something else—the gospel's encounter with the Roman world and its governing authorities. Up to this point in Acts, the main focus of attention has been on the early Church's confrontation with Judaism and its quest for a separate identity *vis-à-vis* its mother faith. Now, although the debate with Judaism does not disappear, the narrative increasingly focuses on Christianity's relationship with the empire that ruled the whole of the area around the Mediterranean.

It is interesting to contrast Paul's troubles at Philippi with his earlier misadventures in Lystra (14:19). There, the Jews had played a leading role in making life difficult for him. Here the persecution is instigated by some sleazy pagan pimps who are affronted by the loss of income which has resulted from one of Paul's acts of healing. Ironically they try to use Paul's Jewish origins to reinforce their case. Paul just cannot win! Yet his and Silas' involuntary encounter with the state facilitates the growth and development of the Christian movement. The Philippian gaoler and his family are almost certainly the first people in Acts to be baptized without any previous knowledge whatsoever of the Jewish faith; they represent the power of the gospel to penetrate further into the Gentile world. And the mention of Paul's Roman citizenship in verse 37 sets the scene for his journey to Rome in the later chapters of Acts. Luke, adopting the viewpoint of the apostle himself in Romans 13, makes the point that Christians like Paul are of good standing in the secular world. They should not be regarded as wild revolutionaries—even when they had the chance to escape from prison, Paul and Silas stayed in their cell. So the gospel they preach can hardly be seen as a threat to the well-being of the Empire.

The ridiculed resurrection   *Acts 17:1–34*

From Philippi, Paul and Silas journeyed west to Thessalonica and Beroea. Here once again we see the familiar patterns of the apostolic mission: Scripture-based preaching in the synagogue, where Paul proclaimed the messiahship of the crucified and risen Jesus; support from some Jews and possibly a greater number of God-fearers; and rejection by other Jews, with the result that the apostles travelled to the next town, where the pattern repeated itself. For his own safety, Paul was forced to go further, as far as Athens, where he intended to wait for his companions.

Paul's ministry in these three centres is linked by his preaching of the resurrection, and the almost total incomprehension he encountered among both the Jews of Thessalonica and Beroea and the Greeks of Athens. At Thessalonica the assertion that the Christ must suffer and then rise from the dead led to a riot; in Athens Paul's views largely met with ridicule. His audience in Athens seem to have misunderstood him from the start: they took his preaching of 'Jesus and the resurrection' (v. 18) as a reference to two deities—one male, one female—as was characteristic of eastern mystery or fertility cults. The sophisticated Athenians, imbued with both Stoic and Epicurean philosophy, regarded such notions as primitive. On the other hand they would have been in general agreement with Paul's views on idolatry in verses 22–23, and in verse 28 Paul actually quotes from two Greek poets and theologians to reinforce his point. In seeking as much common ground as possible with his audience, Paul did what many Christian missionaries have done ever since. If Christians have a proper understanding of God's greatness and his grace, then they should not be afraid to see his hand in non-Christian faiths. But then Paul spoiled his case, at least as far as the Athenian philosophers were concerned, by referring once again to Jesus' resurrection from the dead. We know from Paul's correspondence with the Corinthians that the Greek world found the doctrine of the resurrection of the body, whether of Christ or ordinary mortals, almost incomprehensible. The view that flesh and blood are corrupt and evil was an underlying tenet of Greek thought—why therefore should it be 'resurrected'? Though a belief in the immortality of the soul (the supposedly non-material part of the human person) was widespread, for Paul to preach the resurrection of *flesh* provoked a reaction close to revulsion. At this point the apostle necessarily parted company with most, though not all, of his audience.

In Thessalonica, Paul had been accused of 'turning the world upside down' (v. 6). Ironically the charge is actually correct, for the phrase 'turn upside down' comes from the same Greek word as 'resurrection'. The Christian preaching of the resurrection placed some fundamental question marks over the world-view that prevailed throughout most of the Mediterranean world. Luke stresses how the Athenians buzzed with their love of the 'new' (vv. 19–21). At the same time, it appears that the Judaism which opposed Paul held tenaciously to its 'old' traditions. Resurrection, which linked together the old and the new, was something that neither group was quite prepared to handle.

Gallio and the Gentiles *Acts 18:1–22*

Though Paul's missionary exploits are at the centre of this part of Luke's story, we are not allowed to forget the political world of Rome into which the faith is expanding. The account of Paul's time in Corinth contains two references which help us tie his ministry to specific moments in history. The dates normally given to Paul's letters depend on this historical link.

The decree of Claudius which had forced Aquila and Priscilla to leave Rome is mentioned by the Roman historian Suetonius, and was issued in AD49/50. Interestingly, the decree may well have been issued as a result of the internal strife in the Jewish community in Rome provoked by the preaching of the Christian gospel. From an inscription at Delphi we can date Gallio's pro-consulship as AD51/52. The two references fit together to suggest that Paul's eighteen-month stay in Corinth took place between AD50 and 52. It was a time for consolidation; as Paul later reminded the Corinthians (1 Corinthians 9:6), he spent much of his stay engaged in his trade of tent-making. In some parts of the early Church travelling evangelists were rather too eager to live parasitically off the community—Luke is anxious to show us that Paul wanted to earn his own living as far as possible.

During this period at Corinth an important development occurred. The recurrent hostility to his message led Paul to declare that he was 'innocent' and move in with the Gentile God-fearer Titius Justus. The RSV does not make it clear that 'innocent' in verse 6 and 'clean' in Peter's vision at Joppa (Acts 10:15) both translate the same Greek word. To take up residence with a Gentile would normally make a Jew 'unclean'. Though Paul had done this previously, in Philippi (see 16:15), he had not been altogether comfortable about it. In Corinth he announced that the ritual rules of cleanliness no longer applied to him at all. The significance of Peter's heavenly vision was being worked out on earth.

In verses 18–22 we see that Luke devotes little space to the remainder of Paul's journey, from Corinth back to his base in Antioch. He has written enough to show how Paul forged a path well beyond anything the leaders of the Jerusalem church imagined when they issued their decree.

Spirit and Word once again undergird developments, but in the second missionary journey the progress of the gospel was not as smooth or successful as before. As they opened the door of faith still wider to the Gentiles, Paul and Silas placed greater strain on relations between Christian and Jewish communities with their concern for ritual purity. And wherever the apostles preached to Gentiles who were unfamiliar with the Jewish basis of Christianity, they found it harder to communicate their message. So the relationship between the Church and its Jewish roots was proving to be a mixed blessing. The Scripture-based monotheism and morality of the ancestral faith provided a bridge which enabled the gospel to reach Gentiles who moved in the penumbra of synagogue life. But the Scriptural concern for purity could also be a bind to those impulses within the gospel which sought to overcome age-old divisions and create a new people of God. These ancient issues are found in modern guise, and today's Church continues to struggle with them.

A way to walk

Acts 18:23—19:7

After reading the accounts of Paul's journeys around the eastern Mediterranean, it is a relief to find that for the next two chapters at least, Luke's narrative largely focuses on Ephesus. Here we meet one of the most intriguing figures in Acts, Apollos, whom Paul was to acknowledge as an emissary of the gospel in Corinth (1 Corinthians 1:12, 3:4—6). Alexandria, his home city, was a great centre of Greek learning and also a place where Jews and Greeks learnt each other's wisdom. The most famous Jewish scholar of Alexandria, Philo (c. 20BC– AD45), wove together Greek philosophy and a detailed study of biblical texts to provide creative interpretations which influenced later Christians as well as Jews. Apollos, unusually for a Jew named after the Greek god Apollo, may have been one of Philo's heirs. It has sometimes been suggested that he was the author of Hebrews, which also interprets the Old Testament in a way not dissimilar to Philo.

We may wonder how it was that Apollos only knew about the baptism of John. It is interesting that the 'way of the Lord' in which he had been instructed is the same phrase that appears so prominently in the summary of John's teaching at the beginning of the Gospel (see Luke

3:4). It is possible that the links between John and Jesus and their respective disciples were more complex than the earlier parts of the Gospels imply: the disciples whom Paul encountered at Ephesus (19:1ff) represent groups who continued to identify with the Baptist. Some of these believed that because John preceded Jesus he was the more important of the two. Down to recent times a group called the Mandaeans existed, who particularly venerated John. But those we meet here were evidently more sympathetic to Christian claims about Jesus. Following baptism 'in the name of the Lord Jesus' and the laying on of apostolic hands, they received the hitherto unknown Holy Spirit, as did the Samaritan believers in 8:14–17.

Perhaps the clue to Apollos' genuine though partial knowledge of Jesus is provided by the phrase 'the way of the Lord'. When John first preached those words from Isaiah he was referring to *Israel's* walking in the way the Lord taught, where 'the Lord' was the God of the Jewish Scriptures. But one of the most significant shifts in the development of the Christian Church was the realization that the 'way of the Lord' referred to the way the *Lord Jesus* walked—the way to Jerusalem and the cross. For it was only when Jesus was seen as saviour as well as teacher that Christians could be baptized into his death, and have a share in his risen Spirit. Apollos may have been a former disciple of John who had been drawn into Christianity. Now, through the ministry of Priscilla and Aquila, he is brought into the apostolic circle, and encouraged to use his biblical expertise in the mission in Corinth.

All spells dissolved

Acts 19:8–20

In Ephesus, Paul adopted his regular practice of preaching first in the synagogue. But as in Antioch (13:14ff), Thessalonica (17:2ff) and Beroea (17:10ff), he soon attracted opposition, and his separation from the synagogue eventually brought the gospel to a wider audience. The reference to exorcism here echoes a striking passage in the letter of Ignatius of Antioch, martyred in AD107, to the Christians of Ephesus. He confidently proclaimed that with Christ's coming 'all the power of magic became dissolved and every bond of wickedness was destroyed; human ignorance was taken away, and the old kingdom abolished'. Was magic a particular problem faced by Christianity in Ephesus? Was it a trap into which even some in the Christian community fell?

At Ephesus, Paul seems to have been confronted by the problems of 'half-way believers'. Alongside those who only knew the baptism of John, there were others who treated Jesus' name as a magical talisman. In the Gospel Jesus had pledged, 'If it is by the finger of God that I cast out demons, then the kingdom of God has come upon you' (Luke 11:20). So Paul accompanied his preaching of the kingdom of God by some really spectacular miracles and exorcisms. But some among his audience—perhaps even some of those who have 'heard the word' (v. 10)—misunderstood, thinking that 'Jesus' must be a leading figure in the demonic world who could be activated to play a powerful role in magic spells and incantations. But Jesus himself had made it crystal clear that the kingdom of God had no truck with the kingdom of Satan. The latter had met its match, resulting in the demise of the devil and the death of magic. The exorcisms of Paul and Jesus were possible, not because they were part of the magical world, but because the demons recognized that they were defeated. Ignatius' words describe the situation exactly. So, finally and triumphantly, those who had continued to practise magic even while being counted among the believers saw the error of their ways, and a public book-burning took place. At the end of the day light can have nothing to do with darkness. But sometimes the problems which the 'word of God' encountered were caused by those who did not realize the full implications of the leap of faith they had made.

Journeying to Jerusalem   Acts 19:21–41

Here we are literally and theologically at the mid-point of Paul's career in Acts. Like Jesus, he sets his face resolutely towards Jerusalem (Luke 9:51)—this surely has a deliberate resonance with the Gospel story. And like Jesus, Paul was to travel to Jerusalem by a very convoluted route: to journey from Ephesus via Macedonia and Achaia did not make geographical sense. Paul's letters suggest that part of the reason for this itinerary was his desire to make a collection from his congregations for the Christians of Jerusalem. But unlike Jesus, Jerusalem is not Paul's ultimate goal. He needs to travel through Jerusalem, the traditional city of passion and suffering, to Rome, that second focus of the ellipse which makes up the Book of Acts.

The strife with the silversmiths of Ephesus helps to set the tone for that Roman journey. Ephesus was a magnificent city; its ruins are breathtaking even today, and the theatre where the crowd gathered can still be seen. Its prosperity partly depended on its role as a religious centre for the whole of the province of Asia. A great deal of awe was attached to a meteor which had fallen in the city centuries before, and even more importance was given to the worship of the Ephesian version of the goddess Artemis. The Greek Artemis was venerated as a virgin goddess, but the many-breasted shape of the statues of Artemis of the Ephesians would suggest that here she was worshipped as a great earth mother! Inevitably Paul's preaching was perceived as an economic threat by many.

Luke puts a particular slant on the conflict. On the one hand the silversmiths seem to be greedy charlatans and their supporters are simply an unruly mob. The level of confusion that reigns in the story is remarkable. On the other hand the voice of the authorities, who draw strength from the power of Rome, is one of sweet reason. Luke makes it clear that Paul and the authorities are on the same side. The apostle is no threat to civil order; indeed the Asiarchs, who are responsible in the city for the cult of the emperor, are described as his friends! So as Paul sets off towards Rome, Luke underlines the fact that Rome has nothing to fear from him and his gospel. It is Paul's accusers, not Paul, who are guilty of a breach of the peace.

The feast of the death of death   *Acts 20:1–12*

In the Old Testament (for example, Isaiah 25:6–8; Zechariah 14:16) the Gentiles are invited to bring their gifts to Jerusalem and share in a great feast there. This will be a sign of the kingdom of God. So also in the Gospels, and especially in Luke, there are many stories of common meals (for example, Luke 14:16–24), to which all are or should be invited. They are evidence of the new age which the ministry of Jesus has inaugurated, foretastes of the heavenly banquet prepared for all people.

Accompanying Paul on his journey to Jerusalem are representatives of the congregations which he has founded during his missionary journeys: the ingathering of the Gentiles is beginning. So it is no accident that as it does, a meal is shared, with the breaking of bread. Such a meal formed part of the normal pattern of Christian worship. By this point in time it took place on the 'first day of the week', the day of resurrection— probably on Saturday evening, after the Jewish sabbath had ended. Jewish and Gentile Christians gathered together to celebrate the presence of the risen Lord among them, the one who had revealed himself to his disciples at Emmaus in the breaking of bread. Clearly there were also other elements to the worship: reading of Scripture, singing of hymns and psalms, and teaching. On this occasion the sermon was clearly a very long one! There is a delightful humanity and a reassurance to other preachers about the acknowledgment that even Paul could send people to sleep.

Isaiah 25 also mentions that the feast of the kingdom will take place at a time when death will be swallowed up for ever. For the early Christians the joy of the resurrection was powerfully present as they broke their bread together. It is no surprise then that young Eutychus should be brought back to life to share once more in the kingdom's feast.

Paul's farewell discourse   Acts 20:13–35

The urgency of the journey to Jerusalem intensifies. The very fact that Paul did not have time to go to Ephesus to deliver this important speech, with its justification for his life and ministry, underlines the pressure he is now under. This is reinforced by the language he uses. He is 'bound in the Spirit' and expecting imprisonment. Luke wants to remind us of Paul's earlier career when, before his conversion, he himself had 'bound' disciples and brought them to Jerusalem for persecution (Acts 9:2). It is a powerful and ironic reversal.

Paul's own difficulties then shade into the problems that the Ephesian Christians can expect to face after he is gone (not that Christianity in Ephesus had ever been entirely problem-free, as Acts 19 makes clear). As the vivid impressions of the first preaching of the gospel begin to fade, disagreements over doctrine will divide and weaken the Church. In his speech, Paul is being realistic about the issues that second-generation Christians confronted, and his suggestions are those that second-generation Christianity eventually evolved. Sadly but inevitably, barriers were built, because the first flush of the Spirit's freedom became too dangerous to countenance. Sharp lines had to be drawn between orthodoxy and heresy, and a structured leadership such as the 'overseers' to which Paul refers (v. 28) became necessary.

In his Gospel Luke described the Church as a 'flock' (Luke 12:32). Here he reinforces the image by having Paul depict the overseers as 'shepherding' this flock and protecting it from wolves. Underlying this metaphor is Ezekiel 34:1–24, where the job-description of 'good shepherds' is set alongside the promise that God himself will shepherd his people.

Paul closes his speech with a direct quotation from words of Jesus which do not actually appear in the Gospels. It is the only time since the account of the ascension that Jesus' own words are used, which gives them a special significance. 'It is more blessed to give than to receive' sums up the essence of the message of Acts. Throughout the book the progress of the gospel has regularly been furthered by gracious hospitality and a generous spirit.

A second Gethsemane   *Acts 20:36—21:14*

Often in Acts the Holy Spirit has blazed a trail that is both dynamic and victorious. In Tyre the Spirit speaks with different but no less important tones, of what awaits Paul now less than 150 miles away in Jerusalem.

Luke sometimes gives the impression, particularly in Acts, that the cross of Christ was merely something that Jesus had to endure—almost a kind of mistake—before its apparent failure was reversed on Easter Sunday. But there is more to his understanding of Jesus' Passion than this, for Luke also presents the cross as a powerful model for Christians to follow. We saw this first in the example of Stephen, then James the brother of John. Now it is Paul's turn, as the Spirit of the same Christ who had suffered in Jerusalem foretells both in Tyre (v. 4) and in Caesarea (v. 11) that he is to suffer a similar fate. Note how the words of Agabus verbally echo the final Passion prediction of the Gospel (Luke 18:31–33). But whereas in the Gospel it was stated that Christ's Passion was a fulfilment of the Old Testament prophets, now in the new age of the Church Paul's passion will fulfil the words of this New Testament prophet. Once again the ironic reversal of Paul's earlier life is apparent. Even more strongly than when Paul addressed the elders of Ephesus, the language of 'binding' recalls the overthrown persecutor.

In a sense, we are at Paul's Gethsemane. It is the moment, the last moment when, if he wishes, he can turn back and escape the fate that lies ahead. Like Christ before him he chooses to go on, and it is with the same words of trust in God that he accepts what is to come (compare v. 14 with Luke 22:42).

From Ephesus onwards, both word and Spirit begin to show ever more clearly their true worth. The success story of the earlier chapters enters a new dimension: the painting takes on some new hues.

In Ephesus the 'word' appears to grow, even, or especially, when it encounters difficulties. The sower's seed is actually strengthened by its victory over hostile magic forces. The Spirit, which has so often blazed its route with dynamism and clarity, now leads Paul on a road that will inevitably result in suffering and perhaps death. Like Christ's own ministry which travelled from a Galilean springtime to Jerusalem's Passion, Paul the prophet must journey from his missionary miracles to suffer in the holy city. For the 'word of God' which spans the Testaments is a word that states that Christ and his followers **must** suffer.

It is natural and understandable even for Christians and their leaders to prefer visible success to public failure. This is a particular temptation for an age in which success and control seem to dominate so many spheres of our life. We need to remember that the deepest truth and power of the gospel is to be found not in human hullabaloo, but in what Ignatius of Antioch called the 'deep silence of God', the hidden reserves of divine power which lie beyond human knowledge.

PAUL AND THE AUTHORITIES — IN JERUSALEM —

All things to all people

For one last time we return to Jerusalem. For Luke, Jerusalem had really had its day and its visitation. Ever since the stoning of Stephen, the movement of Acts has steadily been taking us ever further from the city. But it is in Jerusalem that prophets must suffer their final rejection, and for Luke Paul is a prophet as well as so much else. Although we know from Paul's letters and Acts 24:17 that part of the purpose of Paul's journey was to bring alms to the Christian community, it is strange that this not mentioned at this point. Were the recipients of the gifts somewhat grudging in their acceptance?

Luke sees Jerusalem as a has-been city, and in one sense the conservative leaders of the Church there are has-been people. They have tried to understand, to accommodate Paul and his new-fangled developments. But living as they do in Jerusalem they have no more than theoretical acquaintance with the Gentiles among whom the news of the gospel has exploded. They respond to Paul's successes by listing their own. Yet the description they give of these Jewish converts (v. 20) makes it clear that they regard them as being *Jews* first and foremost. The vision of a more inclusive faith, which has been evolving as Paul's missionary work proceeds, is alien to them.

Luke is ambiguous about their demands on Paul and his willingness to comply with them. On the one hand he wants to emphasize that Paul is anxious to foster the harmony and unity of the Church whenever possible. As elsewhere he is also keen to stress Paul's financial generosity. But Luke regards the actual demand—to take part in a complicated Jewish ritual of purification—as something of a retrograde step. Rituals of purification had made sense when the infant Jesus was brought to the temple at the beginning of his Gospel. But since that moment the baby who had been redeemed according to the Law had himself become Israel's redeemer and made such practices no longer necessary. So perhaps there is a perverse logic to fact that Paul's willingness to go 'backwards' on this occasion inadvertently led to his arrest and its aftermath.

A dangerous exclusion   *Acts 21:27–39*

Holy places in the Holy Land are not necessarily the most welcoming spots. Pilgrims are confronted with a long list of noes. And woe betide you if you try to pray in a sanctuary of a different faith—unlicensed prayer is far too dangerous to be tolerated! Even these rules, however, pale into insignificance compared with the restrictions with which entry to the temple of Jerusalem used to be hedged. Archaeological excavations have turned up examples of 'warning stones' that were sited at strategic points around the temple. 'Any Gentile that enters further has only himself to blame for the death that will ensue . . .' is their cheerful message. So the reaction to Paul's presence in the temple was, on one level, understandable. Luke makes it clear, however that the

Jews were mistaken: Paul was no trouble-maker, and he did not flout the law by bringing a Gentile companion into the temple with him. Yet a careful reading of verse 28 suggests that the Jewish grievance against Paul ran deeper—he had taught everywhere against the people and the law and 'this place'. The mistaken assumption that he had brought Trophimus into the temple was merely the spark that lit an already smouldering powder keg. We have of course heard such charges before; they were laid against Stephen and earlier against Christ in very similar terms. And ultimately the charges are not totally wrong. For the temple system depended on exclusion and the maintenance of barriers. Paul, on the other hand, nurturing a seed that went back to the ministry of Christ, had come to realize that 'the dividing wall of hostility' must be broken down (Ephesians 2:14). The two visions were ultimately incompatible.

As in the temple of Artemis at Ephesus, so here, the rumpus created by the unruly crowd contrasts with the order and degree of support for Paul provided by the Roman authorities. Paul's credentials—his knowledge of the Greek language as well as Hebrew, and his birth in the prestigious Greek city of Tarsus—mean that he can move with confidence in the world of the Roman tribune. But towards the conclusion of this episode, which reminds us indirectly of Jesus' own conflict in the temple, the sinister demand is shouted by the crowd, 'Away with him!' The same demand was made in Luke's Gospel before Jesus' crucifixion. And now that the veil of the temple has been rent in two by Jesus' death, will the temple's adherents show any more tolerance to Jesus' follower?

A vision of a faithful Jew   *Acts 21:40—22:21*

The second account of Paul's conversion is worth comparing with the first, in Acts 9:1–30. It is the same story, but told with a different slant. The thrust of the earlier version had been to show how a powerful and hostile enemy of the faith had quite literally been brought to his knees. But notice how the story now subtly aids Paul's defence: it shows how Paul is a faithful Jew, and that his following of the Christian 'Way' is not incompatible with this heritage.

It is emphasized at the outset that Paul has switched from the Greek he used with the tribune to speak to his audience in Hebrew. But it is not only the language which helps him make one with them. The form of address, 'Brethren' (repeated in verse 5), is notable, for the term is normally reserved for members of the Christian community. When he recounts his impeccable Jewish credentials and his zealous persecution of the Christian 'way', Paul further aligns himself with his listeners, thus implying that their viewpoint is reasonable, even if mistaken.

There are only slight differences between the two accounts of the vision on the road. But here there is even more emphasis on the brightness of the light than in 9:3–8—it was far too bright for Paul to fight against it! And this time, Paul indicates that it was Jesus *of the Jewish city of Nazareth* who spoke to him.

In what happened to Paul once he arrived in Damascus we can notice other small but significant details. Ananias is described as so devout a Jew that his Christian discipleship is almost forgotten. Indeed Jesus Christ is not mentioned by name in the words he speaks to Paul. The title 'Just One', used by the very earliest Christians (Acts 3:14) is very similar to expressions used by other Jewish groups. Nor is Paul's commission to the Gentiles mentioned at this point. Instead Paul is told to wash away his sins, with the unspoken implication that the Christian 'Way' is also the path of righteousness for a Jew.

Finally, note how in this account Paul on his return to Jerusalem goes to pray in the temple. Furthermore, his departure from the city and eventual mission to the Gentiles seem not to be of his own volition, but because he himself has now to flee attack. In fact, Paul argues with God about his departure—protesting that his efficiency as a persecutor ought to guarantee his security!

Unlawful lawgiving   *Acts 22:22—23:10*

Superficially it looks as though Paul is on trial here, as Jesus had been before him. But in reality it is the Jewish leaders who stand arraigned by Luke, and the verdict is definitely 'guilty'. The key word in this passage is 'law'. Paul is attacked by the lawful authorities of both Rome and Judaism. But he turns their charges round, and accuses them of contravening the respective laws which they were bound to uphold. In response the Roman tribune Lysias admits the justice of Paul's case while the Jewish high priest and his allies remain obdurate in their illegality.

Paul's Roman citizenship has surfaced earlier, in 16:37. Luke plays it rather like a trump card, to reinforce his picture of Paul and the Christian faith he presents as a way of life that is not intrinsically hostile to the

Roman state. It also suggests both to Lysias and Luke's readers that things are not quite as they seem on the surface. If a Roman citizen is being accused by Jewish leaders, does it say more about the citizen or the leaders?

Paul and the high priest Ananias engage each other by trading quotations and allusions from the Old Testament. Paul begins by making a seemingly innocuous remark about his quality of life to date. But the word translated by 'lived' means 'fulfilled my role in society', and emphasizes his status as a citizen, which does not go down too well with the high priest. Then, struck by the priestly minions, he alludes to Leviticus 19:15 to accuse the high priest himself of breaking the law. And in calling Ananias 'a whitewashed wall' he throws in a probable reference to Ezekiel 13:10–16, a very sinister passage which concludes by predicting the destruction of Jerusalem. Finally, when charged with reviling the high priest, he quotes Exodus 22:28 back to his accusers, but surely ironically. We are left wondering who is the 'the people's leader'—the high priest or Paul? If we end up feeling that Paul knows and observes his Old Testament better than the high priest, we have undoubtedly got Luke's message!

Paul's final remarks reinforce this impression. He presents his credentials as a Pharisee—to the further annoyance of the high priest, who was of the party of the Sadducees. The chaos which follows blackens the image of Ananias still further: if he cannot even preside over a Jewish legal assembly properly then what right has he to accuse Paul of law-breaking?

Providence on the way   Acts 23:11–35

Three messages stand out starkly from these verses: the goodness of Claudius Lysias; the lengths to which the Jewish leaders were prepared to go to rid themselves of Paul; and Paul's total innocence. Linking these messages is the connecting thread of God's providential care for Paul, which will see him safely to Rome. Verse 11 suggests that Paul may well suffer in Rome, as Luke's readers doubtless knew he had: the word 'witness' had been used earlier to refer to Stephen (22:20). Witness and martyr tended to overlap rather too easily in the life of the early Church! But whatever Paul's eventual fate, we can be sure that he is in God's hands and that his life and its end will be in God's time.

To return to the first message: Claudius Lysias is presented not only as well-intentioned but also as efficient: he foils a serious attempt on Paul's life. And he is prepared to listen to Paul—an indirect acknowledgment of Paul's standing. He even sells himself somewhat short when he states that he rescued Paul because he gathered he was a Roman citizen. In fact he rescued Paul well before his citizenship was apparent. He omits to mention in his letter to Felix that he had had Paul bound and beaten, but we can forgive him that, with so much else to his credit.

By contrast the Jewish leaders undermine their own authority still further. They are prepared to connive in murder, which was illegal by any standard of Jewish law. The vow of the would-be assassins in verse 14 reads like a diabolic reversal of Jesus' own vow at the last supper to eat and drink no more until the coming of the kingdom of God (Luke 22:15–18).

The third message concerns Paul. In his Gospel, Luke, even more than the other evangelists, had emphasized Jesus' innocence (Luke 23: 4, 14, 22). Now he does the same for Paul, using the pen of a Roman tribune—as later from the mouths of other Roman officials—to make this crystal clear. Paul had done nothing against the interests of the Roman state, and his continued imprisonment simply serves to protect him from malevolent accusers.

Before his conversion Paul himself had carried letters from the high priest to enable him to persecute Christians: it is a bitter-sweet irony that he should now be protected by the letter of a Roman official from the anger of that high priest's successor.

The Way and the life   Acts 24:1–27

Repeatedly in the last few chapters, Christianity has been described as 'the Way'. The term also appears twice (vv. 14, 22) in this account of Paul's appearance before Felix. What is its significance? It was used by several Christian writers. Mark puns on its literal and symbolic significance as he tells of Christians who follow Jesus 'on the way', often exhibiting behaviour that is not suitable for such a style of life (see Mark 9:33–34). John tells us of a Christ who proclaims 'I am the Way' (John 14:6). Most probably it was an expression that the early Christians made their own from their frequent use of Isaiah 40:3 which tells of one who comes 'to prepare the way of the Lord'. As we noted earlier (18:23–19:7), the term allowed the Christians to venerate Jesus both as a teacher and as one who had suffered. It was also a vivid help in suggesting to Jesus' followers the need to travel in the path he had taken before them, as well as registering the sense of movement which is an integral part of true faith. Importantly for Paul, it also expressed the Christian claim to be the true continuation of the Old Testament faith. The enemies of Christianity tried to dismiss it as a 'sect' (v. 14): by contrast 'the Way' describes a path that travels in a straight and natural line from the Law and the Prophets into the present and future.

Paul's words about the resurrection in verse 21, where he reiterates what he had earlier said before the Sanhedrin, are in step with this view. The resurrection is presented as an authentic and traditional Jewish belief, which it is quite reasonable for Paul as a Pharisee to hold. Of course the Pharisees believed in a general resurrection of all people, 'the just and the unjust' (v. 15), at the end of time. When Paul spoke of resurrection he included, either implicitly or explicitly, his belief in the resurrection of Jesus, which had already taken place. But the two strands are not ultimately incompatible. It is because the resurrection of Christ has *already* happened that the Christian 'hope' of resurrection is justified.

In the accounts of Paul's time in Jerusalem and Caesarea, the Spirit, and perhaps the word too, seem to speak by absence. Mess, chaos and ambiguity dominate this part of Acts.

Was it right for Paul to jump backwards into temple rituals? Why did the leaders of the Jerusalem church not come to his aid in any way—surely they had some influence in the city? Should Paul have sought to set Sadducee against Pharisee in his speech of defence (23:1–10)? Was he dishonest in presenting his Damascus road experience so as to reinforce his credentials as a 'good Jew'? All these questions could be asked but there are even more serious ones of the Jewish leadership who break the law even as they maintain they are upholding it.

For Luke this is Paul's bleakest, darkest moment. Alone and largely friendless, he knows something of the desolation Christ encountered on the cross. As God was absent then, so his Spirit seems absent now. But in the worst moment of Paul's passion, when he has almost been quite literally torn to pieces, the Lord appears to him—a grace that he has not known so directly since that momentous journey to Damascus (23:11). Paul does not hear easy words—for these are not always appropriate—but words of truth and trust and strengthening.

> In the moments of our sharpest pain the truth spoken in love,
> or sometimes no words spoken at all, can be more healing than a
> facile flow. Wounds must not be healed too lightly: yet God is
> with us to bear the pain.

— FROM CAESAREA TO ROME —

'To Caesar you shall go'   *Acts 24:24—25:12*

A major issue in the Gospels concerns the nature of the accusation
which led to Jesus' execution. Was he accused of political offences
against the Romans, such as potential sedition, or religious offences
against the beliefs and practices of Judaism, such as his attitude to the
temple or the Law or possible blasphemy? It is not entirely clear, and
the various Gospel writers may each have looked at the situation in a
slightly different way.

Luke is aware of both dimensions of the charges against Jesus. He
states categorically that the political accusation had absolutely no
substance at all—Pilate dismissed it out of hand (Luke 23:13–16, 22).
Luke held that Jesus was crucified entirely at the initiative of the Jewish
leadership, on religious charges. This illustrated the leaders' own
misunderstanding of, and lack of fidelity to, Jewish tradition. In this
respect, as in so many other, Paul's experience mirrors that of Jesus. As
the apostle's trials unfold in these final chapters of Acts there are many
parallels with the trials of Jesus in Luke's Gospel. In this passage Paul
stands before two governors, Felix and Porcius Festus, and his appeal to
Caesar forms a dramatic assertion of his innocence of any crime against
the Roman empire.

Felix, who had originally kept Paul imprisoned (24:27), was a vicious
and corrupt character—even Roman writers described him as such. He
had murdered one of the high priests, and his liaison with Drusilla, a
Jewish princess of the Herodian family, hardly endeared him to the
people he governed. Tertullus' words to 'most excellent Felix' (24:2–3)
are more than ironic. Little wonder that Felix found remarks about
justice, self-control and future judgment threatening (24:25)—the first
two were singularly absent in his own life.

Festus was different, but by this time the unrest in Judea which was to grow into the Jewish war with Rome of AD62–70 had begun. He could not afford to antagonize the Jewish leadership. So Paul's demand to be heard before Caesar, which was his right as a Roman citizen, must have presented itself as a welcome way out of a difficult situation.

A further inquisition   Acts 25:13—26:3

It is amusing, in spite of the seriousness of his situation, that Paul should now be paraded before Agrippa and Bernice. They were the brother and sister of Drusilla (Felix's wife), and no one could have encountered a family who in their domestic life managed to break the Jewish Law quite as often and as blatantly as they did. Aside from Drusilla's marriage to the seedy Felix, Agrippa and Bernice apparently lived for a time together in an incestuous relationship. Later on Bernice was the mistress of the Roman emperor Titus. Agrippa ruled some areas in the north of the country as a Roman nominee, although he lived mainly in Jerusalem. When the war between the Jews and the Romans eventually broke out their loyalties definitely lay with the Romans. They were worthy relatives of 'that fox' Herod Antipas before whom Jesus had appeared (Luke 23:7–12).

In his introduction of Paul to Agrippa, Festus makes it clear that the issue at stake is a minor internal disagreement between Jewish factions, of no real interest or concern to the Roman authorities. Agrippa, as Paul himself also suggests, is being brought into the picture because he can mediate between Roman and Jewish culture. Though very different from Agrippa, Paul too is at home in both worlds: he knows enough about Roman customs to be aware that it is normal practice to begin a defence speech by flattering one's judges. Thankfully his words about Agrippa (26:2–3) are not quite as exaggerated as Tertullus' nauseating remarks about Felix had been!

As each episode in the story draws to its conclusion, Paul's appeal to Caesar sounds out like the insistent and repetitive rhythm of a drum-beat. Luke does not intend to present this as an error on the part of Paul, but rather as a sign of the apostle's initiative in the events unfolding around him. Whatever end may await Paul in Rome, he—like Christ before him—has consciously chosen the way he is to go.

A resurrection light Acts 26:4–32

Paul begins his defence before Agrippa with the story of his conversion, the third and final reference to it in Acts. Once again a comparison with the earlier accounts illustrates the particular motifs highlighted in the latest re-telling. This time the over-arching theme is Paul's preaching of the resurrection. Though he does not hide his own Jewishness, he does not emphasize it as he did in Acts 22. The repeated references to 'the Jews' serve to distance Paul from them. There is no deep sense of commitment to Judaism as such on Paul's part; rather, he simply maintains that in his faith in the resurrection he stands within the parameters allowed by the Jewish religion, which was in turn a religion allowed by the Romans. As earlier (23:6), he mentions his Pharisaic background in order to justify his 'hope', since the Pharisees themselves were noted for such a belief.

In describing his pre-conversion career, Paul intensifies his hostility to the Church. The deaths that he had so frequently caused were the very antithesis of the resurrection which he would go on to preach. Intensified too is the image of light: it appears three times in the account of the Damascus road experience and the ensuing commission (vv. 13, 18, 23), and even its brightness is magnified—'brighter than the sun'. It is an obvious symbol of resurrection—Christ was the 'sun of Righteousness risen with healing in his wings'.

Above all, the pledge of resurrection is central to Paul's commission and to the words of hope he is to deliver to the Gentiles. The language of the commission and Paul's recapitulation of it in verses 22–23 echo earlier moments from the Gospel and the Old Testament: they reverberate with Paul's own sermon at Antioch in Pisidia (Acts 13:16ff), with the disclosure on the Emmaus road (Luke 24:13ff), with Simeon's *Nunc Dimittis* in the temple (Luke 2:29–32), and with the words about the servant of God in Isaiah 42. The message seems to be— and it is central to Luke—that it is only as we reach back to and understand the past that the future can fully reveal its possibilities for resurrection and renewal. To believe in the resurrection of Christ does not abrogate the Old Testament, but fulfils its deepest meaning.

Passing over from death to life

The beginning of Paul's journey to Rome is preceded by the now-familiar declaration of his innocence, which on this occasion is heavily overlaid with irony: had he not appealed to Caesar, he could have been released. Yet by this apparently wasteful and unnecessary means, the gospel of Jesus Christ is about to spread to the ends of the earth.

After the high drama in Luke's story of Paul, we are not at all surprised by the shipwreck. But there is more to this story than its peril and suspense. At one level there is the common sense and courage of Paul contrasted with the foolhardiness and panic of those who wanted to set sail for Rome in the autumn, after the end of the normal sailing season. At another level Luke offers insights into the meaning of salvation. Words such as 'safe', 'saved', 'safety', which all come from the same root as 'salvation', appear many times in the story.

There are also links with the Scriptures and Luke's Gospel. Paul stands in sharp contrast to Jonah, the other biblical figure who experienced a similarly terrifying experience at sea. Jonah was fleeing west to escape from God, Paul was travelling west to Rome under God's instructions. Jonah's self-concern in the storm is infamous, Paul's concern is for the well-being of his fellow travellers. Both, though, are God's chosen instruments to bring salvation to the Gentiles. Together they illustrate the great variety of ways in which God can work. The storm which put Paul's life at risk appears to be the fulfilment of a prophecy in Luke's Gospel. In words which are without parallel in the other Gospels, Luke 21:25−26 tells of 'fainting with fear' at the 'roaring of the sea and the waves'. But significantly, Luke's readers are told that when these things happen they should 'look up and raise your heads, for your redemption is drawing near'. Does Luke want us to see Paul's escape as an integral part of the story of redemption he has been narrating throughout his two volumes?

The storm that Paul encounters before he reaches Rome is a new crossing of the waters, a new exodus, in the same way as Jesus' own death had also been judged by Luke as an 'exodus' (the Greek word is translated as 'departure' in Luke 9:31). In passing through the storm Paul had, symbolically at least, passed from death to life, to salvation and redemption. It is no accident that Paul on the ship at the darkest moment of despair invites his companions to share in a 'last supper'. He and the others break their long fast as a sign of the dawning of the kingdom of God (compare Luke 22:16). Nor is it coincidental that this feast should take place on the 'fourteenth night' (v. 27), for the Passover, the feast of the first exodus, was held on the fourteenth night of the month Nisan. So, on the journey towards Rome and the future, Luke has Paul reaching back and drawing on the memories of Israel's past. And in arriving at Rome he will reach a promised land. He will arrive at his goal—no more needs to be said.

The grace of generosity

Acts 28:1–16

As Paul reaches Malta, and then journeys on to Rome, Luke finds ways to suggest that the work of Paul—and of Christ—is now done. The good news is finally coming to fruition.

The remarkable hospitality of the people of Malta and their leader Publius is noteworthy. All too often survivors of shipwrecks fell among those who took advantage of their misfortune. Not so the Maltese. They treat Paul and the others with 'unusual kindness' (v. 2); Publius entertains them 'hospitably' (v. 7) for three days, and before the travellers leave they are presented with 'many gifts' and provided with all that is needed (v. 10). The hospitality continues as Paul and his companions travel up the Appian Way towards Rome, though now it is provided by members of the Christian community. What a contrast with the beginning of Luke's Gospel, where the infant Christ found 'no room in the inn'! In Luke's eyes hospitality to strangers was a very important way in which the gospel could be expressed and advanced. And here the hospitality is so warm that we cannot doubt God has finally found a home with human beings.

The strange story of Paul's encounter with the viper underlines the victory of the gospel. Snakes do not get a good press in the Bible: they symbolize the power of evil and Satan. Luke has shown us in Acts that the devil has been defeated by the triumph of Christ. Now in the snake the devil is consigned to the fire and to destruction. Mark 16:18 explicitly states that power over snakes will be a sign of the resurrection gospel. The same is true of the power to cure the sick, demonstrated in Paul's healing the father of Publius. The snake's success in Eden is now undone, and the serpent is well and truly trodden underfoot. Quaint and mistaken though the Maltese may be in describing Paul as a god, they do at least remind us that before Eden's fall our human destiny was to be 'in the likeness of God'. With the work of Christ that original destiny can now begin to be restored.

'Let the eyes of your hearts be opened' *Acts 28:17–31*

The conclusion of Luke's writing is both solemn and triumphant. For one last time Paul sets out before the Jewish leaders, whom he still addresses as 'brethren', the straight facts of his case. He makes it clear that the Roman authorities had no argument with him. He then proceeds to expound the essence of the Christian faith, showing how, as did a stranger on the Emmaus road, the Christ fulfilled both Law and Prophets. But that stranger at the end of the Gospel succeeded in opening the eyes of those who heard him. Not so Paul at the end of Acts: here the eyes and ears that confront him remain firmly closed.

For one last time Luke sets out an extensive quotation from the Old Testament. As we suggested above (see notes to Acts 15:15–16) such quotations occur at moments of particular importance in the narrative. Here we have the infamous quotation from Isaiah 6:9–10 which appears to suggest that the non-belief of the Jewish leaders was somehow predestined by God. Luke's use of these words at this point is telling. Mark and Matthew used them when they recounted the parable of the sower (Mark 4:10–12; Matthew 13:10–15). There they offered an explanation of why Christ taught in parables, and why his hearers responded to them as they did. Luke, however, quite deliberately curtails the Isaiah quotation in his Gospel story (Luke 8:10). The full version is held back until this moment. It is as though he is saying, 'Let us give people every chance—every possible chance—to turn and be healed.' The one who wept over Jerusalem in Luke 19:41–44 will not easily give up on Jerusalem's people. His Spirit will yearn for them throughout the book of Acts. Even Paul, hot-tempered though he could be, must repeat three times his pledge to turn to the Gentiles. First stated, apparently definitively, in 13:46, it must be repeated in 18:6 and now here in 28:28 before the last judgment on the representatives of Judaism can be made. This issue is too serious, too tragic, to be allowed to happen lightly.

For Luke, however, tragedy can be turned to triumph. The last words of Acts are deceptively low key. Yet in his final sentence Luke sums up the essence of his two volumes. There is Paul's preaching of the kingdom of God and of Christ, openly and with boldness. No less significant is his

445

willingness and ability to welcome all who come to him. The ministry of hospitality, which broke down the barriers between Jew and Gentile, was still helping the gospel to spread. The feast of heaven is now spread on earth. Come and share in it!

The voice of the Spirit and the word of God come together in the powerful denouement of the book: 'The Holy Spirit was right in saying to your fathers through Isaiah the prophet . . .' (28:25).

Strangely, in these final chapters, as the gospel and Paul have journeyed towards Rome, we seemed to have turned our attention to the past as well as to the future. Memories of the exodus have been evoked; so too have images of Eden. Even Paul, as he retells for the final time the story of the Damascus road, seems to focus far more than previously on Moses and the prophets (26:22). Luke suggests that by understanding the past more fully we can begin to look forward to the future, and the light of the resurrection can beckon more brightly. The God of resurrection and new life is the same God who has been at work throughout the history of humanity and of Israel.

So it is not surprising that in the final verses Spirit and word are linked in such a way. They stand in some sense for the future and the past, for the new and the old. The Church of Acts needed them both: so too do we.